W9-DEQ-968

The Social Mind

Effective social interaction requires sophisticated mental and motivational strategies. *The Social Mind* reviews and integrates recent psychological research on the relationship between people's thoughts and motives – their "social mind" – and their interpersonal strategies. The research shows that success in personal relationships, group behavior, and strategic interaction is significantly influenced by how individuals interpret and explain the social world around them. The implications of this research for personal adjustment, organizational effectiveness and clinical counseling, and health psychology are also explored.

Joseph P. Forgas is Professor of Psychology at the University of New South Wales, Sydney, Australia.

Kipling D. Williams is Senior Lecturer in Psychology at the University of New South Wales, Sydney, Australia.

Ladd Wheeler is Professor of Psychology at the University of New South Wales, Sydney, Australia.

The Social Mind

Cognitive and Motivational Aspects of Interpersonal Behavior

Edited by

Joseph P. Forgas
University of New South Wales

Kipling D. Williams
University of New South Wales

Ladd Wheeler
University of New South Wales

CABRINI COLLEGE LIBRARY
610 KING OF PRUSSIA ROAD
RADNOR, PA 19087

CAMBRIDGE
UNIVERSITY PRESS

HM
1111
.F67
2000

#43631824

PUBLISHED BY THE PRESS SYNDICATE OF THE UNIVERSITY OF CAMBRIDGE
The Pitt Building, Trumpington Street, Cambridge, United Kingdom

CAMBRIDGE UNIVERSITY PRESS
The Edinburgh Building, Cambridge CB2 2RU, UK
40 West 20th Street, New York, NY 10011-4211, USA
10 Stamford Road, Oakleigh, VIC 3166, Australia
Ruiz de Alarcón 13, 28014 Madrid, Spain
Dock House, The Waterfront, Cape Town 8001, South Africa

http://www.cambridge.org

© Cambridge University Press 2001

This book is in copyright. Subject to statutory exception and to the provisions of
relevant collective licensing agreements, no reproduction of any part may take place
without the written permission of Cambridge University Press.

First published 2001

Printed in the United States of America

Typeface Palatino 10/13 pt.   *System* QuarkXPress [BTS]

A catalog record for this book is available from the British Library.

Library of Congress Cataloging in Publication Data

Forgas, Joseph P.
The social mind : cognitive and motivational aspects of interpersonal behavior /
edited by Joseph Forgas, Kipling D. Williams, Ladd Wheeler.
p. cm.
Includes index.
ISBN 0-521-77092-0
1. Social psychology. 2. Social interaction. 3. Intellect – Social aspects. I. Williams,
Kippling D. II. Wheeler, Ladd, 1937 – III. Title.
HM1111.F67 2000
302 – dc21

ISBN 0 521 77092 0 hardback   00-029268

To Teeshie, Cindy, and Helen

Contents

vii

Contributors

Susan M. Andersen   Department of Psychology, New York University

Kathy R. Berenson   Department of Psychology, New York University

Roy F. Baumeister   Department of Psychology, Case Western Reserve University

Kathleen Catanese   Department of Psychology, Case Western Reserve University

Joel Cooper   Department of Psychology, Princeton University

William D. Crano   Department of Psychology, Claremont Graduate University

Florence Dumas   Laboratoire de Psychologie Sociale de la Cognition, Université Blaise Pascal

Jon Faber   Department of Psychology, Case Western Reserve University

Garth J. O. Fletcher   Department of Psychology, University of Canterbury

Joseph P. Forgas   School of Psychology, University of New South Wales

Lowell Gaertner   Department of Psychology, Texas A & M University

Marie P. Galvaing   Laboratoire de Psychologie Sociale de la Cognition, Université Blaise Pascal

Joel A. R. Harvey   School of Psychology, University of New South Wales

Gordon Hodson   Department of Psychology, The University of Western Ontario

Michael A. Hogg   School of Psychology, University of Queensland

Günter L. Huber   Department of Psychology, Universität Tübingen

Pascal Huguet   Laboratoire de Psychologie Sociale de la Cognition, Université Blaise Pascal

Martin F. Kaplan   Department of Psychology, Northern Illinois University

Norbert L. Kerr   Department of Psychology, Michigan State University

William J. McGuire   Department of Psychology, Yale University

Claire V. McGuire   Department of Psychology, Yale University

Jean-M. Monteil   Laboratoire de Psychologie Sociale de la Cognition, Université Blaise Pascal

John B. Nezlek   Department of Psychology, College of William & Mary

Frederick Rhodewalt   Department of Psychology, University of Utah

Astrid Schütz   Department of Psychology, Technische Universität Chemnitz

Constantine Sedikides   Department of Psychology, University of Southampton

Jeffry A. Simpson   Department of Psychology, Texas A & M University

Richard M. Sorrentino   Department of Psychology, The University of Western Ontario

Dianne M. Tice   Department of Psychology, Case Western Reserve University

Ladd Wheeler   School of Psychology, University of New South Wales

Henk Wilke   Social and Organizational Psychology, Leiden University

Kipling D. Williams   School of Psychology, University of New South Wales

Preface

Social psychology is undergoing some exciting changes at the moment. After decades of interest in devising ingenious *impactful* experiments to study *real* interpersonal behaviors, the last two decades were characterized by the ascendance of research that focused on the cognitive, motivational, and information processing strategies of isolated individuals. This book argues that these two traditions are essentially complementary. The key objective of this volume is to show that a proper understanding of interpersonal behavior requires a careful analysis of social actors' cognitive and motivational strategies. In turn, the study of social cognition and motivation cannot be complete without the study of how these strategies influence real interpersonal processes.

This duality between concern with the *social* and concern with the *individual* has been an enduring feature of social psychology throughout its history. However, the present appears to us a particularly auspicious time to propose an integration between social and individual theories, and between methods that emphasize the cognitive and the interpersonal aspects of social life. Despite extensive interest in social cognitive phenomena in recent years, there have been relatively few attempts to present a comprehensive review and integration of what we know about the links between social cognition, motivation, and interpersonal behavior. This book seeks to provide an informative, scholarly, yet readable overview of recent advances in this field, featuring invited contributions from a select and eminent group of investigators.

We are very much aware that edited books have certain intrinsic strengths and weaknesses. At their best, they should amount to more than the sum of their parts. They can serve as a catalyst and produce new insights and new theoretical approaches that would not have emerged otherwise. This is just what we hope to achieve with this volume, and we have used a number of strategies and procedures to achieve this objective. In other words, this is not simply an edited book in the usual sense. Perhaps a few words are in order about the genesis of this volume, the second in a new series entitled the Sydney Symposium of Social Psychology, organized at the University of New South Wales, Australia. This project has been carefully planned over a two-year period and has benefited from substantial financial support from granting agencies, including a Special Investigator award from the Australian Research Council and support from the University of New South Wales, Sydney, and the Alexander von Humboldt Foundation Research Prize, Germany.

The availability of financial support allowed the careful selection and funding of a small group of leading researchers as contributors. Draft papers by all contributors were prepared well in advance of the symposium and were made available to all participants on a dedicated Web site. A critical part of the preparation of this book has been an intensive face-to-face meeting of all invited contributors during the Second Sydney Symposium of Social Psychology. This three-day meeting allowed free-ranging and critical discussion among all participants, with the objective of exploring points of integration and contrast between the proposed papers. Revised versions of the chapters were prepared soon after the symposium, incorporating many of the points that emerged in our discussions.

Thanks to these intensive collaborative procedures, the book does not simply consist of a set of chapters prepared in isolation. Rather, the volume presents a collaborative effort by this leading group of international researchers intent on producing a comprehensive, up-to-date review of research on the links between social cognition, motivation, and interpersonal behavior. The contributions cover most of the key issues in contemporary research linking social cognition, motivation, and interpersonal behavior. The chapters in Part I of the book discuss the fundamental nature of the relationship between cognitive processes and interpersonal behavior, covering such topics as the nature of socially constructed thought systems, the role of affect in interpersonal behavior, dissonance mechanisms that link attitudes and behavior, and the cognitive and motivational dynamics of everyday social life.

Part II of the book focuses on the role of the social self and individual difference variables such as narcissism and uncertainty orientation in self-presentation and interpersonal behavior. Part III looks at social and motivational processes in personal relationships and analyzes the role of mental representations and cognitive distortions in responding to others. Finally, Part IV looks at the social minds of groups, including self-categorization and social influence processes. A better understanding of how cognitive and motivational processes influence social behavior is also of considerable applied importance, as many of the chapters argue. The interface between social cognition and motivation on the one hand, and social interaction on the other, lies at the heart of many professional applications of psychology, including counseling and clinical psychology, organizational research, health psychology, and marketing and advertising research.

Given the coverage of the book, the main target readers for this volume are practitioners, professionals, students, and researchers in theoretical and applied psychology, sociology, communication studies, and cognitive science. The primary audience is likely to be practitioners and students in social, cognitive, personality, counseling, and clinical psychology at both the undergraduate and graduate levels. The book will also have considerable textbook potential for the growing number of undergraduate and graduate courses dealing with the interpersonal consequences of social cognition and motivation.

We should note that this book is the second in a new and so far highly successful series of publications, the annual Sydney Symposium of Social Psychology volumes. So far, three symposia have been held. Contributions to the First Sydney Symposium have already been published with the title *Feeling and Thinking: The Role of Affect in Social Cognition* (edited by J. P. Forgas and published by Cambridge University Press, 2000). This first symposium featured invited contributions by Robert Zajonc, Jim Blascovich and Wendy Mendes, Craig Smith and Leslie Kirby, Eric Eich and Dawn Macaulay, Leonard Berkowitz, Leonard Martin, Daniel Gilbert and Tim Wilson, Herbert Bless, Klaus Fiedler, Joseph Forgas, Carolin Showers, Tony Greenwald and Marzu Banaji, Mark Leary, and Paula Neidenthal and Jamin Halberstadt.

The forthcoming third volume in this series, edited by J. P. Forgas and Kip Williams, will be titled *Social Influence: Direct and Indirect Processes* and will contain chapters by Robert Cialdini, Eric Knowles, Bibb Latané and Martin Bourgeois, Mark Schaller, Ap Dijksterhuis, Jim Tedeschi, Richard Petty, Herbert Bless, Joseph Forgas, Sik Hung Ng, Fritz Strack, Kip Williams and Lara Dolnik, Chuck Stangor and Gretchen Sechrist, Debbie Terry and Michael Hogg, Stephen Harkins, Barbara David and John Turner, Robin Martin and Miles Hewstone, and Russell Spears and Tom Postmes. The Sydney Symposium of Social Psychology series thus occupies a particular niche in regular international small-group meetings in our discipline. Our objective is to identify and discuss important and emerging middle-level topics in social psychology that are broad enough to be of interest to a cross section of researchers. However, our aim is to bring a tightly argued integrative emphasis to these topics in order to identify commonalities and linkages between related research programs that may not have emerged otherwise. In order to achieve these objectives, each volume in this series has been produced using the same intensive multistage collaborative approach between contributors described earlier.

Last but not least, we want to express our gratitude to several people and organizations that have helped to make the Sydney Symposium of Social Psychology such a resounding success and contributed to this volume in particular. The idea of organizing such an international symposium in Sydney owes much to discussions with, and encouragement by, Kevin McConkey and subsequent support by Chris Fell, Merilyn Sleigh, Sally Andrews, and numerous others at the University of New South Wales. Our colleagues at the School of Psychology at UNSW – Stephanie Moylan, Cheri Robbins, Meg Rohan and Lisa Zadro – as well as many others, have helped with advice, support, and sheer hard work to share the burden of preparing and organizing the symposium and the ensuing book. We are indebted to Julia Hough, Cathy Felgar, and Helen Wheeler at Cambridge University Press, New York, for all their hard work and enthusiasm for this project. Financial support from the Australian Research Council and the University of New South Wales were, of course, essential to get this project off the ground. Most of all, we are grateful for the love and support of our families.

April 2000   Joseph P. Forgas
Sydney, Australia   Kipling D. Williams
                                                                        Ladd Wheeler

1. The Social Mind: Introduction and Overview

JOSEPH P. FORGAS, KIPLING D. WILLIAMS, AND LADD WHEELER

Introduction

Human beings are an intrinsically gregarious species. Much of our remarkable evolutionary success is probably due to our highly developed ability to cooperate and interact with each other (Buss, 1999). It is thus not surprising that the study of interpersonal behavior has long been one of the core concerns of social psychology. Understanding how people relate to each other and how their mental representations about other individuals and groups guide their interpersonal strategies has never been of greater importance than it is today. Throughout most of our evolutionary history, human beings lived in close, face-to-face groups where almost all interaction involved intimately known others. In contrast, with the development of large-scale industrialized societies since the 18th century, our interactions have become increasingly complex and impersonal. Most of our encounters now involve people we know superficially at best (Durkheim, 1956; Goffman, 1972). Effective social interaction thus requires ever more sophisticated and elaborate cognitive and motivational strategies. The scientific study of how people understand and represent the social world around them and how they plan and execute their interactions with others is thus of critical importance.

This work was supported by a Special Investigator award from the Australian Research Council, the Research Prize by the Alexander von Humboldt Foundation to Joseph P. Forgas, and an Australian Research Council grant to Kipling Williams. The contribution of Stephanie Moylan and Lisa Zadro to this project is gratefully acknowledged. Please address all correspondence in connection with this chapter to Joseph P. Forgas, at the School of Psychology, University of New South Wales, Sydney 2052, Australia; email jp.forgas@unsw.edu.au

1

Of course, the study of interpersonal processes has a long and proud tradition in our discipline. However, during the past several decades social psychology has been increasingly dominated by an individual-istic social cognitive paradigm that has focused predominantly on the study of individual thoughts and motivations (Forgas, 1981). Perhaps inevitably, the study of "real" interpersonal processes has declined in relative importance (Wegner & Gilbert, 2000). Although we have made major advances in understanding how people process information about the social world, relatively few attempts have been made to explore how processes of social cognition and motivation may influ-ence interpersonal behaviors. One of our objectives in this volume is to draw on the best of the achievements of recent cognitive and motiva-tional research in social psychology and to show how this knowledge can be applied to understanding interpersonal phenomena.

We argue in this book that a juxtaposition of the "social" and the "individual" in our discipline is neither helpful nor necessary. Any meaningful explanation of interpersonal behavior must be based on a careful analysis of the thoughts and motivations of individual social actors. In turn, social factors such as our personal relationships, group memberships, and culture play a critical role in shaping our mental rep-resentations and motivations. One of the oldest debates in the history of psychology is about whether our discipline should be concerned with the study of "mind" or "behavior" (Hilgard, 1980). It seems to us that any meaningful approach to social psychology necessarily involves paying as much attention to the thoughts, motivations, and feelings of social actors as to their interpersonal behaviors. In other words, the interaction between the mental and the behavioral aspects of social life should be the proper focus of our research. The term *social mind* featured in our title is intended to signify this close interdepen-dence between the mental and the behavioral, the social and the indi-vidual spheres in our discipline. The contributions to this volume all report theories and research that illustrate the benefits of adopting such an integrative approach to the analysis of social cognition and motiva-tion on the one hand and interpersonal behavior on the other.

The substantive task of this book is thus to explore the role of mental representations about the social world in how people under-stand themselves and others, and how cognitive and motivational processes influence their interpersonal behaviors. Of course, the idea that there is a close interdependence between interpersonal behavior on the one hand and cognitive and motivational processes on the other has an interesting history in our discipline, as the next section will argue.

The Background

The close links between symbolic mental processes and interpersonal behavior have long been recognized in social science theorizing. Several influential theories sought to deal with this question. The theories of Max Weber (1947), although rarely invoked in social psychology nowadays, provide one outstanding example of such an approach. Weber assumed a direct relationship between the individual's cognitions, beliefs and motivations – the social mind – and larger social systems and structures. Weber's well-known analysis of large-scale sociohistorical processes, such as his theory linking the advent of capitalism with the spread of the Protestant ethic and values, is fundamentally social psychological in orientation. In this work, as well as most of his other writings, Weber assumes that individual beliefs and motivations – such as the spreading acceptance of the Protestant ethic – are the fundamental force shaping large-scale social and economic processes, such as the advent of capitalist social organization (Weber, 1947). Max Weber's concern with mental representations as the key to understanding interpersonal and societal processes is particularly noticeable in his work on bureaucracies. Here he argues that understanding the mind set of the bureaucrat is essential to understanding how bureaucracies function; on the other hand, the explicit rule systems that define bureaucracies play a critical role in shaping and maintaining the social mind of the bureaucrat that, in turn, governs his or her behaviors.

Weber was also among the pioneers who argued that any understanding of social and interpersonal behavior must involve a study of the externally observable causes of that behavior, as well as the subjectively perceived meanings that are attached to an action by the actor. Weber's methodologies involved an ingenious attempt to combine empirical, quantitative data about social processes with the simultaneous analysis of subjective beliefs and motivations of individuals. Several of the chapters here report important progress in research on the interface of individual minds and social behavior that has a distinctly Weberian flavor (e.g., those of McGuire and McGuire, Nezlek, Baumeister and Catanese, Hogg, and Kerr). Indeed, one could make a plausible case that Max Weber was one of the precursors of the social cognitive approach, and it is rather unfortunate that his work and theories remain largely unrecognized and unappreciated by social psychologists today.

Another important theoretical framework that is highly relevant to the concerns of the present book is symbolic interactionism, and the work of George Herbert Mead in particular. Mead's *social behaviorism*, later to be renamed *symbolic interactionism*, was perhaps the most comprehensive attempt to create a theory of social interaction that would synthesize the behaviorist and the phenomenologist, the environmentalist and the mentalistic approaches to human behavior. Mead argued that interpersonal behavior is best understood as both the product and the source of the symbolic representations and expectations of social actors – their social mind. These mental representations, in turn, are partly "given," determined by prior experiences and symbolic representations of social encounters, and partly "creative," constructed by social actors in the course of their encounters with others. Mead's theory is in a sense an attempt to combine phenomenological concerns with symbolic meanings and intentions with the dominant behaviorist orientation of experimental psychology at that time. According to Mead, by internalizing and symbolically representing the social interactions people participate in, the individual acquires social expertise, which lies at the core of the socialized "me." However, social interactions are not acted out in a repetitive, determinate, stereotypical fashion in everyday life. It is the role of the unique, creative "I" to continuously reassess, monitor, and redefine social interactions as they progress, injecting a sense of indeterminacy and openness into our interactions.

Symbolic interactionism has failed to become a dominant theory within social psychology, probably because the methodologies available at the time did not provide a suitable empirical means for studying individual mental representations. The social cognitive paradigm that has been in ascendancy for at least two decades now has changed much of this. Social cognitive research essentially deals with the same kinds of questions that were also of interest to Mead: How do individual thoughts, beliefs, representations, and motives influence interpersonal behavior, and how are such mental representations constructed and maintained? Social cognitive research has now developed a range of ingenious techniques and empirical procedures that for the first time allow a rigorous empirical analysis of Mead's ideas. Many of the chapters in this book address issues that are directly relevant to symbolic interactionist concerns (e.g., those of Andersen and Berenson, Fletcher and Simpson, Nezlek, Rhodewalt, Sedikides and Gaertner). Like these authors, symbolic interactionists were also interested in these questions: How do people's ideas and beliefs about relationships, the self, or other people influence their interpersonal behaviors? and How are such beliefs created and maintained in the course of social interactions? Symbolic interactionist ideas continue to provide a huge and largely untapped reservoir of theories and hypotheses about the links between social mind and social behavior, and one of the key antecedents to the issues explored in this book.

It is interesting to note that even though the theoretical systems developed by Max Weber and George Herbert Mead had only a weak direct influence on social psychology, within sociology they gave rise to a strong and thriving micro-sociological tradition (Coser, 1971). In fact Weber's and Mead's influence on social psychology has been largely indirect, transmitted to us through the work of writers such as Erving Goffman (1972). Goffman provided some of the most stimulating conceptual accounts of the intricate relationship between an individual's thoughts and motivations, planned self-presentational strategies, and observable public social behavior. Goffman's dramaturgical account of social interaction is essentially based on his extended analysis of the cognitive and motivational strategies that shape the social minds of actors. Consistent with the micro-sociological tradition, Goffman's method of explaining the puzzles of interpersonal behavior was largely based on analytical, interpretive methods. Social psychologists cover much the same ground, relying on the whole armory of empirical methods. The work presented here by Andersen and Berenson, Baumeister and Catanese, Rhodewalt, Schütz, Sorrentino et al., Tice and Faber, and Williams et al. all touches on issues that are directly relevant to our understanding of strategic self-presentation in interpersonal situations, as also analyzed by Goffman.

A further historical tradition that is directly relevant to the theme of our book can be found in the various phenomenological theories in social psychology. Although the introspective method for studying phenomenological mental experiences pioneered by Wundt and Titchener was largely rejected in later psychological research, phenomenological theories continue to exert a great influence on our discipline (Bless & Forgas, 2000). In fact, the phenomenological perspective produced some of our most stimulating and enduring ideas and research paradigms in experimental social psychology. A classic example is Fritz

Heider's pioneering work (Heider, 1958) exploring the kinds of knowledge and motives that social actors need to possess in order to plan and execute strategic interpersonal behaviors successfully.

Heider's work is fundamentally a theoretical analysis of the nature of the social mind: What are the characteristics of social knowledge, how is it acquired and organized, and how does it guide interpersonal behaviors? Heider's phenomenological speculations about the nature and functions of the minds of social actors had a major impact on our discipline and gave rise to some of our most productive empirical research paradigms. Phenomenological ideas provided the initial impetus and defined the scope of such key areas of research as the study of person perception and attribution, balance and dissonance theories, and research on attitude organization and attitude change. Without Heider's commitment to taking seriously and trying to understand the social mind of social actors, social psychology would have developed as an entirely different discipline. Several chapters here report research concerned with the social understanding of actors that show considerable affinity with Heider's theoretical ideas (e.g., those of Cooper, Forgas, McGuire and McGuire, Nezlek, Schütz, Sorrentino et al., and Tice and Faber).

Heider is just one of the key representatives of the phenomenological tradition. Kurt Lewin is another defining figure who also believed that the study of how interpersonal behavior is directed by the mental representations and motivations of individuals should be within the focus of social psychological inquiry. Lewin's field theory in particular represents an explicit affirmation of the principle that the way people mentally represent and experience social situations must be the core research question guiding our discipline. Lewin's ideas have, of course, left an indelible mark on our field. His emphasis on the need to understand the subjective representations of social actors – their social mind – eventually gave us some of our most successful research paradigms, including much research on group dynamics, social influence processes, and cognitive dissonance. One can easily discern a conceptual link between the Lewinian approach to the analysis of social influence and group processes in the work reported here by Crano, Kerr, Huguet et al., and Kaplan and Wilke, as well as that of Williams et al.

This necessarily brief survey of the various historical antecedents of an interest in the social mind is, of course, far from complete. Our purpose in touching on these earlier theories is simply to illustrate that social psychology has a rich tradition of fruitful theorizing that addresses exactly the same questions that contributors to this volume are also concerned with: What are the features and characteristics of thought systems? How are mental representations about the social world, other people, intimate relationships, and the like formed, and how do they, in turn, influence our interpersonal strategies? To what extent can we understand group behavior in terms of the implicit representations people have about the role of their own group and its relative position compared to the positions of other groups? In order to answer questions such as these, we need to be mindful of earlier theories of the social mind that could inform our enterprise today.

However, we are now also in a much better position than earlier researchers to find answers to questions such as these. The past several decades in social psychology have been characterized by the rapid ascendancy of the social cognitive paradigm. For all its failings, this is a framework that clearly accepts that the mental representations, feelings, and intentions of social actors are the key determinants of interpersonal behavior. Social cognitive research has produced an impressive corpus of findings and empirical methods that are directly relevant to studying the social mind. Many of the contributions included here offer excellent illustrations of how social cognitive methods can be applied to study the links between social cognition and motivation and strategic interpersonal behaviors (e.g., the chapters by Andersen and Berenson, Forgas, Huguet et al., Sedikides and Gaertner, Sorrentino et al., and Tice and Faber).

What are the fundamental dimensions that define people's social experiences? Can we identify basic characteristics that play a key role in influencing a wide range of interpersonal plans and behaviors? Several chapters here suggest that the answer to questions such as these may be a cautious "yes." A number of contributors to this volume find that thoughts and concern about being accepted and *liked*, and concern about being *competent*, in control, and respected, appear to be distinct and orthogonal features of the social minds of actors. Interestingly, this dichotomy appears to be important in other areas of social psychology as well. For example, there is considerable evidence from person perception research suggesting that liking (social evaluation) and competence (task and intellectual evaluation) are also fundamental dimensions in the way people are perceived (Rosenberg & Sedlak, 1972). Indeed, it is rather pleasing to find that the same dimensions that define our perceptions of and reactions to others also emerge as critical when it comes to understanding how the thoughts and motivations of social actors influence their social behaviors. The fundamental importance of dimensions such as liking/social acceptance and respect/social control in strategic social behavior is illustrated in a number of chapters here, including those by Andersen and Berenson, Crano, Kerr, Nezlek, Rhodewalt, Schütz, and Williams et al.

Our concern with the social mind as a crucial factor in interpersonal behavior is not an isolated phenomenon. As foreshadowed in the theories of Weber, Mead, Goffmann, Heider, and Lewin, there is a growing recognition in the field that understanding the mechanisms that link people's thoughts, ideas, representations, and motivations with their actual social behaviors is one of the core objectives of social psychology. In a recent volume concerned with the social psychology of subjective experience, Wegner and Gilbert (2000) argued that even though "those of us who constitute the field 'know' that the social interaction of individuals is its intellectual core, in reality the center around which modern social psychology actually turns is the understanding of subjective experience" (p. 4). Even though the study of interpersonal behavior is supposed to be the central territory of social psychology, in fact the most exciting recent developments have taken place in other areas, such as research on social cognition and social motivation that focuses on isolated individuals rather than actual social behavior. As Wegner and Gilbert (2000) note, "a curious by-product of social psychology's expansion has been a kind of urban blight at its official core. Topics such as social interaction, relationships, and groups – which are clearly 'downtown' social psychology in the official story of the field – have suffered massive decay over the last few decades" (p. 7). One of the objectives of this book is to argue that the study of social cognition and motivation on the one hand and interpersonal behavior on the other hand need not be competing endeavors. Rather, interpersonal behavior is best understood through a careful analysis of the thoughts and motivations of social actors – their social minds.

We hope to achieve this objective by discussing four interrelated issues in this book. The chapters included in Part I are concerned with the question of "What is the fundamental nature of social thinking and social motivation, and how do these processes influence interpersonal behavior?" Part II contains contributions that discuss the nature of the socially constructed self and highlight some important individual difference variables involved in strategic interpersonal behavior. Part III deals with the role of social cognition and social motivation in personal relationships, and Part IV looks at the role of these factors in group phenomena.

Part I. The Social Mind: Basic Issues and Processes

The first part of the book considers some *basic conceptual issues* about the interplay of mental representations and interpersonal behavior and contains four chapters. In the first chapter, William and Claire McGuire summarize their integrative theory and empirical research on one of the fundamental questions of the study of social mind: the issue of how *phenomenal thought systems* develop around foci of meaning like oneself and others. Their ingenious experiments analyze how thinkers carry out various directed-thinking tasks, such as listing designated types of characteristics of a target person. The aim of these studies is to discover the content and structure of people's thought systems and how they are affected by cognitive and affective variables. McGuire and McGuire report that the affective qualities of the object of thinking (e.g., likability) are often far more important than cognitive qualities in making judgments. Male and female thinkers also differ on a number of dimensions of thought systems about people. The conceptual framework and methods developed by McGuire and McGuire represents one of the most ambitious and integrative attempts to come to terms with the social minds of social actors, and should have important theoretical and practical implications for how we understand and study interpersonal behaviors.

As McGuire and McGuire demonstrate, affective features are critical in determining how people see and represent the social world around them. This theme is picked up in the next chapter in this part, by Forgas, who analyzes the *role of affective states or moods in strategic interpersonal behaviors*. Although recent research in social cognition has told us much about the role of rational information processing strategies in guiding interpersonal behaviors, the influence of affective states on strategic interaction has been relatively neglected. This chapter argues that even mild and temporary mood states are likely to have a significant and predictable influence on the way people perceive, plan, and execute interpersonal behaviors. Further, extrapolating from the author's Affect Infusion Model (AIM; Forgas, 1995), the chapter develops a theoretical framework that predicts that affect infusion into social interaction should be most likely to occur in social situations that require more elaborate, substantive processing for a behavioral response to be produced. Numerous recent experiments are discussed indicating that positive and negative affective states have a marked influence on the interpretation of social behaviors, responses to approaches from others, the planning and execution of negotiation encounters, and the production and interpretation of strategic interpersonal messages such as requests. The chapter concludes by emphasizing the critical role of affect in how people represent and respond to the social world. These findings also have important implications for applied areas such as organizational, clinical, and health psychology.

Cognitive dissonance research represents one of the most important attempts to come to terms with the dynamic, motivated character of the social mind in social psychology. Surprisingly, the precise motivational basis for the dissonance effects has remained elusive. The chapter by Joel Cooper presents a major review of research on dissonance motivation and develops an integrative explanation of this phenomenon. Since the time of Festinger's original assumption that inconsistency leads to dissonance arousal, influential alternative views have been advanced as to just how or why this occurs. For example, theorists such as Aronson suggested that the self is necessarily involved in dissonance. In contrast, Cooper and Fazio proposed that feeling responsible for aversive or unwanted consequences is the key factor that produces dissonance. Others, such as Steele, echoed Aronson's emphasis on the self and suggested that the need to affirm the self rather than to reestablish consistency is the critical factor driving the effect. This theoretical controversy concerning the fundamental nature of dissonance processes has provided some fascinating insights into the "social mind" and opened up new areas of research such as investigations into hypocritical behavior by Aronson. Nonetheless, there remains little consensus about the primary motivational basis of cognitive dissonance.

The model proposed here by Cooper assumes the existence of a mutual influence between cognition and motivation, as also implied in Festinger's original model. The chapter shows that the degree to which the self is involved in dissonance, versus the degree to which dissonance supersedes the self, is a function of the cognitive accessibility of particular standards. Cooper presents data that show that when people's personal standards for behavior are chronically or situationally accessible, dissonance follows a path predicted by self-consistency theorists. When normative standards are accessible, on the other hand, people's experience of dissonance follows the "New Look" model of

Cooper and Fazio. Cooper's model thus helps to integrate the competing views about the underlying motivational properties of dissonance and represents an important advance in our understanding of how motivational mechanisms influence the social mind and, ultimately, interpersonal behavior.

The question of social motives and their role in the *cognitive dynamics of everyday behavior* is also discussed by John Nezlek. He presents a model describing the relationships between the cognitive and motivational dynamics of day-to-day social life and their relationships to psychological well-being. Nezlek's work focuses on exploring two related areas of social life: (1) day-to-day social interaction and (2) daily plans and their fulfillment. The primary assumption of Nezlek's model is that people's daily lives reflect an integration of two basic needs: the need to belong and the need for control. This dichotomous view of interpersonal motives reappears in several of the other chapters as well. Nezlek's model assumes that people need to *feel* close to others (a motivational task), and they need to *think* they have control (a cognitive task). The model suggests that *what* people do socially each day is best understood as a cognitive phenomenon subject to cognitive processes and constructs; *how* people feel about what they do each day is best understood from a motivational perspective.

Part II. The Social Mind of Individuals: The Role of the Self and Individual Differences

What are the fundamental building blocks of the self and social identity? How do human beings prefer to define themselves in social situations? Is the self primarily an individual, a group, or a collective creation? This is one of the key questions we need to address in trying to understand the social minds of actors, and this is the task undertaken in the chapter by Constantine Sedikides and Lowell Gaertner here. According to these authors, persons seek to achieve *self-definition and self-interpretation* (i.e., identity) in at least three fundamental ways. People may define themselves (1) in terms of their personal traits or those aspects of the self-concept that make them unique in a given social environment (the individual self); (2) in terms of group membership or those aspects of the self-concept that differentiate the group member from members of relevant outgroups (the collective self); and (3) in terms of contextual characteristics, that is, those aspects of the situation that make one self more accessible than the other.

Do these three bases of self-definition carry equal weight? Is one more primary than the others? To address these questions, Sedikides and Gaertner formulated and tested three hypotheses. According to the individual-self primacy hypothesis, the individual self is the most fundamental basis of self-definition. According to the collective-self primacy hypothesis, the collective self provides the most fundamental basis for self-definition. Finally, according to the contextual-primacy hypothesis, neither the individual nor the collective self is primary; instead, self-definition depends upon contextual factors. The chapter reports the results of a series of ingenious experiments addressing this question. Sedikides and Gaertner state that all experiments supported the individual-self primacy hypothesis. These results fundamentally challenge the view that group or collective identities take precedence in defining people's social identity, as suggested, for example, by much research based on social identity theory or self-categorization theory (see also the chapters by Hogg and by Crano in this volume).

Self-presentation is the paramount interpersonal aspect of the self. Ultimately, as Goffman also argued, shaping a particular and desirable image of the self to present to others is one of the crucial tasks of interpersonal life, and the presented self is a powerful tool for relating to other people. The chapter by Dianne Tice and Jon Faber presents an up-to-date review and discussion of *self-presentation* research based on the authors' empirical work. They report that the favorability of self-presentation changes, depending on whether one is presenting oneself to friends or to strangers. Modesty prevails among friends, but self-enhancement seems to be the norm among strangers. Research looking at cognitive load and memory impairment data show that these styles of self-presentation are automatic processes, whereas modest presentation to strangers requires controlled processes.

Tice and Faber also found that when people depart from their familiar style of self-presentation, this may impair their capacity to process new information about the interaction partner. Hence engaging in controlled self-presentation results in less accurate memory for the other person. Of course, people must often choose whether to take risks to enhance their public image or avoid risk so as to protect their image of themselves. Trait self-esteem and self-handicapping contingencies were found to predict how people respond to a risky interpersonal situation. Tice and Faber's evidence also indicates that self-concept change follows from internalizing self-presentations to others – but similar information processing without public self-presentation fails to produce parallel changes. Consistent with the theme of the book, the chapter concludes by highlighting the critical role of cognitive, motivational, and affective processes associated with the self in managing strategic interpersonal behaviors.

What is the role of *self-esteem* in interpersonal behaviors and self-presentational strategies? The chapter by Astrid Schütz reviews new research suggesting that it is often high rather than low self-esteem that is linked to more negative and asocial behaviors. This may be because self-enhancement is less important to low self-esteem people compared to the goal of being perceived as pleasant and likable, a theme that is also reflected in the chapter by McGuire and McGuire. Schütz describes several experiments showing that low self-esteem people are often less critical, are more likely to admit mistakes and seek to be excused, and present themselves as more socially minded and altruistic. In contrast, high self-esteem people may emphasize ways in which they are better than their partners, whereas low self-esteem people describe themselves modestly and their partners positively. As the interactional style of high self-esteem persons focuses on individual achievements and abilities, it can be competitive to the point of criticizing or devaluing others. Low self-esteem, in contrast, leads to more cautious strategies designed to gain liking. Schütz discusses theoretical explanations of the interpersonal consequences of low and high self-esteem, and she concludes that high self-esteem, especially when it is extremely positive or unstable, may be related to socially disruptive behaviors. Overall, the work presented here throws doubt on the widely shared assumption that high self-esteem is always a socially desirable and highly adaptive individual trait.

Recent social psychological research on the self has moved from a focus on the content and structure of one's self-conceptions to a broader focus on how these self-conceptions are related to affect, motivation, and interpersonal behavior. The *social/cognitive model of narcissism* presented by Frederick Rhodewalt is illustrative of this approach. Rhodewalt discusses an overall theory of narcissism incorporating clinical ideas and observations, as well as social psychological research on social/cognitive and interpersonal processes. The model assumes that narcissists are highly invested in maintaining and enhancing a positive view of the self. However, the narcissistic view of the self is not based on reliable past knowledge of real achievements and accomplishments. Rather, for the narcissist, the essential requirement for maintaining a favorable self-representation is to continuously obtain self-affirming, positive on-line feedback from others. According to Rhodewalt's analysis, a significant proportion of the narcissist's interpersonal strategies is aimed at eliciting positive feedback from others. Even if these interpersonal strategies are successful, they rarely produce enduring positive representations in the narcissist, as the value of the positive self-information obtained is compromised by the manipulative way it is elicited. The analysis of the narcissistic self by Rhodewalt provides an excellent illustration of how studying the socially constructed selves – the social mind of the narcissist – can offer new and illuminating insights into the dynamics of interpersonal behavior. Rhodedwalt's work, consistent with some of Schütz's arguments, suggests that the incessant search for self-esteem in our relations with others may produce a number of dysfunctional consequences.

Uncertainty is one of the most universal individual difference characteristics that can influence the social mind. The way people deal with *uncertainty in the interpersonal context* is also an important psychological issue that has a major influence on many kinds of strategic behaviors. The chapter by Richard Sorrentino and colleagues challenges the currently dominant prototype of "humans as rational beings," which implies that people need to know and understand their environment and will engage in cognitive activity or overt behavior in order to resolve uncertainty. Sorrentino et al. argue that certainty-oriented persons are more likely to maintain clarity about their environment rather than engage in or attend to situations that contain uncertainty. Given the tremendous importance of uncertainty in the interpersonal domain, this research program also has important implications for research on interpersonal relations and group dynamics. The evidence presented by Sorrentino et al. suggests that uncertainty orientation is an important moderator of behavior in many areas of strategic social behavior, such as close relationships, attitudes and judgments, group decisions, social identity and self-categorization, minority versus majority influence, social comparison, stereotyping, prejudice, and intergroup conflict. The work presented here suggests that uncertainty orientation is one of the most promising individual difference variables that characterizes the social mind and is an important predictor of how people deal with the social world.

Part III. The Social Mind in Personal Relationships and Interpersonal Behaviors

Symbolic interactionist theories have long assumed that mental representations based on prior experiences of interacting with others should play a key role in influencing our subsequent social behaviors and relationships. This theme is recaptured in the chapter by Susan Andersen and Kathy Berenson, who discuss the way mental representations of significant others, stored in memory, can be activated and applied in new social encounters, with important consequences for thoughts, feelings, and motivations. This process of *transference* can lead social actors to remember things in ways that are distorted toward the significant other in accord with the model of schema-triggered affect. For example, physical resemblance to a significant other may trigger a motivation to be close to such a person. The expectancy of being accepted or rejected by a new person can be triggered by such transference based on past relationship experiences. Similarly, facial affect can be cued by resemblance to a significant other. In sum, Andersen and Berenson's chapter argues that significant other representations and transference are affectively and motivationally laden, and guide our interpersonal strategies in subtle and often counterintuitive ways. The authors' work offers an excellent example of how contemporary social cognitive methods and concepts can help us to better understand interpersonal relationships.

The theme of how mental representations and motivations influence personal relationships is continued in Garth Fletcher's and Jeffry Simpson's chapter, exploring the *structure and function of ideals in close relationships*. What are ideal standards in a relationship? What are the ideal dimensions individuals use to evaluate their partners and relationships? How do such ideal standards develop? And most important, how do ideals influence and guide relationships? Fletcher and Simpson present a comprehensive model analyzing the features and functions of social ideals in close relationships and describe empirical research based on the model. They suggest that ideals have three main functions: They help us to (1) evaluate relationship quality, (2) regulate emotions and behaviors, and (3) explain and predict relationship events. Fletcher and Simpson report a series of studies that explore the content of ideals in romantic relationships, and demonstrate that evaluations of partners are often guided by these ideal standards. Longitudinal research showed how relationship ideals develop and change, and

Fletcher and Simpson also found a close link between relationship ideals and changes in relationship perceptions and satisfaction. These results provide a provocative illustration of how mental representations and ideals can have a tangible influence on our relationships and intimate partners. Fletcher and Simpson interpret these effects in terms of social cognitive mechanisms, and place special emphasis on the role of automatic social comparisons between accessible ideals and actual perceptions. This work offers a particularly nice illustration of the critical role that mental representations play in the maintenance and development of personal relationships.

A special kind of interpersonal relationship is the one created between victims and perpetrators of transgressions. Roy Baumeister and Kathleen Catanese, in their illuminating chapter, analyze the different *accounts of the transgression provided by victims and perpetrators* and the psychological mechanisms responsible for such differences. In a series of studies, Baumeister and his colleagues found that victims produce consistently biased accounts in which (1) the victims were wholly innocent, (2) the perpetrators had no valid reason or justification for their actions, and (3) severe and lasting negative consequences were caused. Further, in victims' accounts, (4) mitigating or extenuating circumstances surrounding the perpetrator's actions were missing, (5) multiple offenses were involved, (6) the victims' reactions were either appropriate or highly restrained, and (7) the transgression is still seen as highly relevant. Despite the widespread assumption that perpetrators lie to protect themselves whereas victims tell the unvarnished truth, Baumeister et al.'s studies show that victims and perpetrators distort information to an equal degree. Both victims and perpetrators distort their accounts significantly more than a control group with no motivational goals to influence their judgments.

Thus, both victim and perpetrator roles contain cognitive and motivational biases that can distort interpretations and memories. Other research by Baumeister also found that perpetrators also alter their speech patterns, use shorter sentences, and avoid grammatical constructions that imply responsibility (e.g., "I decided . . ." vs. "before I knew it . . ."). Perpetrators' accounts also feature their own emotions, rather than those of the victim, and present more antecedent (background) material rather than information about the consequences of their actions. Because victims and perpetrators think about, understand, and remember similar events in very different ways, this makes it far more difficult to resolve certain conflicts after the event. Baumeister and Catanese's work has broad implications for our understanding of the cognitive and motivational distortions that characterize accounts of war crimes, racial oppression, and gender differences in perceptions of rape. This work has important implications for professional practice in forensic, clinical, and counseling psychology, and represents an ingenious illustration of how the study of cognitive and motivational processes can help to illuminate even very intractable social and relationship conflicts.

Interpersonal relationships, especially those involving conflict, often require the exercise of influence tactics, such as the use of ostracism. In their chapter, Williams, Wheeler, and Harvey outline a comprehensive theory of the nature, antecedents, and consequences of social ostracism as an interpersonal strategy. According to the chapter, ostracism occurs when individuals (or sources) ignore and exclude other individuals (or targets). Earlier research in this domain focused primarily on the effects of social ostracism on the target. Specifically, studies explored how targets feel, think, and behave as a consequence of being ignored and excluded by those who are physically present. In contrast, this chapter focuses on individuals who *use* ostracism on others. The needs to belong and to feel control emerge as important motivational themes in understanding the social mind of the ostracizer. According to these studies, ostracizers recognize that by ignoring and excluding others they threaten their target's sense of belonging. Simultaneously, ostracizers perceive a heightened sense of control over their interpersonal environment. The present research employs an event-contingent self-recording method in a micro-longitudinal study to test predictions that social ostracism will be empowering, yet effortful, for sources. In general, the results suggest that some of the very needs that ostracism threatens in targets are the ones that are fortified in the sources of ostracism. The chapter shows that even highly provocative interpersonal tactics, such as ignoring and excluding others, can be adequately analyzed in terms of the cognitive and motivational strategies in the social mind of the ostracizer.

Part IV. The Social Mind of Groups: Group Representations and Group Behavior

The last part of the book contains five chapters that discuss the role that cognitive and motivational processes play in group behavior. Attempts to understand the social minds of group members have a long history in our discipline. Lewin's work on group dynamics established a thriving tradition of research concerned with cognitive and motivational aspects of group behavior. Later, classic work by Festinger, Tajfel, and others gave us new insights into how group membership can shape individuals' mental representations and motivations, and how these processes, in turn, impact on strategic group interactions.

The first chapter in this part, by Michael Hogg, reaches back to Henri Tajfel's seminal work on the role of social identity processes in group behavior. Hogg suggests that one of the main cognitive and motivational functions of group membership may be the reduction of subjective uncertainty through self-categorization processes rather than self-enhancement, as is often assumed. As Hogg points out, ever since Bartlett's presentation of the notion of a human search after meaning, contemporary social psychology has developed an array of constructs that describe a basic human need to reduce subjective uncertainty and render social experience meaningful. Although much of this work focuses on individual differences in the need for certainty or closure (see, for example, the chapter here by Sorrentino et al.), Hogg argues that the experience of subjective uncertainty can also be influenced by the social context. The chapter suggests that *social identification as a group member* is one very effective method of resolving subjective uncertainty and that the cognitive process of self-categorization underlying group identification is well suited to explaining uncertainty reduction. Indeed, uncertainty reduction may be one of the very basic motives for the formation of social groups, an idea that resonates with some of Festinger's earlier notions developed in his social comparison theory. Hogg describes a series of six minimal group experiments that show that identification and intergroup discrimination are stronger among participants who are explicitly categorized under conditions of subjective uncertainty. A series of field studies complements the results of the laboratory experiments. Hogg's work clearly indicates that group membership and group identity can play a critical role in shaping the social minds of individuals, and such representations, in turn, can play a key role in influencing intergroup relations.

The next chapter, by Norbert Kerr, focuses on one of social psychology's most important (but still not satisfactorily resolved) applied questions: How does working in a group affect the task motivation of group members? Specifically, Kerr examines the role of cognitive and motivational processes in producing *motivation gains*. Previous work has shown reliable and predictable motivation losses (i.e., social loafing, free riding) when working in groups, but finding reliable motivation gains has remained elusive. Kerr draws upon his previous work in the search for motivation gains and examines the so-called Köhler effect as a source of motivation gain (an effect produced by how one perceives oneself in relation to group members). Kerr's work shows that it is necessary to understand the workers' social minds to fully understand the links between motivation and performance in work groups. Kerr's approach emphasizes the critical role of conceptions of the self and conceptions of others as they are related to task demands as the key to understanding motivation and performance in groups.

The effects of working among others on an individual's (cognitive) performance is also the topic of the chapter by Pascal Huguet and colleagues. In this discussion, they focus on how mental representations of social situations such as the presence of an audience and their expectations can sometimes dominate even cognitive processes that were previously assumed to be uncontrollable. Huguet et al. present research showing that the automatic cognitive processes that produce Stroop interference are in fact open to social influence and social facilitation in certain social situations. The chapter presents intriguing experimental results from the authors' laboratory showing that performance on the Stroop task can be significantly influenced by social manipulations, such as the presence of an attentive audience or when respondents are engaged in forced upward social comparisons. The authors' findings demonstrate the power of social situations over what has been thought to be invariant automatic cognitive processing. As such, these results appear to challenge the accepted view, reiterated in more than 500 papers on Stroop interference over the past 60 years, that the cognitive mechanisms producing this effect are uncontrollable. The work reported here indicates that even fundamental cognitive processes previously thought to be impervious to control are sensitive to social and environmental influences. In other words, thinking is done by social minds that are always attuned to subtle interpersonal influences.

William Crano's chapter examines another intriguing aspect of the social minds of group members: What is the role of social identity in mediating strategic persuasion processes in groups? In particular, the goals of this chapter are to identify some of the cognitive processes underlying majority and minority influences and to delineate the factors that affect the persistence of attitude change brought about by these different sources of pressure. Crano seeks to provide a plausible theoretical account not only of direct majority influence, but also of delayed and indirect minority-induced change. He reports some fascinating results showing that even when attempts to change a focal attitude through persuasive communication remain overtly unsuccessful, other attitudes associated with the focal attitude may show a spontaneous and delayed change even though not targeted by persuasive messages. The leniency model is developed to explain how the cognitive and motivational mechanisms that allow majority and minority influences to occur may function within groups and mediate these effects. The leniency model builds on earlier research based on the Elaboration Likelihood Model and also considers the role of such factors in persuasion as message strength, outcome relevance, and social identity. The chapter argues that it is only through the integrated analysis of cognitive, affective, and motivational variables that dynamic interpersonal processes such as minority and majority influences on groups can be properly understood.

Decision making by groups involves both cognitive mechanisms, as well as affective and normative variables. The chapter by Martin Kaplan and Henk Wilke explores the conditions that promote task versus relationship motives and analyzes the consequences of such motives for group decision outcomes. All group tasks may be described on a dimension running from purely intellective tasks, which have a demonstrably correct solution, to judgmental tasks, for which solutions are based mainly on opinions and social consensus. Although behaviors guided by task (cognitive) and relationship (social) motives often collide in group decision making and may enhance or inhibit productivity, Kaplan and Wilke also suggest that their effects are frequently interactive. Social motives can affect the approach to a task in terms of the sorts of social decision schemes adopted and the depth of cognitive processing. Kaplan and Wilke present an integrative model of task and social motivational processes in group decision making. This model draws on and synthesizes the dual-process theory of social influence (normative and informational influence) and the dual-process theory of cognitive response (heuristic and systematic reasoning), as well as theories of social decision schemes (SDS) and the social identity theory of intragroup disagreement.

Conclusions

Understanding the way people think, feel, and behave in social situations has always been the core task of social psychology. However, the history of our discipline has been characterized by quite radical swings in interest within this broad domain. For several decades, up to and including the 1960s, the focus of attention was on the study of dynamic interpersonal processes often involving experimentally manipulated strategic social encounters between two or more people. This focus on interactive behaviors produced some of our most dramatic theories and research findings. This highly productive enterprise came to a rather sudden halt with the "crisis" in social psychology in the 1970s. This crisis brought with it a wholesale questioning of the appropriateness of manipulated experiments and ethical doubts about the permissibility of exposing human participants to staged social situations that they might find stressful or demanding. The resolution of the crisis did not involve a rejection of the experimental method and the adoption of qualitative methods. Rather, it produced a shift toward studying the thoughts, ideas, and motivations of isolated social actors, often without exposing them to dynamic interpersonal situations. For the last two decades or so, the social cognitive paradigm has been in ascendancy in our discipline. Critics of this approach often point out that it fails to study real interpersonal behaviors, that it is not truly social, and that it neglects the dynamic, strategic aspects of social life (Forgas, 1981).

Our main purpose in this volume is to suggest that such a stark juxtaposition of social and individualistic paradigms in our discipline is neither necessary nor useful. The chapters included here, in their various ways, all make the point that strategic interpersonal and group behaviors can be explained only if we have a good understanding of the cognitive and motivational processes that guide individuals. In other words, the social minds of individuals should be the key to understanding their strategic social behaviors. The impressive developments during the last two decades in our knowledge of social cognition and motivation offer a sound foundation for reintegrating the social and the indvidual in our discipline. The contributions within each of the four parts of this book were selected to highlight the integrative principles that might help us to accomplish this task.

References

Bless, H., & Forgas, J. P. (Eds.). (2000). *The message within: The role of subjective experience in social cognition and behavior*. Philadelphia: Psychology Press.

Buss, D. M. (1999). *Evolutionary psychology*. Boston: Allyn and Bacon.

Coser, L. A. (1971). *Masters of sociological thought*. New York: Harcourt, Brace, Jovanovich.

Durkheim, E. (1956). *The division of labour in society*. New York: Free Press.

Forgas, J. P. (1981). *Social cognition: Perspectives on everyday understanding*. New York: Academic Press.

Forgas, J. P. (1995). Mood and judgment: The Affect Infusion Model (AIM). *Psychological Bulletin, 116*, 39–66.

Goffman, E. (1972). *Strategic interaction*. New York: Ballantine Books.

Heider, F. (1958). *The psychology of interpersonal relations*. New York: Wiley.

Hilgard, E. R. (1980). The trilogy of mind: Cognition, affection and conation. *Journal of the History of the Behavioral Sciences, 16*, 107–117.

Rosenberg, S., & Sedlak, A. (1972). Structural representations of implicit personality theory. *Advances in Experimental Social Psychology, 6*, 235–297.

Weber, M. (1947). *The theory of social and economic organisation*. (T. Parsons, Ed.). Glencoe, Ill.: Free Press.

Wegner, D. M., & Gilbert, D. T. (2000). Social Psychology: The science of human experience. In H. Bless & J. P. Forgas (Eds.), *The message within: Subjective experience in social cognition and social behavior*. 1–10. Philadelphia: Psychology Press.

PART I

The Social Mind: Basic Issues and Processes

2. Dimensions of the Social Mind: Size, Asymmetries, Congruence, and Sex Differences in Thought Systems Focused on Self or Other Persons

WILLIAM J. McGUIRE AND CLAIRE V. McGUIRE

Thought systems are postulated to develop around important core concepts including those, like the self and significant others, that epitomize the social mind. Self-concepts (i.e., thought systems focused on oneself) are perhaps psychology's most studied topic and deservedly so (James, 1890). Other-person perception, how one thinks and feels about other people, receives less but still substantial study, as in stereotype and impression-formation research. Studies bringing these two topics together to investigate how thought systems focused on self compare and contrast with those focused on others are rarer but not completely neglected (e.g., Duck, Hogg, & Terry, 1998; Griffin & Bartholomew, 1994; Krueger, 1998; Leyens, Yzerbyt, & Rogier, 1997; McGuire & McGuire, 1986; Peeters & De Wit, 1995; Prentice, 1990). The aspects of our research program on thought systems reported in this chapter will, in keeping with the "social mind" theme of this book, concentrate on systems having persons, self or significant others, as their core concepts. In keeping also with this book's motivational and cognitive focus, the research reported in this chapter investigates how the dimensions of such social-mind thought systems are related to affective (e.g., likableness) and cognitive (e.g., familiarity) aspects of the systems' evoking stimulus persons. Our aims include contrasting thought systems focused on the self with those focused on significant others, identifying dimensions of thought systems, untangling positivity asymmetries in the social mind, and identifying differences between how men and women think about people. Earlier studies in our program of research on thought systems include McGuire (1960, 1968,

1984, 1989, 1990), McGuire and McGuire (1986, 1988, 1991, 1992, 1996), and McGuire and Padawer-Singer (1976).

Theory and Predictions Regarding Social Mind

Description of the Thought Systems Studied Here

Despite some views to the contrary (Abelson, 1972; Converse, 1970), our research program shows that people develop organized thought systems, at least around core concepts particularly important to them. Our basic assumption that people organize their thought systems meaningfully agrees with the theorizing of authors of other chapters in this volume, including Andersen's striving-for-meaning assumption, Sorrentino, Hodson, and Huber's uncertainty-orientation notion, Hogg's uncertainty-reduction assumption, Cooper's dissonance-as-aversive theory, and Nezlek's prediction-and-control cognitive focus. We identify the content, structure, and functioning of thought systems by asking participants to focus on a designated core concept important to them (e.g., the self, an intensely disliked person of his or her own sex, a cathected group, a significant event) and then to free associate or carry out a directed-thinking task on this core concept by listing specified types of its characteristics (e.g., list all the desirable characteristics that the stimulus person lacks). We then content analyze the evoked characteristics to identify the dimensions of these person-focused thought systems and to determine the core-concept variables that affect these dimensions. Most self-concept and person-perception studies use reactive approaches that restrict the participant to describing the stimulus person on dimensions presented by the researcher. Such reactive approaches reveal only how the participant would think about the stimulus person on that dimension if he or she ever thought about it without revealing salience information on how often he or she ever does think of it. The open-ended measures used in our research provide information on salience as well.

Independent Variables That Affect Social Mind Thought Systems

In this research program we are especially concerned with how dimensions of thought systems are affected by cognitive (familiarity) and affective (liking) aspects of the stimulus persons who serve as the thought system's evoking core concept, including the self and four types of significant others, intensely liked (versus disliked) familiars of one's own (versus the opposite) sex. A dispositional among-participants independent variable in the design, sex of participants, allows testing of how men and women differ in social mind, particularly in ways they think about people. Andersen, in this volume and elsewhere (Andersen, Glassman, & Gold, 1998), studies effects of similar contrasts in the social mind.

Dependent Variables: Five Significant Dimensions of Thought Systems

These stimulus-person independent variables are predicted to affect five diverse dependent variables, each an interesting dimension of thought systems. We evoked social-mind thought systems by asking participants to focus on a stimulus person of a designated type and to carry out one of four directed-thinking tasks that constitute a 2×2 design: "In the next 3 minutes list as many as you can of the desirable (versus undesirable) characteristics that the person P possesses (versus lacks)." The thought systems so evoked were measured on five dimensions: (1) richness or size of the system (i.e., number of characteristics generated while focusing upon a stimulus person of a designated type averaged across the four directed-thinking tasks); (2) cognitive affirmational bias, or the tendency to think of the stimulus person with an excess of characteristics possessed over those lacked; (3) affective desirability bias, or the tendency to think of people in terms of an excess of desirable characteristics (possessed or lacked) over undesirable ones; (4) evaluative favorability bias, or the tendency to think well of people (i.e., with an excess of desirable characteristics possessed plus undesirable ones lacked, over undesirable characteristics possessed plus desirable ones lacked); and (5) congruence between cognitive and affective manifestations of favorability. The first two are primarily cognitive dimensions; the third and fourth are affective; and the fifth is agreement between cognitive and affective dimensions. Other dimensions of thought systems need study (e.g., distinctiveness and internal organizational dimensions such as connectedness, rigidity, levels, and unicentrality), but the five studied here constitute an ambitious and interesting subset.

Hypotheses

The theorizing about social mind that underlies our research program yields numerous predictions about how the dependent variables, these five dimensions of evoked thought systems, are affected by cognitive and affective independent variables, most of which are manipulated by varying the types of designated stimulus persons that evoke the thought systems. The next section provides operational definitions of the variables, and the subsequent section lays out the theory, derived predictions, and obtained relations between the social-mind independent variables (stimulus-person aspects) and the five dependent variables (thought-system dimensions).

Identifying and Measuring Dimensions of the Social Mind

In the research reported in this chapter all the independent variables except thinker's sex were manipulated by designating contrasting types of stimulus persons to serve as core concepts for evoking social-mind thought systems. Participants were asked to carry out diverse thought-generating tasks while focusing on their selected stimulus person of the designated type to provide measures of the five dependent-variable dimensions of thought systems. This experimental design enabled us to investigate whether variations in stimulus-person characteristics have the predicted effects on the dimensions of the thought systems that the stimulus person evokes.

Variations Among the Stimulus Persons Serving as Thought Systems' Core Concepts

Five categories of stimulus persons were designated, the self plus four designated significant others in a 2×2 design: liked versus disliked others of one's own versus the opposite sex. Participants were asked to select a person they know well in each of the four categories and to rate how much they like the selected person. They were then asked to think about the person selected and to take 3 minutes to write down as many characteristics as possible of a given type (desirable versus undesirable characteristics possessed versus lacked by the designated stimulus person).

Designating the self versus designating one of the significant others as the evoking stimulus person of the thought system was intended to manipulate both a cognitive aspect of the system's core concept (its familiarity) and an affective aspect (its likableness) on the assumption that one both knows and likes oneself more than one does the average others. These familiarity and likableness variables can be unconfounded by testing contrasts between the designated significant other. Specifically, by comparing how thought systems evoked by opposite-sex others differed from those evoked by same-sex others we can test the effects of stimulus-person familiarity on the thought system's dimensions (assuming that one knows one's own sex better). Alternatively, by comparing thought systems evoked by liked others with those evoked by disliked others we can test how stimulus-person likableness affects the dimensions.

Directed-Thinking Tasks That Provided Measures of the Social-Mind
Dependent Variables: The Five Dimensions of Thought Systems

Each participant served in four directed-thinking task conditions, each task focused on a different type of stimulus person (with tasks rotated around stimulus-person types from participant to participant). The four directed-thinking tasks constituted a 2 × 2 design (generating desirable versus undesirable characteristics x that the stimulus person possesses versus lacks). The relative number of characteristics generated in 3 minutes in specified combinations of the four tasks furnished data for measuring the five dependent-variable dimensions of the evoked thought systems. Dimension 1, size of the thought system evoked by each type of stimulus person, is defined here as the mean number of characteristics evoked by that type of stimulus person in 3 minutes across all four tasks.

Dimensions 2, 3, and 4 are dimensions of thought systems concerned with positivity asymmetries that are often confused but are shown here to be distinguishable and conceptually independent of one another in that they constitute orthogonal column, row, and diagonal differences in the 2 × 2 experimental design as regards the task. Dimension 2, cognitive affirmational bias in a thought system focused on a given core concept, is operationally defined as the number of characteristics evoked in the two affirmational directed-thinking tasks ("Write down desirable [undesirable] characteristics possessed by the stimulus person") minus the number evoked in the two negational tasks ("Write down desirable [undesirable] characteristics not possessed"). Dimension 3, affective desirability bias, is defined as the number of characteristics evoked by the two desirable directed-thinking tasks ("Write down desirable characteristics possessed [not possessed] by the stimulus person") minus the number evoked by the two undesirable tasks ("Write down undesirable characteristics possessed [not possessed]"). Dimension 4, favorability bias in thought systems, is defined as the diagonal interaction means in the 2 × 2 directed-thinking design, namely, the number of characteristics evoked in the two favorable tasks ("Write down desirable characteristics possessed" plus "Write down undesirable characteristics not possessed") minus the number evoked in the two unfavorable tasks ("Write down undesirable characteristics possessed" plus "Write down desirable characteristics not possessed").

The fifth dependent variable, Dimension 5, the thought-system's affective-cognitive congruence, is measured by agreement between a cognitive index of stimulus-person evaluation (the excess of favorable over unfavorable characteristics evoked, as in Dimension 4) and an affective index of stimulus-person evaluation (the rated liking for that person).

Procedures and Participants

Each participant worked through an experimental booklet, each of whose five crucial pages called for carrying out one of the four directed-thinking tasks, each on a different stimulus person. At the top of each of these pages were instructions for selecting a designated type of stimulus person: "Choose a person about your own age and the same sex as you are (versus the opposite sex) whom you know well and like (versus dislike) very much. Give that person's initials ——. Indicate how much you dislike or like that person, using a scale from –10 (dislike intensely) to +10 (like intensely) ——." The participant was then given one of the four directed-thinking tasks focused on that person (i.e., told that there would be 3 minutes for writing down as many as possible desirable (versus undesirable) characteristics possessed by (versus lacking in) that stimulus person, writing each new characteristic next to one of the numbers 1 to 20 printed down the left margin of the page. The assignment of directed-thinking tasks to stimulus persons, and the ordering of tasks and persons within the booklets, were systematically rotated from participant to participant.

The 128 participants included 81 women and 47 men, close to the sex ratio of students in the Yale College introductory psychology course from which the students were drawn.

Obtained Relations Between Types of Stimulus Persons and Dimensions of Evoked Thought Systems

The next five subsections report how cognitive and affective differences between stimulus-person core concepts influence the five dependent-variable dimensions of thought systems they evoke: size, cognitive positivity, affective positivity, favorability positivity, and cognitive-affective congruence. A subsequent section describes sex interactions with these five dimensions of social mind.

Factors Affecting Dependent Variable 1, Size of Person-Focused Thought Systems

As regards the size of thought systems evoked by a designated type of core concept (the mean number of thoughts evoked by a specified type of stimulus person across the four thought-generating tasks), a basic Prediction 1a is that thought systems evoked by the self as the stimulus-person core concept will be larger than those evoked by the average of the other persons. This prediction, implied by both cognitive familiarity and affective liking explanations, was confirmed. (See also Sedikides & Gaertner, this volume.) Across the four directed-thinking tasks the self evoked a mean of 9.54 characteristics per task, 1.17 or 14% ($p < .01$) more characteristics than the 8.37 mean evoked by the four other stimulus persons. The cognitive familiarity explanation, that one knows more about oneself than about others, implies a further size Prediction 1b: that others of one's own sex, because one knows one's own sex better, will evoke larger thought systems than others of the opposite sex. There was a slight (3%) difference in this direction, but it was of trivial statistical significance. An alternative affective liking explanation, that one likes the self more and that one thinks more about liked persons, implies size Prediction 1c: that liked others will evoke larger thought systems than will disliked others. This prediction was strongly confirmed ($p < .01$): Liked others evoked 9.03 characteristics, and disliked others evoked 7.71, a substantial 1.32 or 17% difference.

Factors Affecting Dependent Variable 2, Cognitive Affirmational Bias in Thought Systems

The basic cognitive affirmational bias Prediction 2a, that thinkers will generate more characteristics that core concepts have than lack, is paradoxical considering that there are usually far more characteristics that people lack than have (nationality is typical in that an individual tends to have one or two nationalities but to lack hundreds). One explanation is a default process that merely thinking of a characteristic automatically affirms it of the evoking concept unless, by a second operation, one explicitly negates it. Three other explanations (McGuire & McGuire, 1992) involve distinctiveness, a tree diagram organization of the social mind, and confounding with markedness. As predicted, many more ($p < .01$) characteristics were evoked in the "have" than in the "not have" task conditions, the means being 9.46 versus 7.75, respectively, a 22% affirmational bias. Negational thinking, being more difficult, should be especially sparse in thought systems evoked by less familiar stimulus persons, implying Predictions 2b and 2c. Implied Prediction 2b is that cognitive affirmational bias will be greater in thought systems focused on other persons than on self; the obtained difference is in the predicted direction but falls short of .05 significance. Implied Prediction 2c is that because one knows one's own sex better, the cognitive-affirmational bias will be greater for opposite-sex than for own-sex other, but again the obtained difference was trivial.

An alternative affective explanation is that it is friendlier to think of people in terms of what they are rather than what they lack, which implies Predictions 2d, 2e, and 2f. Implied Prediction 2d, that affirmational bias will be greater in thought systems surrounding liked than disliked others, is strongly confirmed ($p < .01$): The obtained cognitive affirmational over negational excess is greater in thought systems focused on liked than disliked others, $10.47 - 7.59 = 2.88$ (38%) versus $8.03 - 7.39 = 0.64$ (9%). Implied Prediction 2e is also confirmed ($p < .05$): Cognitive affirmational bias is greater in thought systems focused on self, $10.30 - 8.78 = 1.52$ (17%), than on disliked others, $8.03 - 7.39 = 0.64$ (9%). Prediction 2f (implied by counter-intuitive Predictions 4i and 4'j that liked others are liked better than the self) is also confirmed in that cognitive affirmational bias is greater ($p < .01$) in systems focused on liked others, $10.47 - 7.59 = 2.88$ (38%) than on the self, $10.30 - 8.78 = 1.52$ (17%). Even though these first two thought-system dimensions, DV1 (size) and DV2 (cognitive affirmational bias), are themselves cognitive more than affective dimensions of thought systems, they are influenced more by affective (liking) than cognitive (familiarity) aspects of the stimulus persons on which the systems focus. (See Forgas and also Nezlek, this volume.)

Factors Affecting Dependent Variable 3, Affective Desirability Bias in Thought Systems

As regards affective asymmetry, our basic Prediction 3a is that social-mind thought systems focused on people, especially in circumstances when self-gratifying autistic thinking is feasible, are richer in desirable than undesirable characteristics possessed or lacked by the social stimulus (because it is less anxiety arousing to think of desirable than undesirable characteristics of persons). Across the four stimulus persons, this predicted excess of desirable over undesirable characteristics did obtain, $8.76 - 7.98 = 0.78$ (10%), $p < .05$. Prediction 3b is that this obtained desirability bias, because it is the net resultant of opposed, mutually canceling forces, will be less than the cognitive affirmational bias (Prediction 2a) that is the outcome of more univalent forces. The 10% obtained affective desirable bias was indeed significantly less ($p < .05$) than the 22% cognitive affirmational bias.

Our theorizing (McGuire & McGuire, 1991) regarding Dimension 3 is that affective desirability bias will be found to the extent that it is safe to indulge in autistically gratifying wishful thinking, for example, when the stimulus-person core concept is low threat. Conversely, an undesirability bias will emerge in thought systems evoked by threatening core concepts that call for realistic coping, such as by damage control and uncertainty reduction. (See Sorrentino et al., Forgas, & Hogg, this volume.) Two interaction predictions follow. For interaction Prediction 3c, that autistically gratifying desirability bias will be greater in thought systems focused on the safer self than on other people, the obtained results are in the predicted direction but are of trivial magnitude. Interaction Prediction 3d, that affective desirability bias will be greater in thought systems focused on safer liked others than on disliked others, was strongly confirmed ($p < .01$). In thought systems evoked by liked others, the desirability bias was $9.87 - 8.20 = 1.67$ (20%), far exceeding the $7.65 - 7.77 = -0.12$ (−2%) undesirable bias in systems focused on riskier disliked others. Forgas's (Chapter 5) Affect Infusion Model could be elaborated to take into account possible asymmetry between infusion of positive and negative affect.

Factors Affecting Dependent Variable 4, Favorability (People Positivity) Bias in Thought Systems

On the assumption that it is gratifying to perceive people with whom one comes into frequent contact as benign, our basic Prediction 4a about a favorability asymmetry is that thought systems focused on people will show an overall favorability bias (Anderson, 1981; Sears, 1983). Across thought systems focused on all four of the stimulus persons there was a preponderance ($p < .01$) of favorable characteristics (desirable ones possessed and undesirable ones lacked) over unfavorable ones (undesirable characteristics possessed and desirable ones lacked), $9.27 - 7.48 = 1.79$, a 24% favorability bias. Prediction 4b, that this 4a favorability bias will be greater than the affective desirability bias (Prediction 3a) that is the resultant of two opposed, mutually canceling forces, is also supported: The obtained favorability bias of 28% is significantly ($p < .01$) greater than the 10% affective desirability bias.

It is not only that liked people evoke a greater excess of favorable over unfavorable characteristics than do disliked people, and not only that liked people evoke an excess of favorable characteristics and disliked people an excess of unfavorable characteristics. Beyond these hypotheses is the nonobvious people positivity asymmetry Prediction 4c, that the excess of favorable characteristics evoked by liked people will be greater than the excess of unfavorable characteristics evoked by disliked people. In confirmation ($p < .01$) the excess DV4 favorability in thought systems focused on liked others, $12.56 - 5.51 = +7.04$ (+128%) was significantly ($p < .01$) greater in absolute value than was the unfavorability excess for disliked others, $5.98 - 9.44 = -3.46$ (-37%). A parallel Prediction 4'd measures favorability by an affective index, namely, the rated likableness of the selected stimulus persons. On a scale of -10 (intensely dislike) to $+10$ (intensely like), the selected liked persons received a mean positive rating of $+8.24$, whereas disliked persons received a smaller mean negative rating of -5.60, this greater polarization of the liked-person ratings being significant at the .01 level. Liked people are rated more likeable than disliked people are rated dislikable. On the whole people are perceived as fundamentally good.

At least three explanations can account for this overall people favorability bias. Evolutionary theory (Buss & Schmitt, 1993) suggests that people favorability would promote approach tendencies that confer a reproductive advantage. This implies Prediction 4e, that an excess of favorable over unfavorable characteristics will be greater in thought systems evoked by opposite-sex others than by own-sex others. The obtained favorability difference is in the predicted direction, 27% versus 21%, but falls short of the .05 significance level.

A second, ego-enhancement (ingroup favoring) or narcissism (see Rhodewalt, this volume) explanation, is that favoring people flatters the self (oneself being a person), implying Prediction 4f, that the excess of favorable characteristics will be greater in thought systems evoked by more similar own-sex others than by opposite-sex others; however, the obtained difference is nonsignificantly in the opposite direction. An obvious implication of ego-enhancement theory, that thought systems evoked by the self will show more favorability excess than those evoked by the four other persons, is confirmed by both cognitive and affective indices. As regards the DV4 cognitive index, the excess of favorable over unfavorable characteristics in thought systems evoked by the self is $11.30 - 7.78 = 3.52$ (45%), whereas in thought systems evoked by the four other persons, the mean is substantially less ($p < .01$), $9.27 - 7.48 = 1.79$ (24%). In terms of the affective rating index of stimulus-person favorability, Prediction 4'h is likewise confirmed. The mean admiration rating on a 1 to 15 scale was 10.48 for the self, higher ($p < .01$) than the mean admiration rating of 7.77 for the four other persons.

A third, wishful-thinking, hero-worship theory explains people-favorability bias as a reassuring outlook enhancing confidence that one's associates are admirable people, likely to help when one is in need, so that one can depend on the kindness of strangers and familiars alike (A. M. McGuire, 1994). This helpfulness explanation implies that thought systems evoked by liked others will be even more favorable than thought systems evoked by the self, both in terms of the DV4 evoked cognitive characteristics index (Prediction 4i) and in terms of the affective rating index (Prediction 4'j). These two predictions, although nonobvious and even counterintuitive, are both confirmed. As regards the DV4 cognitive index of favorability, thought systems evoked by liked others show a favorable-over-unfavorable excess of $12.56 - 5.51 = 7.05$ (128%), higher ($p < .01$) than the favorable excess in systems evoked by the self, $11.30 - 7.78 = 3.52$ (45%), confirming Prediction 4i. Likewise, as regards the affective index of favorability, the mean admiration rating on a 1 to 15 scale was 12.22 for liked others, higher ($p < .05$) than the 10.48 mean admiration rating for the self. In accord with this nonobvious tendency to perceive liked others more favorably than the self are Tice and Faber's discussion in Chapter 7 of a risk-reducing modesty among friends and Schütz's Chapter 8 discussion of low self-esteem participants' rating self more modestly than partners, Sedikides and Gaertner's discussion in Chapter 6 of collective self, and more tenuously Rhodelwalt's proposition in Chapter 9 that narcissism is dependent on positive feedback more than accomplishments.

Factors Affecting Dependent Variable 5, Affective-Cognitive Congruence in Thought Systems

Each of the previous four dependent variables deals with a single dimension of thought systems. A fifth "congruence" dependent variable is more complex, referring to the amount of agreement between two dimensions: the affective favorability rating of the stimulus person and that person's net evocation of favorable over unfavorable cognitions. The basic prediction, that affective and cognitive indices of stimulus persons' favorability will be positively interrelated, is supported ($p < .01$), whether liking is varied by acute manipulation of liking (Prediction 5a) or by correlation with chronic levels of liking (Prediction 5b). As regards manipulating likability of the thought system's core concept (by designating highly liked versus highly disliked stimulus persons as the core concept to evoke the thought system), the excess of favorable over unfavorable characteristics evoked was $12.56 - 5.51 = 7.05$ (128%) for liked stimulus persons; conversely, disliked stimulus persons evoked fewer ($p < .01$) favorable than unfavorable characteristics, $5.98 - 9.44 = -3.46$ (−37%).

Congruence was measured also by how the affective likableness ratings and admiration ratings of the stimulus persons correlated with the cognitive index of favorability (the DV4a excess of favorable over unfavorable characteristics evoked by the stimulus persons). The correlations (Pearson r values) between likableness ratings and the cognitive favorability excess across the 128 participants were +0.73 and +0.46 for number of desirable characteristics possessed and undesirable ones lacked, respectively; and the r values were −.38 and −.66 for undesirable characteristics possessed and desirable ones lacked. The corresponding correlations between admirableness and cognitive favorability excess showed a similar pattern, $r = +.77$ and +.54 and $r = -.48$ and −.25. Each of the eight correlations is significantly in the predicted direction and each, except the last, is individually significant at the .01 level.

Postulating that congruence within the social mind increases with opportunity for editing out inconsistencies and for amassing bolstering cognitions, then congruence of thought systems should increase with familiarity of the core concepts. (See Cooper, this volume.) If so, congruence will be greater in thought systems focused on self than on other people (Prediction 5c) and in those focused on same-sex than on opposite-sex others (Prediction 5d). An alternative, affective explanation of the obtained congruence implies that it will be greater in thought systems focused on liked than disliked others (Prediction 5e) and on liked others than on the self (Prediction 5f). However, none of these four interaction predictions was confirmed at the conventional .05 level, indicating that the high affective-cognitive congruence in thought systems is robust in magnitude across the cognitive and affective manipulations used here.

Sex Differences in Social Mind as Manifested on the Five Dimensions of Thought Systems

For counterbalancing and to enhance generalizability, and because of their ad hoc intrinsic interest, three sex-independent variables were included in the experimental design: sex of the participant who is doing the thinking, sex of the stimulus person on whom the thought system is focused, and the interaction between the two (e.g., the thinker's and the stimulus person's being of the same versus the opposite sex). Sex of participant is predicted to have pervasive main effects on the five thought systems' dimensions on the assumption that women are more people-oriented and people-favorable than men (McGuire & McGuire, 1982, 1988).

Differences Between Male and Female Thinkers on DV1, Richness of People-Focused Thought Systems

The postulate that women are more people-oriented than men implies sex-difference Prediction S1a, that women will generate richer people-focused thought systems than will men. This prediction is confirmed ($p < .01$): The mean number of characteristics per task evoked across the four other-person stimuli is 8.97 for female participants, 22% more than the 7.34 generated by males. The assumption that women's social minds are not only larger than men's but also more favorable yields the further, confirmed ($p < .05$) Prediction S1b, that women's thought systems will be larger than men's more for systems surrounding liked others (about whom more good things can be said) than for those surrounding disliked others. Also confirmed ($p < .05$) is Prediction S1c, that men's thought systems will be more egocentric than women's, the size of self-focused thought systems exceeding the size of those evoked by the liked significant others more in men than in women (See Sedikides & Gaertner, this volume).

These sex differences in the size of thought systems could be due either to women's being more people oriented or to women's being more verbal. McGuire and McGuire (1991) report that as regards thought systems focused on core concepts other than people (e.g., on future eventualities), women's thought systems are not notably larger than men's. Women's greater verbal fluency may be declining (Finegold, 1988) and the sex difference in thought-system richness found here seems attributable to women's greater preoccupation with people rather than to women's greater verbal ability.

Differences Between Male and Female Thinkers on DV2, Cognitive Affirmational Bias

As regards sex differences on DV2, cognitive affirmational bias in thought systems focused on persons, the postulate that women are more favorable to people than are men implies Prediction S2a, a greater affirmational bias in women, it being more friendly to think of significant others in terms of what they are rather than what they lack. In confirmation ($p < .05$ for the interaction), the cognitive affirmational bias (generating an excess of characteristics possessed over those lacked) in thought systems focused on significant others is 28% (10.08 − 7.86 = 2.22) in women and only 13% (7.82 − 6.90 = 0.92) in men. More favorable interpersonal thinking in women than in men is indicated also (Prediction S2b) by women's greater cognitive affirmational bias's showing up almost entirely in thought systems focused on others and hardly at all in self-focused thought systems.

Differences Between Male and Female Thinkers on DV3, Affective Desirability Bias

Predictions about sex differences on the DV3 dependent variable (affective desirability bias) are more ambiguous because our complex theorizing (McGuire & McGuire, 1991) could lead to opposite main-effect predictions that would need interaction effects to disentangle. One could predict an affective desirability bias (i.e., thinking about the stimulus-person core concept in terms of desirable rather than undesirable characteristics possessed or lacked) to the extent that the thinker can afford to indulge in the gratifications of autistic thinking. Conversely, one could predict an affective undesirable bias (i.e., thinking about the core concept in terms of undesirable more than desirable characteristics) to the extent that the situation calls for realistic problem-focused thinking about undesirable possibilities in order to facilitate adaptive coping modes like prevention, uncertainty reduction, and damage control. (See Sorrentino et al., Forgas, and Hogg, this volume.) This theorizing has complex sex-difference implications. Women might show more desirability bias (because women's more favorable view of people would make them feel safer in engaging in pleasant autistic thinking); conversely, women might show more undesirable bias (because women's greater interpersonal concerns would make them feel more vulnerable, so that they would be more effectively realistic in thinking about others). (See Kaplan & Wilke, this volume.) Given these mutually canceling tendencies, it is not surprising that men and women in this study both showed only slight ($p > .05$) main-effect desirability biases.

The stimulus-person design of this research allows these complex, mutually canceling affective desirability (DV3) biases to be untangled by testing for implied interaction effects. Our theory, that in more secure situations an affective desirability bias will occur and in more threatening situations there will be an undesirability bias, implies interaction sex differences in the direction that women will show more desirability bias than men to a greater extent in thought systems focused on safer liked others than on the more dangerous disliked others (Prediction S3a) and to a greater extent in thought systems whose core concept is the safer self rather than riskier other people (Prediction S3b). Both obtained interactions are in the predicted direction, but neither reaches the .05 level of significance.

Differences Between Male and Female Thinkers on DV4, Evaluative Favorability Bias

The postulate that women are more people oriented and friendly than men has clear implications regarding DV4, favorability bias. Basic Prediction S4a is that thought systems evoked across the four other-person core concepts will show a greater excess of favorable over unfavorable characteristics in women than in men. Thought systems focused on other people do show a greater ($p < .05$) favorability excess for female participants (10.11 − 7.83 = 2.28, 29%) than for male particirants (7.81 − 6.87 = 0.94, 14%). Also implied is interaction Prediction S4b, that the favorability bias in thought systems focused on the self will be greater than in those focused on others more in male than in female participants. In confirmation ($p < .05$), for male participants the favorability bias is substantially greater in self-systems than in systems focused on other persons (4.21 versus 0.94), whereas the corresponding self-versus-other favorability excess for female participants is only 4.48 versus 2.28. (See also Tice & Faber, this volume.)

Differences Between Male and Female Thinkers on DV5, Affective-Cognitive Congruence

Affective-cognitive congruence can be measured by the size of the positive relation between affective ratings of the stimulus person and the excess of favorable over unfavorable cognitive characteristics evoked by that person. Prediction S5a is that this excess cognitive favorability in thought systems evoked by liked over disliked stimulus persons will be greater in female than in male thinkers because women's greater people preoccupation will have facilitated their editing out inconsistencies in their perceptions of others. (See Cooper, this volume.) As predicted, the excess of favorable over unfavorable characteristics in thought systems focused on liked versus disliked stimulus persons is greater ($p < .01$) for women (7.78 versus −3.39 for an 11.17 excess) than for men (5.44 versus −3.51 for an 8.95 excess).

In summary, men's and women's people-focused thought systems show similar directions of relations, but women's social minds are larger, more favorable, more cognitively affirmational, and show greater affective-cognitive congruence than men's. More comparative study is needed of the extent to which these thinker sex differences show up only in social mind (i.e., in thought systems focused on people core concepts) or also in thought systems focused on core concepts other than people (McGuire & McGuire, 1991, 1992).

Differences Between Thought Systems Focused on Male Versus Female Stimulus Persons

In contrast to these pervasive differences between male and female thinkers in people-focused thought systems, it makes little difference whether the stimulus people who served as the thought-system core concepts are men or women. Sex of the stimulus persons has few significant main or interaction effects on these five dimensions of thought systems. Only on dimension DV4, favorability bias, did sex of the evoking stimulus person have a significant main effect. Thought systems focused on female stimulus persons more ($p < .01$) than those focused on male stimulus persons show an excess of generated favorable characteristics (desirable ones possessed and undesirable ones lacked) over unfavorable ones (undesirable ones possessed and desirable ones lacked). This greater favoring of female stimulus persons shows up in the thought systems of both male and female thinkers. It shows up only on the subtle cognitive index, DV4, and not on the explicitly evaluative rating index. (See Huguet, Galvaing, Dumas, & Monteil and Crano, this volume.)

Half of the participants rated the stimulus persons on a likableness scale and the other half rated them on an admirableness scale in order to detect any "patronizing partiality" toward women, that is, viewing women as more likable but without regarding their achievements as more admirable (Eagly & Mladinic, 1994; Glick & Fiske, 1996; Haddock & Zanna, 1994). However, on neither the likableness nor the admirableness rating scale were female stimulus persons rated more favorably than male stimulus persons by either men or women thinkers. Schütz in Chapter 8, Rhodewalt in Chapter 9, and Kaplan and Wilke in Chapter 19 discuss possible conflicts between liking and admiration, either for people in general or as a stimulus person sex difference.

Progress Made and Progress Needed

The methodological approach, the theoretical issues raised, and the relations found in the present research program have important theoretical and practical implications. As regards methodological yields, this research program demonstrates the utility of collecting salience information by more open-ended measures and manipulations that allow participants more leeway to respond in their own terms rather than limiting their responses to reactions that place a core concept on some dimension of the researcher's choosing. Reactive approaches reveal only where the participant would think the core concept falls on the experimenter-chosen dimension if he or she ever thought of it; our open-ended approaches reveal also how frequently that dimension occurs to the thinker. These open-ended, thought-generating methods also show that the participant's cognition and affect on a topic can be changed without presenting new information from an outside source but simply by using Socratic questioning or directed-thinking tasks that enhance the salience of material already within the person's own thought system on the topic (McGuire & McGuire, 1991).

Theoretical issues regarding positivity asymmetries, a topic popularized in basic research by Peeters (1971; Peeters & Czapinski, 1992) and by Tversky and Kahneman's (1981) framing theory, are clarified by our decomposing positivity biases into three orthogonal dimensions (cognitive affirmation, affective desirability, and evaluative favorability) that can be manipulated and measured independently, and are shown to be distinguishable among themselves and to relate differently to other variables. Another important aspect of social mind clarified here is how thought systems focused on the self differ from those focused on other people. Other basic theoretical yields of this research program are clarifications of five dimensions of thought systems and of how they are affected by aspects of the stimulus persons who serve as the systems' core concepts. For example, thought systems focused on the self differ from those focused on significant other persons by being richer and more favorable (except that liked others are actually perceived even more favorably than the self). However, self and other perceptions do not differ on cognitive affirmational or affective desirability biases. As regards liked versus disliked significant others, thought systems focused on liked others are richer, more cognitively affirmational, more affectively desirable, and more favorable than those focused on disliked others. Thought systems focused on own-sex stimulus persons do not differ significantly from those focused on opposite-sex stimulus persons on any of the five dimensions. In general, thought systems are influenced by the affective aspects of the stimulus persons (e.g., their likableness) more than by their cognitive aspects (e.g., their similarity or familiarity). Sex of the thinker is shown to have considerable effect on four of the five dimensions of people-focused thought systems, indicating that women think more frequently and more favorably about people than do men. However, sex of the stimulus person who is thought about has little effect (only on the favorability and on that dimension only if a subtle cognitive asymmetry index is used).

As regards practical implications, this program of research clarifies applied issues on the intergroup level such as subtleties of sex stereotypes and whether hostility between outgroups can be more efficaciously reduced by having people think about the outgroup members in terms of desirable characteristics they possess or undesirable ones from which they are free. A practical implication on the intrapersonal clinical level is whether self-esteem can be more effectively enhanced by thinking of desirable characteristics one has or of undesirable characteristics from which one is free (McGuire, 1990; McGuire & McGuire, 1996). In the intimate relationships discussed by Fletcher and Simpson in Chapter 12 favorability might be expressed largely in terms of desirable characteristics possessed, whereas the favorability of casual friends might be expressed more in terms of undesirable characteristics from which they are free.

Promising topics for further research are also indicated. Firstly, study is needed of additional dimensions of thought systems beyond the five investigated here, especially dimensions of internal organization (centrality, hierarchy, complexity, etc.), connectedness, distinctiveness, and other asymmetries (e.g., between costs and benefits or between causes and effects). Secondly, comparative effects on thought systems of cognitive versus affective aspects of core concepts need further study using partial definitions beyond the familiarity versus liking used here. Thirdly, further study is needed of how the relations found here in thought systems evoked by stimulus persons (which most clearly constitute social mind) compare and contrast with the relations found in asocial thought systems focused on core concepts other than people.

References

Abelson, R. P. (1972). Are attitudes necessary? In B. T. King & E. McGinnies (Eds.), *Attitudes, conflicts, and social change* (pp. 19–32). New York: Academic Press.

Andersen, S. M., Glassman, N. S., & Gold, D. A. (1998). Mental representations of the self, significant others, and nonsignificant others: Structure and processing of private and public aspects. *Journal of Personality and Social Psychology, 75*, 845–861.

Anderson, N. H. (1981). *Foundations of information integration theory*. New York: Academic Press.

Buss, D. M., & Schmitt, D. P. (1993). Sexual strategies theory: An evolutionary perspective on human mating. *Psychological Review, 100*, 204–232.

Converse, P. E. (1970). Attitudes and nonattitudes: Continuation of a dialogue. In E. R. Tufts (Ed.), *The quantitative analysis of social problems* (pp. 168–189). Reading, MA: Addison-Wesley.

Duck, J. M., Hogg, M. A., & Terry, D. J. (1998). Perceived self-other differences in persuasibility: The effects of interpersonal and group-based similarity. *European Journal of Social Psychology, 28*, 1–21.

Eagly, A., & Mladinic, A. (1994). Are people prejudiced against women? Some answers from research on attitudes, gender stereotypes, and judgements of competence. In W. Stroebe & H. Hewstone (Eds.), *European Review of Social Psychology* (Vol. 5, pp. 1–35). Chichester, UK: Wiley.

Finegold, A. (1988). Cognitive gender differences are disappearing. *American Psychologist, 43,* 95–103.

Glick, P., & Fiske, S. T. (1996). The ambivalent sexism inventory: Differentiating hostile and benevolent sexism. *Journal of Personality and Social Psychology, 70,* 491–512.

Griffin, D., & Bartholomew, K. (1994). Models of the self and others: Fundamental dimensions underlying measures of adult attachment. *Journal of Personality and Social Psychology, 67,* 430–445.

Haddock, G., & Zanna, M. P. (1994). Preferring "housewives" to "feminists": Categorization and the favorability of attitudes toward women. *Psychology of Women Quarterly, 18,* 25–52.

James, W. (1890). *Principles of psychology.* New York: Holt.

Krueger, J. (1998). Enhancement bias in descriptions of self and others. *Personality and Social Psychology Bulletin, 24,* 505–516.

Leyens, J. P., Yzerbyt, V. Y., & Rogier, A. (1997). Personality traits that distinguish you and me are better memorized. *European Journal of Social Psychology, 27,* 511–522.

McGuire, A. M. (1994). Helping behaviors in the natural environment: dimensions and correlates of helping. *Personality and Social Psychology Bulletin, 20,* 45–56.

McGuire, W. J. (1960). A syllogistic analysis of cognitive relationships. In C. I. Hovland & M. J. Rosenberg (Eds.), *Attitude organization and change* (pp. 65–111). New Haven, CT: Yale University Press.

McGuire, W. J. (1968). Theory of the structure of human thought. In R. P. Abelson, E. Aronson, W. J. McGuire, T. M. Newcomb, M. J. Rosenberg, & P. H. Tannenbaum (Eds.), *Theories of cognitive consistency: A sourcebook* (pp. 140–162). Chicago: Rand McNally.

McGuire, W. J. (1984). Search for self: Going beyond self-esteem and the reactive self. In R. A. Zucker, J. Arnoff, & A. I. Rabin (Eds.), *Personality and the prediction of behavior* (pp. 73–120). New York: Academic Press.

McGuire, W. J. (1989). The structure of individual attitudes and attitude systems. In A. R. Pratkanis, S. J. Breckler, & A. G. Greenwald (Eds.), *Attitude structure and function* (pp. 37–69). Hillsdale, NJ: Erlbaum.

McGuire, W. J. (1990). Dynamic operations of thought systems. *American Psychologist, 45,* 504–512.

McGuire, W. J., & McGuire, C. V. (1982). Significant others in self-space: Sex differences and developmental trends in the social self. In J. Suls (Ed.), *Social psychological perspectives on the self* (pp. 41–70). Beverly Hills, CA: Sage.

McGuire, W. J., & McGuire, C. V. (1986). Differences in conceptualizing self versus conceptualizing other people as manifested in contrasting verb types used in natural speech. *Journal of Personality and Social Psychology, 51,* 1135–1143.

McGuire, W. J., & McGuire, C. V. (1988). Content and process in the experience of self. In L. Berkowitz (Ed.), *Advances in experimental social psychology* (Vol. 21, pp. 97–144). New York: Academic Press.

McGuire, W. J., & McGuire, C. V. (1991). The content, structure, and operation of thought systems. In R. S. Wyer, Jr., & T. K. Srull (Eds.), *Advances in social cognition* (Vol. IV, pp. 1–78). Hillsdale, NJ: Erlbaum.

McGuire, W. J., & McGuire, C. V. (1992). Cognitive-versus-affective positivity asymmetries in thought systems. *European Journal of Social Psychology, 22,* 571–591.

McGuire, W. J., & McGuire, C. V. (1996). Enhancing self-esteem by directed thinking tasks: Cognitive and affective positivity asymmetries. *Journal of Personality and Social Psychology, 70,* 1117–1124.

McGuire, W. J., & Padawer-Singer, A. (1976). Trail salience in the spontaneous self-concept. *Journal of Personality and Social Psychology, 33,* 743–754.

Peeters, G. (1971). The positive–negative asymmetry: On cognitive consistency and positivity bias. *European Journal of Social Psychology, 1,* 455–474.

Peeters, G., & Czapinski, J. (Eds.). (1992). Positive–negative asymmetries. *European Journal of Social Psychology, 22,* whole issues Nos. 5, 6.

Peeters, G., & DeWit, R. (1995). Self–other and third-person anchored mode of thinking in psychological expertise. *International Journal of Psychology, 30,* 317–328.

Prentice, D. A. (1990). Familiarity and differences in self- and other-representations. *Journal of Personality and Social Psychology, 59,* 369–383

Sears, D. O. (1983). The person-positivity bias. *Journal of Personality and Social Psychology, 44,* 233–250.

Tversky, A., & Kahneman, D. (1981). The framing of decisions and the psychology of choice. *Science, 211,* 453–458.

3. Affect and the "Social Mind": Affective Influences on Strategic Interpersonal Behaviors

JOSEPH P. FORGAS

Introduction

Interpersonal behavior is almost never devoid of affect. Indeed, as Zajonc (1980) once argued, affect is probably *the* most fundamental dimension of social interaction. It is rather surprising to find, then, that most of the classic theories interested in the social mind and its role in interpersonal behavior devoted relatively little attention to the analysis of affective states and their role in social life (Hilgard, 1980). It is only as a result of extensive research during the past 20 years or so that it is now recognized that affect and mood constitute an essential component of the social mind, and exert a significant and predictable influence on our thinking as well as our strategic social behaviors. Indeed, there is strong convergent evidence from neuropsychology and psychophyisiology supporting the view that affect is an essential component of adaptive social thinking and motivation (Adolphs & Damasio, in press; Blascovich & Mendes, 2000).

Evidence for the pervasive role of affect in many kinds of social behaviors is all around us. To take one example, in a well-known short story on the game of chess, the writer Thomas Mann describes how chess players will suddenly and unconsciously change their strategies from aggressive to defensive and back again in line with the changing

This work was supported by a Special Investigator award from the Australian Research Council and by the Research Prize awarded by the Alexander von Humboldt Foundation to Joseph P. Forgas. The contribution of Stephanie Moylan and Joan Webb to this project is gratefully acknowledged. Please address all correspondence in connection with this chapter to Joseph P. Forgas at the School of Psychology, University of New South Wales, Sydney 2052, Australia; email: jp.forgas@unsw.edu.au affective tone of the background music they listen to. But how and why should changes in incidental music produce a change in people's strategic behaviors? What are the cognitive mechanisms that are responsible for this subtle link between an upbeat, positive tune, the good mood it induces, and more daring, risky, and optimistic strategic moves?

In many ways, playing chess is an ideal metaphor for understanding the strategies that govern social interaction in real life. Just like chess, social interaction also demands constructive thinking in inherently uncertain situations. Subtle shifts in mood due to changes in background music, for example, may impact on our incidental thoughts and associations, and ultimately will have a significant influence on our interpersonal behaviors. Experimental studies have confirmed the effects of mood on various strategic behaviors, just as described by Thomas Mann. Participants in a good mood seem to behave in a much more confident and even assertive way, whereas participants in a bad mood act in a pessimistic and cautious manner (Forgas, 1999a, 1999b). Thomas Mann's short story also describes just how this might happen. His chess players subconsciously hum along with the tunes they hear, and the words and thoughts that come to their minds either seem associated with positive, lucky, and successful events (happy tunes) or suggest failure, sadness, and loss (sad tunes). As their minds constructively search for the next strategic move in their game, their music-induced thoughts and associations cannot help but infuse their plans about what to do and eventually influence their playing strategies.

How do Thomas Mann's incisive – but fictional – ideas linking music, mood, and chess apply to real-life interpersonal behaviors? Do affective states indeed influence what we do in social situations? Based on recent theories and empirical evidence, this chapter will describe just how and why affect should be considered an integral part of the social mind and how affective states may come to influence many kinds of interpersonal behaviors.

Some Theoretical Issues

Even though the relationship between affect, cognition, and behavior has been the focus of enduring interest and speculation since time immemorial, most of what we know about the links between affect and social behavior have been discovered only during the past 20 years or so. This chapter will emphasize the critical role of *cognitive* processes in mediating affective influences on social behaviors. This emphasis is based on extensive recent evidence – including numerous studies in our Affect Research Laboratory – suggesting that mood effects on attention, thinking, memory, and judgments are critically involved in regulating eventual mood effects on behavior. In other words, this chapter will suggest that it is through affective influences on cognition that subsequent changes in interpersonal behaviors can be best understood. Cognitive accounts are also preferred here because they appear better able to accommodate clear evidence indicating the considerable context and situation sensitivity of affective influences on social behaviors (see also the chapter by McGuire and McGuire).

Motivational Accounts

There is, however, also an alternative view that emphasizes the direct influence of affect on motivation rather than cognition as the primary route to explain behavioral effects. Recent theories by Carver and Scheier (1998), Polivy (1998), and others represent influential examples of such an approach. These theories see affect as essentially an adaptive and functional source of information about motivated goal achievement. It is quite interesting that after decades of ignoring affect as at best irrelevant and at worst a fundamentally disruptive and maladaptive force (Hilgard, 1980), psychological theories have now come full circle, viewing emotions as a source of predominantly functional and adaptive information. For example, Carver and Scheier (1998) suggest that affect mainly functions as a signal indicating progress toward goal achievement and plays a key role in regulating the *intensity* of motivation.

This seems an unduly restrictive conceptualization of the role of affect in social behavior. In fact, much of the evidence to be reviewed here suggests that affect can also have an important independent influence on behavior by colouring people's thoughts, judgments, and interactive strategies. According to this view, affective influences are neither inherently functional nor dysfunctional. As human beings are highly flexible and sophisticated information processors, affective influences on behavior can be best understood in terms of cognitive mediating mechanisms (Bower, 1991; Forgas, 1995a; Smith & Kirby, 2000). Thus, rather than viewing affect as simply a motivational feedback signal (Polivy, 1998), it will be argued here that affect also has a direct and independent influence on behavior that is mediated by cognitive processes.

Affect, Mood, and Emotion

Our primary concern here is with the effects of low-intensity moods on social behaviors. Despite decades of research, it remains unclear how terms such as *emotion, affect, feelings,* or *mood* can best be defined (Fiedler & Forgas, 1988; Forgas, 1992a, 1995a). As we have proposed elsewhere, the term affect will be typically used here as a generic label to refer to both moods and emotions. Moods, in turn, may be defined as "low-intensity, diffuse and relatively enduring affective states without a salient antecedent cause and therefore little cognitive content (e.g., feeling good or feeling bad)," whereas *emotions* "are more intense, short-lived and usually have a definite cause and clear cognitive content" (e.g., anger or fear) (Forgas, 1992a, p. 230). There is evidence that moods, as well as emotions, may influence social behaviors (Forgas, 1991, 1994, 1998a, 1998b, 1998c, 2000). However, nonspecific moods often have a more enduring and insidious influence on the social mind and on subsequent social behaviors than do distinct emotions – precisely because they do lack elaborate cognitive content and thus often escape conscious scrutiny (Fiedler, 1991; Forgas, 1992a, 1992b, 1995a, 1995b, 1999a, 1999b; Mayer, 1986; Sedikides, 1992). This chapter will discuss recent evidence for the influence of moods on how people plan and implement interpersonal behaviors and how they interpret the observed behaviors of others.

Affect, Cognition, and Behavior

There also continue to be fundamental disagreements in the discipline as to whether affect should be treated as part of the cognitive-representational system or should be seen as an entirely separate, primary mental faculty (Fiedler & Forgas, 1988; Hilgard, 1980; Salovey & Mayer, 1990; Zajonc, 2000). There is an influential view that feelings are external to and separate from cognition, and can serve as a source of independent input to subsequent cognitive and behavioral processes, just as Thomas Mann's short story suggested (Clore, Schwarz, & Conway, 1994). Such a *separate-systems* view was proposed by Zajonc (1980, 2000), who argued that affect often precedes, and is distinct from, cognitive processes.

Whether affect is primary or not, the approach developed here assumes that affect and cognition represent closely related and interacting systems allowing affective states to infuse and inform people's thoughts and subsequent social behaviors. The empirical evidence also suggests that affective states will rarely trigger direct and invariant behavioral responses. Quite the contrary: The same affective state can have a congruent, an incongruent, or no effect on subsequent cognition and action, depending on subtle shifts in people's preferred information processing strategies (Berkowitz, Jaffee, Jo, & Troccoli, 2000; Erber & Erber, in press; Forgas, 1991, 1995a; Sedikides, 1994).

Affect Infusion

For the purposes of this discussion, such *affect infusion* may be defined as a process whereby affectively loaded information exerts an influence on and becomes incorporated into a person's cognitive and behavioral processes, entering into his or her constructive deliberations and eventually coloring the outcome in a mood-congruent direction (Forgas, 1995a). Affect infusion occurs because planning and executing complex social behaviors usually requires high-level, constructive, and inferential cognitive processes. As also suggested by Mead's symbolic interactionist theory, social actors can make sense of ambiguous situations, and plan their actions and pursue their goals effectively, only by constructively using their preexisting knowledge, memories, and associations to create a meaningful cognitive representation of the social world. In many situations, the prevailing affective state of a person can become part of the constructive informational base used when interpreting information or when planning and executing a behavior (Fiedler, 1991).

There is evidence that affect infusion is most likely to occur in the course of *constructive processing* that involves the substantial transformation rather than the mere reproduction of existing social knowledge. In other words, affect "will influence cognitive processes to the extent that the . . . task involves the active generation of new information as opposed to the passive conservation of information given" (Fiedler, 1990, pp. 2–3). Research has also shown, however, that affect infusion is not an invariable phenomenon. Frequently, the affective state of a person appears to have no influence on the content of cognition and action, and may even have an inconsistent, mood-incongruent influence (Erber & Erber, in press; Forgas, 1991; Sedikides, 1994). How can we explain these apparently contradictory findings?

The *Affect Infusion Model (AIM)* recently proposed by Forgas (1995a) argues that the nature and extent of affect infusion into behavior and cognition will largely depend on what kind of processing strategy is adopted by a person in dealing with a particular task. This is in marked contrast to the single-process assumptions of many social cognition theories. The AIM predicts that some social tasks such as setting and performing routine, recurrent actions may require little constructive thinking (Fiedler, 1991) and should be impervious to the infusion of affect. In contrast, interpersonal tasks that require the monitoring of ambiguous or indeterminate information and the production of complex responses may require highly constructive and generative cognitive processing that can be readily influenced by affect (Forgas, Bower, & Krantz, 1984).

The AIM identified four alternative processing strategies people might use in social situations, each characterized by different affect infusion potentials. (1) The *direct access* of a preexisting response or (2) *motivated processing* in the service of a preexisting goal both involve highly predetermined and directed information search and behavior patterns that require little generative, constructive processing, limiting the scope of affect infusion. In contrast, when an interpersonal task requires a degree of constructive processing, people may use either (3) a *heuristic*, simplified or (4) a *substantive*, generative processing strategy to plan their actions and produce a response. These are high-infusion strategies that require a degree of open, constructive thinking in which affect may either directly (Clore et al., 1994) or indirectly, through primed associations (Forgas & Bower, 1987), inform the response.

According to the AIM, processing choices should be determined by three categories of variables associated with the *task*, the *person* and the *situation*, respectively. Familiarity, typicality, and complexity are the main *task features* of interest. *Personal factors* include traits, personal relevance, motivational goals, cognitive capacity and affective state. Finally, *situational factors* such as the need for accuracy, public scrutiny, or normative pressures may also influence processing choices. A complete description of the AIM and the evidence supporting it has been presented elsewhere (Forgas, 1992a, 1995a, 2000), so it will not be reviewed in detail here. The major relevance of the AIM is that it provides a framework within which the presence or absence of affect infusion into the social minds of actors, and thus into their interpersonal behaviors, can be explained within an integrated theoretical model.

This distinction between different processing strategies as mediators of affect infusion should have considerable benefits for understanding mood effects on interpersonal behaviors. For example, the direct access strategy recognizes that people possess a rich repertoire of routine, pre-existing social moves and will rely on these whenever more extensive processing is not necessary. Direct access is a low-affect infusion strategy requiring little on-line constructive processing. Motivated processing is a highly selective, guided, and targeted information processing strategy that is also impervious to affect infusion. Indeed, motivated processing may frequently be used to achieve mood maintenance as well as mood repair in social encounters, as several studies have now found (Forgas, 1990).

In contrast, heuristic processing should be adopted when people have no stored action plan or a strong motivation to guide their actions, and they seek to produce a response with the least amount of effort, using whatever shortcuts or simplifications are readily available. This strategy is common when the interaction is of low personal relevance, processing capacity is limited, and the context does not call for greater elaboration. Interpersonal behaviors are sometimes guided by heuristic cues such as irrelevant features of the environment or the superficial characteristics of a person. Heuristic processing can also produce affect infusion into social behavior when actors misinterpret their prevailing affective state as indicative of an evaluative response to the situation (cf. Clore et al., 1994).

Substantive processing is the most constructive and extended strategy for dealing with social situations. It occurs when people need to select, learn, and interpret new information about an encounter, and need to rely on their associative ideas and memories to accomplish this. Affect priming can produce significant affect infusion during substantive processing, as "activation of an emotion node also spreads activation throughout the memory structures to which it is connected" (Bower, 1981, p. 135). Paradoxically, affect infusion may be greater when more extensive and constructive processing is employed, a counterintuitive prediction that has been repeatedly confirmed in recent studies (Fiedler, 1991; Forgas, 1992b, 1994, 1995b, 1999a, 1999b; Sedikides, 1995). This occurs because more extensive and elaborate processing also increases the likelihood that affectively primed information will be inadvertently incorporated into the behavior planning process, as found in several of our recent experiments.

What is the evidence for affect infusion into interpersonal behaviors? In the next section, we shall briefly review some of the recent empirical literature indicating affective influences on how people perceive, plan, and behave in social situations.

Affect and Interpersonal Behavior

As we have seen, affective states can play a complex and interactive role in strategic social behaviors. The AIM suggests that affect may influence both the *content* of people's actions (what they do) and the *processes* they use to think about and respond to social situations. Thus, a full understanding of how affect impacts on behavior requires careful attention to the kinds of information processing strategies people adopt in particular social situations. Empirical evidence supporting these suggestions, including research from our laboratory, will be considered next.

Affective Influences on Behavior Interpretation

Strategic social behavior is necessarily based on people's perception and evaluation of the actions of others and themselves. To the extent that affective states may influence how such judgments are made, they will also influence subsequent social behaviors. Indeed, the on-line interpretation of observed behaviors is one of the most fundamental social-cognitive tasks people face in everyday life (Heider, 1958; Kelly, 1955). Does affect influence the outcome of such simple behavior interpretation tasks? In terms of the AIM, to the extent that making sense of observed behaviors does require some degree of inferential, substantive thinking (Heider, 1958), there should be some evidence for mood-consistent distortions in behavior interpretation.

We performed a particularly challenging test of this hypothesis (Forgas et al., 1984). Rather than analyzing artificial judgments, we provided participants with objective videotaped evidence of their actual social interactions. This study was carried out over 2 consecutive days. On the first day, pairs of participants were videotaped while engaging in four kinds of social encounters (interviews) with female confederates of varying formality and intimacy. The next day, the same people returned for a "social perception experiment." They were hypnotized and induced to feel happy or sad, and were then asked to monitor the videotapes of the interaction episodes from the previous day. Their task was to make frequent evaluative judgments about the observed behaviors, and to identify and score instances of positive, skilled and negative, unskilled behaviors both for themselves and for their partners as they saw it on the videotape.

We found a significant affective bias on this on-line behavior monitoring task, despite the availability of objective videotaped information. Happy subjects saw more positive, skilled and fewer negative, unskilled behaviors both in themselves and in their partners than did sad subjects. Negative mood, in turn, resulted in more negative behavior interpretations for the self but not necessarily for others – a pattern also commonly found in depression. Observers who received no mood manipulation showed no such monitoring biases. These results confirm the existence of a significant mood-induced bias on how interpersonal behaviors are monitored and interpreted even when objective videotaped evidence is readily available. It is quite likely that mood may have an even greater effect on monitoring and interpreting naturally observed social behaviors in everyday circumstances when people are not consciously focusing on videotaped information, as was the case here. According to the AIM, these affective biases should be due predominantly to mood-priming effects in the course of substantive inferential processing. This prediction was supported by recall data showing better memory for positive, easy interactions by happy subjects and negative, difficult interactions by sad subjects.

In several later experiments, we explored the impact of temporary moods on more complex, elaborate inferential judgments about the causes of various social events. Results clearly confirmed that people in a negative mood tended to make more critical, self-deprecatory interpretations and attributions for their own behaviors, whereas those in a positive mood selectively looked for and found lenient and optimistic explanations for identical outcomes (Forgas, Bower, & Moylan, 1990). Surprisingly, such mood-induced distortions of behavior interpretation can even influence evaluations of highly familiar, intimate, and involving interaction episodes, such as real-life conflicts experienced in people's long-term relationships (Forgas, 1994). In these experiments, partners involved in long-term intimate relationships were asked to evaluate behaviors in more or less serious interpersonal conflict episodes while feeling good or bad. Results again showed a significant mood-congruent bias. People in a positive mood selectively preferred lenient, self-serving explanations. Further, in a counterintuitive pattern, these mood effects on behavior monitoring became even greater when judgments were made about more complex and serious conflicts that required more extensive and constructive processing strategies to be adequately explained.

These studies show that affective states are an integral part of the social mind and tend to spontaneously infuse even such mundane tasks as the on-line monitoring of observed social behaviors. To the extent that moods can have a major impact on how social behaviors are interpeted, it is reasonable to expect that the actual performance of interactive behaviors should also show affect sensitivity in circumstances that favor open, constructive processing. We now have evidence for just such effects in a series of more recent experiments.

Mood Effects on Responding to Strategic Situations

Responding to an unexpected request by a stranger is one of the simplest interpersonal tasks in which a rapid reaction involving constructive cognitive processing is required. In a series of recent field experiments (Forgas, 1998b), we looked at the role of temporary affective states in determining how people evaluate and respond behaviorally to more or less polite requests directed at them in a public place. In order to increase the external validity of the design, an unobtrusive strategy was used. Students entering a library found pictures or text placed on their desks designed to induce a good or bad mood. A few minutes later, they were approached by another student (in fact, a confederate) and received an unexpected polite or impolite request for several sheets of paper needed to complete an essay. Their responses were noted. A short time after this incident, a second confederate explained to participants that the request was staged, and asked them to complete a brief questionnaire evaluating their perception and recall of the request and the requester. Results showed that there was a clear mood-congruent pattern in how students behaved in this situation. People in an induced negative mood were more likely to form a critical, negative view of requests and were less inclined to comply than were those in a positive mood (Figure 3.1). In a particularly interesting result, we found a significant interaction between mood state and the level of politeness of the request. Overall, mood effects were significantly greater on the evaluation of and responses to impolite, unconventional requests that required more substantive processing, as confirmed by better recall memory for these messages later on. Conventional, polite requests were apparently processed less substantively, were less influenced by mood, and were also recalled in less detail later on.

This experiment shows that unrelated temporary mood states have a significant mood-congruent influence on the way people respond to unexpected social situations. Further, consistent with the AIM, these results indicate that affect infusion into the planning and execution of impromptu social behaviors is significantly mediated by the kind of

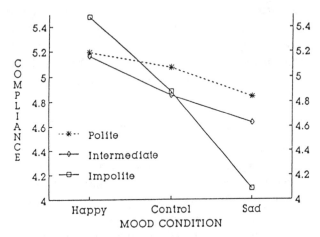

Figure 3.1. Affective influences on strategic responses to a naturalistic request: Positive mood increases and negative mood decreases compliance, and these mood effects are greatest in response to more impolite, unconventional requests that require more extensive processing (after Forgas, 1998b).

processing strategy people employ. These findings indicate that a comprehensive understanding of strategic social behaviors needs to incorporate a detailed consideration of how temporary affective states can impact on people's thoughts, action plans, and subsequent behaviors. Of course, mood may not influence reactions to unexpected encounters alone. In terms of our theoretical framework, mood effects should be even more marked on self-initiated interpersonal moves that are likely to involve more elaborate and extensive cognitive processing, such as the production of strategic verbal messages.

Mood Effects on Strategic Verbal Behaviors: The Case of Requesting

In one series of studies, we explored the effects of mood on strategic goal-oriented behaviors: the way people formulate and use verbal messages such as requests. Requesting is an intrinsically complex behavioral task characterized by goal pursuit and psychological ambiguity. Requests must be formulated with just the right degree of politeness so as to maximize compliance without risking giving offence. We expected that incidental mood should significantly influence the social mindset of requesters and their requesting strategies. We predicted that people will adopt a more confident, direct requesting style when experiencing a positive mood, consistent with the greater availability of positively valenced thoughts and associations in their minds as they constructively assess the situation (Forgas, 1998b, 1999a, 1999b). Further, in terms of the AIM, these mood effects should be particularly strong when the situation is more complex and demanding, and requires more substantive and elaborate processing strategies.

Mood was induced in an allegedly separate experiment by asking people to recall and think about happy or sad autobiographical episodes (Forgas, 1999a, Exp. 1). In a subsequent task, participants selected a more or less polite request formulation that they would use in an easy and a difficult, demanding request situation. Results showed that induced mood had a significant influence on request strategies. Happy participants preferred more direct, impolite requests, whereas sad persons used indirect, polite request alternatives. Further, these mood effects on requesting were significantly greater in the more difficult, demanding request situation that required more extensive, substantive processing strategies.

Very similar procedures were used in a follow-up experiment, but instead of prestructured requests, participants now formulated their own open-ended requests, which were subsequently rated for politeness and elaboration by two independent raters (Forgas, 1999a, Exp. 2). Results again showed that mood had a significant influence on these strategic behaviors. Happy persons produced significantly more impolite and less elaborate requests than did sad individuals, and mood effects were again greater in the more problematic and difficult situational context (Figure 3.2). These results confirm that moods can influence how people perceive and interpret social situations and how they formulate and execute subsequent interpersonal behaviors such as requests. But why should mood effects be greater on requests in a more difficult and demanding social situation? More difficult interpersonal tasks also require more elaborate processing, and according to the AIM, affect infusion should increase proportionally when more substantive processing is required to produce a social response.

This pattern was further confirmed in a third experiment in which participants were asked to select more or less polite request alternatives in a variety of different realistic situations (Forgas, 1999b, Exp. 1). Following an audiovisual mood induction (watching happy or sad films), participants selected more or less polite request forms they would use in each of 16 different request situations. Results showed that mood effects were greatest on decisions about using the most

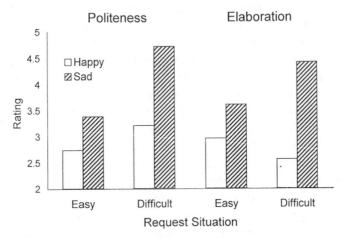

Figure 3.2. Mood effects on producing strategic messages: Negative mood increases and positive mood decreases request politeness and elaboration, and these mood effects are significantly greater in more difficult, demanding social situations that require more extensive processing (after Forgas, 1999b).

direct, unconventional requests that are most likely to violate cultural conventions of politeness and should recruit the most substantive, elaborate processing strategies. These findings indicate that mood effects on interpersonal behaviors are indeed process-dependent, with affect infusion enhanced or reduced, depending on just how much open, constructive processing is required to deal with more or less demanding interpersonal tasks (Fiedler, 1991; Forgas, 1995a).

Nor are these effects restricted to controlled laboratory tasks. Similar effects were also obtained in a fourth, unobtrusive experiment looking at naturally produced requests (Forgas, 1999b, Exp. 2). After an audio-visual mood induction, the experimenter casually asked participants to get a file from a neighboring office while the next experiment was set up. All participants agreed. Their actual words in requesting the file were recorded by a concealed tape recorder, and subsequently were analyzed for politeness and other qualities. Results showed a significant mood effect on these natural, unobtrusively elicited social behaviors. Sad people used more polite, friendly, and elaborate forms, and happy people used more direct and less polite forms. Negative mood also increased the latency of requests. Sad persons delayed making their requests significantly longer than did control or happy persons, and were more polite, elaborate, and hedging, consistent with their

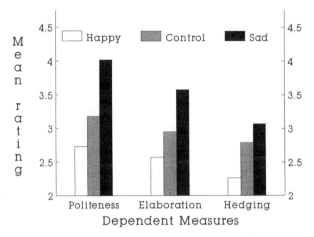

Figure 3.3. Mood effects on naturally produced requests: Positive mood increases and negative mood decreases the degree of politeness, elaboration, and hedging in goal-oriented strategic communications (after Forgas, 1999b).

more cautious, defensive behavioral strategies and the more extensive processing that these unconventional behaviors presumably required (Figure 3.3). An analysis of the subsequent recall of the requests confirmed that unconventional requests were also recalled significantly better. This confirms the predicted more elaborate, in-depth processing of these messages and supports the core prediction of the AIM that the greatest mood effects occur when more elaborate, substantive processing is used by a communicator.

Affective Influences on Strategic Social Encounters

As the previous studies suggest, even mild, temporary mood states can have a significant influence on the way people monitor social behaviors, the way they respond to unexpected situations, and the way they formulate and produce verbal messages such as requests. Is it possible that the same kinds of affective influences also occur in planning more complex, elaborate social encounters? In another series of experiments, we investigated affective influences on the regulation and performance of complex behavior sequences such as negotiating encounters (Forgas, 1998a). Positive, control, or negative mood was induced by giving participants positive, negative, or neutral feedback about their performance on a verbal test. Next, they engaged in an

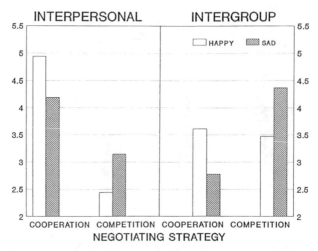

Figure 3.4. The effects of temporary mood on strategic behavior in negotiation: Positive mood increases and negative mood decreases cooperation in both interpersonal and intergroup bargaining encounters; the opposite mood effects were observed for competitive bargaining strategies (after Forgas, 1998a).

informal, interpersonal and a formal, intergroup negotiating task with another team in what they believed was a separate experiment. We were interested in how temporary moods might influence people's goal-setting strategies and behaviors. Results showed that participants who were in an induced positive mood set themselves higher and more ambitious goals, formed higher expectations about the forthcoming encounter, and formulated specific action plans that were more optimistic, cooperative, and integrative than did control or negative-mood participants. Furthermore, individuals who formulated cooperative goals as a result of feeling good actually behaved more cooperatively, and were more willing to make and reciprocate deals, than were those in a negative mood (Figure 3.4). Perhaps the most interesting finding was that these mood-induced differences in goal-setting and bargaining behavior actually resulted in more successful performances. People who felt good did significantly better in this bargaining task than did those who felt bad. These results provide relatively clear-cut evidence that even slight changes in mood due to an unrelated prior event can significantly bias the goals that people set for themselves, the action plans they formulate, and their subsequent interpersonal behaviors.

In terms of the AIM, these mood effects on interpersonal behaviors can be explained as due to the operation of affect priming mechanisms.

Thinking about and planning a bargaining encounter is by definition a complex, indeterminate, and personally involving cognitive task in which substantive processing should be the dominant strategy adopted. Positive mood should selectively prime more positive thoughts and associations, and should ultimately lead to the formulation of more optimistic expectations and the adoption of more cooperative bargaining strategies. In contrast, negative mood should result in more pessimistic, negative thoughts and associations, leading to less ambitious goals and less cooperative and successful bargaining strategies.

Interestingly, the second experiment in this series showed that these mood effects were much less marked for individuals who scored high on individual differences measures such as Machiavellism and need for approval. In terms of the AIM, these individuals should have approached the bargaining task from a more predetermined, motivated perspective that limited the degree of open, constructive processing they employed and thus reduced the effects of affect infusion on their behaviors. In a way, their minds were made up about what to do even before they started, reducing the likelihood of incidental affect infusion. Such individual differences in a person's tendency to use open, constructive or guided, motivated processing strategies may significantly influence the extent to which affective states are likely to infuse social thinking and subsequent social behaviors (Rusting, 1998).

Affect Control and Behavior Control

The evidence so far suggests that even short-term and relatively low-intensity moods may have a strong influence on how people interpret and respond to social situations, as long as some degree of open, constructive processing is required. However, the relationship among affect, cognition, and behavior is not unidirectional. Just as affect can influence social thinking and behavior, changes in information processing strategies and behaviors can produce corresponding changes in the prevailing affective state. In other words, the affective aspects of the social mind exist in a closely interactive relationship with cognitive and behavioral processes.

How do people go about controlling and managing their own affective states? Arguably, one of the most common and important goals people have in everyday life is to maintain a reasonably positive, optimistic affective balance and a controlled state of mind despite the manifold challenges they face. The objectives of mood maintenance and mood regulation (Clark & Isen, 1982) probably play a disproportionately important role in the way many everyday behavioral and cognitive strategies are performed.

Accumulating evidence suggests that people may use a number of motivated strategies to control their affective states. These include selective exposure to mood-incongruent information (Erber & Erber, in press; Forgas, 1992a), recall of mood-incongruent memories (Sedikides, 1994), engaging in mood-incongruent behaviors (Cialdini & Kenrick, 1976), interacting with rewarding partners (Forgas, 1991), or distracting themselves from the source of their mood (Rusting, 1998). Within the AIM framework, the ongoing task of affect management and control can be best understood as the process of routinely and automatically switching between two complementary information processing strategies. Substantive processing typically results in affect infusion and the accentuation of the existing affective state. In contrast, motivated processing inhibits affect infusion and may produce targeted, affect-incongruent outcomes. We recently proposed such a preliminary affect management model (Forgas, Johnson, & Ciarrochi, 1998) based on relevant aspects of the AIM (Forgas, 1995a). A schematic outline of the affect management hypothesis is presented in Figure 3.5.

As this figure shows, the choice of either a substantive (affect infusion) or a motivated (affect control) processing strategy is determined by a combination of personal, situational, and task-related input variables and the extremity of the prevailing affective state. So far, research suggests that a switch to motivated rather than substantive processing is more likely when (1) the task is of direct personal relevance (Forgas, 1991), (2) people are aware of the cause or consequence of their mood (Berkowitz et al., 2000; Clore et al., 1994), (3) they score high on individual differences measures that indicate motivated processing tendencies (Forgas, 1998a), and (4) they experience an extreme or aversive affective state (Ciarrochi & Forgas, 1999; Forgas & Fiedler, 1996). Situational variables may also impact on processing and behavioral choices (Forgas, 1995a). For example, persons who expect to engage in a demanding interaction with a stranger may in fact prefer to tone down their mood by reading articles that are the opposite in affective tone to their own mood (Erber & Erber, in press).

A critical feature of the homeostatic affect management model is that it incorporates a feedback loop between the valenced outcome of the existing processing strategy and behavior and subsequent processing

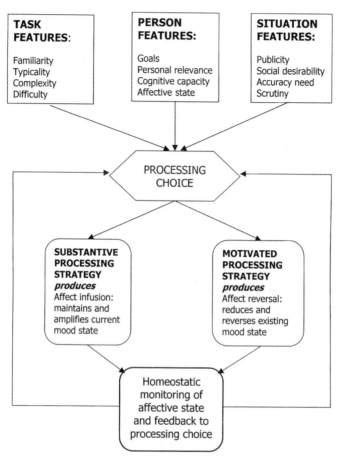

Figure 3.5. The mood management hypothesis: Substantive processing accentuates and motivated processing attenuates the valence of the existing affective state, and automatic switching due to a feedback loop between these two processing modes produces a homeostatic mood management system (after Forgas, Johnson, and Ciarrochi, 1998).

choices. As a consequence, the model provides for the possibility of continuous changes in processing strategies as a function of the prevailing mood state, a suggestion that is also supported by empirical evidence (Clark & Isen, 1982; Forgas, 1995a; Sedikides, 1994). In practical terms, this means that if, as a result of an existing substantive processing strategy and ongoing affect infusion, the level of negativity in a person's thinking and behavior reaches a threshold level, an automatic correction should take place that consists of a switch to motivated processing and a preference for mood-inconsistent thoughts and behaviors (Erber & Erber, in press).

The mood-management model predicts that negative mood initially leads to affect infusion and mood-congruent thoughts until a threshold level of negativity is reached, at which point people should switch to motivated mood control and mood-incongruent associations. Sedikides (1994) found some initial support for such a hypothesis. Recently, we (Forgas & Ciarrochi, 2000) conducted several additional studies to test the hypothesis that affect leads first to affect infusion, followed by a spontaneous switch to a motivated affect control strategy. In Study 1, participants who were feeling good or bad after recalling sad or happy events from their past generated a series of trait adjectives. Negative mood initially produced mood-congruent adjectives, but over time, subjects spontaneously switched to generating mood-incongruent (positive) adjectives consistent with the adoption of a motivated affect control strategy. In Study 2, a word completion task was used to measure mood effects on associations. A time-series regression analysis revealed that sad subjects rapidly changed from affect-congruent to affect-incongruent recall. It appears that once a threshold level of negativity was reached due to affect infusion processes, sad people spontaneously changed their cognitive and behavioral strategies and switched to motivated, incongruent recall as if seeking to control and eliminate their aversive mood (Figure 3.6).

In a further study, we also explored the role of individual difference variables such as self-esteem in affect management strategies. Previous work suggests that people low in self-esteem are less likely than others to engage in conscious affect control (Smith & Petty, 1995). To induce mood, participants received positive or negative feedback about their performance on a spatial abilities task. Next, they completed a series of sentences asking for self-decriptive adjectives. Results again indicated a clear "first congruent, then incongruent pattern," and this result was particularly marked for high self-esteem people. Those scoring high on self-esteem were able to rapidly eliminate a mood-congruent bias in their responses by producing mood-incongruent, positive descriptions after initially negative responses. In contrast, low self-esteem people provided mood-congruent responses throughout the entire task. This finding suggests that traits such as self-esteem may moderate people's ability to adopt motivated behavioral strategies to control their affective states. These studies (Forgas & Ciarrochi, 2000;

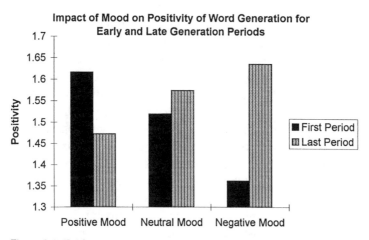

Figure 3.6. Evidence consistent with the automatic mood management hypothesis: Initially, mood-congruent associations are spontaneously reversed, and these effects are greater in a negative than in a positive mood (after Forgas and Ciarrochi, 2000).

Sedikides, 1994) support the notion of a homeostatic feedback-loop model of affect control, suggesting that fluctuating affective states can play an important role in changing processing strategies. Changes in processing style will, in turn, influence the degree of affect infusion and thus control the extremity of the mood state. Other research also suggests that simply making people aware of their mood can trigger motivated affect-control strategies (Berkowitz et al., 2000). In other words, affective states can be seen as integral components of the social mind, influencing our thoughts and actions but also regulated by subtle shifts in processing strategies and behaviors.

Summary and Conclusions

Engaging in strategic interactions with others is a recurrent feature of everyday social life. The ability to form relatively accurate judgments about the social world and to produce appropriate and effective interpersonal strategies is a key requirement for maintaining successful personal and working relationships. The theory of affect infusion and the supporting evidence presented here strongly suggest that mood states have a subtle yet highly significant and largely unrecognized influence on people's thoughts and interpersonal behaviors. As Thomas Mann's short story of the chess players suggests, fluctuating mood states, just like background music, can continuously influence our thoughts and associations and can eventually color our interpersonal behaviors.

These findings tell us something interesting about the social mind. Consistent with the findings of several other contributors to this volume, our results suggest that cognitive, affective, and motivational aspects of the social world are inextricably linked in the way we perceive and respond to other people. In a sense, psychology has suffered from its long-standing tradition of attempting to separate and study in isolation fundamental mental faculties such as cognition, affect, and conation (Hilgard, 1980). Consistent with the objectives of this book and the evidence presented by the other contributions, this chapter argued for a careful reintegration of feeling, thinking, and social behavior within a comprehensive theoretical framework such as the AIM. The research reviewed here documents the highly significant influence that emotions and moods can have on the way people perceive and interpret social situations, the kinds of goals and plans they formulate, and the way they execute and regulate their social behaviors. However, these effects are neither simple nor unidirectional. Cognitive information processing strategies play a key role in mediating mood effects on interpersonal behavior, and changes in thinking and behavior, in turn, can be a key strategy in managing affective states, as the studies on spontaneous mood management reviewed here suggest.

Why has it taken psychologists so long to incorporate affect in their conceptualization of the social mind? The influence of affective states on people's thoughts, judgments, and decisions has long been a source of interest and fascination to laypersons and philosophers alike. Psychologists were relatively late to recognize the importance of this phenomenon, probably because of the traditional separation of affect, cognition, and conation, the three "faculties of mind," throughout most of the history of the discipline (Hilgard, 1980). During the last two decades, considerable empirical evidence has demonstrated mood-congruent influences on learning, memory, and associations (Bower, 1981, 1991). Explanations of these phenomena have evolved from earlier psychoanalytic and conditioning approaches (Clore et al., 1994; Feshbach & Singer, 1957) to the more recent cognitive, information processing accounts. The affect priming hypothesis in particular (Bower, 1981, 1991) offers a particularly simple and parsimonious account of many mood-congruent phenomena, including judgmental and behavioral effects (Forgas & Bower, 1987; Forgas et al., 1984).

One recurring problem with incorporating affective phenomena into explanations of social behavior is that their effects are neither simple nor uniform. There is ample evidence for both mood congruity and incongruity in people's thoughts and behaviors, and these effects appear to be highly context sensitive. We suggested here that multi-process theories such as the AIM (Forgas, 1992a, 1995b) can offer a simple and parsimonious explanation of when and how affective states infuse purposive behaviors. We also reviewed a range of empirical studies illustrating how such principles can be translated into behavioral research, and how affective states can be shown to influence both simple and complex interpersonal behaviors. Mood effects were demonstrated on the formulation of and responses to requests (Forgas, 1998b, 1999a, 1999b), the planning and execution of strategic negotiations (Forgas, 1998a), and the monitoring and interpretation of complex interactive behaviors (Forgas, 1994; Forgas et al., 1984, 1990).

Further, we proposed that the need to control and manage affective states is itself one of the more important and recurring tasks of behavior regulation. We described a preliminary affect management model, which predicts that people may switch between two complementary processing strategies, substantive processing (producing affect infusion) and motivated processing (producing affect control) in an automatic, homeostatic system of mood management. Several experiments illustrating the spontaneous recovery from aversive moods by people engaging in targeted, mood-incongruent behaviors were also described (Forgas & Ciarrochi, 2000). It seems then that a comprehensive theory of the social mind needs to take explicit account of the critical role affect plays in the planning and execution of purposive behaviors.

This chapter aimed to provide a review and integration of mood effects on social judgments and interpersonal behaviors. The evidence suggests that affect infusion into judgments and behaviors is most likely to occur in the course of open, constructive processing. It also appears that affect priming is the mechanism most likely to lead to mood congruence in most everyday interpersonal tasks. Several counterintuitive results showing that more extensive, substantive processing enhances mood congruity provide especially strong support for the AIM (Forgas, 1992b, 1994, 1995b, 1998a, 1998b, 1999a, 1999b). Conversely, other experiments show the disappearance of mood congruity whenever people approach a cognitive task from a highly directed or motivated perspective (Forgas, 1991; Forgas & Fiedler, 1996; Sedikides, 1995). Indeed, the tendency to alternate between substantive and motivated processing strategies, producing affect infusion and affect control, respectively, may be thought of as part of an ongoing homeo-static strategy of controlled mood management (Forgas & Ciarrochi, 2000; Forgas et al., 1998). The kind of affect congruity in interpersonal behaviors demonstrated here may be important in many everyday situations, including the maintenance and management of intimate relationships, interaction in organizations, and clinical situations (Baron, 1987; Forgas & Moylan, 1987; Mayer, Gaschke, Braverman, & Evans, 1992; Salovey, O'Leary, Stretton, Fishkin, & Drake, 1991; Sedikides, 1992). Indeed, the more people need to engage in open, constructive processing, the more likely that affect will infuse their interpersonal responses. Even such highly involved and complex strategic tasks as coping with relationship conflicts showed such mood-congruent biases (Forgas, 1994).

We started this discussion by suggesting that there may be a clear scientific basis for age-old speculations about the infusion of affect into thinking and behavior, as exemplified by Thomas Mann's story of the chess players. We conclude by observing that the social mind is indeed a composite of affective, cognitive, and motivational reactions to social situations, and the relationship between them is complex and multiply determined. By postulating four distinct information processing strategies, the AIM offers a parsimonious account for a variety of mood effects on interpersonal behaviors observed in the literature. We hope that by further clarifying the characteristics and conditions conducive to affect infusion into interpersonal behavior, the present review will encourage growing interest in this important research area.

References

Adolphs, R., & Damasio, A. (in press). The interaction of affect and cognition: A neurobiological perspective. In J. P. Forgas (Ed.), *The handbook of affect and social cognition*. Mahwah, NJ: Erlbaum.

Baron, R. (1987). Interviewers' moods and reactions to job applicants: The influence of affective states on applied social judgments. *Journal of Applied Social Psychology, 16*, 16–28.

Berkowitz, L., Jaffee, S., Jo, E., & Troccoli, B. T. (2000). On the correction of feeling-induced judgmental biases. In J. P. Forgas (Ed.), *Feeling and thinking: The role of affect in social cognition* (pp. 131–152). New York: Cambridge University Press.

Blascovich, J., & Mendes, W. B. (2000). Challenge and threat appraisals: The role of affective cues. In J. P. Forgas (Ed.), *Feeling and thinking: The role of affect in social cognition* (pp. 59–82). New York: Cambridge University Press.

Bower, G. H. (1981). Mood and memory. *American Psychologist, 36*, 129–148.

Bower, G. H. (1991). Mood congruity of social judgments. In J. P. Forgas (Ed.), *Emotion and social judgments* (pp. 31–53). New York: Pergamon Press.

Carver, C., & Scheier, C. (1998). The self-regulation of behavior. In R. Wyer & T. Srull (Eds.), *Advances in social cognition* (Vol. 12, pp. 1–106). Mahwah, NJ: Erlbaum.

Cialdini, R. B., & Kenrick, D. T. (1976). Altruism as hedonism: A social development perspective on the relationship of negative mood state and helping. *Journal of Personality and Social Psychology, 34*, 907–914.

Ciarrochi, J., & Forgas, J. P. (1999). On being tense yet tolerant: The paradoxical effects of trait anxiety and aversive mood on intergroup judgments. *Group Dynamics: Theory, Research and Practice, 3*, 227–238.

Clark, M. S., & Isen, A. M. (1982). Towards understanding the relationship between feeling states and social behavior. In A. H. Hastorf & A. M. Isen (Eds.), *Cognitive social psychology* (pp. 73–108). Amsterdam: Elsevier/North-Holland.

Clore, G. L., Schwarz, N., & Conway, M. (1994). Affective causes and consequences of social information processing. In R. S. Wyer & T. K. Srull (Eds.), *Handbook of social cognition* (2nd ed., Vol. 1, pp. 323–419). Hillsdale, NJ: Erlbaum.

Erber, R., & Erber, M. (in press). The role of motivated social cognition in the regulation of affective states. In J. P. Forgas (Ed.), *The handbook of affect and social cognition.* Mahwah, NJ: Erlbaum.

Feshbach, S., & Singer, R. D. (1957). The effects of fear arousal and suppression of fear upon social perception. *Journal of Abnormal and Social Psychology, 55*, 283–288.

Fiedler, K. (1990). Mood-dependent selectivity in social cognition. In W. Stroebe & M. Hewstone (Eds.), *European review of social psychology* (Vol. 1, pp. 1–32). New York: Wiley.

Fiedler, K. (1991). On the task, the measures and the mood in research on affect and social cognition. In J. P. Forgas (Ed.), *Emotion and social judgments* (pp. 83–104). Elmsford, NY: Pergamon Press.

Fiedler, K., & Forgas, J. P. (Eds.). (1988). *Affect, cognition, and social behavior: New evidence and integrative attempts* (pp. 44–62). Toronto: Hogrefe.

Forgas, J. P. (1990). Affective influences on individual and group judgments. *European Journal of Social Psychology, 20*, 441–453.

Forgas, J. P. (1991). Mood effects on partner choice: Role of affect in social decisions. *Journal of Personality and Social Psychology, 61*, 708–720.

Forgas, J. P. (1992a). Affect in social judgments and decisions: A multi-process model. In M. Zanna (Ed.), *Advances in experimental social psychology* (Vol. 25, pp. 227–275). San Diego, CA: Academic Press.

Forgas, J. P. (1992b). On bad mood and peculiar people: Affect and person typicality in impression formation. *Journal of Personality and Social Psychology, 62*, 863–875.

Forgas, J. P. (1994). Sad and guilty? Affective influences on the explanation of conflict episodes. *Journal of Personality and Social Psychology, 66*, 56–68.

Forgas, J. P. (1995a). Mood and judgment: The affect infusion model (AIM). *Psychological Bulletin, 117*(1), 39–66.

Forgas, J. P. (1995b). Strange couples: Mood effects on judgments and memory about prototypical and atypical targets. *Personality and Social Psychology Bulletin, 21,* 747–765.

Forgas, J. P. (1998a). On feeling good and getting your way: Mood effects on negotiation strategies and outcomes. *Journal of Personality and Social Psychology, 74,* 565–577.

Forgas, J. P. (1998b). Asking nicely? Mood effects on responding to more or less polite requests. *Personality and Social Psychology Bulletin, 24,* 173–185.

Forgas, J. P. (1998c). Happy and mistaken? Mood effects on the fundamental attribution error. *Journal of Personality and Social Psychology, 75,* 318–331.

Forgas, J. P. (1999a). On feeling good and being rude: Affective influences on language use and request formulations. *Journal of Personality and Social Psychology, 76,* 928–939.

Forgas, J. P. (1999b). Feeling and speaking: Mood effects on verbal communication strategies. *Personality and Social Psychology Bulletin, 25,* 850–863.

Forgas, J. P. (Ed.). (2000). *Feeling and thinking: The role of affect in social cognition.* New York: Cambridge University Press.

Forgas, J. P., & Bower, G. H. (1987). Mood effects on person-perception judgments. *Journal of Personality and Social Psychology, 53*(1), 53–60.

Forgas, J. P., Bower, G. H., & Krantz, S. (1984). The influence of mood on perceptions of social interactions. *Journal of Experimental Social Psychology, 20,* 497–413.

Forgas, J. P., Bower, G. H., & Moylan, S. J. (1990). Praise or blame? Affective influences in attributions for achievement. *Journal of Personality and Social Psychology, 59,* 809–818.

Forgas, J. P., & Ciarrochi, J. (2000). Mood congruent and incongruent thoughts over time: The role of self-esteem in mood management efficacy. Manuscript under review.

Forgas, J. P., & Fiedler, K. (1996). Us and them: Mood effects on intergroup discrimination. *Journal of Personality and Social Psychology, 70,* 36–52.

Forgas, J. P., Johnson, R., & Ciarrochi, J. (1998). Affect control and affect infusion: A multi-process account of mood management and personal control. In M. Kofta, G. Weary, & G. Sedek (Eds.), *Personal control in action. Cognitive and motivational mechanisms* (pp. 155–196). New York: Plenum Press.

Forgas, J. P., & Moylan, S. J. (1987). After the movies: The effects of transient mood states on social judgments. *Personality and Social Psychology Bulletin, 13,* 478–489.

Heider, F. (1958). *The psychology of interpersonal relations.* New York: Wiley.

Hilgard, E. R. (1980). The trilogy of mind: Cognition, affection and conation. *Journal of the History of the Behavioral Sciences, 16,* 107–117.

Kelly, G. A. (1955). *The psychology of personal constructs.* New York: W. W. Norton.

Mayer, J. D. (1986). How mood influences cognition. In N. E. Sharkey (Ed.), *Advances in cognitive science* (Vol. 1, pp. 290–314). Chichester, England: Ellis Horwood.

Mayer, J. D., Gaschke, Y. N., Braverman, D. L., & Evans, T. W. (1992). Mood congruent judgment is a general effect. *Journal of Personality and Social Psychology, 63*, 119–132.

Polivy, J. (1998). Behavior inhibition. *Psychological Inquiry, 9*, 185–204.

Rusting, C. L. (1998). Personality, mood, and cognitive processing of emotional information: Three conceptual frameworks. *Psychological Bulletin, 124*(2), 165–196.

Salovey, P., & Mayer, J. D. (1990). Emotional intelligence. *Imagination, Cognition, and Personality, 9*, 185–211.

Salovey, P., O'Leary, A., Stretton, M., Fishkin, S., & Drake, C. A. (1991). Influence of mood on judgments about health and illness. In J. P. Forgas (Ed.), *Emotion and social judgments* (pp. 241–262). Oxford: Pergamon.

Sedikides, C. (1992). Mood as a determinant of attentional focus. *Cognition and Emotion, 6*, 129–148.

Sedikides, C. (1994). Incongruent effects of sad mood on self-conception valence: It's a matter of time. *European Journal of Social Psychology, 24*, 161–172.

Sedikides, C. (1995). Central and peripheral self-conceptions are differentially influenced by mood: Tests of the differential sensitivity hypothesis. *Journal of Personality and Social Psychology, 69*(4), 759–777.

Smith, C. A., & Kirby, E. (2000). Appraisal and memory: Toward a process model of emotion-eliciting situations. In J. P. Forgas (Ed.), *Feeling and thinking: The role of affect in social cognition* (pp. 83–108). New York: Cambridge University Press.

Smith, S. M., & Petty, R. E. (1995). Personality moderators of mood congruence effects on cognition: The role of self-esteem and negative mood regulation. *Journal of Personality and Social Psychology, 68*, 1092–1107.

Zajonc, R. B. (1980). Feeling and thinking: Preferences need no inferences. *American Psychologist, 35*, 151–175.

Zajonc, R. B. (2000). Closing the debate on the primacy of affect. In J. P. Forgas (Ed.), *Feeling and thinking: The role of affect in social cognition* (pp. 31–58). New York: Cambridge University Press.

4. Motivating Cognitive Change: The Self-Standards Model of Dissonance

JOEL COOPER

Cognitive dissonance theory has been an important concept in social psychology for more than 40 years. Although we know a great deal about the effects produced by dissonance and the conditions under which dissonance occurs, the precise motivational basis for the effect has remained elusive. We know that, under the appropriate conditions, choosing between two choice alternatives leads to changes in the evaluation of the alternatives. We know that, under appropriate conditions, behaving in a way that is inconsistent with one's attitude leads to a change in the attitude. What has been considerably more difficult is to achieve consensus on what motivates these changes. This chapter will sketch a way of looking at dissonance that tries to capture the motivational bases for the changes in attitudes and cognitions that have been the hallmark of the phenomenon known as cognitive dissonance.

Dissonance began life as a theory and evolved into a phenomenon. That is, from a simple set of premises, Leon Festinger (1957) presented a theoretical account of people's abhorrence of cognitive inconsistency and the consequences that follow therefrom. In the late 1950s and early 1960s, the theory predicted a number of interesting and nonobvious phenomena. Dissonance theory stood alone in predicting that people would change their attitudes following attitude-inconsistent behavior as an *inverse* function of the magnitude of the incentive (Festinger & Carlsmith, 1959). Very few other theories would have predicted that people would come to like what they suffered to attain – and would like it more, the more they suffered (Aronson & Mills, 1959). And very few theories would have predicted that people would spread their

Address for correspondence: Joel Cooper, Department of Psychology, Princeton University, Green Hall, Princeton, NJ 08544, USA. Email: jcoops@princeton.edu attraction of choice alternatives after making a selection, and that the spreading would be greater for two similarly ranked alternatives than for more disparate ones (Brehm, 1956). The theory predicted these phenomena, and the existence of the effects became evidence for the theory. But was the theory correct?

Upon closer scrutiny, questions were raised about the completeness and accuracy of the theoretical account that predicted the phenomena. Why should people abhor inconsistency? Is it inconsistency per se that produces the dissonance phenomenon? Is the self involved? In this chapter, we shall examine the theoretical controversy that surrounded the progress of dissonance research and suggest a new way of conceptualizing the motivational process that lies at the heart of dissonance.

Dissonance at Its Infancy

From the beginning, dissonance theory stood at the nexus of social cognition and motivation. Festinger used the term *cognition* before it was popular, and he used it in a way that is compatible with modern views of the concept. By cognition, Festinger referred to people's mental representation of their knowledge of themselves and their environment. The relationship among these mental representations had the ability to motivate cognitive changes. Festinger postulated that nonfitting or inconsistent cognitions were not just unpreferred or nonharmonious, in the cooler language of balance and symmetry theories, but rather would be *experienced*. They would be felt as uncomfortable and unpleasant and, just as a drive motivates its own reduction, they would produce activity designed to reduce the inconsistency.

There is little doubt that Festinger was correct in his prediction of the proximal cause of the dissonance phenomenon. The change in mental representations following attitude-discrepant behavior occurs in order to reduce unpleasant arousal. Croyle and Cooper (1983) confirmed Festinger's prediction that people who engage in counterattitudinal behavior do experience physiological arousal, as measured by increases in participants' skin conductance responses. Later, Elliot and Devine (1994) showed that counterattitudinal behavior is characterized by a feeling of measurable psychological discomfort. Losch and Cacioppo (1990) found that physiological arousal and psychological discomfort accompany the dissonance process and that cognitive change occurs in order to reduce the unpleasant psychological state.

But what is the *distal* cause? Festinger's theoretical proposition was that the perception of inconsistency among mental representations was the distal cause. However, that begged the question of *why* inconsistency should lead to psychological discomfort and unpleasant arousal. Perhaps, through the process of social and biological evolution, humans have become hard-wired to feel unpleasantly aroused at the perception of inconsistency. However, researchers in the field have sought other explanations for the distal motivational foundation of dissonance. We will examine some of the major revisions that have been proposed since Festinger's original formulation, briefly present their differences, and suggest a new synthesis that can provide a broad theoretical framework with which to understand the dissonance phenomenon.

The Plot Builds: Alternative Theoretical Conceptions

The Self-Consistency Interpretation

The first significant challenge to the accuracy of the original theory's explanation of the distal motivation for dissonance was provided by Elliot Aronson (1968; see also Aronson & Carlsmith, 1962). It was more of a friendly amendment than a countervailing theory. Aronson believed that in order for a person to feel aroused and bothered by his or her attitude-discrepant behavior, that behavior must seriously challenge a person's sense of self. Aronson (1968, p. 23) wrote, "At the very heart of dissonance theory, where it makes its strongest prediction, we are not dealing with just any two cognitions; rather, we are usually dealing with the self-concept and cognitions about some behavior. If dissonance exists, it is because the individual's behavior is inconsistent with his self-concept."

In the self-consistency view, people are aroused to experience the unpleasant tension state of dissonance when they violate their own expectancies for themselves, particularly in the domains of morality and competence. As an example, consider the original "forced compliance" experiment of Festinger and Carlsmith. In that study, participants changed their attitudes toward a very dull task after they told another student that the task was interesting and exciting. In the self-consistency view, the participant is motivated to change his or her attitude not merely because the participant's behavior was inconsistent with his or her original attitude. Rather, the discomfort arose because the act of lying about the task compromised the participant's own sense of morality. Note, too, that the introduction of the self-concept introduced another variable into the equation. Because people have different self-concepts, different conceptions of competence and morality, and different expectations of themselves, self-consistency necessarily predicts individual differences in the level of the psychological discomfort of dissonance.

The Aversive Consequences Position: A Cure for the "But-Onlys"

Russ Fazio and I provided a very different explanation of the distal motivation for dissonance (Cooper & Fazio, 1984). We observed a conundrum that could only be resolved with a new view of the theoretical foundation of the dissonance phenomenon. On the one hand, it was clear that, as of the mid-1980s, there had been enormous empirical support for the basic predictions of dissonance theory. On the other hand, it appeared that dissonance research had been stricken with a serious case of the "but-onlys": Attitude-discrepant behavior leads to attitude change (as predicted by the original theory),

- but only when commitment is high
- but only under conditions of free choice
- but only when there are consequences to the behavior
- but only when the consequences are foreseeable

In Cooper and Fazio's view, the cure for the "but only's" lay in drawing a new metaphorical straight line through the existing data. And when we did, that straight line did not pass through inconsistency.

The aversive consequence position proposed that dissonance arousal occurs when you behave in such a way as to feel personally responsible for bringing about an aversive consequence, defined as "an event . . . that one would rather not have occur" (Cooper & Fazio, 1984, p. 232). When you are aware that you have acted to bring about such an unwanted event, it causes the unpleasant arousal state known as dissonance. It also motivates you to reduce the arousal. One effective way to reduce the arousal is to change your mental representations so as to render the consequence nonaversive. In brief, you change your attitude so that what you have done is no longer unwanted. If you are responsible for having convinced a friend to favor a candidate for election whom you do not truly favor, you have brought about an unwanted, aversive consequence. You experience the unpleasant state of dissonance arousal. By changing your attitude toward the candidate and deciding that you, too, favor that candidate, you no longer find your friend's new position to be aversive. Thus, in Cooper and Fazio's view, being personally responsible for bringing about an aversive consequence *is* the distal motivation for the dissonance phenomenon. Dissonance occurs not because of inconsistency among mental representations, or because the self has been compromised, but rather because you have acted in such a way as to be personally responsible for the occurrence of an aversive consequence. The motivation to change a mental representation is explicitly to render the consequence of behavior nonaversive. Scher and Cooper (1989) conducted a study that crossed cognitive inconsistency with aversive outcomes and found strong evidence supporting the aversive consequences position.

Restoring Self-Integrity: Dissonance Subsumed by Self-Affirmation

Another powerful theoretical position to explain the distal motivation for dissonance was Claude Steele's self-affirmation theory (Steele, 1988). Steele postulated that creating a positive sense of self, or *affirming* the self, is a master motive that pertains to a wide array of important social and personal behaviors. The dissonance phenomenon is but one manifestation of this master motive that occurs in particular circumstances. When a person commits a dissonant act such as making a counterattitudinal statement, it threatens the self. It causes a need to repair the integrity of the self that has been compromised by the discrepant act. But any repair will do.

According to self-affirmation theory, if you commit a dissonant act, you can repair your damaged self by changing a mental representation of your attitude. From this perspective, what we have been calling the changes associated with the dissonance phenomenon merely represent one possible method of repair. Other repairs are also possible. Steele proposed, "To the extent that self-affirmation motivates consistency restoration, any adaptation that effectively affirms the larger self should be an effective adaptation" (1988, p. 281). The implication of this tenet is that people can be flexible in the method they use to reduce dissonance. Specifically, self-affirmation predicts that if people can call upon other positive aspects of their self-concept when threatened, they will reduce the dissonance without having to confront the issue that caused the threat in the first place. So, you can draw upon your resources as a lover, a fighter, or an artist as a means of affirming your sense of self without ever having to undergo a change of attitude.

Like self-consistency theory, self-affirmation theory finds an important role for differences among individuals in the dissonance process. A person who has more self-resources has more ways of resolving a threat to self-integrity caused by a counterattitudinal act than does a person with fewer self-resources. Steele, Spencer, and Lynch (1993) predicted and found that people who scored high on a self-esteem scale were less likely to change their attitudes following a dissonant act than were people with lower self-esteem. Steele et al. argued that people with limited self-resources (low self-esteem) have few other arrows in their quiver. When confronted with dissonant behavior, they can restore self-integrity only by changing their attitudes. People with high self-esteem, however, can change their attitudes if they so choose, but they can also think of their wonderful qualities that gave rise to their high sense of self-esteem. Thus, self-integrity can be restored by focusing more on positive self-representations and relying less on changing attitudes.

It is interesting that the role accorded differences in self-esteem in self-affirmation theory appears to be precisely opposite to the role of self-esteem in self-consistency theory. In the former, the higher the self-esteem, the less likely a person is to change attitudes when confronted with the implications of inconsistency. In the latter, the higher the self-esteem, the higher the expectations are for the person's actual selves and thus the more uncomfortable a person will become if the negative implications of his or her behavior undermine that expectancy. Although a full resolution of the differences is beyond the scope of this chapter, it should be noted that the two theories are focusing on different aspects of the dissonance process. Recall that in all of the theoretical accounts of the dissonance phenomenon, there is a difference between arousal and reduction of dissonance. Self-consistency theory focuses primarily on the factors that cause dissonance to be aroused; self-affirmation theory focuses mainly on how dissonance is reduced. It may be that high self-esteem, with its concomitant high expectation for how one will behave, leads to a higher level of dissonance arousal. On the other hand, the same high self-esteem, with its concomitant reservoir of positive resources, may facilitate means of dealing with the tension other than a change in attitude.

Seeking a Synthesis

In summary, all three major theoretical revisions of dissonance affirm the existence of the basic dissonance phenomenon. However, each of the three offers a different view of the distal motivation, especially with regard to one major issue: What is the role of the *self* in dissonance processes? We suggest that there is an overall picture and that each of the contemporary revisions describes an important piece of the cognitive dissonance process. It is quite reasonable to suppose that, under some conditions, people are motivated by a desire to uphold important beliefs they have about themselves (i.e., self-consistency); it is equally tenable that, under some conditions, people are motivated to reduce the perceived aversive consequences of their unwanted behavior (i.e., the "New Look"); and it is also the case that under some conditions, people would prefer to think about other positive aspects of themselves rather than face the implications of their behavior (i.e., self-affirmation). Put this way, one can see that the three major revisions are neither synonymous nor simple linguistic translations of one another. Rather, they each describe a distinct and important piece of the overall dissonance process and, in doing so, make a unique contribution to our understanding of cognitive dissonance arousal and reduction. The perspectives are brought together in what Jeff Stone and I have called the *self-standards model* of dissonance (Stone, 1999; Stone & Cooper, 1999).

The Self-Standards Model

Consistent with the Cooper and Fazio (1984) perspective, we believe that the dissonance process begins with behavior and the assessment of the behavioral outcome. Assessing an outcome is not a trivial process. Is the outcome desirable or undesirable? Does it say something positive or negative about me? Or is it hedonically irrelevant? The behavioral outcome takes on meaning only when it is compared to a significant *standard of judgment* – a significant criterion that we use to assess the meaning of our behavior. If I want to know whether the outcome of my behavior was something I wanted or shunned, whether it told me something positive or negative about me, I can answer these questions only by comparing what I have done to a standard of judgment. But what kinds of standards are available?

Ideographic Self-Standards

Multiple standards exist and compete to be used as the significant standard of judgment. One type of self-standard we can call an *ideographic* standard. A person's ideographic standard is unique to himself or herself. It is a standard of judgment based on the individual's personal set of expectations, goals, and desires. One person's ideographic standard may be based on an ideal outcome – for example, never to tell a lie. Another person's may be based on expectations – for example, not to tell more of a lie than he or she usually does. If an individual chooses to use a personal, ideographic self-standard to judge the meaning of a behavioral outcome, then personal issues such as morality and competence will be the bases for judgment. Consequently, as suggested by the self-affirmation and self-consistency theories, differences in self-representations, such as self-esteem, are bound to play a role in the assessment of the meaning of the behavioral outcome.

Let's look at how the process might unfold, leading to individual differences in assessing behavioral outcomes. When people invoke ideographic self-standards, they think about their own unique characteristics on a particular dimension. Let us call this dimension the *actual self*. When people have their actual selves in mind, they think of where they chronically stand vis-à-vis the normative or shared standard for that behavior – that is, they think of how close they typically are to the standard that most people in a given culture view as the desired or ideal benchmark. For example, a student's ideal goal may be to get an A on every test she takes. However, most students do not typically achieve this goal. The A is the desired end of the continuum, and a student's actual standing on this continuum probably lies at some distance from this ideal. Similarly, it is ideal never to say anything that is not true, but most of us have had some experience that violates this ideal. This discrepancy between the actual self and the shared, normative standard for behavior is what I refer to as people's *typical expectation* for themselves. Figure 4.1 portrays two people – one whose actual self leads to high expectations for behavioral outcomes and one for whom low expectations are predominant. People who view themselves as pretty good, positive, competent, moral people expect that they will act in appropriately competent ways relative to the normative standard for that behavior (see Figure 4.1). These positive expectancies are what we mean when we say that a person has high self-esteem. On the other hand, people who think of themselves as not particularly able,

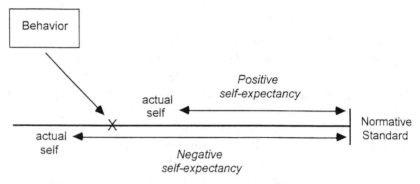

Figure 4.1. The use of self-expectancies to evaluate behavior.

competent, or moral (who have low self-esteem) have negative expectancies about their actual selves. Such people typically expect to behave further away from the normative standard.

If a person is using an ideographic standard of judgment, then a particular behavior – say, duping a fellow student – derives its meaning not only from its violation of a shared ideal standard, but also from the chronic expectancy (i.e., the actual self) that the person has come to love, cherish, or at least live with. As we see in Figure 4.1, a particular behavior can create cognitive dissonance for a person with high self-esteem but not for a person with low self-esteem. That behavior (duping another student) falls within the range of behaviors that a person with low self-esteem expects but outside the range of behaviors that the person with high self-esteem expects.

The Normative Standard

Another standard that can be brought to bear on a behavioral outcome is the normative standard of judgment. The normative standard represents the shared cultural value on a particular dimension. As Figure 4.2 shows, when this standard is applied, a person measures his or her behavioral outcome against the standard to which most people in a culture subscribe. Rather than factoring in where I normally stand on a particular dimension, I invoke society's standard as the measure of meaning.

This will become clear by thinking of a person who acts freely to comply with an experimenter's request in a typical dissonance situa-

Figure 4.2. The use of a normative standard to evaluate behavior.

tion. People know it is considered bad to dupe others by making them eagerly look forward to a task you know is dull. People know it is considered bad to convince others to vote for a candidate whom you do not really favor. It is bad, and people know it is considered bad, to argue for a policy that is contrary to their attitudes and that they think is immoral and unjust. When normative standards of judgment are invoked, people do not consider the frequency with which they usually lie to another student, say things they do not believe, and so forth. To the contrary, the individual differences in behaviors that comprise the actual self are not relevant. A person's level of self-esteem, typical expectancies, and prior behaviors do not enter into his or her assessment. Discrepancy with the culturally shared standard renders the behavioral outcome unwanted and aversive.

Accessibility of the Self-Standards

The interesting and significant question is, what determines which standard of judgment will be used to give meaning to a particular behavioral outcome? When will it be an ideographic standard that will invite issues of self-concept to play an important role in dissonance, and when will it be a shared, normative standard in which self-concept differences are not involved? We believe the answer depends on which standard is accessible in memory at the time the judgment is made.

By *accessibility*, we mean the ease of bringing a particular representation to bear on judgments and perceptions, whether consciously or not. In a given culture, we all have normative and ideographic standards available to us that we can bring to bear on our perceptions and judgments, and we all have standards that are unique to our personal ideographic situations. However, they are not equally accessible in all situations. If shared normative standards are accessible, then we believe people will apply those standards when they judge the outcomes of their behavior. If personal standards are accessible, behavioral outcomes will be assessed according to those standards.

The accessibility of a standard of judgment is mostly a function of the situation that people are in. If a situation evokes thoughts about oneself and one's individual experiences, it increases the accessibility of ideographic standards. If a situation evokes thoughts about norms, ideals, and shared values, it increases the accessibility of normative standards. It is probably true that some people, by virtue of their individual experiences, have chronically accessible standards of either the normative or the ideographic type, but Stone and I think this is rare. We focus instead on the standards that the situation makes salient, regardless of individual differences in chronicity.

Using the tenets of the self-standards model, we are in a position to make a general prediction about the role of the self in the arousal and reduction of cognitive dissonance. If personal ideographic standards are accessible, then the self will play a role and will affect the magnitude of the motivation to reduce dissonance. On the other hand, if shared normative standards are accessible, then the self will not affect the arousal or the reduction of dissonance. In particular, the valence of a person's self-esteem will play no role in the magnitude of dissonance, provided that normative standards are most accessible.

Inducing a Standard

Throughout life, we have learned to judge ourselves in large part by how we act and the consequences of those actions, accumulating occurrence after occurrence (see, for example, Tice and Faber, this volume). We learn that it is important to give meaning to our behaviors and their consequences, and we are motivated to apply a measuring stick or self-standard to convey that meaning. Yet we typically have neither the time nor the resources to consider carefully which standard of judgment to apply. The environment primes us by providing the appropriate cues.

The primes can occur consciously or beyond awareness. In their chapter in this volume, Susan Andersen and Kathy Berenson report that very meaningful transference relationships with significant others can be primed by presenting either overt resemblance cues or sub-liminal resemblance descriptors. Consistent with Andersen and Berenson's work, we conclude that whether conscious or unconscious, obvious or subtle, cues available in the situation can determine the standard that will be used by making that standard more accessible in memory.

Is there a default condition? That is, suppose that there are no subtle or overt cues to make one standard more accessible than another. This can be an important issue in behaviors that lead to dissonance. Assume that a person is asked to perform a counterattitudinal act or must decide between two choice alternatives. If the situation has no elements that induce normative or ideographic standards, which standard are people likely to use? Our suggestion is that normative standards are the default condition. This suggestion is based on the observation that most studies in the literature on cognitive dissonance do not report dif-ferent magnitudes of dissonance reduction with chronic differences in self concept, particularly self-esteem. We venture the speculative guess that when people assess the outcomes of their behavior, they are most likely to judge that behavior as a function of the expectations and standards of the cultural group to which they belong, predisposing them to use normative standards of judgment.

Summarizing the Model

The various revisions of dissonance theory make different predictions about the distal motivation that produces the dissonance phenomenon. The most central difference pertains to the role of the self. In the Self-Standards Model, we make the assumption that people judge the outcome of their behavioral acts by bringing to bear a particular stan-dard of judgment. The use of the standards and their results are depicted in Figure 4.3. When the situation makes ideographic self-standards accessible, people will judge their acts from the perspective of their expectations about themselves that are, in turn, based on their individual past experiences. In short, the self matters. But if normative standards of judgments are made accessible, then people judge their behavior in terms of shared and agreed-upon values. As I mentioned previously, we all know that it is bad or at least inappropriate to lie to a fellow student. When normative standards are accessible, people do not go about the business of recalling their own prior experiences or their generalized state of self-competence, which we refer to as self-

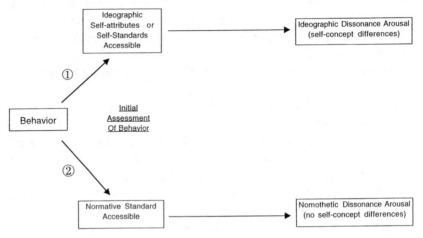

Figure 4.3. The paths to dissonance arousal.

esteem. Rather, they assume that they have done something aversive, negative, or unwanted, and the psychologically uncomfortable tension state of dissonance is aroused.

Ideographic and Normative Standards: Some Preliminary Findings

In order to provide preliminary evidence for the self-standards model, Kimberlee Weaver and I decided to manipulate the accessibility of ideographic and normative standards (Cooper & Weaver, 1999). Our basic hypothesis was that if ideographic standards are made accessible, then people who participate in a standard induced compliance study will manifest the dissonance phenomenon as a function of their level of self-esteem. With ideographic standards accessible, people's assessment of the outcome of their behavior will necessarily involve some assessment of their unique, personal characteristics. A person's self-esteem will matter, and dissonance will be a function of self-esteem. On the other hand, people who engage in the same dissonance-producing act but for whom normative standards are accessible will measure their behavioral outcome against a shared standard. Self-esteem will not matter, and people with both low and high self-esteem will experience a similar level of dissonance, as assessed by attitude change.

Inducing Compliance

The basic framework for our study was similar to the basic induced compliance experiments that have become the major paradigm for studying dissonance. Participants were asked to write an essay taking the position that Princeton University should reduce its funding for facilities for the handicapped. This position was known to be counter-attitudinal for our participants. Moreover, the participants were assured that their essays would be sent to a committee that had the financial power to increase or decrease funding for the handicapped. After writing their essays favoring reduced funding for the handicapped, participants had their attitudes assessed. A change in attitudes represented the reduction of dissonance.

Self-Standards Accessibility

The self-standard that would serve as the measuring stick with which to assess the behavioral outcome (i.e., writing a counter-attitudinal essay whose result may cause a lowering of funding for the handicapped) was systematically manipulated using a priming procedure. Participants had been told that the overall purpose of the study was to investigate issues in "language and cognition." Before the essay-writing task was ever mentioned, participants were asked to perform some mental tasks. One of the tasks was to make a sentence from a set of jumbled words. Each group of words, with one exception, formed a sentence. The participants were to discover the word to omit and then form a sentence with the remaining words. In reality, the task was relatively easy and was designed to form sentences that made the participants think of a particular standard for self-judgment. For participants who were randomly assigned to the *ideographic standards* condition, the sentences were all directed toward making the participants think of things about themselves. For example, the words *things, many, unique, chair, make,* and *me* could be used to form the sentence, "Many things make me unique." Other participants were assigned to the *normative standards* condition. They could unscramble the words *follow, should, people, cat, standards,* and *ethical* to form the sentence "People should follow ethical standards." We also included a condition in which unscrambling the words did not reflect a particular standard. The sentence "The pencil was on the desk" could be constructed from the words *pencil, desk, the, on the, was,* and *tree* and was not expected to serve as a prime for any self-standard.

After the jumbled-word task was completed, the experimenter presented an appropriate cover story about cooperation between the university administration and the researchers to explain why the administration was soliciting opinions about reducing funding for the handicapped. As is typical in induced compliance research, the participants were told that "one of the best ways we have found to understand the opinions for and against a proposal is to have people write the strongest and most forceful essays they can on one side of the proposal." The experimenter explained that she had already obtained a sufficient number of essays against the proposal to reduce funding for handicapped services, and she now needed people to take the position that funding should be reduced. Participants were run under high-choice conditions, and using typical instructions, the experimenter made certain that all participants felt that they were free to decline to write the essay. She also reiterated that the funding committee would find the essays very useful in forming a final policy. At the conclusion, she collected participants' attitudes about the handicapped funding issue.

Earlier in the semester, participants had filled out Rosenberg's (1979) self-esteem scale. Based on their scores on the scale, they were divided into high and low self-esteem groups. Thus, in this 2 × 3 factorial experiment, level of self-esteem (high vs. low) was combined with the manipulation of self-standard (ideographic vs. normative vs. none). The classic signature of the dissonance phenomenon is that attitudes change more for people who engage in counterattitudinal behavior under high-choice conditions than under low-choice conditions. Accordingly, we ran one condition in which people wrote counterattitudinal essays favoring reductions in spending for the handicapped but were told, rather than asked, to do so. Standards were not manipulated in this condition. Rather, the condition served as a benchmark from which to measure attitude change.

Our predictions followed from the self-standard model. Self, as assessed by level of self-esteem, was not expected to make a difference if people freely wrote counterattitudinal essays while their normative standards were activated. However, when ideographic standards were made accessible by the jumbled-word task, the level of self-esteem was predicted to make a difference. Based on our guess about the default condition, when no standard was primed, we hypothesized that the No

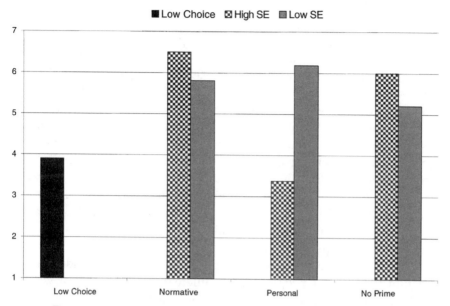

Figure 4.4. Attitude change as a function of self-standard and self-esteem.

Prime condition would have the property of the normative standard condition. Participants would be motivated to change their attitudes, and self-esteem would not make a difference.

The results, presented in Figure 4.4, support this prediction. In the No Prime condition, there is clear evidence of attitude change. The low and high self-esteem conditions did not differ from each other, and participants in both conditions showed significantly greater attitude change than participants in the low-choice condition. This difference is the classic finding in dissonance research and also supports our guess that self-esteem would not make a difference if ideographic standards were not specifically primed. When normative standards were primed, we found almost identical results: Self-esteem did not make a difference, and both self-esteem groups differed significantly from those in the low-choice condition. However, when the scrambled words made people's personal, ideographic characteristics accessible, level of self-esteem made a dramatic difference. As predicted, high and low self-esteem participants differed significantly from each other, and only the low self-esteem group differed from those in the low-choice condition.

Future Agenda

The results of preliminary studies are supportive of the self-standards model of dissonance. In addition to the study by Cooper and Weaver (1999), Stone, Galinsky, and Cooper (1999) had participants complete a free-choice procedure in which they made decisions about two choice alternatives. Following the decision, but before they rated the items a second time, participants were asked to write a short description of a target person who represented either the normative standard for competence or their personal standards for competence. As predicted, the data showed that thinking about personal self-standards caused participants with high self-esteem to justify their choices significantly more than participants with low self-esteem, but thinking about normative self-standards led to significant decision rationalization for *both* self-esteem groups.

The theory also opens up new questions that await evidence. If circumstances cause people to bring different standards to bear when judging their own behavior, is the violation of different standards *experienced* differently? In his work on self-discrepancy theory, Higgins (1989) suggests that different types of behavioral discrepancies may lead to qualitatively different emotional labels applied to dissonance arousal. Following Higgins's suggestion, it may be that when people assess their potentially discrepant behavior against a normative self-standard, they come to experience agitation-related emotions such as anxiety. However, if they apply an ideographic, personal self-standard, they may experience an emotion more like guilt or shame (Higgins, 1990). It may well be that what has heretofore been seen as an undifferentiated negative emotional state may be at least two qualitatively different states, depending on the self-standard that is used as the measuring stick for self-judgment. It would also follow that examining how people perceive their experience of dissonance arousal may be the gateway to understanding the self-standards that they applied. Further research will be needed to see if this is a fertile avenue for study.

A Final Perspective

In establishing the self-standards model of dissonance, I began by indicating that three leading versions of dissonance have all found some support for their point of view. By arguing for a synthesis of the aversive consequence, self-consistency, and self-affirmation models, I am not arguing that each is correct, depending on the circumstances. Rather, I take the position that each model captures a piece of the puzzle, but none of the models has accurately captured the distal motivation of dissonance. What I have called the dissonance phenomenon is not motivated solely by a drive for self-consistency, nor is it motivated by a need for self-integrity. Similarly, it is unduly narrow to argue that the motivation to reduce the aversiveness of behavioral consequences is the sole reason for dissonance arousal, independent of any personal, ideographic considerations about the actor.

Rather, the self-standards model begins with an actor's behavior and his or her motivation to assess the consequences of that behavior. Of course, unless the outcome is attributed to the self, it has little meaning for the actor. Thus, considerations of choice and responsibility are necessary in this model, just as they have been in the myriad empirical studies summarized by Cooper and Fazio (1984). If the attribution is to the self because personal responsibility is high, then the outcome takes on meaning by its comparison to a self-standard. That is where the current model broadens the approach of the aversive consequences model. The standard may be a normative one, as suggested by Cooper and Fazio, but it also may be a personal standard, as suggested by Aronson (1968; Thibodeau & Aronson, 1992).

It is the assessment of the behavioral outcome against whichever standard is accessible that puts the dissonance engine in motion. If the outcome is found to be aversive, unwanted, or undesired, as measured by that standard, then the uncomfortable psychological motivational state is activated. As we have speculated, that state may be experienced differently, depending on the standard that was used. In either case, as Festinger (1957) suggested, its unpleasant psychological property provides the impetus for its own reduction. It motivates the individual to find ways to reduce it. The reduction comes by rendering the outcome nonaversive. If an ideographic self-standard had been used to form the initial judgment, then the self may well play a role in its reduction. If a normative standard had been used, then the aversiveness will be experienced similarly by everyone, and differences in self-concept will not aid in dissonance reduction.

Festinger (1957) was well ahead of his time in arguing that the relationship among mental representations causes motivation for change. His original notion, of course, was that simple psychological inconsistency was the distal motivation that led to the change. On the 25th anniversary of dissonance theory, Festinger spoke to a symposium and expressed his pleasure that his original theory had evolved from its basic tenets. Perhaps he would have felt that the self-standards model was yet another step in the right direction.

References

Aronson, E. (1968). Dissonance theory: Progress and problems. In R. P. Abelson, E. Aronson, W. J. McGuire, T. M. Newcomb, M. J. Rosenberg, & P. H. Tannenbanm (Eds.), *Theories of cognitive consistency: A sourcebook* (pp. 5–27). Chicago: Rand McNally.

Aronson, E., & Carlsmith, J. M. (1962). Performance expectancy as a determinant of actual performance. *Journal of Abnormal and Social Psychology, 65,* 178–182.

Aronson, E., & Mills, J. M. (1959). The effects of severity of initiation on liking for a group. *Journal of Abnormal and Social Psychology, 59,* 177–181.

Brehm, J. W. (1956). Postdecision changes in the desirability of alternatives. *Journal of Abnormal and Social Psychology, 52,* 384–389.

Elliot, A. J., & Devine, P. G. (1994). On the motivational nature of cognitive dissonance: Dissonance as psychological discomfort. *Journal of Personality and Social Psychology, 67*(3), 382–394.

Festinger, L. (1957). *A theory of cognitive dissonance.* Stanford, CA: Stanford University Press.

Festinger, L., & Carlsmith, J. M. (1959). Cognitive consequences of forced compliance. *Journal of Abnormal and Social Psychology, 58,* 203–210.

Cooper, J., & Fazio, R. H. (1984). A new look at dissonance theory. In L. Berkowitz (Ed.), *Advances in experimental social psychology* (Vol. 17, pp. 229–262). Hillsdale, NJ: Erlbaum.

Cooper, J., & Weaver, K. (1999). *Priming self-standards in the dissonance process.* Unpublished manuscript.

Croyle, R. T., & Cooper, J. (1983). Dissonance arousal: Physical evidence. *Journal of Personality and Social Psychology, 45,* 782–791.

Higgins, E. T. (1989). Self-discrepancy theory: What patterns of self-beliefs cause people to suffer? In L. Berkowitz (Ed.), *Advances in experimental social psychology* (Vol. 22, pp. 93–136). Hillsdale, NJ: Erlbaum.

Higgins, E. T. (1990). Personality, social psychology, and person–situation relations: Standards and knowledge activation as a common language. In L. A. Pervin (Ed.), *Handbook of personality theory and research* (pp. 301–338). New York: Guilford Press.

Losch, M. E., & Cacioppo, J. T. (1990). Cognitive dissonance may enhance sympathetic tonus, but attitudes are changed to reduce negative affect rather than arousal. *Journal of Experimental Social Psychology, 26,* 289–304.

Rosenberg, M. (1979). *Concerning the self.* New York: Basic Books.

Scher, S. J., & Cooper, J. (1989). Motivational basis of dissonance: The singular role of behavioral consequences. *Journal of Personality and Social Psychology, 56,* 899–906.

Steele, C. M. (1988). The psychology of self-affirmation: Sustaining the integrity of the self. In L. Berkowitz (Ed.), *Advances in experimental social psychology* (Vol. 21, pp. 261–302). Hillsdale, NJ: Erlbaum.

Steele, C. M., Spencer, S. J., & Lynch, M. (1993). Dissonance and affirmational resources: Resilience against self-image threats. *Journal of Personality and Social Psychology, 64*(6), 885–896.

Stone, J. (1999). What exactly have I done? The role of self-attribute accessibility in dissonance. In E. Harmon-Jones & J. Mills (Eds.), *Cognitive dissonance: Progress on a pivotal theory in social psychology* (pp. 175–200). Washington, DC: American Psychological Association.

Stone, J., & Cooper, J. (1999). *A self-standards model of dissonance.* Unpublished manuscript.

Stone, J., Galinsky, A., & Cooper, J. (1999). *The role of self-standards in dissonance processes: The mirror has many faces.* Unpublished manuscript.

Thibodeau, R., & Aronson, E. (1992). Taking a closer look: Reasserting the role of the self-concept in dissonance theory. *Personality and Social Psychology Bulletin, 18*(5), 591–602.

5. The Motivational and Cognitive Dynamics of Day-to-Day Social Life

JOHN B. NEZLEK

This chapter presents a model describing relationships among the cognitive and motivational dynamics of day-to-day social life and psychological well-being and describes the results of studies supporting parts of the model. The model rests upon three complementary assumptions. The first is that people's daily lives reflect the integration of two basic needs (among others), the need to belong and the need for control and predictability in one's life. Although both of these needs may be thought of as motives, the second tends to be conceptualized in more cognitive terms than the first, which tends to be conceptualized as having a stronger affective component. The second assumption is that understanding people's daily lives requires distinguishing the processes responsible for how people allocate their time (the quantitative components of daily life) from the processes responsible for how people react to daily experience (the qualitative components).

The model further assumes that the needs for prediction and control are related more closely to the quantitative components of day-to-day life than they are to the qualitative components. What people do each day (the people they meet, the activities in which they engage, etc.) is more heavily influenced by cognitive processes and by the needs for prediction and control than are people's reactions to these events. In contrast, the need to belong is related more closely to the qualitative

The model described in this chapter is based upon a body of research that would not have existed without the help and support of the numerous colleagues with whom I have worked over the years. I am grateful to them for their help and inspiration. Equally important, I am indebted to the hundreds of participants who provided the data for these studies. Correspondence regarding this paper should be sent to John B. Nezlek, College of Willian & Mary, Department of Psychology, P. O. Box 8795, Williamsburg, VA 23187-8795, email: john.nezlek@wm.edu components of day-to-day life than it is to the quantitative components. Moreover, such distinctions are more pronounced when considering social events than they are when considering nonsocial events.

The model draws on research and theory on various topics, including day-to-day social interaction, daily plans and their fulfillment, relationships between daily events and day-to-day psychological states, and relationships between life goals and daily behaviors. The model relies on research and theory on these topics because although daily life consists of much more than social life, research using a wide variety of methods indicates clearly that people spend a considerable portion of each day with others. Consequently, understanding the motivational and cognitive dynamics of daily life necessarily provides insight into the motivational and cognitive dynamics of daily interpersonal behavior.

This chapter complements the other chapters in this volume in several ways. First, the present model emphasizes a temporal unit (the day) as an organizing theme, whereas the other chapters use persons, events, or some combination of these as organizing themes. Given the power of the circadian cycle in determining a broad array of human behaviors, it is difficult to imagine that the day is not a powerful organizing unit for human social behavior. Second, the present model places more emphasis on social systems and their norms and roles as influences on social behavior than do most of the other chapters. By definition, social behavior requires the presence of other people, and it seems that people invariably form collectives, collectives that provide a structure within which people behave.

The model also concerns interpersonal behavior at an aggregate level rather than at the level of the specific behavior or interpersonal exchange. This level was chosen because some psychologically meaningful phenomena may exist only within broader temporal and situational contexts. For example, understanding the extent to which people's social lives meet their plans and expectations requires knowing people's plans for various types of activities across time and various situations.

Belonging and Prediction and Control as Dimensions of a Framework

The present model's assumption that two basic motives underlie day-to-day life (and social life) reflects the integration of a broad array of theories and supporting research. Needs or motives for prediction and control have figured heavily in scholarship concerning attribution, task motivation, reactions to stressful events, and a host of other topics. The need to belong has also figured heavily in scholarship on various topics, although with some recent exceptions (Baumeister & Leary, 1995), this need has not been discussed with a focus as sharp as that of discussions concerning the need for prediction and control. Furthermore, few attempts have been made to understand day-to-day social behavior within a conceptual framework relying on two constructs such as these.

The present two-dimensional framework is similar to other two-dimensional typologies, including Freud's classic distinction between *Arbeit* and *Lieb*, as well as more contemporary research on group processes and leadership (instrumental vs. socioemotional functions) and interpersonal style (agency vs. communion). The same distinction has also been made in research on strivings. For example, Emmons (1991) compared people who had achievement and affiliative goals. The parallel between these typologies and the present model is predicated on the correspondence between agentic and instrumental aspects of daily life and cognitively focused needs for prediction and control, and between socioemotional and communal aspects and more affectively focused needs for belongingness.

Quantity and Quality of Day-to-Day Social Interaction and Psychological Well-Being

An important impetus for the present model was a series of studies on day-to-day social interaction using variants of the Rochester Interaction Record (RIR; Wheeler & Nezlek, 1977). Participants in these studies used standardized forms to describe the social interactions they had each day. These descriptions included the others present during the interaction, when the interaction began, and how long it lasted; these data provided measures of the quantity and distribution of social contact. Participants also provided various ratings of their reactions to the interaction, and these ratings constituted measures of the quality of interactions.

Taken together, these studies suggest that quantity and quality of social interaction are markedly different constructs. First, measures of quantity such as interactions per day, and measures of quality such as intimacy and enjoyment, are correlated only weakly, if at all (e.g., unpublished analyses of data presented in Nezlek 1993, 1995, 1999; Nezlek, Hampton, & Shean, 2000; Nezlek, Reis, & Cunningham, 1999). Second, and more important, measures of quantity tend to be unrelated to measures of psychological well-being, whereas measures of quality tend to be positively related to well-being.

For example, in Nezlek, Imbrie, and Shean (1994), college students used a variant of the RIR to describe their day-to-day social interactions. Compared to those who were not at risk for depression, participants who were at risk, as measured by the Center for Epidemiological Studies Depression scale (CES-D) (Radloff, 1977), found their interactions to be less enjoyable and intimate and felt less confident and influential in their interactions. Nezlek et al. (1994) did not find differences in amount of social contact between those at risk and not at risk.

The same pattern of results was found by Nezlek et al. (2000) in a study of adults living in the community, half of whom meet DSM criteria for clinical depression and half of whom served as a control group. The results of hierarchical linear modeling analyses indicated that depressed participants found their interactions to be less enjoyable and intimate and felt less influential in their interactions. Nezlek et al. (2000) did not find differences between the two groups in amount of social contact. Moreover, similar patterns of results have been found in studies of the relationships between social interaction and measures of more specific aspects of adjustment such as body image (Nezlek, 1999) and the use of humor as a coping mechanism (Nezlek & Derks, in press).

Relationships between measures of interaction quality and psychological well-being have also been found in studies of causal relationships between such constructs. Based upon structural equation modeling of data collected in a panel study conducted over 2 years, Nezlek (in press-a) found that changes in social skills (interpreted in part as an indirect measure of social acceptance) were related to changes in a latent factor representing quality of social interaction. There were no relationships between social skills and quantity of social interaction. Similarly, Nezlek et al. (1999) found that a latent factor representing quality of interaction led to changes in a latent factor representing psychological well-being. Nezlek et al. (1999) also found no relationships between well-being and quantity of social interaction.

Null results frequently raise questions about the adequacy of the design, power, and other characteristics of a study, and such questions can be raised about each of the studies just cited. Nonetheless, quantity of social interaction and well-being were found to be unrelated, whereas quality of interaction and well-being were related:

1. in different samples (collegians and adults in the community);
2. across different operationalizations of well-being (subclinical and clinical depression, measures of specific personality constructs, and a multivariate latent construct);
3. across different operationalizations of interaction quality; and
4. across different analytic methods (ordinary least squares, hierarchical linear modeling, and structural equation modeling).

Moreover, in all but one of these studies the sample was larger than 100, and for traditional ordinary least squares analyses a sample of 100 provides a power of approximately .85 to detect effects (expressed as correlations) of .30 or larger. It should also be noted that such a conclusion is consistent with that of Marangoni and Ickes's (1989) review of research on loneliness. They noted that "*qualitative* considerations are more important than *quantitative* considerations in mediating the relationship between social network variables and the experience of loneliness" (p. 97).

From some perspectives, the lack of relationships between interaction quantity and well-being may be counterintuitive. For example, some research on social support suggests that psychological well-being is positively related to the size of people's support networks. The apparent difference between the conclusion of this research and research on social interaction can be understood by considering differences between the two bodies of research in how quantity of social contact is measured. Research on support networks frequently focuses on the number of *supportive* people one *knows* and measures, and by implication, the amount of support one can receive when it is needed. In constrast, research on social interaction measures the number of people with whom one interacts, the number of interactions one has, and the amount of time one spends with others, irrespective of the social support provided or received in an interaction.

People spend time with others for a wide variety of reasons, and supportive interactions, the explicit focus of research on social support, probably constitute a minority of interactions for most people at most times. This contention is supported by two studies. In a study by Sullivan, Nezlek, and Jackson (1996), college student participants maintained a variant of the RIR, and in addition to providing the standard information about each interaction (discussed previously), they indicated how much social support they received during the interaction. In only 14% of interactions did participants report receiving high levels of support (a rating of 4 or more on a 7-point scale), and in 38% they reported receiving no support at all. In a similar study, by Barbee, Felice, Cunningham, and Berry (1993), participants described in detail the social support they provided or received during an interaction if they provided or received support; these additional data were provided for only 25% of interactions.

Regardless of the percentage of interactions that explicitly involve social support, the fact that quantity of social interaction and psychological well-being are unrelated may be somewhat counterintuitive. For example, many psychologists and laypeople think of isolated and lonely people as suffering due to their isolation, and the emphasis in many forms of therapy is to help people become more fully integrated into some form of social network. Yet it is important to note that *none* of the nine A-criteria used in the DSM to diagnose clinical depression refer explicitly to quantity of social contact. The criteria that refer to sociality refer to quality of contact. The DSM criteria are also consistent with research suggesting that quality of support, not quantity, provides a buffer against psychological distress such as depression (e.g., Sheldon & West, 1989).

The lack of relationships between well-being and quantity of social contact, combined with the existence of reliable relationships between well-being and quality of social interaction, suggests that the quantity and quality of social interaction are regulated by or reflect different processes. The present model assumes that more cognitively focused processes centering on needs for prediction and control govern quantitative aspects of social life, whereas qualitative aspects reflect processes centering on the need to belong. Moreover, psychological well-being is related more closely to the satisfaction of the need to belong than to the satisfaction of the need for prediction and control.

A Working Model of the Dynamics of Daily Life

The working model presented in this chapter describes the dynamics of daily life (including daily social life) and the relationships between day-to-day social life and psychological health. Different parts of the model are explained in more detail than others, depending upon the available data and relevant theories. The model, depicted in Figure 5.1, incorporates the following:

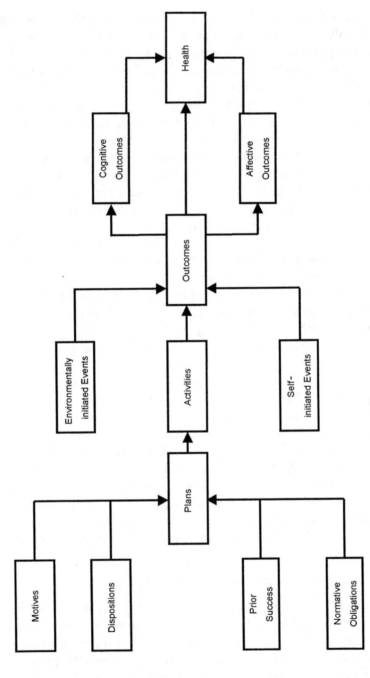

Figure 5.1. The dynamics of day-to-day activities and their relationships to psychological health.

1. People have and make plans for their daily activities.
2. The daily activities in which people engage are primarily the result of these plans.
3. These activities provide various outcomes for people, outcomes that are difficult to plan with certainty.
4. These outcomes influence people's psychological health, both directly and indirectly.
5. Environmentally initiated and self-initiated events that were not planned or anticipated also influence people's psychological health in ways similar to the influence of planned or anticipated events.

In terms of the two organizing themes, the need for prediction and control and the need to belong, the model emphasizes the close relationship between the need for prediction and control and the formulation and enacting of plans, and the close relationship between outcomes of social events and the need to belong. In part, these differences reflect the realities of life and social life. I can much more readily plan what I will do (e.g., a social activity) than I can plan the outcome of that activity. Moreover, the need to belong is probably more affective in nature than it is cognitive, and so it is difficult for this need to be met by more cognitively focused activities such as the fulfillment of plans.

Formation of Plans for Daily Living

Daily plans have not been studied extensively, although they have been discussed. For example, daily plans were highlighted in the first few pages of Miller, Galanter, and Pribam's (1960) influential book *Plans and the Structure of Behavior*. The authors noted, "Whether it is crowded or empty, novel or routine, uniform or varied, your day has a structure of its own – it fits into the texture of your life. And as you think what your day will hold, you construct a plan to meet it" (p. 5). They noted further that these plans may not be exact or precise: "[plans] probably have some relation to how you spend your time during the day . . . [although] you do not draw out long and elaborate blueprints for every moment of the day . . . all you need is the name of the activity that you plan for that moment of the day, and from that you proceed to elaborate the detailed actions in carrying out the plan" (pp. 5–6). Curiously, they did not discuss the construct of a daily plan any further.

The present model assumes that daily plans reflect a combination of individuals' motives and dispositions, their expectations about the likelihood that they can exhibit certain behaviors, their obligations to meet the normative requirements of role occupancy, and their largely unconscious, habitual, ingrained patterns of behavior. Dispositions include a broad array of personality characteristics, particularly those that may be directly relevant to planning and goal setting, such as Kuhl's state and action orientations (Kuhl, 1985). Motives include various constructs, such as personal strivings (Emmons, 1989), life goals (Cantor, 1994), or the need for self-determination (Deci & Ryan, 1985). Expectations refer more to people's beliefs about their ability to exhibit a certain behavior than to their beliefs about whether a certain behavior will lead to a certain outcome.

The present model differs from much previous research in its emphasis on normative expectations and ingrained patterns. As discussed by Katz and Kahn (1978) and other more sociologically focused scholars, a considerable portion of human behavior can be understood in terms of meeting role requirements and obligations. Given the enduring nature of most role obligations, people's daily plans typically incorporate such obligations.

The incorporation of roles into routine plans and behaviors may also be understood within the context of Bargh's (1990) work on automaticity. Bargh has suggested that engaging in a behavior over and over makes the behavior (and accompanying cognitions) more automatic and less subject to conscious control and, by implication, less influenced by changes in motives. Plans and routines combine to produce behavioral regularity, including the regularity of day-to-day social interaction.[1]

Although goals and daily plans share features such as a future orientation, the present model makes important distinctions between them. *Plans* refer to fairly specific activities or behavioral sequences such as "I plan to have dinner with Dick and Jane tonight." In contrast, *goals* usually refer to desired outcomes such as "I want to get to know Dick and Jane better." Such a distinction is important because people can plan what they do much more readily than they can plan or anticipate the outcomes of their behaviors. Having dinner with Dick and

---

[1] Bargh's work also figures prominently in Ouelette and Wood's (1998) discussion of how habit and intention combine to predict behavior. Although Ouelette and Wood were primarily interested in explaining why people exhibit specific target behaviors such as recycling, whereas the present model concerns larger aggregates such as sets or classes of behaviors, Oulette and Wood's conclusions complement the present model.

Jane simply requires eating in their presence, and meeting them at an appropriate place at dinner time constitutes a viable plan. Getting to know Dick and Jane better requires their cooperation, perhaps the mutual recognition of shared values or beliefs, and so on; and it may be difficult, if not impossible, for people to plan this process in the same way they plan more instrumental activities such as allocating one's time at work.

Plans as the Proximal Causes of Day-to-Day Behaviors

The present model assumes that people's plans are the proximal, immediate causes of their day-to-day behaviors. This premise is consistent with numerous theories concerning the roles of intentionality, including the positions advocated by Harré and Secord (1973), Kuhl and Beckman (1985), and Ajzen (1985). Structurally, the proposed relationship between plans and behaviors resembles critical components of Ajzen's (1985) theory of planned behavior. In Ajzen's model, attitudes combine with normative beliefs and perceived control over behavior to form behavioral intentions, and behavioral intentions are the immediate causes of behaviors. In the present model, people's motives and dispositions, their expectations about the likelihood that they can exhibit certain behaviors, and their role obligations combine to create plans that are the immediate causes of day-to-day behaviors.

This is the part of the model most directly concerned with the cognitive dynamics underlying day-to-day social behavior. The model assumes that the primary mechanisms responsible for the distribution of people's time are cognitive in nature. People have plans and expectations for how they will spend their days, and these plans become the causes for their behaviors, social or otherwise. Moreover, assuming that plans are the proximal causes of the distribution of daily activities explains the lack of relationships between quantity of social interaction and psychological well-being. If the distribution of people's time (including the amount of time spent with others) is determined primarily by routinized cognitive constructs such as plans and roles, quantity of interaction and other more socioemotionally focused constructs may be not be closely related.

Daily plans and their relationships to daily activities were examined by Nezlek and Sullivan (1996), and the results of this study support the proposed link between plans and activities. In this study, college student participants described how they allocated their time each day for 14 days, and some participants also described the plans they had for each day.

Using a standard form, all participants described what they did during each of the 72 20-minute segments into which the 24 hours of a day are divided. They described what they were doing using one of eight mutually exclusive activity categories (socializing, relaxation, study, class, work, life necessity, sleep, and religion), categories based on previous research on social interaction (e.g., Nezlek, Wheeler, & Reis, 1983) and on focus groups that met prior to the study. If a segment involved more than one activity, participants recorded the activity that took up the majority of the time in that segment.

To control for potential reactivity of the procedure, four different recording protocols were used. One group of participants recorded only their activities. The second group indicated how well planned each activity was as they recorded their activities. The third group indicated what they thought they would do the next day (by 20-minute segment) while describing their activities for the current day. The fourth group estimated the total amount of time they would devote to each activity the upcoming day (by category) while describing their activities and how well planned they were for the current day (by segment). It should be noted that the procedure was not reactive. There were no differences between conditions in any of the analyses to be discussed or in analyses of the distribution of activities.

Relationships between plans and activities were examined with a series of multilevel random coefficient modeling analyses in which days were nested within people. In the day-level models in these analyses, the amount of time spent per day in each activity was the dependent measure, and the amount of time planned for that activity was the independent measure. These analyses found that people's plans for how they would allocate their time the next day were good predictors of how they did allocate their time. The results of these analyses are summarized in Table 5.1.

One component of the analyses referred to correspondence between plans and activities at the person level, and for all activities, plans accounted for a substantial proportion of the between-individual variance in amount of activity. Planned time accounted for 76% of the variance in socializing and relaxation, for 61% in class attendance, for 65% in life necessity, for 80% in sleep, and for more than 95% in study, work, and religion. Individuals who on average planned to do more of an activity did more on average, and this correspondence was high for

Table 5.1. *Correspondence Between Actual and Planned Activities*

			Variance Accounted for by Plans	
	Actual	*Planned*	*Person Level*	*Day Level*
Socializing	9.40	8.68	76	41
Relaxation	10.31	8.83	76	20
Study	11.03	12.88	97	46
Class	6.70	7.32	61	80
Work	1.88	3.02	99	60
Life necessity	8.20	8.45	65	27
Sleep	23.99	22.34	80	26
Religion	.76	1.15	97	70

Note: The first two columns contain the mean number of 20-minute segments that occurred (Actual) and were planned (Planned) for each day.

socializing, the only activity that by definition involved interacting with others.

The analyses also provided estimates of how closely plans and activities corresponded on a day-by-day basis, controlling for individual differences in mean levels of planned and actual activities. Plans also accounted for a substantial proportion of the day-to-day variance in class attendance (80%), religious activity (70%), and work (60%), a moderate proportion of the day-to-day variance in studying (46%) and socializing (41%), and a smaller proportion of the variance in relaxation (20%), sleeping (26%), and life necessity (27%). It is interesting to note that the lowest day-level correspondence was for relaxation, sleep, and life necessity, the three activity categories that are probably bound the least by social norms. In contrast, for going to class, perhaps the most role-defining and role-defined activity for a student, plans accounted for 80% of the variability in day-to-day attendance.

Although these data do not prove that plans caused behaviors, these results are consistent with a model in which plans are causes of behaviors. It is important to keep in mind that plans were made the day before the behaviors occurred, satisfying at least the temporal requirement for a cause. Moreover, distributions of activities did not vary across conditions, suggesting that participants did not modify their activities because they recorded their plans for the purposes of the study.

As discussed earlier, plans, as presently defined, concern activities or behavioral sequences, not goals or outcomes. This separation of goals and activities distinguishes the present conceptualization of plans from some others. For example, Gollwitzer (1990) discusses plans primarily in terms of how people plan and enact action goals. Within Gollwitzer's conceptualization, planned behaviors are not goals in themselves; they are means to ends. Such a conceptualization would seem to be most applicable to situations in which goals can be clearly articulated, in which action plans can be established, and in which relationships between behaviors and goals are fairly unambiguous and consistent.

Conceptualizing plans in terms of action goals may not be applicable, however, when behaviors are not means to ends but are ends in themselves, and people may frequently encounter such situations in day-to-day life. Role-prescribed behaviors such as arriving at a job punctually may eventually serve some higher goal (not getting fired), but in people's immediate phenomenology, the exhibition of the behavior per se (being on time) is the planned behavior.

Another class of behaviors that would appear to fall outside the class of "means to ends" consists of behaviors that Deci (1972) termed *intrinsically motivated*, behaviors for which the reward (or goal) is the exhibition of the behavior itself. I may play the piano simply because I enjoy playing the piano.[2] This characteristic means that plans to exhibit such behaviors function as goals in the sense that exhibiting the behavior (fulfilling the plan) is the reward.

A third class of behaviors for which an action goal analysis may not be particularly applicable consists of behaviors for which action goal sequences are difficult to formulate. Within a model such as Gollwitzer's, when goals have been identified, action plans are created and action sequences are initiated. What does one do, however, when one's goals are unclear or when goals are not entirely appropriate ways of

---

[2] Admittedly, one could argue narrowly that playing the piano is a means to an end (feeling good), but such reductionism leads nowhere or to propositions that cannot be refuted. That is, every behavior is a means to an end (feeling good). However valid such a position may be from some perspectives, it would appear that there is some value to assuming that some behaviors or actions are functionally ends in themselves.

representing desired states? For example, it may be quite difficult for people to plan successful interpersonal relationships or encounters. People may not know what they want from their friends, and many may deny (at least consciously) wanting anything more than friendship itself under normal circumstances.

Simple affiliation may be the most important consideration in planning many social activities. People may not know what else they want from social activities if they want anything else at all. Or it may be too difficult for people to formulate goals with sufficient clarity to permit the creation of action plans. Even if goals can be formulated, people may not know enough to create action plans to guide them. The murkiness of interpersonal encounters may make the connection between the exhibition of behaviors and desired outcomes sufficiently tenuous to render behaviors and goals relatively independent.

The foregoing discussion was not intended to argue that people do not have, set, or pursue interpersonal goals. Rather, the primary point is that in terms of their day-to-day behaviors (interpersonal and otherwise), people may not be that consciously and explicitly goal-oriented when goals are defined as some sort of desired end state produced by and separable from their behaviors. When trying to understand the dynamics of day-to-day life, plans themselves, not various sorts of ulterior motives or goals, may be the reason why people engage in certain behaviors.

Finally, for those who cannot imagine that people behave without goals, it may be useful to think of behavioral sequences as proximal goals and outcomes as distal goals. Such a sequence would be more consistent with (although not the same as) models such as Gollwitzer's. Nonetheless, given the qualitative difference between such types of goals, it may be more useful to describe them with different labels while recognizing their similarities within some frameworks.

Outcomes of Activities

In parallel to the present model's distinction between plans and goals, the model also distinguishes activities and outcomes. Having dinner with Dick and Jane is an activity. Enjoying dinner with them and getting better acquainted with them are outcomes that are separable from the activity itself. *Outcomes* are defined as changes that occur in an individual, and as depicted in Figure 5.1, they can take various forms. Outcomes may be more cognitive in nature, such as perceptions of control, or more affective in nature, and some may not fit easily into either category but may still affect well-being.

Research on reactivity to daily events concerns this component of the model. The dominant focus of this research has been the relationships between negative events (stressors) and mood, and in general, these studies have found that daily negative mood covaries with negative events (e.g., Bolger & Schilling, 1991). On days when people experience more stressors, their moods are more negative.

Although informative, this research has important limitations, two of which are particularly relevant to the parameters specified in the present model. First, these studies have focused exclusively on moods as outcomes. Although mood is an important construct, there are other constructs that merit attention due to their relationships with well-being. Second, these studies have not distinguished social and achievement events, and given the important distinctions that have been drawn between these domains in other literatures, such a distinction should be informative.

A recent series of studies by Nezlek and colleagues addressed such concerns by studying the covariation between daily social and achievement events and psychological states other than mood. In these studies, participants indicated which events occurred during a day, and they provided measures of various psychological states. These data were analyzed with multilevel random coefficient modeling analyses that examined the day-level covariation between psychological states and daily events. In general, these studies support components of the proposed model in that the covariation between social events and well-being was stronger than the covariation between negative events and well-being.

In one study, by Nezlek and Gable (1999), participants provided data every day for 3 weeks. The primary analyses found that both affectively and cognitively focused measures of psychological well-being (self-esteem, anxiety, depressive thinking, perceived control over the environment, and causal uncertainty) covaried positively with positive events and negatively with negative events. Unpublished analyses of these data that distinguished social and achievement events found that although daily well-being covaried with both daily social and achievement events, this covariation tended to be stronger for social events than for achievement events.

In a similar study, by Nezlek and Plesko (2000), participants provided data twice a week for up to 10 weeks. These measures included daily events, self-esteem, anxiety, depressive thinking, and positive and negative mood. Consistent with the results of Nezlek and Gable (1999), the authors found that daily well-being covaried positively with positive events and negatively with negative events and that this covariation tended to be stronger for social events than for achievement events. The distinction between social and achievement events also figured prominently in a study on day-to-day covariation in self-consciousness. Nezlek (2000) found that daily private and public self-consciousness covaried with daily social events, whereas neither covaried with daily achievement events.

Although informative, these studies do not address the roles played by plans. Such relationships were examined by Nezlek (in press-b) in a paper that presents additional analyses of some of the data discussed by Nezlek and Gable (1999). In addition to measures of well-being, participants in the Nezlek and Gable study provided measures of how well their plans for social and achievement-related activities had been realized each day. Participants' psychological well-being was higher on days when their plans were realized more fully than on days when their plans were realized less fully. Moreover, well-being covaried more strongly with the fulfillment of social plans than with the fulfillment of achievement plans.

The stronger covariation between day-to-day well-being and the fulfillment of social plans suggests that psychological well-being is more closely related to social activities than to achievement activities, a possibility that supports components of the present model. If social plans are not met, if others do not appear when they are supposed to, or if a social event does not turn out as planned, people may begin to feel less secure about their social relationships.

This study was somewhat limited by the fact that no measure of planned activities was collected, a shortcoming addressed by Nezlek and Elia (1998). In this study, each day participants described up to three goals or plans they had for the upcoming day, and they indicated how fully the plans they had made the previous day had been fulfilled. The data were analyzed with a series of multilevel random coefficient modeling analyses in which days were nested within people. Preliminary analyses have found that people who were more poorly adjusted, as measured by the CES-D, accomplished fewer goals (fulfilled fewer plans). Interestingly, more poorly adjusted people also set more difficult goals that they believed would take longer to meet, results consistent with the negative relationships between plan fulfillment and trait adjustment reported in Nezlek (in press-b) and in Nezlek and Hampton (1996).

Integration and Summary

Although the present model relies upon a different level of analysis than the research and theory described in the other chapters in this volume, it shares features with much of this work. For example, the two needs that serve as the foundation for the present model, the need for control and prediction and the need to belong, figure prominently in research serving as the basis for Andersen and Berenson's chapter in this volume and are part of the model upon which Williams, Wheeler, and Haurey's discussion of ostracism is based, and the need to belong is central to Tice and Faber's discussion of self-presentation.

In terms of focus and level of analysis, the ostracism research discussed by Williams et al. is the most relevant to the present model, and at first glance, it would appear that the two bodies of research are in conflict. Williams et al. suggest that ostracism, the withdrawal of social contact, is associated with various negative outcomes, whereas the present model suggests that social contact per se is not related to psychological well-being. Nevertheless, differences in these conclusions may reflect differences between the two approaches in how social contact is operationalized.

Ostracism, by definition, is the intentional withdrawal of social contact, a withdrawal that may not be desired by the target. In contrast, the social interactions that are the focus of the present model include (and are probably dominated by) events that people choose or plan to have, or, in the case of people with no or few interactions, not to have. It is quite possible that part of the reason some people have relatively few interactions is that others have ostracized them. Nonetheless, it is likely that the bulk of the variability in social activity is determined by factors others than ostracism. This analysis does not imply that ostracism is unimportant. In fact, ostracism's influence on well-being may be inversely related to its frequency – less frequent events may be more influential for various reasons.

Myriad factors influence the course of people's daily lives and people's reactions to their daily lives. Research has tended to focus on relationships between day-to-day life and various motives, goals, and dispositions. The present model complements this research by focusing on relationships between plans and the course of people's daily lives and reactions to daily life. Moreover, the studies described in this chapter provide preliminary support for some components of the proposed model. Clearly, demonstrating the explanatory power of the proposed model will require further research and deliberation. Nevertheless, the work described in this chapter suggests that such a demonstration is possible.

References

Ajzen, I. (1985). From intentions to actions: A theory of planned behavior. In J. Kuhl & J. Beckman (Eds.), *Action-control: From cognition to behavior* (pp. 11–39). Heidelberg: Springer-Verlag.

Ajzen, I. (1996). The directive influence of attitudes on behavior. In P. M. Gollwitzer & J. A. Bargh (Eds.), *The psychology of action* (pp. 385–403). New York: Guilford Press.

Barbee, A. P., Felice, T., Cunningham, M. R., & Berry, M. (1993, June). *Studying supportive and nonsupportive interactions in daily life.* Paper presented at a symposium entitled "Current research using social interaction diaries," organized by John Nezlek. International Network on Personal Relationships Conference, Milwaukee, WI.

Bargh, J. A. (1990). Auto-motives: Preconscious determinants of thought and behavior. In E. T. Higgins & R. M. Sorrentino (Eds.), *Handbook of motivation and cognition* (Vol. 2, pp. 93–130). New York: Guilford Press.

Baumeister, R. F., & Leary, M. R. (1995). The need to belong: Desire for interpersonal attachments as a fundamental human motivation. *Psychological Bulletin, 117,* 497–529.

Bolger, N., & Schilling, E. A. (1991). Personality and the problems of everyday life: The role of neuroticism in exposure and reactivity to daily stressors. *Journal of Personality, 59,* 355–386.

Cantor, N. (1994). Life task problem solving: Situational affordances and personal needs (Division Eight Presidential Address, 1993). *Personality and Social Psychology Bulletin, 20,* 235–243.

Deci, E. L. (1972). *Intrinsic motivation.* New York: Plenum.

Deci, E. L., & Ryan, R. M. (1985). *Intrinsic motivation and self-determination in human behavior.* New York: Plenum.

Emmons, R. A. (1989). The personal striving approach to personality. In L. A. Pervin (Ed.), *Goal concepts in personality and social psychology* (pp. 87–126). Hillsdale, NJ: Erlbaum.

Emmons, R. A. (1991). Personal strivings, daily life events, and psychological and physical well-being. *Journal of Personality, 59,* 453–472.

Gollwitzer, P. M. (1990). Action phases and mind sets. In E. T. Higgins & R. M. Sorrentino (Eds.), *Handbook of motivation and cognition: Foundations of social behavior* (Vol. 2, pp. 53–92). New York: Guilford Press.

Gollwitzer, P. M. (1996). The volitional benefits of planning. In P. M. Gollwitzer & J. A. Bargh (Eds.), *The psychology of action* (pp. 287–312). New York: Guilford Press.

Harre, R., & Secord, P. (1973). *The explanation of social behaviour.* Totowa, NJ: Littlefield, Adams.

Katz, D., & Kahn, R. L. (1978). *The social psychology of organizations* (2nd ed.). New York: Wiley.

Kuhl, J. (1985). Volitional mediators of cognition–behavior consistency: Self-regulatory processes and action versus state orientation. In J. Kuhl & J. Beckman (Eds.), *Action control: From cognition to behavior* (pp. 100–128). Heidelberg: Springer-Verlag.

Kuhl, J., & Beckman, J. (Eds.). (1985). *Action-control: From cognition to behavior.* Heidelberg: Springer-Verlag.

Marangoni, C., & Ickes, W. (1989). Loneliness: A theoretical review with implications for measurement. *Journal of Social and Personal Relationships, 6,* 93–128.

Miller, G. A., Galanter, E., & Pribam, K. H. (1960). *Plans and the structure of behavior.* New York: Henry Holt.

Nezlek, J. B. (1993). The stability of social interaction. *Journal of Personality and Social Psychology, 65,* 930–942.

Nezlek, J. B. (1995). Social construction, gender/sex similarity, and social interaction in close personal relationships. *Journal of Social and Personal Relationships, 12,* 503–520.

Nezlek, J. B. (in press-a). Causal relationships between perceived social skills and day-to-day social interaction. *Journal of Social and Personal Relationships.*

Nezlek, J. B. (1999). Body self-evaluation and day-to-day social interaction. *Journal of Personality, 67,* 793–817.

Nezlek, J. B. (2000). *Day-to-day relationships between self-consciousness, daily events, and anxiety.* Manuscript submitted for publication.

Nezlek, J. B. (in press-b). Psychological well-being and the planfulness of day-to-day behavior. *Journal of Social and Clinical Psychology.*

Nezlek, J. B., & Derks, P. (in press). Use of humor as a coping mechanism, psychological adjustment, and social interaction. *Humor.*

Nezlek, J. B., & Elia, L. (1998). *Daily goal fulfillment and psychological well-being.* Manuscript in preparation.

Nezlek, J. B., & Gable, L. S. (1999). *Daily events, day-to-day psychological adjustment, and depressive symptoms.* Manuscript submitted for publication.

Nezlek, J. B., & Hampton, C. P. (1996, March). *Depression and the predictability of daily routine.* Paper presented at the annual meeting of the Eastern Psychological Association, Washington, DC.

Nezlek, J. B., Hampton, C. A., & Shean, G. D. (2000). Clinical depression and everyday social interaction in a community sample. *Journal of Abnormal Psychology, 109,* 11–19.

Nezlek, J. B., Imbrie, M., & Shean, G. D. (1994). Depression and everyday social interaction. *Journal of Personality and Social Psychology, 67,* 1101–1111.

Nezlek, J. B., & Plesko, R. M. (2000). *Trait adjustment as a moderator of the interactive effects of positive and negative daily events on daily psychological adjustment.* Manuscript submitted for publication.

Nezlek, J. B., Reis, H. T., & Cunningham, W. A. (1999). *Everyday social interaction, social acceptance, life satisfaction, and psychological symptoms: A causal model.* Manuscript in preparation.

Nezlek, J. B., & Sullivan, L. A. (2000). *The planfulness of daily behavior.* Manuscript submitted for publication.

Nezlek, J., Wheeler, L., & Reis, H. (1983). Studies of social intersction. In H. Reis (Ed.), *Naturalistic approaches to studying social interaction.* New Directions for Methodology of Social and Behavioral Science, No 15 (pp. 57–75). San Francisco: Jossey-Bass.

Ouelette, J. A., & Wood, W. (1998). Habit and intention in everyday life: The multiple processes by which past behavior predicts future behavior. *Psychological Bulletin, 124,* 54–74.

Radloff, L. S. (1977). The CES-D scale: A self-report depression scale for research in the general population. *Applied Psychological Measurement, 1,* 385–401.

Sheldon, A. E. R., & West, M. (1989). The functional discrimination of attachment and affiliation: Theory and empirical demonstration. *British Journal of Psychiatry, 155,* 18–23.

Sullivan, L. A., Nezlek, J. B., & Jackson, L. (1996). *Social interaction and emotional social support: Reciprocity and sex differences.* Unpublished manuscript. College of William & Mary.

Wheeler, L., & Nezlek, J. (1977). Sex differences in social participation. *Journal of Personality and Social Psychology, 35,* 742–754.

PART II

The Social Mind of Individuals: The Role of the Self and Individual Differences

6. The Social Self: The Quest for Identity and the Motivational Primacy of the Individual Self

CONSTANTINE SEDIKIDES AND LOWELL GAERTNER

The theme of this volume is the social mind. The volume aspires to unravel the tangled web of interconnections between the individual and the social environment. This ambition represents a time-honored and cherished tradition of theorizing, echoed by pivotal works in social sciences such as those of Cooley (1902), Mead (1934), Durkheim (1950), and Weber (1964).

From a social and personality psychology perspective, the interconnections between the individual and the social environment manifest themselves in life transitions, concerns, and objectives, which have received several labels such as *personal strivings* (Emmons, 1986), *personal projects* (Little, 1983), *life tasks* (Cantor, Markus, Niedenthal, & Nurius, 1986), and *possible selves* (Markus & Nurius, 1986). In this chapter, we conceptualize these transitions, concerns, and objectives as direct or indirect endeavors to clarify and articulate the self. We conceptualize them as the quest for self-definition or identity.

The quest for identity is perhaps the most central, persistent, and challenging component of human development (Breytspraak, 1984; Damon, 1983). Success or failure in achieving a well-articulated identity has implications for a variety of key psychological functions such as self-regulation, the processing of self-referent information, the experience of affect, the setting of goals, the perception of others, and the behavior toward others (for a review, see Sedikides & Strube, 1997).

Identity can be derived from several within-person sources, such as the individual self, the relational self, the familial self, and the

Corresponding author's address: Constantine Sedikides, Department of Psychology, University of Southampton, Highfield Campus, S017 1BJ Southampton, England, UK (E-mail: c.sedikides@soton.ac.uk).

collective (i.e., ingroup) self. These four cognitive representations are relatively independent (Andersen and Berenson, this volume; Brewer & Gardner, 1996; Gaines et al., 1997; Trafimow, Silverman, Fan, & Law, 1997; Trafimow & Smith, 1998; Trafimow, Triandis, & Goto, 1991). In the present chapter, we will concentrate on two of these representations or sources of identity: the individual self and the collective self. Additionally, we will be interested in features of the social context that shape the self – what we call the *contextually determined self*.

Sources of Identity

The Individual Self

The *individual self* refers to personal characteristics. These are traits or attributes that distinguish the person from other ingroup members. These aspects of the self-concept make the person unique and set him or her apart from other members of the ingroup. Stated otherwise, the individual self is an identity that is independent of group membership.

There is a lot to be said for the view that the individual self constitutes the primary basis for identity (*individual-self primacy hypothesis*). The core conceptions of the individual self are relatively stable (Bem & Allen, 1974; Pelham, 1991), resistant to change (Sedikides & Strube, 1997), and susceptible to confirmation rather than disconfirmation (Swann, 1990) – especially when the self-conceptions are positive (Sedikides, 1993).

Existing literature is supportive of the privileged status of the individual self in identity-seeking. For example, persons evaluate the individual self more positively than the ingroup (Lindeman, 1997; Lindeman & Sundvik, 1995), regard the self as more resistant to media propaganda than the ingroup (Duck, Hogg, & Terry, 1995), and take personal credit for the achievements of the ingroup while denying personal blame for the failures of the ingroup (Mullen & Riordan, 1988). Furthermore, persons accentuate intragroup differences to a greater degree than intragroup similarities (Simon, Pantaleo, & Mummendey, 1995).

The Collective Self

The *collective self* refers to characteristics that an individual assumes as a group member. These traits or attributes differentiate the group member from members of antagonistic outgroups. These aspects of the self-concept are shared by members of a given ingroup and distinguish the ingroup members from members of the outgroup. Stated otherwise, the collective self is an identity that is dependent exclusively on group membership.

A compelling case can be made for the thesis that the collective self constitutes the primary basis of identity (*collective-self primacy hypothesis*). The behavior of individual group members is shaped substantially by the group, as attested to by phenomena such as social influence (Asch, 1951; Crano, this volume), group decision making and performance (Kaplan & Wilke, this volume; Kerr, this volume; Myers & Lamm, 1976), social facilitation (Zajonc, 1965), and ostracism (Williams, Wheeler, & Harvey, this volume). In fact, it has been argued that the collective self provides the optimal level of self-definition, as it affords both assimilation with the ingroup and differentiation from outgroups (Brewer, 1991; Hornsey & Hogg, 1999).

Extant research backs the collective-self primacy hypothesis. For example, persons consider negative traits as more descriptive of the self than of the ingroup (Biernat, Vescio, & Green, 1996, Study 1) and feel worse following an ingroup as opposed to an individual performance failure (Hirt, Zillman, Erickson, & Kennedy, 1992, Exp. 2).

The Contextually Determined Self

There is an alternative to the previously mentioned hypotheses: the *contextual primacy hypothesis*. According to this hypothesis, the kind of self (i.e., individual or collective) that will be used for self-definition is dependent on characteristics of the social context. These characteristics are situational features that render one self momentarily more accessible than the other self. The self that is rendered cognitively accessible at any particular moment will guide self-definition. Momentary accessibility of the self, in this case, is equated with self-definitional primacy.

This position also enjoys theoretical and empirical support. The working self-concept (i.e., the part of the chronic self-concept that is temporarily active in working memory) is malleable and amenable to contextual variation (Markus & Kunda, 1986; McGuire, McGuire, & Cheever, 1986). This point has been refined and extended by self-categorization theory (Turner, Hogg, Oakes, Reicher, & Wetherell, 1987; Turner, Oakes, Haslam, & McGarty, 1994). Whether persons will define themselves as unique individuals versus interchangeable group members depends on social contextual contrasts. These can be summarized through the principle of meta-contrast: Social categories become salient to the extent to which the average perceived difference between stimulus aggregates exceeds the average perceived difference within stimulus aggregates. This principle predicts that self-definition fluctuates toward the individual self in intragroup contexts and toward the collective self in intergroup contexts. Indeed, persons are more likely to use the collective self as a basis for self-definition in intergroup than intragroup settings (Hogg & Turner, 1987) and when the ingroup is a numerical minority rather than a majority (Simon & Hamilton, 1994).

Will the Most Primary Self Please Stand Up? Testing the Relative Merit of the Three Hypotheses

Clearly, there is merit to all three theoretical views when each is considered individually. However, in our research program, we asked a different set of questions: Which view affords the most satisfactory account of the quest for identity? Which self constitutes the primary basis for identity? Do persons "care" for one self more than the other? Are persons more likely to *protect* one self more than the other in the face of adversity (e.g., threatening feedback)? If so, which self are persons more likely to protect? Does context determine which self is protected?

To begin answering these questions, a researcher would need to engage in competing hypothesis testing. Thankfully, as our review so far indicates, such testing exists. However, we have several misgivings about the conclusiveness of these tests. Before we state our misgivings, though, we acknowledge that, more often than not, the objective of prior research was to test hypotheses that differed from the ones that we presently assess. We take the liberty to view this prior research from our own tilted perspective.

We will express our misgivings in the form of guidelines toward achieving conclusiveness in competing hypothesis testing. We will introduce four guidelines. *First,* feedback to the individual self should be relevant only to this self; likewise, feedback to the collective self should be relevant only to this self. This provision ensures a valid assessment of the strength of the independent motivational properties of each self. Past research (e.g., Biernat et al., 1996; Mullen & Riordan,

1988) has been unclear on this issue. *Second*, the two selves should receive feedback on the same domain, and the domain should be of equal importance to the two selves. Providing feedback on domains that are dissimilar for the two selves (e.g., Hirt et al., 1992) confounds target of threat (i.e., individual vs. collective self) with domain importance. *Third*, the impact of feedback on the two selves should be measured immediately rather than after a delay. Delayed assessment (e.g., Moghaddam, Stolkin, & Hutcheson, 1997) can mask the impact of feedback, as equilibrium processes may take place. *Fourth*, the accessibility of each self should be controlled or manipulated. This guideline is responsive to the proposition of the contextual primacy hypothesis that primacy varies with relative accessibility.

With these guidelines in mind, we designed several experiments to test the motivational primacy of the bases for identity (see Gaertner, Sedikides, & Graetz, 1999, for a more detailed exposition). In our research, (1) the feedback was directed at either the individual or the collective self, (2) the feedback was identical and pertained to the same self-aspect, (3) the reactions to feedback were measured immediately, and (4) the accessibility of the two selves was either controlled or manipulated. We will describe this research subsequently.

Which Self Is Protected?

The collective self in our first experiment was University of North Carolina at Chapel Hill (UNC-CH) women. Our initial task was to derive traits that UNC-CH women would regard as most typically positive or negative of their ingroup. In a pilot study, we asked UNC-CH women to generate group-stereotypic positive and negative traits. In a second pilot study, we asked a new sample of UNC-CH women to rate the previously generated traits for group-stereotypic positivity/negativity. The two pilot studies revealed that UNC-CH women regarded the trait "emotionally expressive" as the most positive group-stereotypic trait, whereas they regarded the trait "moody" as the most negative group-stereotypic trait.

To overview our experiment, we directed either unfavorable or favorable feedback at either the individual or the collective self. Specifically, participants were informed that the experiment was conducted by the Department of Psychology on behalf of the (fabricated) Office of Student Affairs (OSA). We made every effort to prime both the individual and the collective self. In order to prime the individual self, we told participants that students at UNC-CH are "extremely diverse; after all, each one of you is an individual with your own unique background, personality traits, skills, abilities, and hobbies." In order to prime the collective self, we told participants that "you also share membership with other students in various social groups. . . . [O]ne of the most important social groups to which people belong is gender. That is, you are female, and you share membership in the social group UNC-CH women." Furthermore, we mentioned to participants that the OSA has authorized the Psychology Department to collect information about the characteristics of the female student body (priming of the collective self). To accomplish this, each participant would need to complete a computerized version of the Berkeley Personality Inventory (BPI). The BPI was described as a "reliable and valid measure of personality characteristics and traits" (priming of the individual self).

Participants were informed that the BPI consisted of two parts. In the first part, participants responded to 30 statements that were related vaguely (but nondiagnostically) to the trait emotional or moody (e.g., "One of my favorite pastimes is sitting in front of a crackling fire," "Sad movies touch me deeply"). In the second part, participants indicated how frequently, during the last month, they felt each of 30 emotions (e.g., cheerful, sad). Next, participants were informed that the computer would begin scoring their responses. While they waited, we initiated the manipulations.

The computer provided participants with feedback that was either favorable or unfavorable and was directed at either the individual or the collective self. Participants in the *unfavorable feedback directed at the individual self* condition were informed that the BPI assesses the trait moodiness. Moodiness was defined ("inability to control one's mood state"), and its negative consequences (e.g., disrupting social interactions) were described. Furthermore, the importance of moodiness was overstated, as the trait was said to predict future poor adjustment as well as personal and professional failure. Next, participants were informed that scoring of the BPI was completed and, according to their individualized profile, they were "excessively moody." Participants in the *favorable feedback directed at the individual self* condition were told that the BPI assesses the trait of emotional expressiveness. This trait was defined ("one's ability to express appropriately a wide array of emotions"), and its positive consequences (e.g., facilitating social interactions) were described. Furthermore, emotional expressiveness was said to predict future adjustment as well as personal and professional success. Next, participants were told that scoring of the BPI was completed and, according to their individualized profile, they were "very emotionally expressive."

Participants in the *unfavorable feedback directed at the collective self* condition were instructed that they would not receive personalized feedback because their responses had already been forwarded directly to the OSA, given that OSA required anonymity in responding. Instead, they would receive feedback pertaining to all UNC-CH women tested so far, excluding their own score. Subsequently, the trait moodiness was defined, and its negative consequences and predictive power were emphasized. Finally, participants received feedback on the BPI in aggregate form (i.e., "UNC-CH women are excessively moody"). Participants in the *favorable feedback directed at the collective self* condition were also told that only feedback pertaining to UNC-CH women as a group (excluding their own scores) was available. After learning all about the ostensible merits of emotional expressiveness, participants received feedback that "UNC-CH women are very emotionally expressive."

In the end, participants responded to three sets of questions. The *first set* assessed the degree to which participants perceived themselves as similar to the group (i.e., "I am very similar to UNC-CH women," "My personality attributes are quite similar to the attributes of UNC-CH women," "My beliefs and values are quite similar to the beliefs and values of UNC-CH women") or perceived themselves as unique individuals (i.e., "I am a unique individual," "My personality attributes are totally unique," "My beliefs and values are totally unique"). The *second set* of measures assessed the degree to which participants identified with the group (i.e., "I strongly identify with the group UNC-CH women," "I am proud to belong to the group UNC-CH women," "I value my membership in the group UNC-CH women") or identified with the individual self (i.e., "I only identify with myself," "I am proud to just be myself," "I value being myself"). Note that these two sets of measures have been used successfully to index the collective self in previous research from a self-categorization theory perspective (e.g., Simon et al., 1995; Simon, Hastedt, & Aufderheide, 1997; Turner et al., 1987). In our research, we adapted these measures slightly and implemented them as indicators of both the collective and the individual self. The *third set* of measures assessed participants' perceptions of the severity of feedback (i.e., "Was the feedback you received negative or positive?"; "How displeased or pleased with the feedback did you feel when you received it?").

The three theoretical views make contrasting predictions. According to the *individual-self primacy hypothesis*, the individual self has a higher motivational value for identity-seeking than does the collective self. Hence, participants will regard a threat to the individual self as more severe than a threat to the collective self. When the individual self is threatened, participants will use the collective self as a protective buffer for the individual self; that is, participants will derive identity from the collective self. However, when the collective self is threatened, participants will not move to derive identity from the individual self. We label this absence of identity-seeking *motivational apathy* or *indifference*. According the *collective-self primacy hypothesis*, the collective self has higher motivational value for identity-seeking than does the individual self. Consequent, participants will regard a threat to the collective self as more severe than a threat to the individual self. When the collective self is threatened, participants will use the individual self as a protective buffer of the collective self. However, a threat against the individual self will be accompanied by motivational apathy. Finally, according to the *contextual primacy hypothesis*, threats against the individual self and the collective self will be perceived as equal in severity. As a result, participants will be likely to use either self as a protective buffer. When the collective self is threatened, identity will be derived from the individual self, and when the individual self is threatened, identity will be derived from the collective self.

The results of the experiment were consistent with the *individual-self primacy hypothesis*. To begin with, participants regarded unfavorable feedback to the individual self as a more serious threat (i.e., they perceived it as more negative and were more displeased with it) than unfavorable feedback to the collective self. More important, participants buffered their threatened individual self by redefining themselves in terms of their collective self. No such shift occurred in response to the threatened collective self.

Let us elaborate on this latter pattern. First, we will consider the case in which feedback was directed at the individual self. Participants were more likely to indicate similarity with the ingroup and identify more strongly with the ingroup when the feedback was unfavorable than when it was favorable. In the face of threat, participants resorted to the ingroup and used it as a buffer to protect the individual self. This identity shift was not evident when feedback was directed at the collective self. Unfavorable feedback did not affect participants differently than favorable feedback. They did not use the individual self as a protective buffer for the collective self. Participants manifested motivational apathy.

We wondered about the self-definitional immovability of participants who received feedback at the collective-self level. Why were they apathetic? One explanation is group solidarity. Participants remained with the ingroup in the face of threat as an expression of solidarity. In fact, it is likely that unfavorable information "becomes a source of pride at the group level – a badge of distinction rather than a mark of shame" (Brewer, 1991, p. 481). However, this explanation is rendered rather implausible by our results. If participants manifested solidarity, (1) they should be more likely to define themselves in accordance with the group in the unfavorable rather than the favorable feedback condition, and at the very least, (2) they should define themselves as group members in absolute terms (i.e., compared to the scale midpoint). Neither of these two predictions was borne out.

Nevertheless, our findings may be qualified by a relevant individual difference variable: group identification. High group identifiers are persons who identify strongly with the ingroup, whereas low group identifiers are persons who identify weakly with the ingroup. By definition, the collective self is more primary than the individual self for high identifiers, whereas the individual self is more primary for low identifiers. Research findings are consistent with this proposition: High identifiers are more likely to protect the group identity (e.g., through outgroup derogation or expression of higher ingroup homogeneity) under conditions of threat than nonthreat, whereas low identifiers do not exhibit such group-identity enhancement strategies (Branscombe & Wann, 1994; Spears, Doojse, & Ellemers, 1997).

In summary, our first experiment provided preliminary evidence for the primacy of the individual self. However, a conclusion in favor of the individual-self primacy hypothesis may be premature given the possibility that group identification moderates self-definitional primacy. A new experiment is needed. The finding that high group identifiers are more likely to use the collective rather than the individual self as a basis for self-definition will give the contextual primacy hypothesis a boost. On the other hand, the finding that the motivational importance of the individual self does not differ in high and low group identifiers will be in line with the individual-self primacy hypothesis. Finally, the finding that the collective self is of equal motivational importance to high and low group identifiers will support the collective-self primacy hypothesis.

Does Group Identification Moderate Identity Preferences?

We addressed the question of whether group identification moderates identity preferences in a second experiment. Specifically, we examined the reactions of high and low group identifiers to unfavorable feedback directed at either the individual or the collective self. These reactions were mood states and feedback derogation. We reasoned that a threat targeted at the more primary self will result in stronger feedback derogation and more negative mood states than a threat targeted at the less primary self.

The pertinent collective self was UNC-CH students. We classified participants into high and low group identifiers based on their responses to the following three questions: "How important is your university to you?", "To what extent does being a member of your university reflect an important aspect of who you are?", and "How much do you identify with your university?" We mentioned to participants that the experiment was conducted allegedly on behalf of a national testing agency that gathered data on creativity. They would be tested on a valid creativity test. (Note that we gathered pretest data on the perceived importance of creativity for both the individual self and the collective self, and we controlled statistically for preexisting differences.) Next, we administered a face-valid creativity test, the "Lange-Elliot" creativity test (Sedikides, Campbell, Reeder, & Elliot, 1998). We presented participants with the names of two objects (*brick* and *candle*), one at a time. Participants were given 5 minutes to generate as many functionally distinct uses as possible for each object. They wrote each use on a slip of paper, folded the paper, and dropped it in a box next to them. In the end, the experimenter summed up the total number of functionally distinct uses that each participants had generated. This sum constituted the overall creativity score. Next, the experimenter delivered to participants uniformly unfavorable feedback.

In the case of *threat to the individual self*, participants were informed that "Your total score . . . was calculated to be at the 31st percentile. This means that your score is worse than 69% of the creativity scores in the normative reference sample." In the case of *threat to the collective self*, participants were informed that, for ethical reasons, we could not give personalized feedback, but we could give feedback about the average

performance of UNC-CH students, excluding their own score. Participants were told that "UNC-CH's total score . . . was calculated to be at
the 31st percentile. This means that UNC-CH's score is worse than 69%
of the creativity scores in the normative reference sample."

We gauged feedback derogation by asking participants to rate the
perceived importance of the test outcome either for "you" (individual
self) or for "UNC-CH" (collective self). High derogation was taken as
an indicator of higher motivational primacy of the relevant threatened
self. We gauged mood states by asking participants to respond to 14
mood adjectives. Seven of the adjectives (i.e., *annoyed, angry, bitter, frustrated, irritated, threatened,* and *upset*) measured agitation, whereas the
remaining seven adjectives (i.e., *blue, disappointed, down, gloomy, low,
miserable,* and *sad*) measured dejection. We will report the pooled mean,
as responses to the two sets of adjectives were essentially identical
(i.e., they were highly correlated). Increasingly negative mood states
are taken as an indicator of the motivational primacy of the relevant
threatened self.

In a conceptual replication of our previous experiment, the results were consistent with the individual-self primacy hypothesis. We
observed no significant difference in the responses of high versus low
group identifiers. Specifically, both high and low group identifiers were
more likely to devalue the importance of the creativity test when its
unfavorable outcome threatened the individual rather than the collective self. Additionally, both high and low group identifiers felt worse
when the unfavorable feedback was directed at the individual rather
than at the collective self. Group identification did not moderate the
preference for an individual-level identity.

Toward a More Balanced Test of the Contextual Primacy Hypothesis

The contextual primacy hypothesis states that identity shifts toward
the individual self in interpersonal contexts and shifts toward the
collective self in intergroup contexts. In a third experiment, we varied the social context. Specifically, we directed either unfavorable or
favorable information to either the individual self in an interpersonal
context or to the collective self in an intergroup context. In a sense, we
maximized the accessibility of one self while minimizing the accessibility of the other. Thus, we were able to observe and compare the reactions to unfavorable information (i.e., an insult) on the individual self
and the collective self in settings in which each self was maximally

accessible. Self-reported anger served as an indicator of motivational primacy.

The three theoretical views make contrasting predictions. For illustrative purposes, we will formulate these predictions only for the case of unfavorable feedback. According to the *individual-self primacy* hypothesis, an insult to the individual self will instigate more anger than an insult to the collective self. According to the *collective-self primacy* hypothesis, an insult to the collective self will induce more anger than an insult to the individual self. Finally, according to the *contextual primacy* hypothesis, insulting information will make participants angry, regardless of the type of self (i.e., individual or collective) to which the feedback is targeted.

We solicited participants in aggregates of six for an experiment on "social decision making." Our first task was to create an interpersonal versus intergroup context. We established the *interpersonal context* (i.e., individual-self condition) by dividing the participants randomly into three 2-person dyads. After the division into dyads, each participant was escorted to a separate room. Participants anticipated interacting with their partner in a Prisoners Dilemma Game (PDG). We established the *intergroup context* (i.e., collective-self condition) by dividing the participants randomly into two 3-person groups. Subsequently, we escorted ingroup members into a common room. Each group anticipated interacting with the opposing group in a PDG.

Participants were told that they could expect to earn money as a result of their interactions with the other person (group). The interactions would occur on a three-choice PDG matrix. Each person (group) was given a copy of the matrix, examples, and a decision record sheet on which they would presumably record their decisions for 10 trials. Next, participants completed a matrix comprehension exercise in an alleged effort to increase their understanding of the payoff matrix. In particular, participants completed three sentences of the form "A person (group) would choose "X" ("Y" or "Z") if they (he/she) wanted to . . ." In the individual-self condition, each person completed the sentences separately. In the collective-self condition, each group completed the task as a whole. Participants also completed a prefeedback measure of anger.

Then the experimenter told participants that, in the interest of saving time, they would evaluate their opponents' comprehension exercise. Each person (group) received an evaluation form and a comprehension exercise completed allegedly by their opponent. Participants rated their opponent's comprehension of the PDG matrix and were given the option of providing written comments.

The experimenter collected all forms and returned the original comprehension exercises and bogus evaluations. Participants in the *unfavorable feedback* condition received a low score and a disparaging comment ("This person [group] did not do well. He/She [they] must be a little slow"). Participants in the *favorable feedback* condition received a high score and praise ("This person [group] did well. He/She [they] really seems to know what's going on"). Finally, all participants completed (in their private cubicles) a postfeedback measure of anger.

In the interpersonal context condition, we used the individual as the unit of analysis, whereas in the intergroup context condition, we used the group as the unit of analysis. No differences were observed among the four conditions as far as the prefeedback measure of anger is concerned. Importantly, however, differences were obtained in the post-feedback anger measure.

The pattern of results supports the *individual-self primacy* hypothesis. Unfavorable feedback instigated more anger when it referred to the individual rather than the collective self. (Favorable feedback aroused equally low levels of anger regardless of whether it referred to the individual or the collective self.) Even in social contexts (i.e., interpersonal and intergroup) that maximize the accessibility of each self, a threat to the individual self generates more anger than a threat to the collective self.

Discussion

We began this chapter by paying tribute to the social mind and, by implication, to the social self. The self has its origins in social context and operates within a social context. The content of the self is fundamentally social (Markus, 1983; Stryker & Statham, 1985).

At the same time, however, we have acknowledged that the individual and the collective self compose two relatively independent and robust cognitive structures (Brewer & Gardner, 1996; Trafimow & Smith, 1998; Trafimow et al., 1991, 1997; see also Simon, 1997). This acknowledgment served as the springboard for our research, as we were able to pose the question of self-definition or identity. How do human adults know who they are? When in a state of relative threat (e.g., when receiving unfavorable feedback), how do they go about seeking and achieving self-definition? On which self do they rely the most? Which self do they rush to protect?

Summary of Findings

We formulated and comparatively tested three hypotheses. The *individual-self primacy* hypothesis emphasizes the privileged status of the individual self (i.e., attributes that are unique and independent of group membership) in identity-seeking. The *collective-self primacy* hypothesis emphasizes the relevance of the collective self (i.e., attributes that are shared by other members of the ingroup) in the quest for identity. Finally, the *contextual primacy* hypothesis stresses the importance of context (i.e., interpersonal vs. intergroup) in determining whether identity will be derived from the individual or the collective self.

In three experiments, we controlled for several potential confounding variables, such as feedback domain, importance of feedback domain, independence of feedback for each type of self, delay of measurement, and accessibility of the two selves (i.e., rendering each self simultaneously accessible). More important, we manipulated key variables such as feedback referent (individual vs. collective self), feedback valence (unfavorable vs. favorable feedback), level of group identification (high vs. low), and context (interpersonal vs. intergroup). Furthermore, across experiments, we varied the relevant collective self. In particular, we used collective selves that were contingent upon membership in an ascribed group (i.e., women, Experiment 1), an achieved group (i.e., UNC-CH students, Experiment 2), and a context-dependent group (i.e., a minimal group, Experiment 3). Finally, we examined a multiplicity of responses to feedback, such as identity preferences, perception of feedback, derogation of feedback, mood state, and level of anger.

We made a critical assumption, one that is empirically substantiated (Campbell & Sedikides, 1999; see also Andersen and Berenson, this volume): A threat to the more primary basis of self-definition elicits more severe reactions than a threat to the less primary basis of self-definition. Despite variations in methodology, the three experiments provided converging results. Compared to a threat directed at the collective self, a threat directed at the individual self (1) led to an increased preference for using the collective self as a source of identity (i.e., participants deemphasized their personal uniqueness and identified more strongly with the ingroup), (2) was considered more severe, (3) produced a more negative mood state, (4) elicited more anger, and (5) led to stronger source derogation. These results constitute compelling support for the *individual-self primacy* hypothesis. The individual self is the most potent source of identity.

Qualifications and Alternative Hypotheses

Nevertheless, our findings are arguably subject to qualifications and alternative hypotheses. We will consider these possibilities in the following section.

Qualifications: Individualism Versus Collectivism. Our research was conducted in a Western, individualistic culture. To what extend do our findings generalize to collectivistic (e.g., Asian) cultures? Some cross-cultural research indicates that fundamentally different self-processes are at work in these two types of culture (Markus & Kitayama, 1991). For example, Australians are more likely than Japanese to use the first-person pronoun in conversations (Kashima & Kashima, 1997). Also, Americans are likely to self-enhance, whereas Japanese are not (Heine & Lehman, 1997). If anything, Japanese are more likely to self-criticize (Kitayama, Markus, Matsumoto, & Norasakkunkit, 1997).

The implication of this counterpoint is that the cultural value orientations of individualism and collectivism moderate the primacy of the individual self. The individual self likely serves as the primary identity basis for persons high on individualism, whereas the collective self likely serves as the primary identity basis for persons high on collectivism.

We tested this moderational argument (Gaertner et al., 1999, Experiment 4). In a preliminary session, we assessed participants' levels of individualism and collectivism using Singelis's (1994) self-construal scale. A week later, we asked these participants to list 20 self-descriptions that "generally describe you." We reasoned that, if the individual self is the primary identity basis, participants would generate more descriptions pertaining to the individual self than to the collective self, regardless of the level of individualism or collectivism. However, if self-definitional primacy is moderated by the level of cultural value orientation, individual-self primacy would be limited to persons high on individualism. Persons high on collectivism would instead generate more descriptions pertaining to the collective self than to the individual self. Interestingly, participants listed more traits that referred to the individual self than to the collective self. This finding is consistent with the individual-self primacy hypothesis. Regardless of the levels of individualism and collectivism, the individual self serves as the primary forum of identity-seeking.

Indeed, we claim that the individual self is highly prevalent in collectivistic societies. Implicit measures have detected self-enhancement in Japan: Letter and number evaluation tasks show a greater preference for letters and numbers occurring in one's own name and birth date, respectively (Kitayama & Karasawa, 1997). Cross-cultural comparisons of exchange principles make a similar point. Finjeman, Willemsen, and Poortinga (1996) measured expected inputs to and outputs from various relationships (e.g., parents, siblings, cousins, close friends, acquaintances, strangers) in individualistic countries (the Netherlands and the United States) and collectivistic countries (Greece, Hong Kong, and Turkey). Regardless of culture, willingness to provide for others was related to expectations of what would be received from others. The operation of basic exchange principles, equity and reciprocity, indicates that even in collectivistic cultures there is a surprisingly strong concern for self-interest. In a related vein, although persons of color (i.e., African Americans, Asian Americans, and Latinos) score higher than Anglos on measures of collectivism, they score as high as Anglos on measures of individualism (Freeberg & Stein, 1996; Gaines et al., 1997).

These research findings converge on an important principle. Although level of collectivism can be rather easily influenced by culture (e.g., norms), level of individualism is relatively invariant. Individualism is less amenable to cultural variation. To us, this principle is yet another substantial indicator of the primacy of the individual self.

Alternative Hypotheses. We will consider three alternative hypotheses that speak to potential differences between the individual and the collective self: differences in uncertainty orientation, differences in strength of identification, and structural differences. These differences may have accounted for our findings.

DIFFERENCES IN UNCERTAINTY ORIENTATION. Two chapters in this volume (by Hogg and by Sorrentino, Hodson, & Huber) make a compelling case for the role of uncertainty orientation in information processing. This perspective has implications for our research.

Arguably, the results of Gaertner et al. (1999, Experiment 1) are due to differences in uncertainty orientation. According to this argument, participants were more certain about the individual self than about the collective self. Consequently, they reacted more defensively against negative feedback directed at the individual self than at the collective self.

Although this issue is best addressed empirically, we doubt that uncertainty played a critical role in our research. To begin with, Gaertner et al. (1999, Experiment 1) preselected traits that were typical of the *ingroup*, not of the individual. As such, participants likely were more certain about the collective self than about the individual self. More important, differential uncertainty was not an issue in Gaertner et al.'s (1999) Experiment 3; interestingly, this experiment replicated conceptually the results of Experiment 1.

DIFFERENCES IN STRENGTH OF IDENTIFICATION. The strength of identification alternative advocates that participants protected the individual self at the expense of the collective self because they identified weakly or marginally with the collective self. We addressed this issue empirically (Gaertner et al., 1999, Experiment 2). Furthermore, we conducted a meta-analysis (Gaertner, Sedikides, Vevea, & Iuzzini, 2000) in which we also failed to obtain evidence that strength of identification moderates the primacy of the individual self; that is, participants use the collective self as a buffer for the protection of the individual self, regardless of strength of identification with the ingroup.

In fact, the line of argument for this alternative can be easily reversed. We found that participants are primarily interested in protecting the individual self even on traits that are typical of the ingroup but not necessarily typical of the individual self (e.g., Gaertner et al., 1999, Experiments 1 and 2). We believe that attempts to protect the individual self will be magnified on traits that are typical of the individual self rather than of the ingroup. Additionally, we maintain that attempts to protect the individual self likely will be increased among individuals who have a relatively strong sense of individual self, such as high self-esteem persons (Schütz, this volume) or narcissists (Rhodewalt, this volume).

STRUCTURAL DIFFERENCES. According to the structural differences alternative (P. P. Costanzo, April, 1999, personal communication), our findings may be due to the possibility that the two selves have different structural properties. The collective self likely has a categorical structure; that is, a person either belongs or does not belong to a group. The individual self, on the other hand, likely has a dimensional, trait-based structure; that is, trait self-descriptions differ only in degree.

We would like to challenge the plausibility of the structural differences alternative. To begin with, we controlled for type of individual-self versus collective-self structure: In our first three experiments (Gaertner et al., 1999, Experiments 1–3) the two selves were set to have a dimensional structure, whereas in our fourth experiment (Gaertner et al., 1999, Experiment 4) the two selves were set to have a categorical structure. But, of course, this experimental setup does not address directly the criticism.

The structural differences alternative would gain in plausibility if the structures of the two selves differed naturalistically. We do not believe, however, that this is the case. The structure of the collective self (i.e., group membership) is not necessarily categorical. As we have mentioned repeatedly, ingroup identification is a matter of degree. One can be a member of a group to varying degrees, from leading the group to existing on the fringes of the group. Additionally, it is not clear that the structure of the individual self is dimensional. Most theoretical and empirical statements pertaining to structural properties of the individual self advocate a categorical structure (Kihlstrom & Cantor, 1984; Kihlstrom & Klein, 1994), and the representation of other persons is categorical as well (Anderson & Sedikides, 1991; see also Gannon & Ostrom, 1996).

Concluding Remarks

We believe that we have illustrated a basic personality and social psychological phenomenon, namely, the higher motivational value of the individual self than the collective self. Our theoretical thesis and empirical documentation are consistent with several other lines of research. Self-determination theory emphasizes individual strivings for autonomy and competence and gives secondary importance to the role of social context (Deci & Ryan, 1985). Self-regulation theories also make the point that the social context serves as the background within which the individual acts (Baumeister & Catanese, this volume; Baumeister & Heatherton, 1996; Carver & Scheier, 1998; Higgins, 1996). The self-aspect model of the individual self and the collective self states that aspects of the individual self that are positive and important form the basis for the collective self (Simon, 1997; Simon & Hastedt, 1999).

Perhaps a reason for the motivational importance of the individual self is the volume, availability or accessibility, and inescapability of private feelings and thoughts (Andersen, 1984; Andersen, Glassman, & Gold, 1998; Andersen, Lazowski, & Donisi, 1986).

We have considered the self as predominantly an individual structure. Our approach stands in sharp contrast to several other theoretical formulations, including social identity theory (Tajfel & Turner, 1986) and self-categorization theory (Turner et al., 1987). The implications of this contrast are important. Conceptualizing the self as predominantly an intergroup structure leads to the derivation that social antagonism (i.e., stereotyping, prejudice, and discrimination) is omnipresent and inevitable (Ehrlich, 1973; Hamilton, 1979; Tajfel, 1981). However, conceptualizing the self as predominantly an individual structure allows for a drastically different (and far more optimistic!) conclusion. Social antagonism is fundamentally a function of differences in the structure of the individual self (Duckitt, 1992). When the individual self is prone toward social differentiation (i.e., "How different am I from others?"), stereotyping, prejudice, and discrimination are likely to result. However, when the individual is prone toward social integration (i.e., "How similar to others am I"), social tolerance (i.e., the absence of stereotyping, prejudice, and discrimination) will be the likely outcome (Phillips & Ziller, 1997).

Consistent with an individual-self primacy analysis of intergroup discrimination, research subsequent to the development of social identity theory located the origin of intergroup discrimination in motives of individual self-interest rather than social-identity enhancement (Gaertner, 1999; Insko et al., 1992; Rabbie, Schot, & Visser, 1989). For example, Gaertner (1999; Experiments 2 and 3) unconfounded outcome dependence and social categorization in the minimal group paradigm and found that category members allocated more money to the ingroup than to the outgroup only when their own earnings could have been influenced by fellow ingroup members. That is, category members discriminated only when they could have maximized their personal earnings by reciprocating favorable allocations with ingroup members. If category members were concerned with enhancing their social identity (i.e., collective self), they should have favored the ingroup regardless of whether they were outcome dependent upon other ingroup or outgroup members. In line with the individual-self primacy perspective, intergroup discrimination is rooted in concern for the welfare of the individual self.

References

Andersen, S. M. (1984). Self-knowledge and social inference: II. The diagnosticity of cognitive/affective and behavioral data. *Journal of Personality and Social Psychology, 46,* 294–307.

Andersen, S. M., Glassman, N. S., & Gold, D. A. (1998). Mental representations of the self, significant others, and nonsignificant others: Structure and processing of private and public aspects. *Journal of Personality and Social Psychology, 75,* 845–861.

Andersen, S. M., Lazowski, L. E., & Donisi, M. (1986). Salience and self-inference: The role of biased recollections in self-inference processes. *Social Cognition, 4,* 75–95.

Anderson, C. A., & Sedikides, C. (1991). Contributions of a typological approach to associationistic and dimensional views of person perception. *Journal of Personality and Social Psychology, 60,* 203–217.

Asch, S. E. (1951). Effects of group pressure upon the modification and distortion of judgments. In H. Guetzkow (Ed.), *Groups, leadership, and men.* Pittsburgh: Carnegie Press.

Baumeister, R. F., & Heatherton, T. F. (1996). Self-regulation failure: An overview. *Psychological Inquiry, 7,* 1–15.

Bem, D. J., & Allen, A. (1974). On predicting some of the people some of the time: The search for cross-situational consistencies in behavior. *Psychological Review, 81,* 506–520.

Biernat, M., Vescio, T., & Green, M. L. (1996). Selective self-stereotyping. *Journal of Personality and Social Psychology, 71,* 1194–1209.

Branscombe, N. R., & Wann, D. L. (1994). Collective self-esteem consequences of outgroup derogation when a valued social identity is on trial. *European Journal of Social Psychology, 24,* 641–658.

Brewer, M. B. (1991). The social self: On being the same and different at the same time. *Personality and Social Psychology Bulletin, 17,* 475–482.

Brewer, M. B., & Gardner, W. (1996). Who is this "We"? Levels of collective identity and self representations. *Journal of Personality and Social Psychology, 71,* 83–93.

Breytspraak, L. (1984). *The development of self in later life.* Boston: Little, Brown.

Campbell, K. W., & Sedikides, C. (1999). Self-threat magnifies the self-serving bias: A meta-analytic integration. *Review of General Psychology, 3,* 23–43.

Cantor, N., Markus, H., Niedenthal, P., & Nurius, P. (1986). On motivation and the self-concept. In R. M. Sorrentino & E. T. Higgins (Eds.), *Motivation and cognition: Foundations of social behavior* (pp. 96–127). New York: Guilford Press.

Carver, C. S., & Scheier, M. F. (1998). *On the self-regulation of behavior.* New York: Cambridge University Press.

Cooley, C. H. (1902). *Human nature and the social order.* New York: Scribner's.

Damon, W. (1983). *Social and personality development: Infancy through adolescence.* New York: Norton.

Deci, E. L., & Ryan, R. M. (1985). *Intrinsic motivation and self-determination in human behavior.* New York: Plenum.

Duck, J. M., Hogg, M. A., & Terry, D. J. (1995). Me, us and them: Political iden-tification and the third-person effect in the 1993 Australian federal election. *European Journal of Social Psychology, 25,* 195–215.

Duckitt, J. (1992). *The social psychology of prejudice.* New York: Praeger.

Durkheim, E. (1950). *The rule of sociological method.* New York: Free Press.

Ehrlich, H. J. (1973). *The social psychology of prejudice.* New York: Wiley.

Emmons, R. A. (1986). Personal strivings: An approach to personality and sub-jective well-being. *Journal of Personality and Social Psychology, 51,* 1058–1068.

Finjeman, Y. A., Willemsen, M. E., & Poortinga, Y. H. (1996). Individualism-collectivism: An empirical study of a conceptual issue. *Journal of Cross Cul-tural Psychology, 27,* 381–402.

Freeberg, A. L., & Stein, C. H. (1996). Felt obligation towards parents in Mexican-American and Anglo-American young adults. *Journal of Social and Personal Relationships, 14,* 457–471.

Gaertner, L. (1999). *Intergroup discrimination in the minimal group paradigm: Categorization, reciprocation, or fear?* Unpublished doctoral dissertation, University of North Carolina at Chapel Hill.

Gaertner, L., Sedikides, C., & Graetz, K. (1999). In search of self-definition: Motivational primacy of the individual self, motivational primacy of the collective self, or contextual primacy? *Journal of Personality and Social Psy-chology, 76,* 5–18.

Gaertner, L., Sedikides, C., & Vevea, J. (1998). *The I, the we, and the when: A meta-analysis of motivational primacy in self-definition.* Unpublished manuscript, University of North Carolina at Chapel Hill.

Gaines, S. O., Jr., Marelich, W. D., Bledsoe, W., Steers, W. N., Henderson, M. C., Granrose, C. S., Barajas, L., Hicks, D., Lyde, M., Takahashi, Y., Yum, N., Rios, D. I., Garcia, B. F., Farris, K. R., & Page, M. S. (1997). Links between race/ethnicity and cultural values as mediated by racial/ethnic identity and moderated by gender. *Journal of Personality and Social Psychology, 72,* 1460–1476.

Gannon, K. M., & Ostrom, T. M. (1996). How meaning is given to rating scales: The effects of response language on category activation. *Journal of Experi-mental Social Psychology, 32,* 337–360.

Hamilton, D. L. (1979). A cognitive-attributional analysis of stereotyping. In L. Berkowitz (Ed.), *Advances in experimental social psychology* (Vol. 12, pp. 53–84). New York: Academic Press.

Heine, S. J., & Lehman, D. R. (1997). The cultural construction of self-enhancement: An examination of group-serving biases. *Journal of Personality and Social Psychology, 72,* 1268–1283.

Higgins, E. T. (1996). The "Self Digest": Self-knowledge serving self-regulatory functions. *Journal of Personality and Social Psychology, 71,* 1062–1083.

Hirt, E. R., Zillman, D., Erickson, G. A., & Kennedy, C. (1992). Costs and benefits of allegiance: Changes in fans' self-ascribed competencies after team victory versus defeat. *Journal of Personality and Social Psychology, 63,* 724–738.

Hogg, M., & Turner, J. C. (1987). Intergroup behavior, self-stereotyping and the salience of social categories. *British Journal of Social Psychology, 26,* 325–340.

Hornsey, M. J., & Hogg, M. A. (1999). Subgroup differentiation as a response to an overly-inclusive group: A test of optimal distinctiveness theory. *European Journal of Social Psychology, 29,* 543–550.

Insko, C. A., Schopler, J., Kennedy, J. F., Dahl, K. R., Graetz, K. A., & Drigotas, S. M. (1992). Individual–group discontinuity from the differing perspectives of Campbell's realistic group conflict theory and Tajfel and Turner's social identity theory. *Social Psychology Quarterly, 55,* 272–291.

Kashima, E. S., & Kashima, Y. (1997). Practice of the self in conversations: Pronoun drop, sentence co-production and contextualization of the self. In K. Leung, U. Kim, S. Yamaguchi, & Y. Kashima (Eds.), *Progress in Asian social psychology* (pp. 165–179). Singapore: Wiley.

Kihlstrom, J. F., & Cantor, N. (1984). Mental representations of the self. In L. Berkowitz (Ed.), *Advances in experimental social psychology* (Vol. 17, pp. 1–47). New York: Academic Press.

Kihlstrom, J. F., & Klein, S. B. (1994). The self as a knowledge structure. In R. S. Wyer, Jr. & T. K. Srull (Eds.), *Handbook of social cognition* (Vol. 1, pp. 153–208). Hillsdale, NJ: Erlbaum.

Kitayama, S., & Karasawa, M. (1997). Implicit self-esteem in Japan: Name letters and birthday numbers. *Personality and Social Psychology Bulletin, 23,* 736–742.

Kitayama, S., Markus, H. R., Matsumoto, H., & Norasakkunkit, V. (1997). Individual and collective processes in the construction of the self: Self-enhancement in the United States and self-criticism in Japan. *Journal of Personality and Social Psychology, 72,* 1245–1267.

Lindeman, M. (1997). Ingroup bias, self-enhancement and group identification. *European Journal of Social Psychology, 27,* 337–355.

Lindeman, M., & Sundvik, L. (1995). Evaluative bias and self-enhancement among gender groups. *European Journal of Social Psychology, 27,* 269–280.

Little, B. R. (1983). Personal projects: A rationale and method for investigation. *Environment and Behavior, 15,* 273–309.

Markus, H. (1983). Self-knowledge: An expanded view. *Journal of Personality, 51,* 543–565.

Markus, H., & Kitayama, S. (1991). Culture and the self: Implications for cognition, emotion, and motivation. *Psychological Review, 98,* 224–253.

Markus, H., & Kunda, Z. (1986). Stability and malleability of the self-concept. *Journal of Personality and Social Psychology, 51,* 858–866.

Markus, H., & Nurius, P. (1986). Possible selves. *American Psychologist, 41,* 954–969.

McGuire, W. J., McGuire, C. V., & Cheever, J. (1986). The self in society: Effects of social contexts on the sense of self. *British Journal of Social Psychology, 25,* 259–270.

Mead, G. H. (1934). *Mind, self, and society.* Chicago: University of Chicago Press.

Moghaddam, F. M., Stolkin, A. J., & Hutcheson, L. S. (1997). A generalized personal/group discrepancy: Testing domain specificity of a perceived higher effect of events on one's group than on oneself. *Personality and Social Psychology Bulletin, 23,* 743–750.

Mullen, B., & Riordan, C. A. (1988). Self-serving attributions for performance in naturalistic settings: A meta-analytic review. *Journal of Applied Social Psychology, 18*, 3–22.

Myers, D. G., & Lamm, H. (1976). The group polarization phenomenon. *Psychological Bulletin, 83*, 602–627.

Pelham, B. W. (1991). On confidence and consequence: The certainty and importance of self-knowledge. *Journal of Personality and Social Psychology, 60*, 518–530.

Philips, S. T., & Ziller, R. C. (1997). Toward a theory and measure of the nature of prejudice. *Journal of Personality and Social Psychology, 72*, 420–434.

Rabbie, J. M., Schot, J. C., & Visser, L. (1989). Social identity theory: A conceptual and empirical critique from the perspective of a behavioral interaction model. *European Journal of Social Psychology, 19*, 171–202.

Sedikides, C. (1993). Assessment, enhancement, and verification: Determinants of the self evaluation process. *Journal of Personality and Social Psychology, 65*, 317–338.

Sedikides, C., Campbell, W. K., Reeder, G., & Elliot, A. J. (1998). The self-serving bias in relational context. *Journal of Personality and Social Psychology, 74*, 378–386.

Sedikides, C., & Strube, M. J. (1997). Self-evaluation: To thine own self be good, to thine own self be sure, to thine own self be true, and to thine own self be better. In M. P. Zanna (Ed.), *Advances in experimental social psychology* (Vol. 29, pp. 209–269). New York: Academic Press.

Simon, B. (1997). Self and group in modern society: Ten theses on the individual self and the collective self. In R. Spears, P. J. Oakes, N. Ellemers, & S. A. Haslam (Eds.), *The social psychology of stereotyping and group life* (pp. 318–335). Oxford: Basil Blackwell.

Simon, B., & Hamilton, D. L. (1994). Self-stereotyping and social context: The effects of relative in-group size and in-group status. *Journal of Personality and Social Psychology, 66*, 699–711.

Simon, B., & Hastedt, C. (1999). Self-aspects as social categories: The role of personal importance and valence. *European Journal of Social Psychology, 29*, 479–487.

Simon, B., Hastedt, C., & Aufderheide, B. (1997). When self-categorization makes sense: The role of meaningful social categorization in minority and majority members' self-perception. *Journal of Personality and Social Psychology, 69*, 106–119.

Simon, B., Pantaleo, G., & Mummendey, A. (1995). Unique individual or interchangeable group member? The accentuation of intragroup differences versus similarities as an indicator of the individual self versus the collective self. *Journal of Personality and Social Psychology, 69*, 106–119.

Singelis, T. M. (1994). The measurement of independent and interdependent self-construals. *Personality and Social Psychology Bulletin, 20*, 580–591.

Spears, R., Doosje, B., & Ellemers, N. (1997). Self-stereotyping in the face of threats to group status and distinctiveness: The role of group identification. *Personality and Social Psychology Bulletin, 23*, 538–553.

Stryker, S., & Statham, A. (1985). Symbolic interactionism and role theory. In G. Lindzey & E. Aronson (Eds.), *Handbook of social psychology* (Vol. 2, pp. 311–378). New York: Random House.

Swann, W. B. (1990). To be adored or to be known? The interplay of self-enhancement and self-verification. In E. T. Higgins & R. M. Sorrentino (Eds.), *Handbook of motivation and cognition: Foundations of social behavior* (Vol. 2, pp. 408–448). New York: Guilford Press.

Tajfel, H. (1981). *Human groups and social categories: Studies in social psychology.* Cambridge: Cambridge University Press.

Tajfel, H., & Turner, J. C. (1986). The social identity theory of intergroup behavior. In S. Worchel & W. G. Austin (Eds.), *Psychology of intergroup relations* (pp. 7–24). Chicago: Nelson-Hall.

Trafimow, D., Silverman, E. S., Fan, R. M., & Law, J. S. F. (1997). The effects of language and priming on the relative accessibility of the private self and the collective self. *Journal of Cross-Cultural Psychology, 28,* 107–123.

Trafimow, D., & Smith, M. D. (1998). An extension of the "two basket" theory to Native Americans. *European Journal of Social Psychology, 28,* 1015–1019.

Trafimow, D., Triandis, H. C., & Goto, S. G. (1991). Some tests of the distinction between the private self and the collective self. *Journal of Personality and Social Psychology, 60,* 649–655.

Turner, J. C., Hogg, M. A., Oakes, P. J., Reicher, S. D., & Wetherell, M. S. (1987). *Rediscovering the social group: A self-categorization theory.* Oxford and New York: Basil Blackwell.

Turner, J. C., Oakes, P. J., Haslam, S. A., & McGarty, C. (1994). Self and collective: Cognition and social context. *Personality and Social Psychology Bulletin, 20,* 454–463.

Turner, J. C., Wetherell, S., & Hogg, M. A. (1989). Referent informational influence and group polarization. *British Journal of Social Psychology, 28,* 135–147.

Weber, M. (1964). *Basic concepts in sociology.* New York: Citadel Press.

Zajonc, R. B. (1965). Social facilitation. *Science, 149,* 269–274.

7. Cognitive and Motivational Processes in Self-Presentation

DIANNE M. TICE AND JON FABER

Self-presentation is one of the paramount interpersonal aspects of the self, involving how persons present themselves to others. Ultimately, shaping a particular and often desirable image of the self to present to others is one of the crucial tasks of interpersonal life. In this sense, the presented self is a powerful tool for relating to other people and an important aspect of the social mind.

The importance of self-presentation is reflected in how pervasive the motivations are. There is a strong and pervasive desire to make a positive impression on others (e.g., Jones & Wortman, 1973; see also Leary & Kowalski, 1990; Sedikides, 1993) or at least to create a desired, if not desirable, impression. (e.g., Leary, 1995; Swann, 1987). In this chapter, we will review some of the cognitive and motivational processes involved in self-presentation.

Self-presentation is an explicitly public phenomenon. Although it can have private implications and consequences, self-presentation is defined as behavior that occurs in a public rather than a private setting. Thus, social interactions are necessary for self-presentation, and, in keeping with a long tradition (e.g., Cooley, 1902; James, 1890; Mead, 1934), most researchers of the self acknowledge the importance of social interaction in constructing and modifying the self-concept. Because the self is publicly constructed and exists in relation to others, public events have greater impact on the self-concept than private events. Public behavior implicates the self more than private behavior: Private behavior can be canceled, ignored, or forgotten, but public behavior cannot because other people know about

Address for correspondence: Dr. Dianne M. Tice, Department of Psychology, Case Western Reserve University, Cleveland, OH 44106-7123, USA. Email: dxt2@po.cwru.edu it. Presenting the self in social interactions, then, constructs and affects the social mind.

Motivations of Self-Presentation

Self-presentation includes two components or goals – a self-construction goal for which the person builds the self by presenting certain images to others, and the more familiar goal that entails managing the impressions others form of oneself (Baumeister, 1982; cf. Leary, 1995; Leary & Kolwalski, 1990). Self-presentation can focus on one or the other of these goals, or sometimes both can be accomplished at once. For example, I may present myself as a skier eager to ski the most difficult black-diamond trails. I may do so because I want the people I am skiing with (or people I tell the stories to afterward) to see me as a risk-taking, athletic adventurer. I may choose to ski these trails because I would like to see myself as a risk-taking, athletic adventurer, and can hold this opinion of myself better if I skied these trails. It may sometimes be the case, however, that I am accomplishing both of these goals at the same time. I ski these difficult trails to convince both myself and others that I am the kind of person who takes these risks. In the remainder of this chapter, we will first cover some issues relevant to the impression management goal and then discuss issues related to the self-constructive goal of self-presentation.

   In addition to these two goals, Leary (1995) has added a third goal – emotion regulation. Making a good impression can increase positive feelings and decrease negative feelings; thus people may present themselves positively to others in order to feel better about themselves. People who are distressed self-disclose more (Stiles, 1987, Stiles, Shuster, & Harrigan, 1992), apparently in an attempt to regulate their emotions through interpersonal contact and self-presentations.

Goals of Impression Management

Need to Belong. A number of chapters in this volume have referred to fundemental needs (e.g., Anderson and Berenson's chapter refers to the needs for connectedness, autonomy, mastery, meaning, and security; Nezlek's chapter concludes that people are motivated by the need to belong and are cognitively influenced by the need for control and predictability). The major reason people try to present a desired view of themselves is to make themselves fit into a group or at least to fit into a role within the group. People want to be liked, respected, or at least feared or pitied. Fitting into a group or belonging is one of the most fundamental human needs (Baumeister & Leary, 1995). People are motivated by this fundamental need to present themselves in ways that will ensure their belongingness. Self-presentation is thus motivated by the need to belong.

Belonging to a group not only satisfies an interpersonal need, but it is also a prerequisite for satisfying most of life's basic safety and material needs (Baumeister & Leary, 1995). Few people have been able to be entirely sufficient at any time in history; we need others to help us satisfy our most basic needs. In order to procure what we need from the group, we need to be part of a group, and so we present ourselves in ways that will enhance our group membership or status. Thus, self-presentation is important for winning material and financial consequences, as well as for satisfying our interpersonal needs (in fact, as a result of satisfying the interpersonal needs, we satisfy our material or financial concerns). People who present themselves as likable and competent are more likely to win job promotions and be selected for other financial rewards. People who present themselves in an intimidating fashion may be able to bully others into giving them what they want, and people who present themselves in a pitiable fashion may be able to elicit gifts from the group (Jones & Pittman, 1982).

Specific Goals. Although the overarching goal of self-presentation may be motivated by the need to belong, people may attempt to achieve belongingness thorough a number of more specific motivations or strategies. People may be motivated to present themselves using the specific strategies of self-enhancement, self-protection, self-verification, accuracy, intimidation, supplication, or exemplification.

Given the desire to make a good impression, one might assume simply that people would always present themselves in a maximally favorable light and make extremely favorable claims about themselves. This is not the case, however, often because of the constraints of plausibility (Schlenker, 1975, 1980; Schlenker & Leary, 1982): Excessively favorable claims about the self will not be believed. They may even be counterproductive because one will lose face if one's claims become discredited (Baumeister, Tice, & Hutton, 1989; Tice, 1991; 1993; Tice & Baumeister, 1990). Moreover, highly favorable statements about the self may be perceived as arrogant and conceited, which are negative traits (Schlenker & Leary, 1982).

Hence, self-presentation faces a constant trade-off between one's desired image and plausibility (Schlenker, 1980, 1985, 1986). One is constrained by the limits of what one's audience or interaction partner will be willing or likely to believe. It is only within those limits that one will tend to present oneself as close to the desired image as possible.

Enhancement Versus Protection. Certain situations present interpersonal risks, and people must choose whether to take the risks in order to have a chance at enhancing their favorable public image of themselves – as opposed to avoiding risk so as to protect the image of themselves. We have shown that trait self-esteem and self-handicapping contingencies predict how people respond to such an interpersonal risk situation (Tice, 1991, 1993; Tice & Baumeister, 1990).

Self-handicapping is a strategic ploy used to manipulate the impression that an audience forms of the handicapper (e.g., Berglas & Jones, 1978; Jones & Berglas, 1978; Kolditz & Arkin, 1982). Self-handicappers place barriers in the way of their own success, thereby jeopardizing their performance. If they fail, the failure can be blamed on the handicap and not on lack of ability, whereas if they succeed despite the handicap, they receive additional credit for overcoming the obstacle. Self-handicapping thus achieves two self-presentational goals with one strategy. Putting barriers in the way of one's own success both provides a protective excuse for failure and enhances credit for success. Some individuals may self-handicap for both motives – that is, they desire both the enhancement and protection benefits of the strategy. However, we found than an individual may engage in self-handicapping behavior primarily for one of the two motives; he or she simply receives the benefits of the other as a bonus (Tice, 1991).

Our findings suggested that high self-esteem people were more likely than low self-esteem people to choose a behavioral self-handicap (either eschewing practice or choosing a performance-impairing musical tape) in order to enhance success. Low self-esteem people were more likely to choose a behavioral self-handicap in order to protect against the esteem-threatening implications of failure rather than to enhance success. Additionally, high self-esteem people were more likely to endorse and agree with a statement describing the enhancement of success benefits of self-handicapping than were low self-esteem people. Low self-esteem people were more likely to endorse and agree with a statement describing the protection-from-failure benefits of self-handicapping. In Schütz's chapter in this volume, she also reports that high and low self-esteem people present themselves using different styles of self-presentation.

Thus, people with different levels of self-esteem are all motivated to create a positive impression in others, but they are motivated to use different strategies to do so. High self-esteem people are motivated to try to look outstanding, whereas low self-esteem people are motivated to try to protect themselves from looking like failures.

Presenting a Desired but Unflattering View of the Self. Jones and Pittman (1982) suggested that most self-presentation falls into one of five categories. People present themselves as likable, competent, intimidating, pitiful, or morally superior. Whereas presenting oneself as likable, competent, or moral may create a positive impression in the audience, presenting oneself as intimidating or pitiful will not. Jones and Pittman argued that creating a desirable impression is not the real reason we try to manage the impression we make; rather, we use self-presentation to gain power over other people in order to get them to do what we want them to do (to get them to behave in the ways we desire). One possible means of gaining power over people is to try to get them to like or respect us, but other means can accomplish this goal as well.

Swann (e.g., 1987) has suggested that people often try to make sure that the impression they are creating in the audience is consistent with their self-views, even if that means contradicting a positive impression and replacing it with something more negative, a strategy he has termed *self-verification*. He has recently found that people are much more likely to seek self-verification in private and seek to create positive images in public (Swann & Pelham, 1991). It may be that creating a positive image is a motivation for impression management and verifying one's true view of oneself is a motivation for self-construction.

Self-Construction Goals

Self-presentation is one of the fundamental and important processes by which people negotiate identities for themselves in their social worlds. An important goal of self-presentation (along with impression management) is to construct a social self. In the privacy of one's own mind, perhaps, one may be relatively free to imagine oneself having any sort of identity, but serious identity claims generally require social validation by other people, and so the construction of identity requires persuading others to see one as having desired traits and qualities (e.g., Baumeister, 1982; Schlenker, 1980; Wicklund & Gollwitzer, 1982).

Examples of people who come to see themselves in a new light because of the way they behaved abound in literature and other media. One example can be found in Mario Puzo's novel *The Godfather*. At the beginning of the story, the Godfather's son Michael (played by Al Pacino in the movie version) had high ideals and has lived a clean, legitimate life. However, he became involved in family dealings once, and soon he came to accept himself as a vicious criminal. How could such a change in his self-concept occur? Part of it was undoubtedly the fact that he was involved in killing people and committing other crimes, even if the initial impetus was high-minded family loyalty, self-defense, and retaliation. Stories such as this suggest that the lesson is that "you are what you do." Just as Michael Corleone's self-concept changed to fit his newly violent and illegal acts, so may other people's self-concepts shift to internalize the implications of their actions.

In Hogg's chapter in this volume, he provides evidence suggesting that people often present themselves in a manner that falls in line with the expected behaviors of a desired group, as Michael Corleone's did. This normative self-presentation gives the individual a positive sense of self and, possibly more important, a clear set of norms and expected behaviors and attitudes. Likewise, in Kerr's chapter in this volume, he reviews evidence that people decrease their effort on tasks that may lead to undesired self-constructions or self-presentations.

Universality of the Motivation. Self-presentation frequently has a negative connotation in some people's understanding of the term. Many people report that they never manage the impressions that others form of them, and that to do so involves unsavory, manipulative, or deceptive actions. Psychologists as well as laypeople often take only the most negative view of self-presentation (e.g., Buss & Briggs, 1984), and view self-presentation as a deceptive, manipulative attempt to fool the audience into believing in a false image of the presenter.

The 1960s popularized the view that one should not be concerned with self-presentational conformity (although many hippies dressed alike and spouted similar political rhetoric) and that one should be true to oneself and not care about the evaluations of others. Many young people today express the belief that self-presentational concerns are inauthentic and profess to avoid all self-presentation. Most individuals who hold the belief that self-presentation is evil are likely to focus only on the impression management component and misunderstand a number of ideas central to self-presentation.

First, self-presentation usually involves telling the truth, not lying, about the self. As Jones, Rhodewalt, Berglas, and Skelton (1981) pointed out, it is possible to be honest and accurate about oneself and yet still be either self-enhancing, modest, or self-derogating. Second, since self-presentation has a self-constructive component as well as an impression management component, we create who we are as well as communicate who we are through our self-presentations. Third, we all engage in self-presentational acts frequently. The young person who claims to be unconcerned with what others think of him may spend hundreds of dollars in order to have the "right" clothes, and may suffer great social anxiety if his friends see him going to the mall with his uncool parents. Andersen and Berenson make similar points in their chapter in this volume, emphasizing the construction of different selves in different contexts and reviewing evidence suggesting that multiple selves are based on social context, motivations, social roles, relationships, situations, and standards.

Self-Presentational Effects on the Self-Concept. A number of researchers have demonstrated that behavior can be internalized; that is, behaving in a given manner can lead to a self-concept change in which one comes to think of oneself as the kind of person who engages in the behavior (e.g., Fazio, Effrein, & Falender, 1981; Gergen, 1965; Jones et al., 1981; Kulik, Sledge, & Mahler, 1986; Rhodewalt & Agustdottir, 1986; Schlenker & Trudeau, 1990). A person who was induced to behave in a shy manner will come to think of himself as more of a shy person than a person who was induced to behave in an outgoing manner. In Cooper's chapter in this volume, it is noted that a similar effect may occur for some of the dissonance findings. In some of the dissonance work, people's public behavior that is dissonant with their values or beliefs results in attitude change so that people's self-concepts and attitudes become more similar to their public behaviors (although internalization of the self-presentation cannot account for all of the dissonance findings; see Cooper's chapter in this volume).

We have conducted a number of studies to demonstrate that the internalization of behavior is affected by the self-presentational motivations of self-construction (Tice, 1992). Specifically, the studies were designed to show that people will internalize their behavior more when the behavior is performed publicly than when the same behavior is performed in private.

In the first study (Tice, 1992), participants were asked to portray themselves as either emotionally stable or emotionally reactive, either in a public self-presentation or privately and anonymously for a tape-recorded response. Participants were subsequently asked for their true ratings of themselves on emotional lability. Behavior performed as a self-presentation in front of others was internalized more fully than behavior performed in more anonymous settings. Despite the fact that all participants drew upon past experiences of their own behavior in answering the questions, those who portrayed themselves to another person in a highly identified, public manner showed more internalization than those who portrayed themselves anonymously.

In the second study, participants were again asked to describe themselves in either a public self-presentation or a private and anonymous tape recording. In this study, participants were asked to describe themselves as either introverts or extraverts. Study 2 replicated the self-report findings of Study 1 and supplemented the self-report measures with behavioral measures collected without the participants' awareness. On both self-report and behavioral measures, there was more self-concept change in the public condition than in the private condition. Subjects who had been led to describe themselves *publicly* as extraverted later sat closer to the confederate and spoke to the confederate more often than subjects who had been led to describe themselves as introverted. But similar self-descriptions given privately and anonymously had no effect on subsequent behavior. Study 2 suggests that the internalization of behavior following self-presentation in Study 1 was not simply a superficial or deliberate repetition of verbal labels but rather a true alteration in self-conception that was strong enough to produce changes in behavior in a subsequent situation without the participant's awareness.

Thus, one of the motivations of self-presentation is the construction of self. Self-presentations can lead to more self-concept change than an identical behavior performed privately. People who present themselves in a given fashion are more likely to internalize their behavior and change their self-concepts to reflect the self-presentation than people who perform the same behavior privately.

Self-Presentation Motivations in Relationships. One of the first studies to examine self-presentation in existing relationships was conducted by Leary et al. (1994), who found that, in same-sex relationships, greater familiarity led to lower self-reported impression management. In opposite-sex relationships, however, greater familiarity led to increased self-reported impression management.

Schlenker and Leary's (1982) studies of how audiences reacted to self-presentations help to clarify some of the issues in self-presentation within relationships. They varied whether the audience knew about the actor's past performance and the actor's description of his or her own performance. Subjects who either knew or did not know how well an actor had performed on a task (the performance was described as very poor, poor, average, well, or very well to those subjects who were informed about the performance) heard the actor describe that performance of his or hers as either very poor, poor, average, well, or very well. With one exception, if the audience knew about the actor's performance, they tended to like the actor better if the actor described the performance accurately rather than inaccurately. However, actors were liked best if they were modest in their description of their superior performance. In other words, if the audience believed that the actor had done well and was modest about it, they liked the actor more than if the actor gave an accurate description of the performance (and therefore sounded boastful). If the audience is not informed about an actor's achievements, however, modest self-presentation may result in less favorable impressions of the actor than self-enhancing self-presentations.

Taking a slightly different approach, Godfrey, Jones, and Lord (1986) showed that people who were instructed to try to present themselves as especially competent succeeded in being perceived as more competent but also less likable (see also Schütz, 1997, and her chapter in this volume). People do not like being the target of upward social comparisons (Exline & Lobel, 1999). Thus, the disclosure of highly favorable information about oneself does entail some loss of likability.

We have done some work suggesting that the favorability of self-presentation changes depending on whether one is presenting oneself to friends or strangers, with modesty prevailing among friends but self-enhancing favorability occurring among strangers (Tice, Butler, Muraven, & Stillwell, 1995). We conducted a series of five studies to examine self-presentational motivations within relationships. Studies 1 and 2 found that when interacting with strangers, people presented themselves in a self-enhancing fashion, but when interacting with friends, they shifted toward greater modesty.

Study 3 examined how well people could recall the details of an interpersonal interaction as a function of how they had been instructed to present themselves because more familiar, habitual, and presumably automatic styles of self-presentation should free up more cognitive resources for encoding the interaction and should therefore result in better memory. It was found that people recalled the interaction best when they had presented themselves either modestly to friends or very favorably to strangers, consistent with the view that these are the habitual and automatic ways of acting. In contrast, being modest with strangers or being self-enhancing with friends resulted in impaired memory for the interaction. Study 4 replicated the results of Study 3 and showed that the effects are not merely an artifact of informational differences between friends and strangers.

Although modest self-presentations increased memory for interactions with friends, Study 5 found that negative (i.e., quite self-deprecatory) self-presentations were not automatic and did not increase memory with any audiences. Thus, it is not simply that people tend to be positive about themselves with strangers and negative with friends. Rather, the optimal and presumably familiar and automatic way of presenting oneself to friends is an intermediate level of favorability (modesty). We will discuss the role of automaticity further in the section on cognitive issues.

The finding that people are more self-presentationally positive with strangers and modest with friends suggests underlying motivational differences, such as the motivation to achieve equity and maintain good relations with friends versus the motivation to make a good impression on strangers. Relationships can thus affect the motivations for self-presentation. People try to manage the impressions of both friends and strangers, but their self-presentational goals change, depending upon the audience.

Summary. The overriding motivation for self-presentation is the need to belong. People present themselves in a manner that makes them appealing to the group (whatever group they are currently interested in). Self-presentation consists of two often overlapping motivations: the goal of managing the impressions others have of you and the goal of constructing the self by presenting it to others. People may pursue this need to belong using a variety of strategies. High self-esteem people seem motivated to make themselves look good by enhancing their positive features, whereas low self-esteem people seem motivated to make themselves look good by protecting themselves from the implications of failure. People seem motivated to make highly positive impressions on strangers and more modest but not negative impressions on friends.

Cognitive Issues in Self-Presentation

Self-presentation has been studied mainly as a motivational process, and years of research have given us a better understanding of the motivations involved. During the historical time that self-presentational issues increased in prominence in the fields of social and personality psychology, these fields and the field of self psychology were dominated by a strong cognitive approach. It is thus ironic that the cognitive processes involved in self-presentation received so little attention until recently. Considerable research has treated cognitive and self-presentational explanations of behavior as antithetical (e.g., Tedeschi, 1981). In Tetlock and Manstead's (1985) review of the self-presentation literature, they suggested that researchers begin to focus on the cognitive consequences of self-presentation. A key point in their discussion of the field of self-presentation was that impression management and intrapsychic cognitive processes are not mutually incompatible forms of explanation.

Self-Presentations Influence the Behavior of Others

One person's self-presentations can affect the way others present themselves. This influence is often undetected, leading to a bias or distortion in the perception of interactions. Baumeister, Hutton, and Tice (1989) conducted a set of studies to demonstrate that one person's self-presentation can alter the behavior of others in the situation, but that neither the original self-presenter nor the audience whose behavior was changed is aware of the self-presenter's influence.

Participants were paired with a partner they did not know and engaged in an exchange of information about themselves. Prior to the dyadic interaction, one member of each pair, the protagonist, was requested to present himself or herself either favorably or modestly during the interaction to help out the experimenter. The other member of each pair (the naive participant) received no special instructions. Results were consistent with the hypothesis that one person's self-presentation can implicitly set the norms that then influence the behavior of others. Self-promotion by the protagonist elicited self-promotion in the naive participant, whereas modesty elicited modesty in return. Protagonists were aware of altering their own self-presentations (as the experimenters had requested) but seemed unaware that their behavior had affected their partners. Specifically, protagonists inferred their partners' level of self-esteem directly from their partners' behavior, without correcting for how protagonists themselves had altered the partners' behavior.

Thus, an important cognitive consequence for self-presentational behavior is that it can lead to biased or distorted perceptions. People may fail to make adequate interpretive adjustments when their self-presentations alter the behavior of others.

Self-Presentations Consume Cognitive Resources

Managing the impressions one makes on others requires considerable cognitive resources. Engaging in deliberate self-presentation can produce cognitive distortions and misperceptions, not just in the audience but also in the self-presenter. To the extent that self-presentation occupies one's cognitive resources, it should impair one's capacity to encode and recall the entire interaction.

In the studies just described demonstrating that self-presentations alter the behavior of others, we (Baumeister et al., 1989) also demonstrated that deliberate acts of self-presentation consume cognitive resources, leaving fewer resources available for processing the interaction. When people presented themselves modestly, they showed impaired memory for the interaction, suggesting that deliberately unfavorable self-presentation reduces the automatic nature of self-presentation and consumes cognitive resources that are otherwise available for processing information about the social interaction.

Automatic Versus Controlled Self-Presentations

Paulhus (1993) directly examined the idea that the cognitive concept of automaticity might apply to self-presentation. Although people may present themselves in a deliberate, conscious fashion, self-presentation may also occur in a more habitual or automatic fashion, without conscious attention.

According to Paulhus (1993), automatic self-presentation is likely to occur when an individual is under a cognitive load and has few attentional resources remaining to concentrate on managing the impression he or she is making. As attentional resources dwindle (due to affective or cognitive loads), self-presentation becomes more automatic (Paulhus, 1993; Paulhus, Graf, & Van Selst, 1989). In the studies of self-presentation to friends versus strangers (Tice et al., 1995) described earlier in the section on motivations to present the self modestly versus self-enhancingly, we replicated Paulhus et al.'s (1989) finding that self-enhancing self-presentation is more automatic when one is presenting oneself to strangers. However, when one is presenting oneself to friends, a modest style is more automatic (Tice et al., 1995). We examined how well people could recall the details of an interpersonal interaction as a function of how they had been instructed to present themselves because more familiar, habitual, and presumably automatic styles of self-presentation should free up more cognitive resources for encoding the interaction and should therefore result in better memory. We found that people recalled the interaction best when they had presented themselves either modestly to friends or very favorably to strangers, consistent with the view that these are the habitual and automatic ways of acting. In contrast, being modest with strangers or being self-enhancing with friends resulted in impaired memory for the interaction. We demonstrated that the effects are not merely an artifact of informational differences between friends and strangers, and that being negative about oneself, rather than modest, was not an automatic self-presentational style for any audience.

When people depart from their familiar style of self-presentation, they must abandon the efficiency of automatic processes in favor of controlled ones, and these impair the capacity to process new information about the interaction partner. Thus, engaging in a controlled self-presentation (in this case, modest with strangers or self-enhancing with friends) results in less accurate memory of the other person.

Self-Presentational Effects on the Self-Concept

In the previous section on the motivation for self-construction, we discussed a couple of the studies demonstrating that public self-presentation has a stronger impact on the self-concept – that is, creates more change in the self-concept – than identical behaviors performed privately and anonymously (Tice, 1992).

Schlenker, Dlugolecki, and Doherty (1992) likewise found that public interpersonal behavior led to self-concept change and behavioral change. They found that subjects who presented themselves as sociable to an interviewer demonstrated self-concept changes reflecting an increase in sociability and behavioral changes reflecting an increase in sociable behavior (such as speaking sooner, more frequently, and longer than subjects who had not presented themselves as sociable). Schlenker et al. also found that public commitment to the identity portrayed in the self-presentation was the crucial antecedent of changes in the self-concept; biased self-perceptions were not sufficient to produce the changes. Directing subjects' thoughts toward congruent or incongruent prior experiences (thereby affecting the biased scanning of relevant information) had no impact on self-concept changes. Changes in self-concept were produced only when subjects had a public commitment to the behavior.

The studies by Schlenker et al. (1992) demonstrate quite conclusively that a biased scanning of the self-concept was not a sufficient explanation for the differences in self-concept change following self-presentation versus private behavior. The cognitive mechanism that leads to greater self-concept change following self-presentation than following other behavior remains to be fully explained.

Nonconscious Self-Presentation

Not all self-presentational behavior is conscious and deliberate. Not only do some styles of self-presentation become habitual, such as being modest with friends and positive with strangers, as described earlier (Tice et al., 1995), but the behaviors themselves may become so habitual that we may not even be aware that we are self-presenting. Earlier we discussed the studies conducted by Leary et al. (1994), who found that, in same-sex relationships, greater familiarity led to lower self-reported impression management. (In opposite-sex relationships, however, greater familiarity led to increases in self-reported impression management.) It is possible that their subjects reported less impression management in same-sex interactions because the forms of self-presentation had become so automatic in their friendships that they no longer were consciously aware of their self-presentational motivations.

If the self-presentations were more automatic in same-sex friendships and more controlled in opposite-sex friendships, the subjects might have been better able to report their impression management attempts in opposite-sex interactions. Likewise in the studies described earlier demonstrating that self-presentations alter the behavior of others, we found that participants were not aware of factors influencing the behavior (Baumeister et al., 1989).

Even when we are doing other things and self-presentation is not our primary goal, our behavior is still constrained by self-presentational concerns. For examples, when I'm giving a talk or lecture, my primary motivation may be to get the information across to my students or colleagues, but I also try to avoid looking stupid or boring; when I am going to a movie, my primary goal may be to be entertained or enlightened, but I still dress nicely, don't push ahead of other people in line, and don't buy the biggest bucket of popcorn available because I don't want people to think I am greedy.

Summary

Cognitive factors do appear to influence self-presentation, and the adversarial stance between cognition and self-presentation is no longer viable (e.g., Tetlock & Manstead, 1985). Self-presentation requires some cognitive resources; if these resources are unavailable, the self-presentation will not be as finely tuned (Paulhus, 1993) and memory for the interaction will be impaired (Baumeister et al., 1989). Well-practiced self-presentation can become more automatic and consume fewer resources (e.g., Paulhus et al., 1989; Tice et al., 1995). This may be why some people deny that they self-present; their actions are so habitual that they do not even realize that they are acting in a manner to preserve their public image. One person's self-presentation can influence the self-presentational behavior of others without the awareness of either the self-presenter or the audience (Baumeister et al., 1989).

Concluding Remarks

The "looking-glass self" emerges as actively rather than passively constructed and as shaped by powerful motivational and cognitive factors. Self-presentation is motivated by the need to belong, but people engage in self-presentation for a number of specific reasons, such as the motivation to construct their self-concepts and the motivation to manage the impressions that others hold of them. People can tailor their self-presentations to their audiences and seem motivated to do so in a manner that maximizes their belongingness. Self-presentation consumes cognitive resources, and people can reduce the cognitive requirements by engaging in more automatic forms of self-presentation.

References

Baumeister, R. F. (1982). A self-presentational view of social phenomena. *Psychological Bulletin, 91,* 3–26.

Baumeister, R. F., Hutton, D. C., & Tice, D. M. (1989). Cognitive processes during deliberate self-presentation: How self-presenters alter and misinterpret the behavior of their interaction partners. *Journal of Experimental Social Psychology, 25,* 59–78.

Baumeister, R. F., & Leary, M. R. (1995). The need to belong: Desire for interpersonal attachments as a fundamental human motivation. *Psychological Bulletin, 117,* 497–529.

Baumeister, R. F., Tice, D. M., & Hutton, D. G. (1989). Self-presentational motivations and personality differences in self-esteem. *Journal of Personality, 57,* 547–579.

Berglas, S., & Jones, E. E. (1978). Drug choice as self-handicapping strategy in response to non-contingent success. *Journal of Personality and Social Psychology, 36,* 405–417.

Buss, A. H., & Briggs, S. R. (1984). Drama and the self in social interactions. *Journal of Personality and Social Psychology, 47,* 1310–1324.

Cooley, C. H. (1902). *Human nature and the social order.* New York: Scribner's.

Exline, J. J., & Lobel, P. (1999). The perils of outperformance: Sensitivity about being the target of a threatening upward comparison. *Psychological Bulletin, 125,* 307–337.

Fazio, R. H., Effrein, E. A., & Falender, V. J. (1981). Self-perceptions following social interactions. *Journal of Personality and Social Psychology, 41,* 232–242.

Gergen, K. J. (1965). Interaction goals and personalistic feedback as factors affecting the presentation of self. *Journal of Personality and Social Psychology, 1,* 413–424.

Godfrey, D. K., Jones, E. E., & Lord, C. G. (1986). Self-promotion is not ingratiating. *Journal of Personality and Social Psychology, 50,* 106–115.

James, W. (1890). *The principles of psychology.* New York: Holt.

Jones, E. E., & Berglas, S. C. (1978). Control of attributions about the self through self-handicapping strategies: The appeal of alcohol and the role of underachievement. *Personality and Social Psychology Bulletin, 4,* 200–206.

Jones, E. E., & Pittman, T. S. (1982). Toward a general theory of strategic self-presentation. In J. Suls (Ed.), *Psychological perspectives on the self* (pp. 231–263). Hillsdale, NJ: Erlbaum.

Jones, E. E., Rhodewalt, F., Berglas, S., & Skelton, J. A. (1981). Effects of strategic self-presentation on subsequent self-esteem. *Journal of Personality and Social Psychology, 41,* 407–421.

Jones, E. E., & Wortman, C. (1973). *Ingratiation: An attributional approach.* Morristown, NJ: General Learning Press.

Kolditz, T. A., & Arkin, R. M. (1982). An impression management interpretation of the self-handicapping strategy. *Journal of Personality and Social Psychology, 43,* 492–502.

Kulik, J. A., Sledge, P., & Mahler, H. I. M. (1986). Self-confirmatory attribution, egocentrism and the perpetuation of self-beliefs. *Journal of Personality and Social Psychology, 50,* 587–594.

Leary, M. R. (1995). *Self-presentation: Impression management and interpersonal behavior.* Madison, WI: Brown & Benchmark.

Leary, M. R., & Kowalski, R. M. (1990). Impression management: A literature review and two-component model. *Psychological Bulletin, 107,* 34–47.

Leary, M. R., Nezlek, J. B., Downs, D., Radford-Davenport, J., Martin, J., & McMullen, A. (1994). Self-presentation in everyday interactions: Effects of target familiarity and gender composition. *Journal of Personality and Social Psychology, 67,* 664–673.

Mead, G. H. (1934). *Mind, self, and society.* Chicago: University of Chicago Press.

Paulhus, D. L. (1993). Bypassing the will: The automatization of affirmations. In D. M. Wegner & J. W. Pennebakers (Eds.), *Handbook of mental control* (pp. 573–587). Englewood Cliffs, NJ: Prentice-Hall.

Paulhus, D. L., Graf, P., & Van Selst, M. (1989). Attentional load increases the positivity of self-presentation. *Social Cognition, 7,* 389–400.

Puzo, M. (1969). *The Godfather.* New York: Putnam.

Rhodewalt, F., & Agustdottir, S. (1986). Effects of self-presentation on the phenomenal self. *Journal of Personality and Social Psychology, 50,* 47–55.

Schlenker, B. R. (1975). Self-presentation: Managing the impression of consistency when reality interferes with self-enhancement. *Journal of Personality and Social Psychology, 32,* 1030–1037.

Schlenker, B. R. (1980). *Impression management.* Monterey, CA: Brooks/Cole.

Schlenker, B. R. (1982). Translating actions into attitudes: An identity-analytic approach to the explanation of social conduct. In L. Berkowitz (Ed.), *Advances in experimental social psychology* (Vol. 15, pp. 193–247). New York: Academic Press.

Schlenker, B. R. (1985). Identity and self-identification. In B. R. Schlenker (Ed.), *The self and social life* (pp. 65–99). New York: McGraw-Hill.

Schlenker, B. R. (1986). Self-identification: Toward an integration of the private and public self. In R. Baumeister (Ed.), *Public self and private self* (pp. 21–62). New York: Springer-Verlag.

Schlenker, B. R., Dlugolecki, D. W., & Doherty, K. (1992). The impact of self-presentations and behavior: The power of public commitment. *Personality and Social Psychology Bulletin, 20,* 20–33.

Schlenker, B. R., & Leary, M. (1982). Audiences' reactions to self-enhancing, self-denigrating, and accurate self-presentations. *Journal of Experimental Social Psychology, 18,* 89–104.

Schlenker, B. R., & Trudeau, J. V. (1990). Impacts of self-presentations on private self-beliefs: Effects of prior self-beliefs and misattribution. *Journal of Personality and Social Psychology, 58,* 22–32.

Schütz, A. (1997). Self-presentational tactics of talk-show guests: A comparison of politicians, experts, and entertainers. *Journal of Applied Psychology, 27,* 1941–1952.

Sedikides, C. (1993). Assessment, enhancement, and verification determinants of the self-evaluation process. *Journal of Personality and Social Psychology, 65,* 317–338.

Stiles, W. B. (1987). "I have to talk to somebody": A fever model of self-disclosure. In V. J. Derlaga & H. J. Berg (Eds.), *Self-disclosure: Theory, research, and practice* (pp. 257–282). New York: Plenum.

Stiles, W. B., Shuster, P. L., & Harrigan, J. A. (1992). Disclosure and anxiety: A test of the fever model. *Journal of Personality and Social Psychology, 63,* 980–988.

Swann, W. B., Jr. (1987). Identity negotiation: Where two roads meet. *Journal of Personality and Social Psychology, 53,* 1038–1051.

Swann, W. B., Jr., & Pelham, B. W. (1999). *The pragmatics of self-verification and positivity strivings.* Manuscript in preparation.

Tedeschi, J. T. (1981). *Impression management theory and social psychology research.* New York: Academic Press.

Tetlock, P. E., & Manstead, A. S. (1985). Impression management versus intrapsychic explanations in social psychology: A useful dichotomy? *Psychological Review, 92,* 59–77.

Tice, D. M. (1991). Esteem protection or enhancement? Self-handicapping motives and attributions differ by trait self-esteem. *Journal of Personality and Social Psychology, 60,* 711–715.

Tice, D. M. (1992). Self-presentation and self-concept change: The looking-glass self is also a magnifying glass. *Journal of Personality of Social Psychology, 63,* 435–451.

Tice, D. M. (1993). The social motivations of people with low self-esteem. In R. Baumeister's (Ed.), *Self-esteem: The puzzle of low self-regard* (pp. 37–53). New York: Plenum.

Tice, D. M., & Baumeister, R. F. (1990). Self-esteem, self-handicapping, and self-presentation: The strategy of inadequate practice. *Journal of Personality, 58,* 443–464.

Tice, D. M., Butler, J. L., Muraven, M. B., & Stillwell, A. W. (1995). When modesty prevails: Differential favorability of self-presentation to friends and strangers. *Journal of Personality and Social Psychology, 69,* 1120–1138.

Wicklund, R. A., & Gollwitzer, P. M. (1982). *Symbolic self-completion.* Hillsdale, NJ: Erlbaum.

8. Self-Esteem and Interpersonal Strategies

ASTRID SCHÜTZ

The way in which people evaluate themselves has important implications for how they perceive things and how they behave. Positive evaluations of the self are often considered part of healthy psychological functioning (e.g., Alloy & Abramson, 1979; Sorembe & Westhoff, 1985; Taylor & Brown, 1988). The effects of self-esteem on individual functioning has been a popular research topic, but interpersonal strategies related to individual self-esteem have not received much attention in research so far. Likewise, negative aspects of positive self-evaluation have only recently been documented (Baumeister, Heatherton, & Tice, 1993; Baumeister, Smart, & Boden, 1996; Bushman & Baumeister, 1998; Tice, 1993). In this chapter, I will address the question of how positive self-evaluation is related to evaluation of others and to interaction styles. In addition, I will show how others evaluate the behavioral patterns associated with high or low self-esteem. Interpersonal problems associated with high self-esteem are discussed.

Sources of Self-Esteem

Parents' acceptance of children is often mentioned as an important early experience in the development of self-esteem. More generally, three sources of self-esteem are described in the literature: self-

A travel grant from Deutsche Forschungsgemeinschaft made participation in this international conference possible. Thanks are also extended to Nina Gegenfurtner, Karola Haupt, Natalie Heinermann, Nina Müller, and Angelika Seidel, who served as experimenters or interviewers, as well as to Helene Weiß and Thomas Kauper, who were responsible for coding the interviews. Address for correspondence: Prof. Dr. Astrid Schütz, Institut für Psychologie, TU Chemnitz, 09107 Chemnitz, Germany. Email: astrid.schuetz@phil.tu-chemnitz.de

perception of performances, social feedback, and social comparison (e.g., Filipp & Frey, 1988; Franks & Marolla, 1976; Schoeneman, 1981; Schwalbe, 1985). For example, Schwalbe and Staples (1991) used items describing experiences in the workplace. This study, like virtually all studies on the issue, is based on closed-ended questionnaires. Participants are presented with hypothetical scenarios and rate the personal significance. Although this procedure has the advantages of precision and comfortable analysis, it is quite possible that certain facets that may be important to the individual are not captured with prefabricated items. This gives no answer to the question of what sources of self-esteem people would name if left to their own devices.

The study by Schwalbe and Staples (1991) focuses on the experience of competence. The experiences described self-perceived competence (e.g., solving a challenging problem), reflected appraisal (e.g., getting praise from the boss), and social comparisons (e.g., doing a better job than someone else). However, there are other things to be proud of. For example, Leary, Tambor, Terdal, and Downs (1995) emphasize social sources of self-esteem and argue that the level of self indicates how fully an individual is socially accepted. The need to belong has also been emphasized in other recent studies (e.g., Andersen & Berenson, this volume; Baumeister & Leary, 1995). Recently, several authors have argued that there are both independent and interdependent ways of constructing the self. Independent self-concepts rely heavily on individual accomplishments. Interdependent self-concepts are based on an individual's feeling of being socially integrated. Interdependence has been observed especially in women and in Eastern cultures (Josephs, Markus, & Tafarodi, 1992; Markus & Kitayama, 1991).

In my first study in the series presented here, participants were asked open-ended questions about the sources of their self-esteem (Schütz, in press). Answers were tape-recorded, transcribed, and categorized based on the procedure of qualitative content analysis (Mayring, 1997). The resulting categories in the present study sorted by frequency were individual abilities, relations, social skills, self-acceptance, and superiority. (1) *Individual abilities* and successes were the most frequently named sources of self-esteem (e.g., "I am smart," "I am a good dancer," "I am successful"). The first category represents an independent self-concept and the second, most frequent category represents interdependence. (2) *Relations*: People in this category said that they derived their self-esteem from being involved in a happy romantic relationship, from sharing mutual trust with friends, and from helping friends. (3) *Social skills* as a source of self-esteem involved abilities in getting to know people and in entertaining others. (4) *Self-acceptance* as a source of self-esteem is a basic belief in a person's worth independent of performance. (5) *Superiority*: A number of people derived their self-esteem from depicting themselves as being ahead of others ("I can influence people," "I am smarter than others," "I can handle idiots at my job in a bar").

The results show that individual abilities, which symbolize an independent self-concept, were mentioned more frequently than social relations, which symbolize an interdependent self-concept. This matches the findings presented by Sedikides and Gaerther (this volume), who present data suggesting the primacy of the individual self over the collective self.

I also compared whether the sources named by people with high self-esteem differed from those mentioned by people with low self-esteem (distinguished by a median split). Overall, the number of sources did not differ between the groups. However, people with high self-esteem tended more often than their low-self-esteem counterparts to derive their feeling of self-worth from having social skills or from being superior to others. Thus, having high self-esteem may also be interpreted as a feeling of being *better* than others. This result shows that self-esteem is not only an attitude about the self, it may also imply certain attitudes about others. If the subject is superior to others, this also means that others are inferior, an attitude that may not be appreciated by interaction partners and may lead to interpersonal conflict. This result suggests that high self-esteem has the potential to be socially disruptive.

Self-Esteem and Styles of Self-Presentation

High self-esteem means describing the self positively. Recent research suggests that self-esteem affects self-presentation. For example, high self-esteem people often take more self-presentational risks and present themselves in a more self-enhancing fashion than low self-esteem people, who present themselves more self-protectively (Baumeister, Tice, & Hutton, 1989; Tice, 1991, 1993; see also Wood, Giordano-Beech, Taylor, Michela, & Gaus, 1994). Similarly, Schlenker, Weigold, and Hallam (1990) found that high self-esteem people become more self-aggrandizing as social evaluative pressures increase, whereas low self-esteem people become more self-presentationally cautious under the same circumstances.

Past research has demonstrated that high self-esteem people generally present themselves more positively than low self-esteem people. Researchers have also begun to deconstruct self-presentation into different styles and strategies. For example, Jones and Pittman (1982) identified a number of self-presentational strategies such as self-promotion (presenting oneself as having high abilities), exemplification (presenting oneself as morally sound), and supplication (presenting oneself as helpless). Brown, Collins, and Schmidt (1988) distinguished between direct and indirect forms of self-enhancement. In this chapter, I will examine in more detail the specific self-presentational strategies used by high and low self-esteem people.

It has been suggested that low self-esteem is related to a general negativity bias, which would imply that low self-esteem people evaluate not only themselves in a relatively negative fashion, but others as well (Crocker & Schwartz, 1985). However, it has to be considered that evaluating objects or people – if it is done in public – may also evoke self-presentational concerns. For example, criticizing others can make the self look superior, and praising people with whom one is associated may also shed favorable light on the self (Cialdini & Richardson, 1980). In a similar vein, positive or negative evaluations of objects also convey impressions about the evaluator, who by being critical may appear competent and by offering positive evaluations may appear likable (Amabile, 1983; Folkes & Sears, 1977).

Describing Romantic Partners: Indirect Self-Enhancement

Low self-esteem people may be more reluctant than high self-esteem people to make risky, self-enhancing claims about themselves, but they may use other methods of self-presentational self-enhancement. Brown et al. (1988) proposed that low self-esteem people may use a more indirect style of self-presentation than high self-esteem people. In an effort to satisfy competing demands between self-enhancement desires and self-consistency, low self-esteem people enhance feelings of self-worth indirectly via association with others. Participants in the Brown et al. (1988) study were grouped with other subjects, and the experimenters ascertained whether the participants engaged in direct or indirect self-enhancement. Low self-esteem people were more likely than high self-esteem people to use indirect self-enhancement and display favoritism when they were not directly involved in the group tasks, but high self-esteem people were more likely to use direct self-enhancement and display favoritism when they were directly involved in the group tasks (see also Cialdini & DeNicholas, 1989).

In a similar manner, low self-esteem people may be more likely than high self-esteem people to attempt to enhance their self-esteem by glorifying their close relationship partners. Brown et al. (1988) demonstrated that low self-esteem people show group favoritism when they are not involved in the group processes, and the second study presented here examines whether another form of indirect self-enhancement may consist in presenting one's relationship partner in a highly positive manner.

Cialdini and Richardson (1980) argued that, with respect to indirect self-presentation, there is another strategy besides associating with famous or popular others: the strategy of derogating others (blasting the opposition). By criticizing others, one may claim expert status and present oneself as superior (see also Amabile & Glazebrook, 1982; Cialdini and De Nicholas, 1989; Schütz, 1998a; Schütz & DePaulo, 1996). This strategy of indirect self-enhancement can be regarded as rather risky, for it may result in losing sympathy (Amabile, 1983). As the willingness to accept self-presentational risks has been observed in high self-esteem rather than in low self-esteem subjects, it may be expected that criticism as a self-presentational strategy should be more frequent in high-self-esteem subjects.

The study presented here is concerned with indirect ways of self-enhancement and analyzes how people describe themselves and their romantic partners (Schütz & Tice, 1997). Participants gave written descriptions of themselves and their partners. This was done either in a private or a public setting. That is, we either told participants to write their description down and place them in a box or we told them to write them down and to expect to read them to the group later. These descriptions can be analyzed in terms of indirect self-presentation. Describing the partner and comparing the self to the partner indirectly conveys an impression of the self.

The results suggest that both high and low self-esteem people attempt to make positive impressions but use different strategies to attain this general goal. High self-esteem people tend to describe themselves in a highly positive manner. Although they say positive things about their partners, they explicitly emphasize the things they are better at than their partners.

Low self-esteem people, on the other hand, describe themselves modestly and their partners positively. We computed the number of

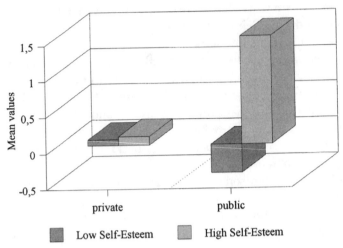

Figure 8.1. Number of self-serving minus partner-serving comparisons in different groups.

partner-serving comparisons (e.g., "He is always in a good mood. I, however, have to battle with mood swings") and the number of self-serving comparisons (e.g., "He is smart, but I am even smarter"). A joint analysis of variance with self-esteem and publicness as between-subjects factors and the number of upward versus downward comparisons as a repeated measurement factor revealed a three-way interaction of all factors. Figure 8.1 illustrates the results in presenting difference scores of the number of comparisons favoring the self minus the number of comparisons favoring the partner. It can be seen that comparisons favoring the partner were especially frequent in public with low self-esteem subjects and comparisons favoring the self were especially frequent in public with high self-esteem subjects. As those effects were typical of the public condition, it may be assumed that they are due to self-presentational concerns (see Tice & Faber, this volume). Under these circumstances, they use devaluation of the partner as a form of indirect self-enhancement. On the other hand, low-self-esteem subjects, who compared their partners favorably with themselves and frequently also emphasized how much their partners adored them, obviously used an indirect strategy of self-enhancement in basking in the reflected glory of their partners (Cialdini & Richardson, 1980).

Evaluating Art: Presenting the Self as Competent or Presenting the Self as Likable?

Three of the five self-presentational strategies described by Jones and Pittman (1982) are related to positive impressions and thus potential goals of self-enhancement efforts: likable, morally worthy, competent. The strategies have different implications. A person who claims competence aims at being admired (Schütz & De Paulo, 1996) but at the same time risks losing sympathy. As Godfrey, Jones, and Lord (1986) have shown, people who try to appear competent are perceived as less likable (see also Amabile, 1983). By describing oneself as a good person and social-minded, one aims at being liked (Schütz, 1997).

In evaluating things or persons, one can basically choose between the self-presentational goals of competence and likability. Voicing critical comments usually creates an impression of competence. However, negative evaluators are often disliked (Amabile & Glazebrook, 1982). On the other hand, praising others and evaluating things favorably makes the actor look friendly and likable. But if it is commonly assumed that the respective objects of evaluation do differ in quality, positive comments may also make the evaluator look somewhat stupid or ignorant (Folkes & Sears, 1977). Thus it appears that there is something of a self-presentational dilemma between the impression of competence and the impression of likability.

In one of our own studies, we were interested in how different self-presentational strategies were related to levels of trait self-esteem (Schütz & DePaulo, 1996). First, participants privately evaluated paintings (on a 9-point scale); then they discussed them with another participant. When evaluations were done in private, there was no difference between low and high self-esteem participants. But in public, low-self-esteem participants spoke more favorably about the paintings, whereas high-self-esteem participants spoke more negatively (see Figure 8.2). Because the differences were observed in the public context, they may be regarded as self-presentational. To low self-esteem subjects, who are less convinced of being accepted by others and who typically avoid self-presentational risks (Arkin, 1981; Baumeister et al., 1989), it may be more tempting to try to be liked by acting like a liker than to attempt the riskier strategy of trying to be respected by acting more critically (Amabile, 1983). It appears that the goal of low self-esteem subjects was to be positive and pleasant, to avoid any negativity or unpleasantness; more colloquially, they seemed to be

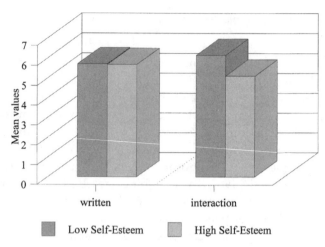

Figure 8.2. Positivity of evaluation of art in different groups.

trying to "make nice." The high self-esteem subjects, possessing sufficient self-confidence, took the chance of reaching for respect and admiration.

In addition, we looked at the style of their comments and counted how many comments were phrased as personal opinions (e.g., "I don't like the fence on the picture"; "The colors of the picture make me feel good") or impersonal evaluations ("The replication of this shape works well"; "The background is blurred"). With respect to positive comments, we did not find any differences in the style of comments. However, with respect to negative comments, there was an interaction. People with low self-esteem tended to phrase negative comments more frequently in personal than in impersonal terms, whereas the reverse was true for high self-esteem subjects. The conclusion we drew from these and some other results was that high self-esteem is related to efforts to impress others by showing competence, but low self-esteem is related to attempts to act in a friendly manner in order to gain liking. Low self-esteem subjects were reluctant to make critical comments in an impersonal, factual, expertlike fashion. Instead, when they had something unkind to say, they phrased their criticism as their own opinion or as their personal feeling about the picture.

Compared with their low self-esteem counterparts, high self-esteem subjects obviously were unafraid to state criticism and to state it as a fact. They did not settle for the safe goals but were willing to take risks:

for example, the risk of being rejected or regarded as cruel for making negative evaluations in order to establish an impression of competence (Amabile, 1983). By making critical evaluations about their own and other people's work, they seemed to aim at being regarded as experts and competent critics of art (Amabile, 1983; Amabile & Glazebrook, 1982).

The conversational style of the low self-esteem subjects in the highly evaluative context of the present experiment is similar to the pattern of *innocuous sociability*, which has been described as characterizing the behavior of people who are socially anxious (Schlenker & Leary, 1982). And in fact, social anxiety is negatively correlated with self-esteem (Cheek, Melchior, & Carpentieri, 1986) and may be causing some of the effects we observed. Socially anxious individuals tend to smile and nod, to express agreement with others and ask them questions, and to refrain from interrupting (Schlenker & Leary, 1982). When called upon to talk about themselves in evaluative situations, they do so in ways that are less revealing, less unique, and less vivid than do people who are not socially anxious (DePaulo, Epstein, & LeMay, 1990). They play it safe and refrain from taking risks.

It can be argued that the self-esteem groups also differed qualitatively in terms of the self-presentational goals to which they aspired: Low self-esteem subjects seemed above all to want to be liked or to be regarded as nice persons, whereas high self-esteem subjects seemed above all to want to be admired or regarded as competent. Similar differences have been found in two other recent studies (Schütz, 1998b; Schütz & Tice, 1997). Arguing in terms of the sociometer hypothesis (Leary et al., 1995), we may say that high self-esteem subjects are confident that they will be liked, so they do not worry about that and focus on other goals. They even risk being disliked by making harsh comments. Low self-esteem subjects, on the other hand, are much more unsure about whether they will be accepted by others. So their primary goal does not seem to be to impress others with their competence but simply to be liked.

Evaluating the Self and Being Evaluated by Others

Possessing high self-esteem means evaluating the self positively. It is, however, not clear whether people who evaluate themselves positively will also be evaluated positively by interaction partners. At least in part, positive self-evaluations may be illusory in that they are not validated through perceptions of interaction partners (see John & Robins, 1994; Kruglanski, 1989).

The next study correlated self-esteem with self-evaluations and with evaluations of others. It used a sample of 40 German psychology students who knew one another from classes (Schütz, in press). These students participated in groups of six to eight persons. They were asked to sit in a circle to the right of a person they knew but were not special friends with. The participants then completed the Fleming and Courtney (1984) Self-Esteem scale and confidentially rated themselves and the person sitting on their left-hand side.

Self-esteem correlated positively with the various self-ratings. Significant correlations emerged for the dimensions of self-efficacy (.38) and attractivity (.53). *Self-efficacy* referred to the ability to achieve one's own goals in social interactions. Interpersonal *attractivity* referred to how easy it would be for people to get others to like them. High self-esteem people were especially likely to describe themselves as efficient and attractive. The correlations between self-esteem and partner ratings were lower and did not reach significance. With the dimension of attractivity, the difference between the correlation of self-esteem with self-rating (.53) and self-esteem with partner rating (.13) was significant ($p < .01$).

The results show that self-esteem is related to positive self-evaluation of various social skills. Based on partner ratings, however, these correlations are reduced or nonexistent. (To avoid effects of judgment style, partner ratings were residual correlations controlling for the raters' self-esteem.) We may conclude that high self-esteem is related to overestimating one's interpersonal attractiveness. This conclusion matches findings reported by Brockner and Lloyd (1986) and by Gabriel, Critelli, and Ee (1994).

A second study tackled the problem of coping with threats to self-esteem (Schütz, in press). The literature on coping and self-esteem informs us that, based on self-reports, people with high self-esteem cope better. However, behavior may be regarded differently from actors' and observers' perspectives. We interviewed 25 young couples in their homes. Each partner was interviewed privately. One partner, the subject, was asked to describe an event in which his or her self-esteem was lowered by being rejected or criticized by someone who was *not* the romantic partner. The respective partner was then interviewed independently about his or her perception of the same episode. So with each couple we have two independent descriptions of an event that threatened one person's self-esteem. In addition to the interview, each partner alone completed a questionnaire about the event.

There were reports of having been criticized by the boss, of a friend canceling a visit without a good reason, and of distant or cold behavior of a colleague. The results show that attributions for the problem were related to self-esteem. Subjects with high self-esteem felt little responsibility for the event ($r = -.33$). Their partners did not share this view, though. Partners' attributions were not related to subjects' self-esteem ($r = .09$), which suggests that the subjects' external attributions can be regarded as self-serving (the difference between $-.33$ and $.09$ is significant at $p < .05$). Another factor covered in the questionnaire was how subjects had coped and how the effectiveness of the coping strategy was evaluated. We distinguished different outcomes and found that high self-esteem was related to higher outcome efficiency only when the criterion was individual well-being ($r = .38$). When the criterion was the effect of the person's coping efforts on the relationship, low self-esteem was related to higher efficiency ($-.22$). This suggests that high self-esteem is related to taking effective care of individual needs and that low self-esteem is associated with a more social style. In other words, high self-esteem people reacted in a way that was beneficial to themselves but harmful to the relationship, whereas the opposite was true for their low self-esteem counterparts. The style associated with high self-esteem may be considered egotistical; the style associated with low self-esteem may be considered altruistic but inefficient in personal terms.

On the whole, the data lead to the conclusion that high self-esteem is associated with a view of the self that is more positive than respective perceptions of interaction partners. High self-esteem people are convinced that they are very attractive to others, whereas the ratings of interaction partners show no significant correlation with the self-esteem of the actors. Likewise, high self-esteem is associated with not feeling responsible for interpersonal conflicts. But partners (who were not involved in the conflict) did not share that view. What are the implications of these results? Having positive illusions about the self may be effective in creating positive emotions. Positive illusions have been described as adaptive phenomena (Taylor & Brown, 1988). However, this general view has been criticized (Asendorpf & Ostendorf, 1998; Colvin & Block, 1994; Colvin, Block, & Funder, 1995, see also Taylor & Brown, 1994). Critics have pointed out that positive illusions may also be associated with negative effects. As to the issue presented here, it may be true that self-serving illusions may have the positive effect of boosting the subject's self-esteem; negative effects may be observed in the social domain. Interaction partners may regard such behavior as conceited. It can be argued that extremely positive illusions about the self will probably create problems in social interactions; but moderate illusions may not create conflict and may just have the positive effect of boosting the person's self-esteem (Baumeister, 1989).

Another issue in evaluation consisted of assessing the burden or help that one partner constituted for the other. Each partner was asked to rate how considerately the other partner had acted in the situation; that is, the person under stress rated how considerate his or her partner was in helping or not helping in that situation, and the person not under stress rated how considerately his or her stressed partner had acted. Correlations of those evaluations with trait self-esteem of the person evaluated point to opposite effects. These correlations were computed while the effect of the evaluator's level of self-esteem was controlled. Uninvolved partners, some of whom offered support to their partners under stress and some of whom created even more stress by telling the partner that he or she should not make such a big fuss about a trifling matter, were rated by their stressed partners. Here a negative correlation with self-esteem emerged ($r = .32$). Partners with high self-esteem were not evaluated as very supportive or considerate by stressed individuals. When stressed subjects were rated, however, the correlation was not significant but was slightly positive ($r = .15$). The difference between the two correlations approached significance ($p < .10$). Again, this points to the fact that self-esteem is related to effective handling of individual matters (see also Schütz, 1998c) but is not related to prosocial behavior. The result may be explained by the fact that high self-esteem was associated with an individualistic style of coping. High-self-esteem people tended to solve their problems alone, without asking their partners for help. When their partners were under stress, high-self-esteem people were less supportive and considerate than their low-self-esteem counterparts, who were rather attentive to their partners' needs.

Does Loving the Self Imply Loving Others?

Many clinical theories claim that you can love others only if you love yourself. Therefore, self-love is often seen as a prerequisite for social adaptiveness. I doubt whether this is true in the general sense and checked this idea (Schütz, in press) by having people complete a self-esteem scale (Deusinger, 1984) and a scale on acceptance of others (Berger, 1952). Sample items for acceptance of others are: "I regard it as useless to do something for a person who cannot do anything for me" and "There are people I despise strongly." The results show that the level of self-esteem was unrelated to the level of acceptance of others ($r = .03$). This view questions the customary assumption that liking the self is a prerequisite for liking others (for a similar argument, see Baumeister & Campbell, 1999). Instead, it seems that in both self-esteem groups there are people who are very kind and helpful to others, as well as people who foster a negative attitude toward other human beings.

The next study related evaluation of others to different personality variables (Schütz, in press). Besides self-concept variables, we included relevant traits such as aggressiveness and altruism (measured with the German version of the Personality Research Form; Stumpf, Angleitner, Wieck, Jackson, & Beloch, 1985). We had 40 psychology students evaluate videotapes of therapeutic interactions. The participants first completed a series of personality questionnaires including scales on self-esteem, narcissistic grandiosity, aggressiveness, and altruism. The participants also rated themselves on a list of adjectives representing surgency, agreeableness, and culture (John, Goldberg, & Angleitner, 1984). They completed the list twice and described themselves both as they perceived themselves (real) and as they desired to be (ideal). Self-discrepancies were used as a predictor (for similar procedures, see Andersen & Berenson, this volume). State self-esteem was measured twice, with a time interval of about 3 weeks. A difference score was used as the measure of esteem instability. Then the authors evaluated the therapists' behavior. Those interactions were role-played by more advanced students, and the participants were informed about the role play. We had two therapists who had started training in psychotherapy but who were still rather inexperienced. The participants were asked to rate how likable the therapists were, how similar they were to themselves, and how competent they were. Finally, the participants commented on how they evaluated the therapists in their own words.

Multiple regression analyses were computed to determine the effect of the subjects' personality variables on how they evaluated the therapists. As a first dependent variable, we used the tone of evaluation. Raters judged whether the comments were written in a friendly or a negative-aggressive style. The results show that narcissistic grandiosity

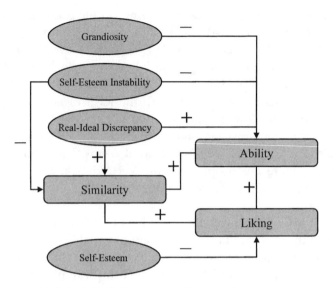

Figure 8.3. Impact of observer variables on judgments of similarity, ability, and liking in targets.

was related to an aggressive tone of evaluation. Participants who described themselves in a highly positive manner tended to be rather aggressive and devaluating when judging the inexperienced therapists' performance. The second dependent variable was how the subjects rated the therapists' competence. Liking for the therapists and judgment of similarity between the self and the therapists were positively related to judgments of competence. The subjects' personality variables show a complex pattern of relations with these variables, which is summarized in Figure 8.3. Interestingly, self-concept variables such as narcissistic grandiosity were better predictors than aggressiveness, which made no additional contribution. This finding is in accordance with previous research on narcissism (see Bushman & Baumeister, 1998; Rhodewalt, this volume). High self-esteem people felt less similar to the therapists and evaluated them more negatively. Although this pattern of positive self-evaluation is based on distinguishing the self from others and on emphasizing superiority, clinical approaches often claim that people who evaluate themselves positively feel no need to put others down. To reconcile this apparent contradiction, it may be argued that the high self-esteem group consists of distinct subgroups that differ in their social attitudes. This hypothesis was then tested.

Different Types of High Self-Esteem

In an effort to explain why people who report positive attitudes about the self perform in ways that do not conform to the patterns usually expected in high self-esteem people, theorists have proposed the concept of *defensive self-esteem*, which suggests that low self-esteem is hidden behind a façade of arrogance (Cohen, 1959; Horney, 1964). Some efforts have been made to validate this concept empirically (Coopersmith, 1959; Schneider & Turkat, 1975), but the results remained somewhat inconclusive. Another way of distinguishing different types of self-esteem was suggested by Michael Kernis and his colleagues (1989, 1993). They suggested that esteem stability is more relevant for a person's adjustment than level of self-esteem.

The literature on self-esteem shows problems or controversial results mostly with respect to three issues: (1) How stable is self-esteem, and is esteem instability an important predictor (Kernis, Cornell, Sun, Berry, & Harlow, 1993)? (2) Does high self-esteem go along with describing the self positively and negating personal flaws, or is a positive view of the self a necessary precondition for the ability to admit individual shortcomings (Rogers, 1961)? (3) Is high self-esteem related to feeling superior and devaluating others or to accepting others and being closely integrated into social groups (Berger, 1952; Leary et al., 1995)? In our own study, we used a detailed analysis of interviews to test whether subjects varied on these dimensions and whether different types of high self-esteem can be identified.

From a large sample of couples who were interviewed about marital conflicts ($N = 400$; Laux & Schütz, 1996), a sample of five couples in which both partners scored in the upper third of the self-esteem scale (Deusinger, 1984) was chosen for detailed analysis. We had interviews from both partners, so we did have two perspectives on all reports. For the analysis, we used a qualitative approach and a bottom-up perspective. We read the interviews in detail and then tried to find similarities and differences with respect to the controversial issues previously mentioned. Transcripts were coded to find out how the self was described, how the partner was described, and how responsibility for conflicts was attributed. Inductively, several dimensions were derived on which some individuals in the group (all of whom had reported rather high self-esteem) showed similarities and others showed differences: positivity of the presented self, stability, independence, and attribution of conflicts.

Three groups of subjects were identified: (1) *Stable self-acceptance*: People in this group appeared to accept themselves while admitting to having flaws and weaknesses. When talking about relationship conflicts, they accepted responsibility for the problem. They spoke in a benevolent fashion about their partners. (2) *Unstable self-esteem*: People in this group experienced ups and downs in their feeling of self-worth. They were very sensitive to criticism and were easily hurt by negative evaluations. To boost their self-esteem, they depended on external praise or approval. When talking about problems, they tended to blame both themselves and their partners. (3) *Egocentric self-enhancement*: People in this group described themselves in a highly positive manner, and tended to defend their own behavior and blame others for problems.

In conclusion, I would like to rephrase my main arguments. High self-esteem, which may be beneficial in many respects, also has the potential to be socially disruptive. It is related to presenting the self positively by criticizing others. It is related to overaccentuating a competitive self-presentation and devaluating when judging others. It is related to overestimating one's personal attractiveness and underestimating one's responsibility for social conflicts. These trends seems to be true especially for certain types of high self-esteem – unstable self-evaluation and extremely positive or grandiose self-evaluation – which fits in well with earlier findings (e.g., Bushman & Baumeister, 1998; Colvin et al., 1995; Kernis, Grannemann, & Barclay, 1989; Paulhus, 1998; Raskin, Novacek, & Hogan, 1991; Rhodewalt & Morf, 1995).

References

Alloy, L. B., & Abramson, L. (1979). Judgment of contingency in depressed and nondepressed students: Sadder but wiser? *Journal of Experimental Psychology: General, 108*, 441–485.

Amabile, T. M. (1983). Brilliant but cruel: Perceptions of negative evaluators. *Journal of Experimental Social Psychology, 19*, 146–156.

Amabile, T. M., & Glazebrook, A. H. (1982). A negativity bias in interpersonal evaluation. *Journal of Experimental Social Psychology, 18*, 1–22.

Arkin, R. M. (1981). Self-presentation styles. In J. T. Tedeschi (Ed.), *Impression management theory in social psychological research* (pp. 311–333). New York: Academic Press.

Asendorpf, J. B., & Ostendorf, F. (1998). Is self-enhancement healthy? Conceptual, psychometric and empirical analysis. *Journal of Personality and Social Psychology, 74*, 955–966.

Baumeister, R. F. (1989). The optimal margin of illusion. *Journal of Social and Clinical Psychology, 8,* 176–189.

Baumeister, R. F., & Campbell, W. K. (1999). Is loving the self necessary for loving another? An examination of identity and intimacy. In G. Fletcher & M. Clark (Eds.), *Blackwell handbook of social psychology* (Vol. 2, pp. 210–221). London: Blackwell.

Baumeister, R. F., Heatherton, T. F., & Tice, D. M. (1993). When ego threats lead to self-regulation failure: Negative consequences of high self-esteem. *Journal of Personality and Social Psychology, 64,* 141–156.

Baumeister. R. F., & Leary, M. R. (1995). The need to belong: Desire for interpersonal attachments as a fundamental human motivation. *Psychological Bulletin, 117,* 497–529.

Baumeister, R. F., Smart, L., & Boden, J. M. (1996). Relation of threatened egotism to violence and aggression. The dark side of high self-esteem. *Psychological Review, 103,* 5–33.

Baumeister. R. F., Tice, D. M., & Hutton, D. G. (1989). Self-presentational motivations and personality differences in self-esteem. *Journal of Personality, 57,* 547–579.

Baumgardner, A. H., Kaufman, C. M., & Levy, P. E. Regulating affect interpersonally: When low self-esteem leads to greater enhancement. *Journal of Personality and Social Psychology, 56,* 907–921.

Berger, E. M. (1952). The relation between expressed acceptance of self and expressed acceptance of others. *Journal of Abnormal and Social Psychology, 47,* 778–782.

Brockner, J., & Lloyd, K. (1986). Self-esteem and likability: Separating fact from fantasy. *Journal of Research in Personality, 20,* 496–508.

Brown, J. D., Collins, R. L., & Schmidt, G. W. (1988). Self-esteem and direct versus indirect forms of self-enhancement. *Journal of Personality and Social Psychology, 55,* 445–453.

Bushman, B. J., & Baumeister, R. F. (1998). Threatened egotism, narcissism, self-esteem, and direct and displaced aggression. Does self-love or self-hate lead to violence? *Journal of Personality and Social Psychology, 75,* 219–229.

Cheek, J. M., Melchior, L. A., & Carpentieri, A. M. (1986). Shyness and self-concept. In L. M. Hartman & K. R. Blankstein (Eds.), *Perception of self in emotional disorder and psychotherapy. Advances in the study of communication and affect* (Vol. 11, pp. 113–131). New York: Plenum.

Cialdini, R. B., & DeNicholas, M. E. (1989). Self-presentation by association. *Journal of Personality and Social Psychology, 57,* 626–631.

Cialdini, R. B., & Richardson, K. D. (1980). Two indirect tactics of image management: Basking and blasting. *Journal of Personality and Social Psychology, 39,* 406–415.

Cohen, A. (1959). Situational structure, self-esteem, and threat-oriented reactions to power. In D. Cartwright (Ed.), *Studies in social power.* Ann Arbor: University of Michigan Press.

Colvin, C. R., & Block, J. (1994). Do positive illusions foster mental health? An examination of the Taylor and Brown formulation. *Psychological Bulletin, 116,* 3–20.

Colvin, C. R., Block, J., & Funder, D. C. (1995). Overly positive self-evaluations and personality: Negative implications for mental health. *Journal of Personality and Social Psychology, 68*, 1152–1162.

Colvin, C. R., Block, J., & Funder, D. C. (1996). Psychometric truths in the absence of psychological meaning: A reply to Zuckerman and Knee. *Journal of Personality and Social Psychology, 70*, 1252–1255.

Coopersmith, S. (1959). A method for determining types of self-esteem. *Journal of Abnormal and Social Psychology, 59*, 87–94.

Crocker, J., & Schwartz, I. (1985). Prejudice and ingroup favouritism in a minimal intergroup situation: Effects of self-esteem. *Personality and Social Psychology Bulletin, 11*, 379–386.

DePaulo, B. M., Epstein, J. A., & LeMay, C. S. (1990). Responses of the socially anxious to the prospect of interpersonal evaluation. *Journal of Personality, 58*, 623–640.

Deusinger, I. (1984). *Die Frankfurter Selbstkonzept-Skalen*. Göttingen: Hogrefe.

Filipp, S. H., & Frey, D. (1988). Das Selbst [The self]. In K. Immelmann, K. R. Scherer, C. Vogel, & P. Schmoock (Eds.), *Psychobiologie. Grundlagen des Verhaltens* (pp. 415–454). Stuttgart: Gustav Fischer Verlag.

Fleming, J. S., & Courtney, B. E. (1984). The dimensionality of self-esteem: II. Hierarchical facet model for revised measurement scales. *Journal of Personality and Social Psychology, 46*, 404–421.

Folkes, V. S., & Sears, D. O. (1977). Does everybody like a liker? *Journal of Experimental Social Psychology, 13*, 505–519.

Franks, D. D., & Marolla, J. (1976). Efficacious action and social approval as interacting dimensions of self-esteem: A tentative formulation through construct validation. *Sociometry, 39*, 466–482.

Gabriel, M. T., Critelli, J. W., & Ee, J. S. (1994). Narcissistic illusions in self-evaluations of intelligence and attractiveness. *Journal of Personality, 62*, 143–155.

Godfrey, D. K., Jones, E. E., & Lord, C. G. (1986). Self-promotion is not ingratiating. *Journal of Personality and Social Psychology, 50*, 106–115.

Horney, K. (1964). *The neurotic personality of our time*. New York: Norton.

John, O. P., Goldberg, L. R., & Angleitner, A. (1984). Better than the alphabet: Taxonomies of personality descriptive terms in English, Dutch and German. In H. Bonarius, G. van Heck, & N. Smid (Eds.), *Personality psychology in Europe* (pp. 83–100). Lisse, the Netherlands: Swets & Zeilinger.

John, O. P., & Robins, R. W. (1994). Accuracy and bias in self-perception: Individual differences in self-enhancement and the role of narcissism. *Journal of Personality and Social Psychology, 66*, 206–219.

Jones, E. E., & Pittman, T. S. (1982). Toward a general theory of strategic self-presentation. In J. Suls (Ed.), *Psychological perspectives on the self* (pp. 231–263). Hillsdale, NJ: Erlbaum.

Josephs, R. A., Markus, H. R., & Tafarodi, R. W. (1992). Gender and self-esteem. *Journal of Personality and Social Psychology, 63*, 391–402.

Kernis, M. H., Cornell, D. P., Sun, C.-R., Berry, A., & Harlow, T. (1993). There's more to self-esteem than whether it is high or low: The importance of stability of self-esteem. *Journal of Personality and Social Psychology, 65*, 1190–1204.

Kernis, M. H., Grannemann, B. D., & Barclay, L. C. (1989). Stability and level of self-esteem as predictors of anger arousal and hostility. *Journal of Personality and Social Psychology, 56*, 1013–1022.

Kruglanski, A. W. (1989). The psychology of being "right": The problem of accuracy in social perception and cognition. *Psychological Bulletin, 106*, 395–409.

Laux, L., & Schütz, A. (1996). *Streßbewältigung und Wohlbefinden in der Familie* [Coping and well-being in families]. Stuttgart: Kohlhammer.

Leary, M. R., Tambor, E. S., Terdal, S. K., & Downs, D. L. (1995). Self-esteem as an interpersonal monitor: The sociometer hypothesis. *Journal of Personality and Social Psychology, 68*, 518–530.

Markus, H. R., & Kitayama, S. (1991). Culture and the self: Implications for cognitions, emotion and motivation. *Psychological Review, 98*, 224–253.

Mayring, P. (1997). *Qualitative Inhaltsanalyse* (6. durchges. Aufl.). Weinheim: Deutscher Studien Verlag.

Paulhus, D. L. (1998). Interpersonal and intrapsychic adaptiveness of trait self-enhancement: A mixed blessing? *Journal of Personality and Social Psychology, 74*, 1197–1208.

Raskin, R., Novacek, J., & Hogan, R. (1991). Narcissistic self-esteem management. *Journal of Personality and Social Psychology, 60*, 911–918.

Rhodewalt, F., & Morf, C. (1995). Self and interpersonal correlates of the narcissistic personality inventory: A review and new findings. *Journal of Research in Personality, 29*, 1–23.

Rogers, C. R. (1961). *On becoming a person*. Boston: Houghton Mifflin.

Schlenker, B. R., & Leary, M. R. (1982). Social anxiety and self-presentation: A conceptualization and model. *Psychological Bulletin, 92*, 641–669.

Schlenker, B. R., Weigold, M. F., & Hallam, J. R. (1990). Self-serving attributions in social context: Effects of self-esteem and social pressure. *Journal of Personality and Social Psychology, 58*, 855–863.

Schneider, D. J., & Turkat, D. (1975). Self-presentation following success or failure. Defensive self-esteem models. *Journal of Personality, 43*, 127–135.

Schoeneman, T. J. (1981). Reports of the sources of self-knowledge. *Journal of Personality, 49*, 284–294.

Schütz, A. (1997). Interpersonelle Aspekte des Selbstwertgefühles: Die Beschreibung der eigenen Person im sozialen Kontext [Interpersonal aspects of self-esteem]. *Zeitschrift für sozialpsychologie, 28*, 92–108.

Schütz, A. (1998a). Assertive, offensive, protective and defensive styles of self-presentation: A taxonomy. *Journal of Psychology, 132*, 611–628.

Schütz, A. (1998b). Autobiographical narratives of good and bad deeds: Defensive and favorable self-description moderated by trait self-esteem. *Journal of Social and Clinical Psychology, 4*, 466–475.

Schütz, A. (1998c). Coping with threats to self-esteem: The differing patterns of subjects with high versus low trait self-esteem in first person accounts. *European Journal of Personality, 12*, 169–186.

Schütz, A. (in press). *Psychologie des Selbstwertgefühls. Von Selbstakzeptanz bis Arroganz*. [Psychology of self-esteem. Types of self-esteem between self-acceptance and arrogance]. Stuttgart: Kohlhammer.

Schütz, A., & DePaulo, B. M. (1996). Self-esteem and evaluative reactions: Letting people speak for themselves. *Journal of Research in Personality, 30,* 137–156.

Schütz, A., & Tice, D. M. (1997). Associative and competitive patterns of indirect self-enhancement. *European Journal of Social Psychology, 27,* 257–273.

Schwalbe, M. L. (1985). Autonomy in work and self-esteem. *Sociological Quaterly, 26,* 519–535.

Schwalbe, M. L., & Staples, C. L. (1991). Gender differences in sources of self-esteem. *Social Psychology Quarterly, 54,* 158–168.

Sorembe, V., & Westhoff, K. (1985). *Skala zur Erfassung der Selbstakzeptierung.* Göttingen: Hogrefe.

Stumpf, H., Angleitner, A., Wieck, T., Jackson, D. N., & Beloch, T. H. (1985). *Deutsche Personality Research Form (PRF).* Göttingen: Hogrefe.

Taylor, S. E., & Brown, J. (1988). Illusion and well-being: Some social psychological contributions to a theory of mental health. *Psychological Bulletin, 103,* 193–210.

Taylor, S. E., & Brown, J. (1994). Positive illusions and well-being revisited: Separating fact from fiction. *Psychological Bulletin, 116,* 21–27.

Tice, D. M. (1991). Esteem protection or enhancement? Self-handicapping motives and attributions differ by trait self-esteem. *Journal of Personality and Social Psychology, 60,* 711–725.

Tice, D. M. (1993). Social motivations of people with low self-esteem. In R. F. Baumeister (Ed.), *Self-esteem. The puzzle of low self-regard* (pp. 37–53). New York: Plenum.

Wood, J. V., Giordano-Beech, M., Taylor, K. L., Michela, J. L., & Gaus, V. (1994). Strategies of social comparison among people with low self-esteem: Self-protection and self-enhancement. *Journal of Personality and Social Psychology, 67,* 713–731.

9. The Social Mind of the Narcissist: Cognitive and Motivational Aspects of Interpersonal Self-Construction

FREDERICK RHODEWALT

Narcissism: An Individual Difference Approach to the Study of Social Self-Construction

According to myth, the handsome Narcissus was punished by the gods for his callous rejection of the nymph Echo. His punishment was to fall in love with his own image, as mirrored in a mountain pool. But the perfect image was unattainable, for when he tried to embrace it, the water rippled and the image became distorted and fragmented. Unable to attain this perfect image, Narcissus fell into despair and ended his life. Beginning with the writings of Havelock Ellis (1898), the myth of Narcissus has become a metaphor for pathological self-love. Following this theme, there is now a voluminous clinical literature on narcissism. However, as Pulver (1970) observed, the concept of narcissism is one of psychoanalysis's most important contributions but also one of its most confusing.

The perspective and supporting research presented in this chapter attempt to reduce some of this confusion by casting narcissism in a social/cognitive, self-regulation framework. Consistent with the theme of this volume, I have sought to understand the relationship between narcissists' mental representations of the self and the social world and their strategic interpersonal behavior. This research program has several objectives but is fundamentally concerned with the cognitive

I would like to thank my students Carolyn Morf, Brian Tschanz, Stacy Eddings, and Michael Tragakis for their invaluable contributions to the research reported in this chapter and Susan Andersen for her thoughtful comments on an earlier draft. Address correspondence to Dr. Frederick Rhodewalt, Department of Psychology, University of Utah, 390 S. 1530 East, Rm 502, Salt Lake City, UT, 84112-0251 or via email at rhodewalt@psych.utah.edu and interpersonal processes involved in the social construction and maintenance of the self. In the present view, narcissism is a convenient marker for a number of variables of interest to self researchers. It allows one to track specific self-representations and self-evaluative needs that may influence or be influenced by social interaction. More important, the research offers the potential for a higher-level integration of the cognitive, affective, motivational, and interpersonal self processes and constructs that fall under the umbrella of the self. This program of research has also fostered the bridging of the psychoanalytically grounded construct of narcissism to contemporary perspectives in personality and social psychology. The purpose of this chapter is to describe the model and relevant research, and to illustrate the ways in which the study of narcissism affords the opportunity to investigate processes and outcomes of social self-construction.

Narcissism: Theory and Description

The topic of narcissism has occupied a long and controversial position in the annals of psychoanalytic theory and practice. An in-depth treatment of this literature is beyond the scope of this chapter, and the reader is directed to excellent overviews by Pulver (1970), Akhtar and Thompson (1982), and Cooper (1985). However, an important jumping-off point for our purposes is the work of Kohut and Kernberg, the two most influential theorists in the area of narcissism. Both theorists focus on disturbances in early social (parental) relationships as the genesis of adult narcissistic personality disorder. Like Freud (1914), Kohut (1971) views narcissism as part of normal early development. The child's self develops and gains maturity through interactions with others (primarily the mother) that provide the child with opportunities to be mirrored (gain approval and enhancement) and to idealize (identify with perfect and omnipotent others). Empathic parents contribute to the healthy development of the self in two ways. First, they provide mirroring that fosters a more realistic sense of self. Second, parents reveal limitations in themselves that lead the child to internalize the idealized image, gaining a personal set of ideals and values. Things go awry when parents are unempathic and fail to provide appropriate mirroring and idealization opportunities. According to Kohut, narcissism is in effect developmental arrest in which the self remains grandiose and unrealistic. At the same time, the child continues to idealize others in order to maintain self-esteem through association.

Kernberg (1976) paints a different portrait of the development of narcissism. In his view, narcissism stems from the child's reaction to cold and unempathic parents, usually the mother. This "emotionally hungry" child is enraged by his parents and comes to view them as even more depriving. Narcissism, in this view, is a *defense* reflecting the child's attempt to take refuge in some aspect of the self that his or her parents value. This defense results in a grandiose sense of self. Perceived weaknesses in the self are split off into a separate hidden self. Although their perspectives are different in many respects, Kernberg and Kohut both describe individuals with a childhood history of unsatisfactory social relationships who, as adults, possess a *social mind* incorporating grandiose views of the self that embody a conflicted psychological dependence on others. Despite these similarities, there are important differences between the two perspectives in terms of defensiveness and the meaning of key characteristics and behaviors that have led to considerable debate in the psychoanalytic literature.

Just as there has been considerable theoretical discussion and disagreement with regard to the etiology of narcissism, there has also been wide discussion about its definition. One might speculate that it was this inability to agree on its defining features that delayed narcissism's inclusion as a diagnostic category until the 1980 edition of the *Diagnostic and Statistical Manual of Mental Disorders* (DSM; American Psychiatric Association, 1980 [DSM-III], 1986). According to the most recent DSM-IV (1994), narcissism involves a pervasive pattern of grandiosity, self-importance, and uniqueness.[1] Narcissists are preoccupied with fantasies of unlimited success, wealth, beauty, and power. They are exhibitionistic and require attention and admiration from others while responding to criticism or a threat to self-esteem with feelings of rage, shame, or humiliation. In addition, there is a set of characteristics that collectively contribute to interpersonal difficulties. For example, narcissists display entitlement and expect special treatment from others without the need to reciprocate. They are also exploitive of others. They tend to have relationships that oscillate between idealization and devaluation. Finally, narcissists are either unable or unwilling to empathize with others. According to the DSM-IV, in narcissism "self-esteem is almost invariably very fragile; the person may be preoccupied with how well he or she is doing and how well he or she is

---

[1] The defining characteristics of narcissism differ trivially across the three editions of the DSM in which it has been included.

regarded by others. . . . In response to criticism, he or she may react with rage, shame, or humiliation" (1994, p. 350).

The picture of narcissism that emerges is one of an individual who is invested in receiving, if not creating, attention, positive regard, and admiration from others and who experiences intense emotions in reaction to such input. In fact, in a review, Westen (1990) concluded that narcissism should be strictly defined as "a cognitive-affective preoccupation with the self, where 'cognitive preoccupation' refers to a focus of attention on the self; 'affective preoccupation' refers to a preoccupation with one's own needs, wishes, goals, ambitions, glory, superiority, or perfection; and 'self' refers to the whole person, including one's subjective experience, actions, and body" (p. 227).

The DSM diagnostic criteria provide a consensual definition of narcissism from which one may operationalize the construct for research purposes. A number of "face valid" scales have been developed since the DSM criteria were published. Of these scales, the Narcissistic Personality Inventory (NPI; Raskin & Hall, 1979; see also Emmons, 1987; Raskin & Terry, 1988; Rhodewalt & Morf, 1995) has received the most research attention and is the one used almost exclusively in our research. The scale provides an index of degree of narcissism reflecting extreme manifestations that represent pathological narcissism, as well as less extreme forms thought to reflect narcissism as a personality trait (Emmons, 1987).[2]

Social/Cognitive Self-Regulation Model

Agreement among clinicians with regard to narcissism's defining characteristics and the corresponding development of measures has

---

[2] Although the NPI has received considerable empirical validation, it may fail to capture the complete essence of narcissism. For example, Akhtar and Thompson (1982) surveyed the wide range of symptoms that have been included in clinical descriptions of narcissism. From their review, they conclude that narcissism is best characterized as deficits in functioning in six areas: (1) self-concept, (2) interpersonal relationships, (3) social adaptation, (4) ethics, standards, and ideals, (5) love and sexuality, and (6) cognitive style. Moreover, each area of dysfunction has overt and covert facets that appear to characterize conflict or inconsistency within the area of functioning. For example, the narcissistic self-concept is overtly haughty, grandiose, and entitled and covertly fragile, plagued with feelings of inferiority and worthlessness. The research presented in this chapter has been guided by the DSM-III definition of narcissism. I mention the Ahktar and Thompson description of narcissism because it highlights the conflict and lack of internal coherence that seem central to the narcissistic personality but are not emphasized in the DSM-III description of the syndrome.

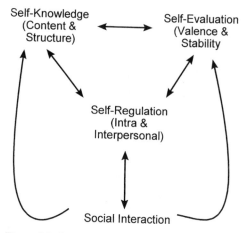

Figure 9.1. Social/cognitive self-regulatory model of narcissism.

spawned renewed interest in the topic as well as an increase in research. Much of the research (including some from this laboratory) has been in the form of validation studies demonstrating, for example, that NPI-defined narcissists are self-focused (Raskin & Shaw, 1988) or possess high self-esteem (Rhodewalt & Morf, 1995). There are, however, a number of more compelling questions regarding the psychology of narcissism. Why would a person simultaneously have high self-regard but be hypersensitive to criticism? Why would this same individual expect special treatment from others but be unwilling to give it in return? Is there a relationship between narcissists' inflated self-views and their interpersonal relations? And, most fundamentally, how might a pervasive "cognitive-affective" preoccupation with the self be cast in contemporary social cognitive personality terms?

The model depicted in Figure 9.1 is our initial attempt to address these questions from within a social cognitive framework. The model is strongly indebted to contemporary social and personality perspectives on the self. Moreover, we view the narcissistic self as having an organization and a process similar to those of the normal self. In the model, the self has three components: self-knowledge, self-evaluation, and self-regulation. The self-knowledge component of the model is what is known about the self, the Jamesian "me." It is the *cognitive self* (Linville & Carlston, 1994); the mental repository of autobiographical information reflected appraisals, self-ascribed traits and competencies, possible selves, and ideals and goals. It is somewhat ironic that the clinical literature often characterizes the narcissistic self as empty or lacking in coherence given that so much psychological investment is placed on the self by narcissistic individuals.

In terms of self-evaluation, the model is concerned with both the valence and the stability of feelings of self-worth. Narcissists claim to have high self-esteem. But this claim undoubtedly masks a more complicated aspect of narcissistic self-regard. The question of interest is whether these reports of high self-regard convey true self-esteem or reflect defensive self-enhancement (cf. Raskin, Novacek, & Hogan, 1991a). What is the basis of narcissistic self-esteem? Westen (1990) maintains that narcissistic self-esteem depends less on the absolute qualities of the self-concept than on the discrepancies between these perceived qualities and the grandiose ideals that the individual holds for himself or herself. Narcissistic hypersensitivity to social feedback should contribute to vulnerable or unstable self-esteem and self-affect. High but unstable self-esteem should make the narcissist more dependent on social feedback in an attempt to gain clarity about the self (Kernis, 1993).

The self-regulation component refers to both intra- and interpersonal strategies used to protect or enhance positive self-views. This type of self-regulation casts narcissists as active manipulators of the social feedback with which they are so concerned. Intrapersonal strategies include distorted interpretations of outcomes and selective recall of past events. Interpersonal regulation covers a multitude of self-presentational gambits and social manipulations also in the service of engineering positive feedback or blunting negative feedback about the self.

The model has heuristic value in terms of organizing research questions. However, it is not implied that the three components are discrete entities, nor are they static. On the contrary, the model clearly embodies reciprocally determined influences in that narcissists actively operate on their social environment, which, in turn, feeds back on their sense of self and self-worth. The arbitrariness of these distinctions and the intertwining of components and processes will become apparent in the following sections, where findings pertaining to self-knowledge, self-evaluation, and self-regulation are reviewed.

Finally, although the model is couched in terms of social cognitive theory and constructs, it has much in common with earlier psychoanalytic statements about the narcissistic personality process. For example, Reich (1960) contends that the narcissistic defect is the inability of a mature ego to test reality and develop an accurate sense of self.

Rather, the narcissist engages in a pathological form of self-esteem regulation in which the narcissist must chronically perform compensatory self-inflation in order to support a megalomanic self-image. Our research creates a portrait of the narcissistic individual whose self-images are transient, dependent on social validation, and largely context dependent.

Narcissistic Self-Concept

Most clinical commentators note that, although generally positive, narcissistic self-conceptions are fragile, internally inconsistent, poorly organized, and unstable. For example, Bach (1977) has argued that the "narcissistic state of consciousness" reflects deficits in the areas of perception of self, language and thought organization, intentionality, and volition, as well as regulation of mood and the perception of time. More recently, Emmons (1987) has suggested that narcissists' self-representations may be organized such that they are low in complexity, which, in turn, accounts for the emotional lability that is a hallmark of narcissism. Drawing upon these characterizations of narcissism, we (Rhodewalt & Morf, 1995, 1998; Rhodewalt, Madrian, & Cheney, 1998; Tschanz & Rhodewalt, in press) have approached the self-knowledge issue from two perspectives: a deficit model and a structural model.

Deficit Model or "Empty" Self

Using the deficit approach, we tested the notion that narcissists' self-conceptions are less accessible and less confidently held than those of less narcissistic individuals. In short, something is lacking. According to this model, narcissists' positive self-concepts are poorly formed, unstable, and not as automatically accessible as they are in others. Consequently, it would follow that narcissists are more reliant on and reactive to social and contextual feedback about their self-worth.

Although not exhaustive, our research on the deficit model of narcissistic self-conceptions permits several conclusions. First, self-knowledge appears to be no more or less accessible in narcissists than in other individuals. In a number of investigations, Brian Tschanz and I (in press) recorded reaction times to make me–not me judgments about trait descriptors. For example, in one study, we primed self-judgments with retrieval of either autobiographical information

("Have you behaved in a friendly way in the past month") or social reputation information ("Does your mother think you're friendly?"; cf. Lord, Deforges, Chacon, Pere, & Clubb, 1992). There were no effects for level of narcissism in any of these studies. Narcissists were neither faster nor slower to make unprimed self-judgments, and they were not differentially responsive to the effects of priming. In one investigation we found that social knowledge was more accessible in narcissists, as indicated by faster response latency to social reputation questions, but we failed to observe this effect in other studies.

Rhodewalt and Morf (1995) examined a variety of self-report, self-concept measures. In particular, we were interested in the confidence and clarity with which self-views were held. Across a variety of measures, the picture that emerges is that NPI-defined narcissists hold self-views that are more positive and about which they report being more certain than do less narcissistic persons. Campbell (1990) indexed what she terms *self-concept clarity* with measures of internal consistency, temporal stability, and extremity of self-concept reports. None of these dimensions of self-concept clarity were related to narcissism (Rhodewalt & Regalado, 1996).

Several theorists claim that narcissists hold unrealistically high standards toward which they are constantly striving (Akhtar & Thompson, 1982). Carolyn Morf and I (Rhodewalt & Morf, 1995, Study 3) administered the Higgins Selves Questionnaire to a group of participants who had also completed the NPI. The Selves Questionnaire provides measures of the discrepancies between the actual self and the ideal and ought selves. The measure does not permit one to examine the comparative level of the standards that people hold for themselves. However, we did find that narcissists displayed a higher correspondence between their actual and ideal selves (i.e., they were *less* self-discrepant) than did less narcissistic participants. Low actual–ideal self-discrepancy is usually associated with positive adjustment; however, as Raskin and Terry (1988) suggest, narcissists' ideal selves may be pathological because they are overly aggrandized and aggressive. Thus, what on the surface appears to be evidence of positive adjustment may reflect the defensive embracing of unrealistic standards for the self.

The question of unrealistic self-standards is important but one that remains for future research. Existing evidence indicates that the chronic belief that one is failing to met his or her standards does not appear to be a characteristic of narcissism. Of course, it may be that high standards interact with anticipated or perceived threat to engender the negative emotions so frequently displayed among narcissists.

In sum, we have found little evidence to support the deficit model of narcissistic self-representation. Self-knowledge appears to be as accessible among narcissists as among others. Moreover, they report being confident and certain of their self-evaluations. There is one potentially important qualification to these conclusions. All of these results have been generated in relatively uninvolving and nonthreatening testing situations. Given our speculation that the narcissistic self is highly context dependent and vulnerable to threat, it may be that cognitive elements of the self would be most sensitively examined across contexts and levels of threat. It may well be that the narcissistic self depicted in the clinical literature would emerge more clearly in circumstances that mirrored the clinical setting. There may be other methods of investigating the self that would reveal differences in self-content between narcissists and others. For example, McGuire and McGuire's (this volume) method of analyzing thought systems might be sensitive to narcissistic views of self and other.

The Structural Model or "Disorganized" Self

The structural hypothesis specifies that although the content and general accessibility of narcissists' self-knowledge may not differ from those of other individuals, it does differ in terms of its organization. This hypothesis gains plausibility when one considers that differences in organization of self-knowledge have been linked to emotional reactivity (Linville, 1985; Showers, 1992a,b), and emotional reactivity is a defining characteristic of narcissism. For example, Emmons (1987) reported that the NPI was positively correlated with both positive and negative affect variability. In discussing these findings, Emmons suggested that self-complexity may serve as the mediator of narcissistic emotional reactivity. Self-complexity describes the extent to which aspects of one's self-concept are differentiated. Moreover, persons with complex self-representations display relatively stable moods compared to those with simplistic representations (Linville, 1985). Alternatively, narcissists' self-knowledge may be more compartmentalized along positive and negative evaluative dimensions. Showers (1992a,b) coined the term *evaluative integration* to capture this dimension, and has demonstrated that the impact of positive and negative information about the self has less emotional impact on those high in evaluative integration (low compartmentalization of good and bad self-knowledge) than on those low in evaluative integration (high compartmentalization).

We have obtained little evidence that narcissism is related to less complex or more compartmentalized self-representations. Rhodewalt and Morf (1995, Study 1) found the predicted high NPI–low self-complexity association ($r = -.27, p < .05$) but failed to replicate this association in five independent samples (Rhodewalt & Morf, 1998; Rhodewalt & Regalado, 1996; Rhodewalt et al., 1998). Likewise, we have failed to find an association between NPI-defined narcissism and low evaluative integration in three independent samples (Rhodewalt & Regalado, 1996; Rhodewalt et al., 1998). The picture is more complex, however, in that we found that evaluative integration but not self-complexity moderates the relation between narcissism and emotional responsiveness to social feedback, a point to which I will return momentarily.

Before ending this section, we should mention that there may be other ways in which self-concept organization is related to narcissism. For instance, narcissists may possess selves that are highly differentiated along roles or social contexts (i.e., high self-concept differentiation; Donahue, Robins, Roberts, & John, 1993), a fact that might also confound the accurate assessment of self-complexity. According to Donahue et al., self-concept differentiation is the tendency to see oneself as possessing different traits in different social roles. Higher self-concept differentiation is related to greater intrapersonal and interpersonal distress. At present, the evidence suggests that narcissism cannot be reduced to a pathological form of underdifferentiated self-concept organization. However, a number of intriguing hypotheses are yet to be explored. I will suggest several in subsequent sections.

Distorted Self-Processes

The clinical literature suggests an alternative way in which self-knowledge may be biased and therefore more dependent upon external validation. This difference is captured by Akhtar and Thompson (1982), who describe the narcissistic self-concept and cognitive style as characterized by inflated self-regard and an egocentric perception of reality. From a social psychological perspective, we would argue that narcissists possess a self-aggrandizing attributional style (Rhodewalt & Morf, 1995; Rhodewalt, Tragakis, & Finnerty, 1999; see also Emmons, 1987, and John & Robins, 1994). A substantial literature documents that individuals make self-serving attributions in order to protect or enhance self-esteem (Bradley, 1978; Miller & Ross, 1975). People in general take credit for success and externalize failure. Narcissists, in contrast, take more credit for positive outcomes than do less narcissistic individuals. For example, Rhodewalt and Morf (1995) found that although narcissism was unrelated to attributions for hypothetical negative outcomes (narcissists externalized bad outcomes to the same extent as did others), narcissists made more self-aggrandizing attributions for hypothetical successes than did low narcissists. In laboratory investigations, narcissists infer greater ability from success feedback, even when that feedback is response noncontingent (Rhodewalt & Morf, 1998; Rhodewalt et al., 1999).

It is likely that this self-aggrandizing attributional style has several implications for narcissistic self-conceptions, affect, and behavior. First, with regard to self-conceptions, viewing one's positive and negative outcomes in attributionally extreme ways may contribute to the tendency to have highly compartmentalized self-conceptions. Kernberg (1976) contends that narcissists frequently engage in "splitting" or dramatic shifts in self-evaluation and thereby avoid the conflicts in dealing with one's strengths and weaknesses. Thus, the defense of splitting should contribute to low evaluative integration among narcissists (and perhaps high self-concept differentiation). With regard to affect, our research (Rhodewalt & Morf, 1998) indicates that negative feedback has a greater impact on high-NPI participants' feelings of self-worth and anger than it does on the feelings of low-NPI participants. Moreover, these extreme emotional reactions to negative feedback are most pronounced when the negative feedback follows a success for which the narcissist has taken credit. Finally, with regard to behavior, the narcissist's tendency to self-aggrandize may plant the seeds of doubt when he or she is called upon again to display competencies and talents. Consistent with this prediction, narcissists are more likely to self-handicap than are less narcissistic individuals (Rhodewalt et al., 1999).

Narcissism and Self-Esteem

The one area where clinical observation and empirical evidence agree is with regard to narcissists' self-aggrandizing, positive views of the self. Across a number of studies using a variety of measures, narcissism is consistently associated with high self-esteem (Emmons, 1984, 1987; Kernis & Sun, 1994; Morf & Rhodewalt, 1993; Raskin et al., 1991a;

Raskin & Terry, 1998; Rhodewalt & Morf, 1995, 1998; Rhodewalt et al., 1998; Watson, Taylor, & Morris, 1987). The meaning of these inflated self-evaluations is less clear. At the heart of the issue is whether these positive self-evaluations reflect a true sense of high self-worth or an expression of defensiveness. In a direct examination of this issue, Raskin et al. (1991a) asked participants to complete measures of narcissism, true self-esteem, and what they termed *defensive self-enhancement*. Defensive self-enhancement had two forms, grandiosity (the need to be admired and adored) and social desirability (the need for the approval of others). Narcissism was related to grandiose self-esteem but not socially desirable self-esteem. In other words, to the extent that narcissists' self-descriptions are positive, they reflect a desire to be admired but not necessarily liked. Raskin et al. noted that "according to most clinical accounts, grandiosity involves two contradictory belief systems, namely an aggrandized version of the self (ideal self) and a self that corresponds to actual experience (actual self). Moreover, when threatened with failure, the grandiose person tends inconspicuously to adopt a posture consistent with his or her aggrandized self" (p. 33).

There is a second dimension to self-esteem that is important in understanding the psychology of narcissism. A theme running through most discussions of narcissists is that they are extremely reactive to feedback about the self. This fact suggests that narcissists' self-evaluations, although generally positive, should also be highly unstable. We have provided support for this prediction in both laboratory (Rhodewalt & Morf, 1998) and survey studies (Rhodewalt et al., 1998). For example, Rhodewalt and Morf (1998) provided participants with success and failure feedback on successive tests of intelligence. The impact of this feedback produced greater changes in the self-esteem of high-NPI participants than it did among low-NPI participants. We have also conducted two studies in which participants provided descriptions of the events of their day and state self-esteem across a series of days (Rhodewalt et al., 1998). In both studies, narcissists displayed greater self-esteem variability than did less narcissistic individuals. Interestingly, in both studies, this relation was moderated by the participant's level of evaluative integration: Narcissists who were also low in evaluative integration displayed the greatest self-esteem variability.

We believe that the evaluative integration findings may provide a key to understanding one type of narcissism. The basic assumption behind the evaluative integration construct is that the accessibility of pertinent self-knowledge mediates the affective responses to positive and negative feedback. Evaluatively integrated people do not over-generalize the implications of good or bad outcomes because the outcomes make salient a balanced set of self-knowledge. Among low evaluatively integrated people (especially narcissists), positive feedback makes accessible exclusively positive information about the self and negative feedback makes accessible exclusively negative information about the self. The consequence of feedback-consistent self-knowledge should be an increased tendency to make internal attributions for the outcome. That is, the more one can think of corroborating self-knowledge, the more one should conclude that the new piece of information says something about the self. A consequence of low evaluative integration is that any feedback will be construed as self-defining and thus will contribute to the instability of self-esteem. Kernberg (1976, 1980) contends that narcissists frequently engage in splitting or dramatic shifts in their self-evaluation and thereby avoid the conflict of dealing with one's strengths and weaknesses. The defense of splitting should also contribute to self-concepts that are low in evaluative integration.

There are a number of parallels between our findings for narcissists and Kernis's research on high but unstable self-esteem individuals. Kernis (1993) contends that high but unstable self-esteem is associated with enhanced sensitivity to evaluative events, increased concern about one's self-image, and an overreliance on social sources of evaluation. Moreover, the goal of high, unstable self-esteem people is to build more stable self-views and to enhance positive self-feelings. Thus, they are especially sensitive to both positive and negative social feedback, reacting to both with more extreme affective responses than do stable self-esteem individuals. They react favorably to positive feedback and have strongly adverse reactions to negative feedback including derogation of the evaluator and evaluation techniques (Kernis et al., 1993). Research also indicates that unstable, high self-esteem individuals are more hostile and angry (Kernis et al., 1992).

Like unstable, high self-esteem individuals, narcissists are also more likely to display antagonism toward and cynical mistrust of others (Rhodewalt & Morf, 1995). They react to self-esteem threats by derogating the source of those threats (Morf & Rhodewalt, 1993) and devaluing the negative feedback (Kernis & Sun, 1994). Narcissists engage in biased self-enhancement (Gabriel, Critelli, & Ee, 1994; John & Robins, 1994; Rhodewalt & Morf, 1995) and view positive feedback as more valid and the evaluator as more competent than do less narcissistic individuals (Kernis & Sun, 1994).

Kernis contends that unstable self-esteem develops in individuals who place substantial importance on self-evaluative information. To the extent that one encounters episodes of potentially contradictory evaluative information and the more one's self-esteem is contingent on such information, the more unstable one's self-esteem is. Thus, it is noteworthy that theories of narcissism also point to difficulties with interpersonal sources of evaluation and inconsistencies in the coherence of self-concepts. Although their emphases are different, the theories of Kernberg (1976) and Kohut (1976) both argue that deficiencies in self-evaluative aspects of parent–child interactions (insufficient feedback) lay the foundation for adult narcissism. Thus, narcissism and self-esteem instability may both have their origins in capricious, inconsistent, or neglectful reinforcement histories that impede the development of confidently held, stable self-conceptions and require constant vigilance for self-defining information.

The Rhodewalt et al. (1998) studies provide what is perhaps an even more illuminating finding. Not only did narcissists display greater day-to-day fluctuations in their self-esteem, the relation between daily self-esteem and the positivity or negativity of social interactions was significantly stronger for narcissists than it was for less narcissistic individuals. That is, narcissists' self-worth is more entrained to the quality of their most recent social interactions, whereas the self-worth of less narcissistic people is more stable and less dependent on social context.

Narcissism and Intra- and Interpersonal Self-Esteem Regulation

The research reviewed thus far portrays narcissists as individuals who hold highly positive, if not inflated, views of their attributes and accomplishments and as people who are highly sensitive to, and reliant upon, social feedback to maintain these positive images of themselves. The final component of the model focuses on the self-regulatory aspect of narcissism. Following from Reich's observation that narcissism is essentially interpersonal self-esteem regulation, the model proposes that narcissists actively employ a variety of intra- and interpersonal mechanisms in order to manipulate their social worlds to sustain the inflated view of who they are. Rather than being passively at the mercy of friends and strangers to provide self-evaluative feedback, narcissists pursue a pathological form of chronic self-verification (cf. Swann, 1983).

At the *intra*personal level, narcissists construct internal models of their social environment and their place in it that corroborates and shores up their grandiose self-views. For example, John and Robins (1994) had individuals participate in "managerial" group discussions and then rate the contributions of each of the five members, including themselves. The NPI significantly predicted the self-enhancement bias in that narcissists significantly overestimated their contributions relative to group ratings (as well as independent judges' ratings) of their contributions (see also Gabriel et al., 1994). As noted, one of the narcissist's intrapersonal strategies is his or her self-aggrandizing attributional style. It is particularly significant that narcissists interpret response-noncontingent positive outcomes as evidence of superior competence (Rhodewalt et al., 1999). Such a tendency should contribute to a fragile sense of self and a continued need for self-verifying feedback.

At the same time, narcissists hold negative views of others, especially when those others are the source of negative feedback (Kernis & Sun, 1994; Morf & Rhodewalt, 1993). Collectively, these findings support the NPI's construct validity in terms of identifying narcissistic self-aggrandizing behavior. In addition, the NPI is positively associated with the Cook-Medley Hostility Scale and negatively associated with agreeableness on the NEO-PI measure of personality (Rhodewalt & Morf, 1995). According to Costa and McCrea (1985), NEO-Agreeableness reflects a positive or negative orientation toward other people, and Smith and Frohm (1985) provided evidence that the Cook-Medley scale captures a cynical mistrust of others. Taken together these findings suggest a set of self and person perception processes that lead to the construction of positive models of self and negative models of others.

Rhodewalt and Eddings (2000) provide additional evidence of intrapersonal self-esteem regulation. In response to threat, narcissists edit or distort recall of their autobiographical memories. Specifically, narcissists who were led to experience a romantic rejection recalled personal romantic histories that were more self-aggrandizing than the histories they reported 1 week prior to the rejection. More important, the greater the positive distortion in recall, the more their self-esteem was buffered from the rejection. Among less narcissistic individuals, the romantic rejection led to a recall of a more humble past and lower self-esteem. It is likely that the narcissists defensive recall and restructuring of past events contribute to the clinical impression of a lack of coherence and continuity of the self.

There is also evidence of narcissistic *inter*personal self-esteem regulation. Morf and Rhodewalt (1993) examined narcissism and the use of self-evaluation maintenance (SEM) strategies (Tesser, 1988). According to Tesser, people relate to psychologically close others in ways that enhance or maintain positive self-evaluations. Such a concern about one's friend's outcomes can be potentially threatening the more relevant the friend's performance is to one's self-definition, especially when the friend's performance is superior to one's own. Most individuals will do something to reduce the comparison. One avenue of threat reduction is to devalue or derogate the friend on some other dimension. Morf and Rhodewalt (1993) believed that narcissists would be especially likely to engage in this form of SEM because of their sense of entitlement and tendency to be exploitive of others.

In the Morf and Rhodewalt (1993) investigation, high- and low-NPI participants were either slightly or substantially outperformed on an ego-relevant task. Participants then had the opportunity to make personality evaluations of the person who outperformed them. Cross-cutting the relative performance manipulation was a manipulation of the publicity of the personality evaluation; half of the participants believed that the evaluation was anonymous and unseen by the target, and half believed that they would have to evaluate the target in a face-to-face interaction. Our intent was to explore the extent to which narcissists would engage in self-esteem protective acts at the expense of others. As expected, narcissists were more negative in their views of threatening others (compared to a nonthreatening control target). Although threatened narcissists' public evaluations of the target were somewhat less negative than their private evaluations, the public face-to-face feedback given by narcissists was significantly more negative than the feedback offered in any other public condition.

Morf and Rhodewalt (1993) said that the SEM findings suggest a way in which narcissistic concern for the self translates into the disturbed interpersonal relationships characteristic of the narcissistic syndrome. Two additional findings corroborate this speculation. First, Rhodewalt and Morf (1998) reported that narcissists respond to threatening feedback with anger, a finding reminiscent of the "narcissistic rage" so prevalent in the clinical literature. Second, Bushman and Baumeister (1998) recently reported that narcissists respond to threat with greater interpersonal aggression than do less narcissistic individuals.

A different line of research also highlights the narcissist's employment of interpersonal self-esteem regulation. Rhodewalt et al. (1999) have demonstrated that narcissists engage in self-handicapping behavior more routinely than low narcissists. Self-handicaps are impediments to success created by the individual in anticipation of performing (Jones & Berglas, 1978). The self-handicap permits one to externalize failure and claim added credit for success. Several aspects of our findings are noteworthy. First, self-handicapping is thought to be in the service of protecting positive but uncertain self-conceptions. Based on evidence of the narcissistic self-aggrandizing style reviewed previously, we suspect that narcissists create for themselves the type of noncontingent success history that promotes concern about future performance and thus fosters the motivation to self-handicap. Second, Rhodewalt et al. (1999) manipulated whether the handicap was public or private, and this manipulation had no effect on the self-handicapping behavior of narcissists. Self-handicapping among narcissists appears to be in the service of defensive self-deception rather than self-presentation. Finally, other research has found that observers of self-handicapping targets do not like them (Rhodewalt, Sanbonmatsu, Feick, Tschanz, & Waller, 1995). Thus, narcissists' propensity to engage in self-handicapping is another factor that is likely to contribute to strained interpersonal relationships.

In sum, there is accumulating evidence that narcissists are actively engaged in manipulating their social interactions so as to generate positive or at least nonthreatening information about the self. Moreover, these efforts are in the service of being admired rather than adored, which has the effect of eroding the quality of the very relationships upon which they are so reliant.

Interpersonal Self-Construction and the Narcissistic Self

The social cognitive self-regulatory model of narcissism depicted in Figure 9.1 and sketched out in this chapter was a starting point in my attempt to study motivated interpersonal self-construction. As noted previously, the model served a heuristic function in guiding research, and I believe that it has productively served its purpose. A number of findings corroborate the view that the narcissist's sense of self is tied to on-line feedback from others. There is also evidence that narcissists attempt to manipulate this social feedback in the service of self-aggrandizement. More generally, the research informs us about the pitfalls of investment in the self and reliance on others to support that investment.

But it is evident that some revision of the model is in order. In this concluding section, I will describe a revised framework suggested by our research to date. It does not appear accurate to characterize narcissism as a fundamental deficiency in self-knowledge availability or accessibility. Rather, the findings suggest that a more active set of processes contribute to the narcissist's dependence on and sensitivity to social feedback. The research indicates that narcissists scan their social contexts for evidence that supports their inflated sense of self. These *positive self-illusions* are often constructed in the absence of objective evidence. The narcissistic self-enhancement bias (Gabriel et al., 1994; John & Robins, 1994) and self-aggrandizing attributional style (Rhodewalt & Morf, 1995, 1998) contribute to the lack of contingency between behavior and self-knowledge, accomplishment and claim. In the absence of objective evidence of self-worth, the narcissist turns to social reality for confirmation. Here the narcissist actively manipulates, or at least attempts to manipulate, his or her social interactions to create the self-verifying reflected appraisals.

These self-evaluative and interpersonal processes should combine with several consequences. First, the narcissist's sense of self should be positive but fragile, and subject to self-doubt and uncertainty, because it is based on dubious interpretations of ambiguous objective feedback. Moreover, the very act of social self-construction should introduce complications in the life of the narcissist. It is likely that repeated attempts to self-aggrandize undermine social relationships and create conflict. A separate problem is caused by the fact that the very act of eliciting social feedback calls into question the veracity of that feedback. In a sense, narcissists must discount positive feedback because of the hand they had in its generation. This fact may account for why the narcissist is only momentarily satisfied by acclaim and accomplishment. Each success requires replication in order to clarify its meaning. In the end, the narcissist must maintain the cycle of social self-construction in order to socially verify the desired self-image. Mapping this cycle and understanding its consequences is the challenge of our present research.

The "Isotope" Approach to the Social Mind: Tracking Cognition, Motivation, and Interpersonal Behavior

The focus of this chapter has been on the application of social cognitive and motivational concepts and research paradigms to the understanding of narcissistic thought and behavior. I would like to conclude by suggesting that individual differences in narcissism provide a vehicle by which one may study the dynamic interplay among the cognitive self, motivation, and interpersonal behavior. Just as the physician introduces radioactive material into the body to track physical systems, the use of individual differences in narcissism as a "hot marker" of ego involvement, reactivity to social feedback, and sensitivity to social context may be useful to a number of researchers represented in this volume. For example, Andersen and Berenson's social cognitive model of transference (this volume) portrays a self that is highly context bound. I have suggested that narcissists' self-aggrandizing attributional style and indiscriminate pandering for positive social feedback create a self that is very context dependent. Narcissists also display exaggerated emotional reactions to their relationship partners. Thus, a consideration of individual differences in narcissism may provide a tool for examining the process of emotional reactivity, cognition, and transference, just as the phenomenon of transference may provide a useful venue for the study of narcissism. Likewise, the examination of the role of narcissism in the study of strategic self-presentation (Tice & Faber, this volume), the interpersonal aspects of self-esteem (Schütz, this volume), and emotion and interpersonal behavior (Forgas, this volume) would undoubtedly offer insight into the bridges between individual difference and social and personality processes.

References

Akhtar, S., & Thompson, J. A. (1982). Overview: Narcissistic personality disorder. *American Journal of Psychiatry, 139,* 12–20.

American Psychiatric Association. (1980). *Diagnostic and statistical manual of mental disorders* (3rd ed.) [DSM-III].

American Psychiatric Association. (1986). *Diagnostic and statistical manual of mental disorders* (3rd ed. rev.) [DSM-III-K]. Washington, DC: Author.

American Psychiatric Association. (1994). *Diagnostic and statistical manual of mental disorders* (4th ed.) [DSM-IV]. Washington, DC: Author.

Bach, S. (1977). On the narcissistic state of consciousness. *International Journal of Psycho-Analysis, 58,* 209–233.

Bradley, G. W. (1978). Self-serving biases in the attribution process: A reexamination of the fact or fiction question. *Journal of Personality and Social Psychology, 36,* 56–71.

Bushman, B., & Baumeister, R. F. (1998). Threatened egotism, narcissism, self-esteem, and direct and displaced aggression: Does self-love or self-hate lead to violence? *Journal of Personality and Social Psychology, 75,* 219–229.

Campbell, J. D. (1990). Self-esteem and clarity of the self-concept. *Journal of Personality and Social Psychology, 59,* 538–549.

Cooper, A. (1985). Narcissism. In A. P. Morrison (Ed.), *Essential papers on narcissism* (pp. 112–143). New York: New York University Press.

Costa, P., & McCrea, R. (1985). *The NEO-PI/FFI manual supplement*. Odessa, FL: Psychological Assessment Resources.

Donahue, E. M., Robins, R. W., Roberts, B. W., & John, O. P. (1993). The divided self: Concurrent and longitudinal effects of psychological adjustment and social roles on self-concept differentiation. *Journal of Personality and Social Psychology, 64*, 834–846.

Ellis, H. (1898). Autoeroticism: A psychological study. *Alienist and Neurologist, 19*, 260–299.

Emmons, R. A. (1984). Factor analysis and construct validity of the Narcissistic Personality Inventory. *Journal of Personality Assessment, 48*, 291–300.

Emmons, R. A. (1987). Narcissism: Theory and measurement. *Journal of Personality and Social Psychology, 52*, 11–17.

Gabriel, M. T., Critelli, J. W., & Ee, J. (1994). Narcissistic illusions in self-evaluations of intelligence and attractiveness. *Journal of Personality, 62*, 143–155.

John, O. P., & Robins, R. (1994). Accuracy and bias in self-perception: Individual differences in self-enhancement and the role of narcissism. *Journal of Personality and Social Psychology, 66*, 206–219.

Jones, E. E., & Berglas, S. (1978). Control of attributions about the self through self-handicapping strategies: The appeal of alcohol and the role of underachievement. *Personality and Social Psychology Bulletin, 4*, 200–206.

Kernberg, O. F. (1976). *Borderline conditions and pathological narcissism*. New York: Jason Aronson.

Kernberg, O. F. (1980). *Internal world and external reality*. New York: Jason Aronson.

Kernis, M. H. (1993). The roles of stability and level of self-esteem in psychological functioning. In R. Baumeister (Ed.), *Self-esteem: The puzzle of low self-regard* (pp. 167–182). New York: Plenum.

Kernis, M. H., Cornell, D. P., Sun, C. R., Berry, A. J., & Harlow, T. (1993). There's more to self-esteem than whether it is high or low: The importance of stability of self-esteem. *Journal of Personality and Social Psychology, 65*, 1190–1204.

Kernis, M. H., Grannemann, B. D., & Barclay, L. C. (1989). Stability and level of self-esteem as predictors of anger arousal and hostility. *Journal of Personality and Social Psychology, 56*, 1013–1023.

Kernis, M. H., & Sun, C.-R. (1994). Narcissism and reactions to interpersonal feedback. *Journal of Research in Personality, 28*, 4–13.

Kohut, H. (1971). *The analysis of the self*. New York: International Universities Press.

Linville, P. W. (1985). Self-complexity and affective extremity: Don't put all of your eggs in one cognitive basket. *Social Cognition, 3*, 94–120.

Linville, P. W., & Carlston, D. (1994). Social cognition and the self. In P. Devine, D. L. Hamilton, & T. Ostrom, (Eds.), *Social cognition: Its impact on social psychology* (pp. 143–193). San Diego, CA: Academic Press.

Lord, C. G., Deforges, D. M., Chacon, S., Pere, G., & Clubb, R. (1992). Reflections on reputation in the process of self-evaluation. *Social Cognition, 10*, 2–29.

Miller, D. T., & Ross, M. (1975). Self-serving biases in the attribution of causality: Fact or fiction? *Psychological Bulletin, 82*, 213–225.

Morf, C. C., & Rhodewalt, F. (1993). Narcissism and self-evaluation maintenance: Explorations in object relations. *Personality and Social Psychology Bulletin, 19,* 668–676.

Pulver, S. (1970). Narcissism: The term and concept. *Journal of the American Psyho-Analytic Association, 18,* 319–341.

Raskin, R., & Hall, C. S. (1979). A narcissistic personality inventory. *Psychological Reports, 45,* 590.

Raskin, R., & Hall, C. S. (1981). The narcissistic personality inventory: Alternative form reliability and further evidence of construct validity. *Journal of Personality Assessment, 45,* 159–162.

Raskin, R., Novacek, J., & Hogan, R. (1991a). Narcissism, self-esteem, and defensive self-enhancement. *Journal of Personality, 59,* 20–38.

Raskin, R., Novacek, J., & Hogan, R. (1991b). Narcissistic self-esteem management. *Journal of Personality and Social Psychology, 60,* 911–918.

Raskin, R., & Shaw, R. (1988). Narcissism and the use of personal pronouns. *Journal of Personality, 56,* 393–404.

Raskin, R., & Terry, H. (1988). A principal-components analysis of the Narcissistic Personality Inventory and further evidence of its construct validity. *Journal of Personality and Social Psychology, 54,* 890–902.

Reich, A. (1960). Pathologic forms of self-esteem regulation. *Psychoanalytic Study of the Child, 18,* 218–238.

Rhodewalt, F., & Eddings, S. (2000). *Motivated memory distortions: Do narcissists reinvent their pasts?* Manuscript in preparation.

Rhodewalt, F., Madrian, J. C., & Cheney, S. (1998). Narcissism, self-knowledge organization, and emotional reactivity: The effect of daily experiences on self-esteem and affect. *Personality and Social Psychology Bulletin, 24,* 75–87.

Rhodewalt, F., & Morf, C. C. (1995). Self and interpersonal correlates of the Narcissistic Personality Inventory: A review and new findings. *Journal of Research in Personality, 29,* 1–23.

Rhodewalt, F., & Morf, C. C. (1998). On self-aggrandizement and anger: A temporal analysis of narcissism and affective reactions to success and failure. *Journal of Personality and Social Psychology, 74,* 672–685.

Rhodewalt, F., & Regalado, M. (1996). *NPI-defined narcissism and the structure of the self.* Unpublished data, University of Utah.

Rhodewalt, F., Sanbonmatsu, D., Feick, D., Tschanz, B., & Waller, A. (1995). Self-handicapping and interpersonal trade-offs: The effects of claimed self-handicaps on observers' performance evaluations and feedback. *Personality and Social Psychology Bulletin, 21,* 1042–1050.

Rhodewalt, F., Tragakis, M., & Finnerty, J. (1999). *Narcissism and self-handicapping: Linking self-aggrandizement to behavior.* Manuscript submitted for publication.

Showers, C. (1992a). Evaluatively integrative thinking about characteristics of the self. *Personality and Social Psychology Bulletin, 18,* 719–729.

Showers, C. (1992b). Compartmentalization of positive and negative self-knowledge: Keeping bad apples out of the bunch. *Journal of Personality and Social Psychology, 62,* 1036–1049.

Smith, T. W., & Frohm, K. D. (1985). What's so unhealthy about hostility? Construct validity and psychosocial correlates of the Cook-Medley Ho scale. *Health Psychology, 4,* 503–520.

Swann, W. B. (1983). Self-verification: Bringing social reality into harmony with the self. In J. Suls & A. G. Greenwald (Eds.), *Psychological perspectives on the self* (Vol. 2, pp. 33–66). Hillsdale, NJ: Erlbaum.

Tesser, A. (1988). Toward a self-evaluation maintenance model of social behavior. In L. Berkowitz (Ed.), *Advances in experimental social psychology* (Vol. 21, pp. 181–227). San Diega, CA: Academic Press.

Tschanz, B. T., & Rhodewalt, F. (in press). Autobiography, reputation, and the self: On the role of evaluative valence and self-consistency of the self-relevant information. *Journal of Experimental Social Psychology.*

Watson, P. J., Taylor, D., & Morris, R. J. (1987). Narcissism, sex roles, and self-functioning. *Sex Roles, 16,* 335–350.

Westen, D. (1990). The relations among narcissism, egocentrism, self-concept, and self-esteem: Experimental, clinical, and theoretical considerations. *Psychoanalysis and Contemporary Thought, 13,* 183–239.

10. Uncertainty Orientation and the Social Mind: Individual Differences in the Interpersonal Context

RICHARD M. SORRENTINO, GORDON HODSON, AND GÜNTER L. HUBER

Given the contents of this book, it is clear that interest in intragroup, intergroup, and interpersonal relations is again on the rise. We are excited not only about this resurgence itself, but also about the key role awarded to uncertainty in these phenomena. In the area of interpersonal relations, for instance, Berger and Calabrese (1975) argue that the entire goal of interpersonal communication is to reduce uncertainty about both the message conveyed and the relations between the communicators. Holmes and Rempel (1989) view uncertainty reduction as the central goal in establishing trust between partners. A strong contingent of social identity researchers (e.g., Turner, Haslam, McGarty, Oakes, and Hogg) are continuing from where Tajfel left off. These theorists argue that perceptions of ingroups and outgroups are based on our need to form a strong (and positive) sense of self and group identity. In other words, perceptions of ingroups and outgroups aid in dealing with uncertainty about who we are. In the area of group dynamics Hogg and Abrams (1993; Hogg, this volume) perceive uncertainty reduction as the central goal of group membership, achieved via ingroup identification. Similarly, Brewer and Harasty (1996) cite uncertainty reduction as a major force behind the need for perceived group entitativity and the feeling of belonging to a group. Other researchers have focused on the resolution of intergroup conflict (e.g. Sherif, Pettigrew, C. Stephan, and W. Stephan). These researchers believe that contact with the outgroup will lead to improved intergroup relations by reducing uncertainty about the outgroup. In this chapter,

Direct all correspondence to Richard Sorrentino, Department of Psychology, University of Western Ontario, London, Ontario, Canada N6A 5C2. email: rsorrent@julian.uwo.ca we will show how the theory of uncertainty orientation (Sorrentino & Roney, 2000; Sorrentino & Short, 1986) may serve as a springboard for relating theories of motivation and cognition to the interpersonal and group context.

The Theory of Uncertainty Orientation

The theory of uncertainty orientation (Sorrentino & Roney, 2000; Sorrentino & Short, 1986) suggests that there are individual differences in self-regulatory styles that are relevant to strategies of coping with uncertainty. At the extreme ends of a continuum are those considered uncertainty-oriented (UOs) or certainty-oriented (COs). For UOs, the preferred method of handling uncertainty is to seek out information and engage in activity that will directly resolve the uncertainty. These are the "need to know" type of people who seek to understand and discover aspects of the self and the social world about which they are uncertain. COs, on the other hand, develop a self-regulatory style that circumvents uncertainty confrontation. Given the choice, such persons will undertake activity that does not involve uncertainty; when confronted with uncertainty, they will rely on others and/or heuristic devices over more direct methods of resolving uncertainty (such as systematically processing the uncertain information). Although UOs generally prefer to handle uncertainty by attaining clarity and COs prefer to handle it by maintaining clarity, this is not always the case. In situations where persons are negatively motivated (e.g., where persons are also afraid of failure or social rejection), their preference for uncertainty or certainty will actually enhance their negative motivation (see Sorrentino & Roney, 2000; Sorrentino, Walker, Hodson, & Roney, in press). It is only in situations where persons' motivational state is normally positive that the UOs and COs will engage their defining self-regulatory styles (more on this later).

Finally, it is important to note that the theory of uncertainty orientation relies on a broad definition of uncertainty, as specified by Kagan (1972). Kagan considered uncertainty reduction a primary motive, with uncertainty originating from incompatibility between (a) two cognitions, (b) a cognition and experience, or (c) a cognition and a behavior, or simply as the inability to predict the future. Using this definition of uncertainty, and the preceding distinction between UOs and COs, our research group has published several studies along two main streams of research: (a) a performance model of achievement behavior and (b) an information processing model (see Sorrentino, 1996; Sorrentino, Raynor, Zubek, & Short, 1990; Sorrentino & Short, 1986). As we shall attempt to demonstrate here, both models have implications for the interpersonal and group contexts. In what follows, we shall show how the theory of uncertainty orientation may be considered in terms of close relationships, cooperative learning, groupthink, persuasion, and ingroup favoritism specifically, and categorization and identification processes more generally.

Uncertainty Orientation and Close Relationships

Upon investigating the interpersonal context, we were excited to find that the domain of trust and close relationships abounds with the concept of uncertainty (see Sorrentino, Holmes, Hanna, & Sharp, 1995). Some authors have argued that coping with uncertainty is a critical challenge in relationships and serves as a major motivational force in shaping individuals' mental representations of their partners (cf., Brehm, 1988; Brickman, 1987; Holmes & Rempel, 1989; Murray & Holmes, 1993). Accordingly, trust is the antithesis of doubt, and is conceputalized as a perceived state of security that marks at least a temporary resolution of uncertainty (Sorrentino et al., 1995).

In the Sorrentino et al. (1995) study, 77 couples living together participated in a three-part investigation. They first completed the uncertainty orientation measure (Sorrentino, Roney, & Hanna, 1992) and various other measures such as those dealing with trust and psychological well-being. In Part 2, individuals recorded their descriptions and ratings of any "emotionally significant" interpersonal events that occurred during each of 12 recording days extending over a 3-week period. Daily summary ratings of mood and relationship satisfaction were also recorded. In Part 3, a positive and a negative event were randomly selected from individuals' diaries. Approximately 5 weeks after the target events had occurred, participants were given brief descriptions of each event, in their own words, and asked to recall their feelings about and attributions for each event at the time it had occurred.

As expected, there was a quadratic relation between uncertainty orientation and trust. UOs were significantly more likely to have *moderate* levels of trust than COs, and COs were higher in both low and high levels of trust. This is the same pattern we found in our research on risk-taking (Sorrentino, Hewitt, & Raso-Knott, 1992). Given that moderate risk is the most uncertain outcome, UOs should prefer moderate risk to low or high risk, where as COs should prefer low *or* high risk to moderate risk. Here we see that this pattern translates into trust in close relationships. UOs, being hypothesis testers (see Roney & Sorrentino, 1995), apparently continue to test their relationship with their partner and avoid absolute statements about their trust for their partner. COs, on the other hand, find ambiguity regarding their partner an anathema and avoid moderate trust or ambivalence toward their partner. Interestingly, it was also found that for UO females, low trust was associated with the most negative psychological symptoms (psychoticism, neuroticism, depression, phobic anxiety, obsessive-compulsive behavior, and overall psychopathology), whereas symptoms under moderate trust typically resembled those for high trust. For CO females, moderate trust is associated with the most severe symptoms, whereas symptoms under low and high trust are similarly less severe. In other words, it is in the moderate trust range that CO women report the highest levels of psychological disturbance. Although males did not show direct evidence of psychological disturbance across levels of trust, CO males showed evidence of such disturbance indirectly on several measures when they were ambivalent toward their partners. Finally, when asked to recall instances listed in their diaries earlier, and to report their feelings regarding those instances at the time, both CO men and CO women used their current feeling of trust for their partner as a heuristic device, distorting their memories of the actual situation to be consistent with their current level of trust. UO men and women showed no evidence of memory distortion or reliance on heuristics.

Subsequent research by Carswell and Sorrentino (2000) expanded on this research by including adult attachment styles as part of their research. They not only replicated the findings for uncertainty orientation and trust in long-term relationships, but also found that differences in trust and ratings of relationship satisfaction between securely and insecurely attached adults were most pronounced under conditions congruent with a person's uncertainty orientation. That is, for UOs, those who were securely attached had the greatest trust in and satisfaction with their partners, and those who were insecurely attached had the lowest trust in their partners when they were uncertain about their relationship. For COs, these differences were greatest when they were certain about their relationship. These results are similar to our findings in the achievement domain, where differences between success-oriented and failure-threatened individuals are heightened under conditions that are congruent with their uncertainty orientation (see Sorrentino & Roney, 1986; Sorrentino, Short, & Raynor, 1984).

Uncertainty Orientation and Cooperative Learning

Our research program has recently extended to the domain of group processes. We initially noted that in the education literature, many theorists embrace the idea that course instruction should arouse epistemic curiosity in students. Drawing on ideas from Berlyne (1960), Vygotsky (1962), Piaget (1972), and Weiner (1972), one could argue that teachers should encourage self-discovery through group-learning methods, conflict situations, or situations involving pure uncertainty, in which students should be more motivated to learn. Such approaches therefore argue that uncertainty about the self and the environment is motivation to *all* students.

Huber, Sorrentino, Davidson, Epplier, and Roth (1992) conducted a series of studies to discover if there are, in fact, individual differences in the preferences, learning, and enjoyment of cooperative learning over other, more traditional forms of instruction. These studies employed Aronson's (1978, 1984) jigsaw method, which requires participants to complete individual assignments and to regroup later to work as a team. This introduces a high potential for self-discovery and uncertainty. In Study 1, samples of university students in Canada, Germany, and Iran preferred cooperative learning to competitive, individualistic, traditional styles of learning. These data are generally consistent with those from Australia (Owens, 1983) and the United States (Johnson, Johnson, & Anderson, 1978). The results, however, are subsumed by a predicted higher-order uncertainty orientation by learning style pattern of interaction ($p < .001$), in which the preference for cooperative over traditional learning styles was greater for UOs than for COs.

Huber et al. (1992) went on to examine attitudes toward the jigsaw method itself more closely. Study 2 addressed attitudes toward different learning situations, Study 3 addressed performance in different learning situations, and Study 4 placed actual student teachers in a jigsaw-type situation. Study 2 essentially replicated Study 1 with four classrooms of *Hauptschule* (high school). In addition to replicating Study 1, Huber et al. found that after 5–8 weeks of learning cooperatively in teams, UOs were more positive about the learning situation

Table 10.1. *Mean Perfomance Scores with Traditional (Trad) Versus Cooperative (Coop) Teaching for UO Versus CO Students*

	Term Tests		Final Exam		Final Grade	
	Trad	*Coop*	*Trad*	*Coop*	*Trad*	*Coop*
UO (*n* = 12)	68.33	71.25	68.83	71.17	72.00	75.17
CO (*n* = 13)	60.76	57.11	61.23	57.31	68.15	66.76

Source: "Uncertainty Orientation and Cooperative Learning: Individual Differences Within and Across Cultures," by G. L. Huber, R. M. Sorrentino, M. A. Davidson, R. Epplier, and J. W. H. Roth, 1992, *Learning and Individual Differences, 4*, p. 14. Copyright 1992 by JAI Press, Inc. Adapted with permission.

than COs overall. UOs also reported more gains from "learning in their own way" and "finding their own solutions," whereas CO students gained less.

Study 3 was conducted in Canada. Students were taught part of a real science course using the jigsaw method. Individual performance was assessed through term tests throughout the 8-week program, final exams for each term, and a final grade given for that term. The final grade included other aspects of the student's behavior (e.g., turning in homework) in addition to actual performance. Huber et al. (1992) compared the performance of students in these cooperative learning sessions with their scores from the previous term, when a traditional science course was taught by the same instructor.

Table 10.1 presents the mean performance scores for Uncertainty Orientation × Teaching Type combinations on the three measures of performance. Note first that UOs performed better than COs, regardless of the teaching technique employed. This probably reflects the fact that this performance is in a learning context, which may favor UOs in general. More important, however, the performance scores of UOs are even higher using the cooperative jigsaw method than the traditional expository teaching techniques on all three performance indices. Cooperative learning situations are thus better than traditional expository techniques for UOs. What is of major significance, however, is the performance of the CO students. Note that their performance is *lower* under the jigsaw method than with traditional techniques.

Huber et al. (1992, Study 4) found that UO teachers were quite receptive to cooperative learning methods but that CO teachers were very resistant to such teaching styles. If CO student teachers have such negative attitudes about their own role in a cooperative learning situation, then we must ask how we can expect them to use cooperative learning strategies successfully in their own classrooms. Huber and colleagues believe that CO teachers should be less likely to use cooperative learning techniques and, if forced to do so, may use them to the detriment of the students (see Huber & Roth, 1988, for case studies of UO and CO teachers and their students).

In sum, the research by Huber et al. (1992) has serious implications for those advocating discovery-based learning through team methods (in general) or the jigsaw method (specifically). It appears that only UOs would benefit from this approach. More important, COs might actually suffer under these approaches compared to more traditional expository methods of teaching. One can only wonder whether the jigsaw method, originally developed as a tool for reducing prejudice, might in fact do more harm than good for COs in that domain as well.

Uncertainty Orientation and Groupthink

Given that uncertainty orientation plays an important role in how we view significant others in the interpersonal domain, it was a natural progression to tackle some of the hard issues in the field of group dynamics. One of our favorite theories, albeit sadly lacking in empirical support, is that of *groupthink* (Janis, 1982). According to Janis, groups succumb to groupthink when they are more motivated to seek concurrence on a decision than assess critically the full range of options and information available to them. Specifically, groupthink is defined as the "deterioration of mental efficiency, reality testing, and moral judgment that results from in-group pressures" (Janis, 1982, p. 9). This is portrayed as an unconscious process in which pressures toward group unity take precedence over rational decision making. Such poor decision making is usually "ripe" under conditions combining closed (or directive) leadership styles and high group cohesion.

As with the jigsaw method discussed earlier, there is no consistent empirical evidence supporting the groupthink concept (see Hodson & Sorrentino, 1997, for a review). Hodson and Sorrentino (1997) argued that individual differences in uncertainty orientation might help clarify the situation for the following reasons. When groupthink occurs, information is processed in a biased manner. We reasoned that differences in one's uncertainty orientation should determine the degree of influence of open (i.e., nondirective) and closed (i.e., directive) leaders. By stating their opinions early and establishing a group norm, closed leaders should provide more certainty to the group dynamic than open leaders. Open leaders, by helping to avoid the establishment of an early group norm, increase the likelihood that new information will be disclosed. Given that COs are more likely to defer to the expert's opinion under high (vs. low) relevance situations (Sorrentino, Bobocel, Gitta, Olson, & Hewitt, 1988, Study 2), and that CO students show a stronger preference for the more directive nature of the leader (or teacher) than do UOs (Huber et al., 1992), it was predicted that although closed leadership would lead to more groupthink and biased decision making than open leadership overall, this difference would be greater for CO than UO groups, and this pattern would be greater under high than low cohesion conditions.

Sixty-eight four-person groups (introductory psychology students) conducted a legal decision-making task (based on Thibaut & Walker, 1975). Three of the group members were homogeneous with regard to uncertainty orientation (i.e., UO or CO), and the leader, for control reasons, was always moderate in uncertainty orientation. From a bogus questionnaire administered in pretesting, group members were led to believe that their group was either high or low in cohesion. High-cohesion groups were told that they were selected to work together because they shared common personalities, interests, attitudes, goals, opinions, and group dynamic preferences, and that their groups were special and likely to be cohesive. Low-cohesion groups were told that they were randomly selected to work together.

Participants were instructed to play the role of legal investigators, with one of them being assigned to play the role of discussion leader. Groups acted on behalf of a legal firm representing the plaintiff, with the goal of assessing the lawfulness of the defendant's actions and deciding whether or not the case should proceed to court. The experimental design was a 2 (Uncertainty/Certainty Orientation) × 2 (Closed/Open Leadership) × 2 (Low/High Group Cohesiveness) between-groups factorial design with 7–11 groups per cell.

Each group was led to believe that the assigned leader had demonstrated during pretesting that he or she possessed characteristics most suitable for the group leader role, when in reality the leader was simply a moderate in uncertainty orientation. Each group member was given separate information about the case, which, if considered, should lead them to settle out of court. The leaders' information was biased toward going to court. Leaders in the open and closed leadership conditions were instructed to state their opinions early or late in the discussion, respectively. Groups were given 20 minutes to complete the task.

Hodson and Sorrentino (1997) found a marginally significant effect ($p = .07$) in that groups with closed leaders made more biased decisions (23 out of 32), whereas open-leader groups were equally likely to make either biased or unbiased decisions. This is consistent with Janis's (1982) theory. This effect is due mostly to the CO groups, however. In closed-leadership conditions, 14 out of 17 CO groups reached a decision biased in the direction of the leader's information. Under open leadership, only 7 of the 18 groups reached this biased decision. The UO groups demonstrated little change as a function of leadership style, with groups being somewhat in favor of going to court in either case (9 of 15 for closed leadership, 11 of 18 for open leadership). This is consistent with past findings in situations where UOs preferred the uncertainty associated with risky behavior (Sorrentino, Hewitt, & Raso-Knott, 1992) such as going to court. As predicted, this Uncertainty Orientation × Leadership pattern of interaction was found to be significant ($p < .05$).

Analyzing the consideration of case facts by group members also yielded interesting results. These analyses dealt with the extent to which groups devoted attention to the facts of the case. In short, uncertainty orientation interacted with cohesion: COs increased their discussion of case facts (regardless of the position of the facts argued) under high (vs. low) cohesion, whereas UOs showed a nonsignificant tendency in the opposite direction. In retrospect, we suspect that the high-cohesion condition, being manipulated via ingroup similarity, produced a high degree of certainty, motivating COs to consider the facts under these relatively "safe" or related conditions. Results of the Hodson and Sorrentino (1997) study thus provide mixed support for Janis's (1982) groupthink theory, suggesting that group-based personality characteristics, specifically those relating to uncertainty orientation, play a critical role regarding its efficacy.

Categorization, Group Homogeneity Perceptions, and Uncertainty Orientation

More recently, we have turned our attention to the role uncertainty orientation plays in social categorization processes (Hanna & Sorrentino,

2000). One such domain of interest is that of perceptions of group homogeneity. In the absence of a comparison outgroup, self-categorization theory (Turner, Hogg, Oakes, Reicher, & Wetherell, 1987) predicts that people will judge the typicality of traits for group members relative to the self. Because the individual perceives the self as different from others, he or she does not perceive the ingroup as homogeneous. However, when given a basis of comparison with other groups, the individual recognizes his or her strong social identity with the ingroup compared to the outgroup and then perceives the ingroup as homogeneous (see Haslam, Oakes, Turner, & McGarty, 1996). This entire process should work well for a person who is using the group as a source of information relevant to the resolution of uncertainty concerning the self, that is, the UO person. But, as argued earlier, this process does not work well for the CO, because he or she already perceives the ingroup as homogeneous. For the CO, group identity is a source for clarity maintenance, not self-assessment. Indeed, when the CO is asked to compare his or her group with an outgroup, we should see no real change with regard to the ingroup but perhaps an even stronger bias against the outgroup. As predicted, an Uncertainty Orientation × Comparative Context interaction emerged (see Figure 10.1). In accordance with general predictions from self-categorization theory, UOs rated the ingroup as less homogeneous in the within-groups comparison condition (i.e., in the absence of a salient outgroup) than in the between-groups condition. COs behaved in the opposite manner, perceiving their ingroups as highly homogeneous in the within-groups condition, but this perception decreased when the judgment was made in the face of a salient outgroup category. In other words, predictions from self-categorization theory were supported only for UO participants. COs, who saw their ingroup as homogeneous when no comparisons were made with another group, appeared to be confused when forced to make such a comparison.

Social Categorization, Information Processing, and Uncertainty Orientation

Contemporary persuasion models such as the Elaboration Likelihood Model (Petty & Cacioppo, 1981) and the Heuristic-Systematic Model (Chaiken, 1980) have proposed dual-route explanations of attitude change. The central (Petty & Cacioppo, 1981) or systematic (Chaiken, 1980) modes of processing are characterized by careful consideration

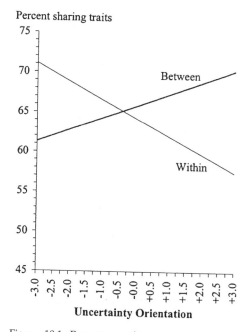

Figure 10.1. Percentage of ingroup members estimated to share typical and positive traits as a function of comparative context (within vs. between) and uncertainty orientation (lower scores = certainty-oriented; higher scores = uncertainty-oriented).

and elaboration of message arguments. These processing styles typically occur under conditions of high personal relevance or importance and result in enduring attitudes with strong attitude–behavior links (see Eagly & Chaiken, 1993). On the other hand, persuasion via the peripheral (Petty & Cacioppo, 1981) or heuristic (Chaiken, 1980) route is much less labor-intensive, arguing that people conserve mental energy whenever possible (Fiske & Taylor, 1991). As a result, when the personal relevance of the situation is low, people should be influenced by factors external to the message arguments (e.g., judgment heuristics, attractiveness of the speaker).

Van Knippenberg (1999, p. 315) asserts that these "cognitive theories of persuasion generally tend to neglect the social context in which persuasion typically takes place" (see also Hogg & Abrams, 1999).[1]

---

[1] Petty and Wegener (1999) argue that perspectives such as these grossly misrepresent and simplify these social cognition theories.

According to Van Knippenberg, these models assume that systematic or central route information processing reflects careful argument scrutiny *regardless* of the message source or social setting. Likewise, heuristic or peripheral route processing is typically characterized by reliance on cues that are *external* to the message, where argument quality is seen to exert less influence. Researchers have begun to question these assumptions. The research presented in this section addresses the impact of the message source (ingroup vs. outgroup) on subsequent information processing.

Mackie and her colleagues (Mackie, Gastardo-Conaco, & Skelly, 1992; Mackie, Worth, & Asuncion, 1990) note that an ingroup category can potentially influence information processing in two very different ways. On the one hand, an ingroup category may serve as a heuristic cue (i.e., a judgment shortcut) concerning the validity of a message. That is, because ingroups are attractive to group members (Kelman, 1961; Pallack, 1983) and provide a socially shared sense of reality (Festinger, 1950; Hardin & Higgins, 1996; Kelman, 1961; Turner et al., 1987), the ingroup category may play a heuristic role in persuasion. Indeed, one could argue that the social identity theory and self-categorization theory perspectives suggest this to be true (e.g., Abrams & Hogg, 1990; Turner et al., 1987). From this perspective, being "correct" in one's judgment and belonging in a group become intertwined, so that the ingroup category provides an easy guideline for judging the acceptance of information and serves to define reality. According to Mullin and Hogg (1998), for instance, the most widely recognized explanation of ingroup favoritism under minimal group situations is social identity theory's position that "group members rely on the category label as a heuristic cue and identify with the minimal categorization" (p. 346). This coincides with Kelman's (1961) position that identifying with an ingroup increases the likelihood of accepting a persuasive message, and this message acceptance may not be based heavily on message content. Although reliance on a group category is an entirely reasonable and appropriate process under certain circumstances (e.g., Haslam et al., 1996), Abrams and Hogg (1990, p. 199) also suggest that "it may be but a short step to argue that social categorization is also heuristic in that it specifies who should and should not be attended to for appropriate information."

On the other hand, an ingroup category might promote the use of systematic information processing. Some have argued that information provided by an ingroup source might be more relevant to the individual (e.g., Festinger, 1950; Mackie et al., 1990, 1992). In line with current models of information processing (e.g., Chaiken, 1980; Petty & Cacioppo, 1981), therefore, high personal relevance should promote the use of careful information processing (given that the resources and capability are present), allowing individuals to distinguish more markedly between strong and weak arguments more for ingroup than outgroup messages, consequently affecting attitudes.

Research by Sorrentino et al. (1988) contested the previously presented models of information processing and showed that only UOs increase their systematic processing and decrease their heuristic processing of information under conditions of high as opposed to low personal relevance. COs actually decrease their systematic processing and increase their heuristic processing under conditions of high as opposed to low personal relevance. Personal relevance here has to do with resolving uncertainty about one's ability (whether or not to take a comprehensive exam in order to graduate).

A recent study by Hodson and Sorrentino (2000b) extended the preceding findings to the group situation. Here, past research informs us that social categorization can create uncertainty when group members disagree with their ingroup (McGarty, Turner, Oakes, & Haslam, 1993; see also Turner, 1985). In addition, group members expect a high degree of similarity with ingroup attitudes and dissimilarity with outgroup attitudes (Allen & Wilder, 1979; Tajfel, Sheikh, & Gardner, 1964; Turner, 1985; Wilder, 1984). An uncertain context can be conceputalized, therefore, as one that is inconsistent with one's expectation based on social categorizations. To the extent that social categorization conflicts can create uncertainty (Turner, 1985) and that uncertainty is the key to group behavior (Hogg & Abrams, 1993; Hogg, this volume), UOs should be the ones to process information systematically. This should be reflected by a marked differentiation between strong and weak arguments (showing increased favorability toward strong arguments) under relatively more uncertain conditions (i.e., when disagreeing with the ingroup and agreeing with the outgroup). Under conditions of relative certainty (i.e., ingroup agreement, outgroup disagreement), UOs should process more heuristically, showing little differentiation between strong and weak arguments. This prediction is in keeping with the work of Driscoll, Hamilton, and Sorrentino (1991), in which UOs showed a marked advantage over COs in the recall of expectancy-incongruent (vs. expectancy-congruent) information, suggesting an increase in processing of the inconsistent information. Following the uncertainty orientation model, COs should behave in a manner opposite to UOs, increasing reliance on systematic processing under certain conditions and increasing heuristic processing under uncertain conditions. These ideas are consistent with the notion that groups serve different functions for different people, with UOs using groups for purposes of discovery and uncertainty resolution and COs using groups as a basis of subjective judgment, particularly under conditions of high uncertainty (see Hodson & Sorrentino, 1999a).

The design of the Hodson and Sorrentino (2000b) study is a 2 (Uncertainty Orientation: CO vs. UO) × 2 (Source: ingroup vs. outgroup) × 2 (Argument Quality: weak vs. strong) × 2 (Position: counterattitudinal vs. proattitudinal) between-participants factorial analysis of variance (ANOVA) design. This study was based largely on Mackie et al. (1990). Participants were told that the Ministry of Education was considering the implementation of comprehensive exams for graduating students. Participants then read weak or strong arguments from an ingroup or outgroup source and rated a variety of dimensions (e.g., favorability of comprehensive exams, the strength of arguments used, qualities of the speaker). These arguments were pro- or counterattitudinal based on initial attitude reports.

Across several measures, support was found for predictions. That is, UOs more strongly favored strong over weak arguments, signaling the use of systematic (vs. heuristic) information processing under conditions of relatively high uncertainty (disagreeing with the ingroup, agreeing with the outgroup) than low uncertainty (agreeing with the ingroup, disagreeing with the outgroup). COs showed the reverse pattern, increasing their systematic processing under certain conditions moreso than uncertain conditions. As seen in Figure 10.2, UOs reported more favorable attitudes following strong than weak arguments, signaling argument scrutiny and systematic processing under high (vs. low) uncertainty. When the situation was more certain and consequently less motivating for UOs, they simply went along with their initial attitudes. COs showed the reverse pattern (see Figure 10.3). In fact, the only significant contrast ($p < .05$) between the strong and weak argument conditions was found under the highest certainty cell (i.e., agreeing with the ingroup). The ratings of message persuasiveness clearly mirror this pattern. Again, UOs rated messages as more persuasive following strong than weak arguments (showing systematic processing) under uncertain (vs. certain) conditions (see Figure 10.4). COs behaved in the opposite manner, demonstrating the greatest strong-versus-weak argu-

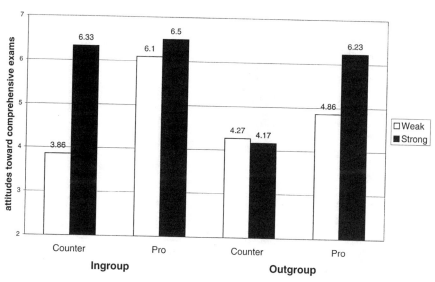

Figure 10.2. UO participants' attitudes toward comprehensive exams as a function of the source and quality of the message and the initial position of the attitude (Pro = proattitudinal; Counter = counterattitudinal).

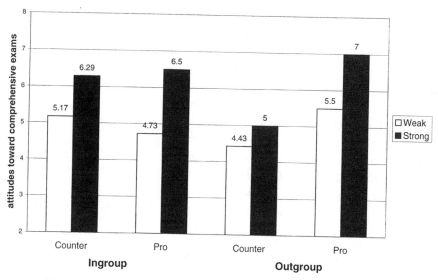

Figure 10.3. CO participants' attitudes toward comprehensive exams as a function of the source and quality of the message and the initial position of the attitude (Pro = proattitudinal; Counter = counterattitudinal).

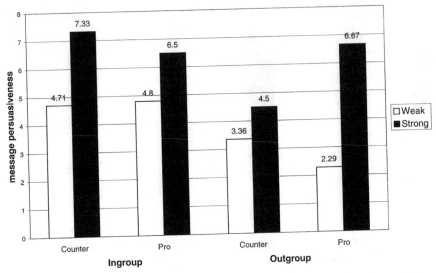

Figure 10.4. UO participants' persuasiveness ratings as a function of the source and quality of the message and the initial position of the attitude (Pro = proattitudinal; Counter = counterattitudinal).

ment differentiation under conditions of high (vs. low) certainty (i.e., ingroup agreement, outgroup disagreement; see Figure 10.5).

The results of Hodson and Sorrentino (2000b) reveal that, as expected, the nature of information processing following reception of ingroup or outgroup messages depends on the uncertainty orientation of audience members. In keeping with the uncertainty orientation model, UOs processed information more systematically under conditions of uncertainty, whereas COs increased such processing under conditions of certainty. This would seem to have some serious implications for theories that espouse the significance of ingroups or outgroups in determining the type of information processing. Obviously, both the position of the sender and the uncertainty orientation of the receiver have much to do with how one handles the message. That is, how a person deals with uncertainty derived from violations of socially based expectations appears to affect the influence process.

Uncertainty Reduction in Groups: The Role of Categorization

The Hodson and Sorrentino (2000b) study demonstrated the importance of social identity in the creation of uncertainty. A study by

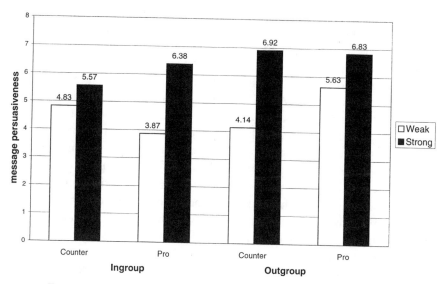

Figure 10.5. CO participants' persuasiveness ratings as a function of the source and quality of the message and the initial position of the attitude (Pro = proattitudinal; Counter = counterattitudinal).

Hodson and Sorrentino (2000a) focused on how group members use social categories as decision-making tools when faced with uncertainty not directly related to group membership. Tajfel (1969; Tajfel & Billig, 1974) initially held that stereotyping and other forms of intergroup behavior might represent the motivated need to search for coherence (i.e., a set of consolidated and consistent ideas about a social category). Tajfel (1972) soon replaced his emphasis on the coherence-seeking motive with the self-enhancement motive, arguing that group members make their ingroup category distinct from the outgroup category along dimensions that are relevant and positive in terms of social (and self) identity. Among others, Abrams and Hogg (1988) have questioned the motivational role of self-esteem in intergroup behavior, raising the issue of whether self-esteem is a cause or a consequence of categorization and intergroup behavior (see also Hogg & Abrams, 1993; Hogg & Sunderland, 1991; Jetten, Spears, & Manstead, 1997; Lemyre & Smith, 1985; Lindeman, 1997; Rubin & Hewstone, 1998). Abrams and Hogg (1988, p. 328) conclude that "another motive which deserves attention is the search for meaning." This view reasserts Tajfel's (1969) view that the motive for group structure or integrity is fundamental to group behavior. From this perspective, group identities primarily function to provide meaning and coherence in the social environment. This conclusion is generally in keeping with the self-categorization perspective that social identities are meaningful because they help individuals make sense of the world.

Hogg and colleagues (see Hogg, this volume; Hogg & Abrams, 1993; Hogg & Mullin, 1999; Mullin & Hogg, 1998) have thus reintroduced the motive for coherence (or uncertainty reduction) in social identification processes. They argue that all people seek certainty, achieved via identification with an ingroup. Other motives (e.g., self-esteem, affiliation) are considered secondary motives under the auspices of uncertainty reduction. This model, based on self-categorization theory (Turner et al., 1987), stipulates that under conditions of high uncertainty, group members should identify with their ingroups and engage in intergroup behavior (e.g., ingroup bias or favoritism) in order to reduce uncertainty.

Using the so-called Tajfel matrices (resource allocation tasks), ingroup bias has indeed been found primarily under conditions of high uncertainty (Grieve & Hogg, 1999, Expts. 1 and 2; Hogg & Grieve, in press; Mullin & Hogg, 1998; but see Tajfel & Billig, 1974). The mechanisms underlying this process, however, remain unclear. Categorization under uncertainty was accompanied by increased identification in some studies (Grieve & Hogg, 1999, Expts. 1 and 2; Mullin & Hogg, 1998) but not in others (Hogg & Grieve, in press) and failed to serve as a mediator in others (e.g., Mullin & Hogg, 1998). Reduced uncertainty was found in one study (Hogg & Grieve, in press) but not in others (Grieve & Hogg, 1999, Expt 1; Mullin & Hogg, 1998). In addition, Hogg and Grieve (in press) found that ingroup bias was accompanied by increased self-esteem, whereas other investigators did not (Grieve & Hogg, 1999, Expts. 1 and 2; Mullin & Hogg, 1998).

We anticipated that uncertainty orientation would moderate the process and help us to understand the processes and mechanisms underlying such discriminatory behavior. Recall that under conditions of high uncertainty, UOs increase their use of careful, systematic processing, whereas COs increase their use of heuristic processing (e.g., Sorrentino et al., 1988, Expts. 1 and 2). Hodson and Sorrentino (1997) found COs to be highly biased by group leaders (a possible heuristic cue, e.g., "leaders are to be trusted") when making decisions. Considering that leaders are often perceived as prototypes for social categories (Fielding & Hogg, 1997), it stands to reason that COs should be more likely than UOs to turn to an ingroup category when faced with a situation demanding the resolution of uncertainty.

Hodson and Sorrentino (2000a) therefore conducted a study based on Mullin and Hogg (1998). The experiment was a 2 (Uncertainty Orientation: CO vs. UO) × 2 (Categorization: categorized vs. uncategorized) × 2 (Task Uncertainty: low vs. high) between-participants design. It was expected that ingroup bias, reflected by ingroup favoritism, would be stronger for categorized than uncategorized participants, and that this difference would be greater under conditions of uncertainty than certainty, in keeping with findings by Hogg and colleagues. These predictions, however, were expected to apply particularly to the CO person, who should use heuristics (an ingroup favoritism rule of thumb) when the situation is relatively uncertain.

Participants were tested individually, and all privately received the same identification number. They were informed that they would be assigning points to individuals later on. A sample matrix was completed to ensure instruction comprehension. Those in the low-uncertainty condition were given (a) detailed instructions on task requirements; (b) six practice matrices to "familiarize" them with procedures; and (c) instruction that there were no correct answers. In the high-uncertainty condition, participants completed a filler task. Baseline levels of reported uncertainty were collected. Categorized participants were randomly assigned to Group Z (vs. Group Y). This group label appeared on the covers of their booklets (i.e., Z34), and they were asked to remember their group assignment. Uncategorized participants simply kept their original identification number (i.e., #34). Categorized participants allocated points to members of Group Y versus Group Z, whereas uncategorized individuals allocated points to individuals.

A booklet of payment matrices (Tajfel matrices; for more details, see Bourhis, Sachdev, & Gagnon, 1994) was given to each participant, the objective being to allocate points to specific individuals. Each matrix consisted of 13 boxes (or columns), with each box containing two numbers (each number referring to points to be allocated to one each of the individuals listed). Participants selected 1 of 13 boxes as a strategy. One matrix was presented on each page across 12 pages. Tajfel matrices allow researchers to examine different point allocation strategies employed. Three strategies are discriminatory (FAV on P; FAV on MJP; MD on MIP + MJP) and represent Ingroup Bias, whereas three are not (P on FAV; MIP + MJP on MD; MJP on FAV). These strategies are "pitted" against one another, allowing examination of preferred strate-

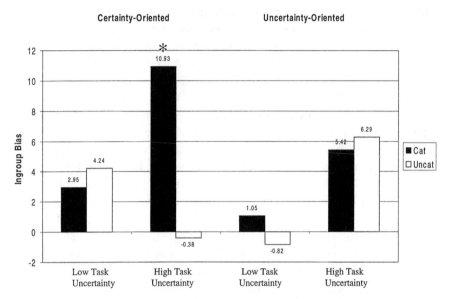

Figure 10.6. Ingroup bias as a function of uncertainty orientation, categorization, and task uncertainty (Cat = categorized; Uncat = uncategorized). *Cell differs from zero. $p < .05$.

gies, reflected in the measurement of *pull scores* (see Bourhis et al., 1994). Upon completion of the matrices, participants rated (9-point rating scales) (a) reported uncertainty (see earlier), (b) ingroup identification (five items), (c) social consciousness (three items), and (d) self-esteem (one item).

The main dependent measure of interest was the extent to which participants adopted allocation strategies in favor of the ingroup (vs. the outgroup). This general ingroup favoritism was an aggregation of the three discriminatory strategies available (FAV on P; FAV on MJP; MD on MIP + MJP). Although a 2 (Uncertainty Orientation: CO vs. UO) × 2 (Categorization: categorized vs. uncategorized) × 2 (Task Uncertainty: low vs. high) ANOVA on this measure revealed no significant interactions, specific comparisons demonstrated significant results in support of predictions.

As predicted, Ingroup Bias was found in only one cell – *when COs were categorized under high task uncertainty* (see Figure 10.6). COs under high Task Uncertainty conditions were the only participants to demonstrate a significant difference in Ingroup Bias between the categorized ($M = 10.93$) and uncategorized ($M = -0.38$) conditions, $t(139) = 1.70$,

Table 10.2. *Mean "Pulls" of Distribution Strategies Selected as a Function of Uncertainty Orientation, Categorization, and Task Uncertainty*

	Certainty-Oriented				Uncertainty-Oriented			
	Low Task Uncertainty		High Task Uncertainty		Low Task Uncertainty		High Task Uncertainty	
Strategies	Uncat	Cat	Uncat	Cat	Uncat	Cat	Uncat	Cat
Parity								
P on FAV	8.77**	7.42**	11.43***	7.6**	7.53*	12.86***	8.47**	7.11*
Discrimination								
FAV on P	.50	.37	.31	6.13‡	0	−.23	1.41	4.16
FAV on MJP	2.29	1.16	1.31	4.67‡	−.35	.73	2.94	.79
MD on								
MIP + MJP	1.45	1.42	−2.0	.13	−.47	.55	1.94	.47
Joint Profit								
MIP + MJP on								
MD	1.00	1.00	−1.13	4.27	2.59	2.73	−.18	.05
MJP on FAV	−1.98	−1.58	1.44	0	.94	.27	−.35	1.00

Note: $*p < .05$, $**p < .01$, $***p < .001$ (two-tailed); $‡p < .02$ (one-tailed) on Wilcoxon Matched Pairs tests. Mean pull scores for each matrix range from −24 to +24. Uncat = uncategorized; Cat = categorized.

$p < .05$ (one-tailed). In fact, the CO Categorized High Uncertainty cell is the only experimental cell with an Ingroup Bias mean significantly greater than zero, showing evidence of a consistent pattern of discriminatory response, $t(14) = 2.08$, $p < .025$ (one-tailed). As predicted, therefore, the only evidence of Ingroup Bias was found for CO participants categorized as group members and finding themselves in a situation of high task uncertainty. The pull scores (see Bourhis et al., 1994; Turner, 1978) shown in Table 10.2 reveal that only COs categorized under high uncertainty showed consistent use of discriminatory strategies for two of the three strategies (FAV on P; FAV on MJP, $ps < .02$), in support of the hypotheses.

No significant interactions were found for Identification, Change in Certainty, or Self-Esteem. A significant three-way interaction for Social Consciousness, $F(1, 136) = 5.98$, $p = .016$, revealed that COs categorized under high uncertainty were particularly conscious of others. Indeed, mediational analyses suggest that Social Consciousness may be a stronger mediator of the Categorization–Bias relationship than Identification under these same conditions.

As predicted, only *COs categorized under high uncertainty* showed ingroup bias via the Tajfel matrices. This favoritism, however, was not accompanied by increased ingroup identification, certainty, or self-esteem. While these findings are contrary to *predictions* of social identity theory (SIT) and self-categorization theory (SCT), they are consistent with some earlier studies by SIT and SCT researchers. A review by Hinkle and Brown (1990) also found little evidence linking ingroup identification and ingroup bias (defined as ingroup positivity; but see criticisms by Perreault & Bourhis, 1999). The present findings suggest the heuristic use of ingroup categorization. That is, a simple "look out for your own" judgment rule appears to have been employed by categorized COs under high uncertainty. Note that ingroup bias was more a function of social consciousness than ingroup identification and that perceptions of experimenter observation did not mediate the effect, ruling out demand concerns. Being conscious of others probably increased the salience of the ingroup heuristic (or norm). This interpretation is consistent with the fact that these COs only employed discriminatory strategies that were least harmful to the outgroup (i.e., no use of MD on MIP + MJP). Not knowing what to do, they adopted a strategy favoring their group. Although UOs showed no consistent ingroup favoritism under these minimal group conditions, they might show such bias under other situations. In the present case, the task uncertainty could not actually be resolved by group membership, possibly defeating the prime objective of group life for UOs.

The Hodson and Sorrentino (2000a) investigation found an ingroup bias strategy only for categorized COs under conditions of uncertainty. The findings conflict with SIT and SCT because (a) personality differences moderated the effect (cf. Abrams & Hogg, 1990; Hogg & Mullin, 1999) and (b) ingroup bias was not accompanied by increased identification, self-esteem, or certainty. We suggest that COs, in a form true to character, employed a simple heuristic (ingroup favoritism) when faced with uncertainty.

General Conclusions

Taking the research we have conducted so far, we are prepared to make these initial conclusions. Ingroups are attractive for COs as a source of subjective judgment and reality. They provide a source of social reality and can be relied upon, like other important heuristics, for guidance as to how one should behave. The primary role of the ingroup for the UO, however, centers on discovery of new aspects of the self, others, and the world, where a group is valued to the extent that it provides this service. Only when the ingroup disconfirms an expectancy is it attended to with great care. Further, it does not appear to be any more valuable to the UO than is an outgroup that also disconfirms its expectancies. In the former case, the ingroup disagrees with the UO; in the latter case, the outgroup agrees.

These ideas are closely related to those presented by Brewer and Harasty (1996, p. 365), who suggest that "perceived entitativity may be greater for certainty-oriented than uncertainty-oriented individuals (Sorrentino & Short, 1986), and . . . that certainty-oriented individuals may be particularly motivated to perceive ingroups as coherent social entities." This is an important link for us. Whereas UOs will engage in group activity as a source of information, COs will engage because the group is an essential source for maintenance and verification of reality and self-identification. Likewise, we predict a greater need for social reality by COs than UOs. Even more intriguing implications, however, emerge for self-categorization theory. Recall that the basic difference we are arguing for between UOs and COs is that whereas UOs utilize the group as a means of *attaining* clarity about the self (i.e., as a source of information about the self), COs utilize the group as a means of *maintaining* clarity about the self (i.e., in order to avoid having to engage in further self-assessment). These notions hinge on the idea of uncertainty. Note that self-categorization theory is essentially a self-assessment theory in which self-categorization is a means of establishing one's social identity. Although self-assessment is a primary goal of UOs, COs avoid it like the plague (so to speak). Whereas UOs want to find out information about the self regardless of the positive or negative implications of the information, COs avoid self-relevant information even in life-threatening situations (see Brouwers & Sorrentino, 1993; Sorrentino & Hewitt, 1984). In fact, they would probably rely on the group's judgment rather than their own in critical situations. If we are correct, then this is the fundamental difference between UOs and COs: the importance of the ingroup as a source of information as opposed to a source of belongingness. As a consequence, there should be fundamental differences in self-categorization processes, information processing of communications, and ingroup biases based on one's cognitive style. We believe that the studies presented in this chapter illustrate the important role of uncertainty orientation for a wide array of social behaviors, including interpersonal trust, cooperative learning, group decision making, information processing, and ingroup favoritism. We also believe that it is but a small step to expand this research to include prejudice and intergroup conflict. Research on these possibilities is underway.

References

Abrams, D., & Hogg, M. A. (1988). Comments on the motivational status of self-esteem in social identity and intergroup discrimination. *European Journal of Social Psychology, 18*, 317–334.

Abrams, D., & Hogg, M. A. (1990). Social identification, self-categorization and social influence. In W. Stroebe & M. Hewstone (Eds.), *European review of social psychology* (Vol. 1, pp. 195–228). Chichester, England: Wiley.

Ainsworth, M., Blehar, M. C., Waters, E., & Wall, S. (1978). *Patterns of attachment: A psychological study of the strange situation.* Hillsdale, NJ: Erlbaum.

Allen, V. L., & Wilder, D. A. (1975). Categorization, belief similarity, and intergroup discrimination. *Journal of Personality and Social Psychology, 32*, 971–977.

Allen, V. L., & Wilder, D. A. (1979). Group categorization and attribution of belief similarity. *Small Group Behavior, 10*, 73–80.

Aronson, E. (1978). *The jigsaw classroom.* Beverly Hills, CA: Sage.

Aronson, E. (1984). Forderung von Schulleistung, Selbstwert und prosozialem Verhalten. In G. L. Huber, S. Rotering-Steinberg, & D. Wahl (Eds.), *Kooperatives lernen* (pp. 48–59). Weinheim: Beltz.

Berger, C. R., & Calabrese, R. (1975). Some explorations in initial interactions and beyond: Toward a developmental theory of interpersonal communication. *Human Communication Research, 1*, 99–112.

Berlyne, D. E. (1960). *Conflict, arousal, curiosity.* New York: McGraw-Hill.

Bourhis, R. Y., Sachdev, I., & Gagnon, A. (1994). Intergroup research with the Tajfel matrices: Methodological notes. In M. P. Zanna & J. M. Olson (Eds.), *The psychology of prejudice: The Ontario symposium* (Vol. 7, pp. 209–232). Hillsdale, NJ: Erlbaum.

Brehm, S. S. (1988). Passionate love. In R. J. Sternberg & M. L. Barnes (Eds.), *The psychology of love* (pp. 232–263). New Haven, CT: Yale University Press.

Brewer, M. B., & Harasty, A. S. (1996). Seeing groups as entities: The role of perceiver motivation. In R. M. Sorrentino & E. T. Higgins (Eds.), *Handbook of motivation and cognition: The interpersonal context* (Vol. 3, pp. 347–370). New York: Guilford Press.

Brickman, P. (1987). *Commitment, conflict, and caring.* Englewood Cliffs, NJ: Prentice-Hall.

Brouwers, M. C., & Sorrentino, R. M. (1993). Uncertainty orientation and protection motivation theory: The role of individual differences in health compliance. *Journal of Personality and Social Psychology, 65*, 102–111.

Carswell, J. J., & Sorrentino, R. M. (2000). *Adult attachment and uncertainty orientation: Affective and informational influences on trust and relationship satisfaction.* Manuscript in preparation.

Chaiken, S. (1980). Heuristic versus systematic information processing and the use of source versus message cues in persuasion. *Journal of Personality and Social Psychology, 39,* 752–766.

Driscoll, D. L., Hamilton, D. M., & Sorrentino, R. M. (1991). Uncertainty orientation and recall of person-descriptive information. *Personality and Social Psychology Bulletin, 17,* 494–500.

Eagly, A. H., & Chaiken, S. (1993). *The psychology of attitudes.* Fort Worth, TX: Harcourt Brace Jovanovich.

Festinger, L. (1950). Informal social communication. *Psychological Review, 57,* 271–282.

Fielding, K. S., & Hogg, M. A. (1997). Social identity, self-categorization, and leadership: A field study of small interactive groups. *Group Dynamics: Theory, Research, and Practice, 1,* 39–51.

Fiske, S. T., & Taylor, S. E. (1991). *Social cognition* (2nd ed.). New York: McGraw-Hill.

Grieve, P., & Hogg, M. A. (1999). Subjective uncertainty and intergroup discrimination in the minimal group situation. *Personality and Social Psychology Bulletin, 25,* 926–940.

Hanna, S. E., & Sorrentino, R. M. (2000). *Personal relevance, comparative context, and uncertainty orientation as determinants of perceived ingroup homogeneity.* Manuscript in preparation.

Hardin, C. D., & Higgins, E. T. (1996). Shared reality: How social verification makes the subjective objective. In R. M. Sorrentino & E. T. Higgins (Eds.), *Handbook of motivation and cognition: The interpersonal context* (Vol. 3, pp. 28–84). New York: Guilford Press.

Haslam, S. A., Oakes, P. J., Turner, J. C., & McGarty, C. (1996). Social identity, self-categorization, and the perceived homogeneity of ingroups and outgroups: The interaction between social motivation and cognition. In R. M. Sorrentino & E. T. Higgins (Eds.), *Handbook of motivation and cognition: The interpersonal context* (Vol. 3, pp. 182–222). New York: Guilford Press.

Hinkle, S., & Brown, R. J. (1990). Intergroup comparisons and social identity: Some links and lacunae. In D. Abrams & M. A. Hogg (Eds.), *Social identity theory: Constructive and critical advances* (pp. 48–70). New York: Harvester-Wheatsheaf.

Hodson, G., & Sorrentino, R. M. (1997). Groupthink and uncertainty orientation: Personality differences in reactivity to the group situation. *Group Dynamics: Theory, Research, and Practice, 1,* 144–155.

Hodson, G., & Sorrentino, R. M. (2000a). *Just who favors the ingroup? Personality differences in reactions to uncertainty in the minimal group paradigm.* Manuscript under review.

Hodson, G., & Sorrentino, R. M. (2000b). *Uncertainty orientation in the group context: Categorization effects on persuasive message processing.* Manuscript under review.

Hogg, M. A., & Abrams, D. (1993). Towards a single-process uncertainty-reduction model of social motivation in groups. In M. A. Hogg & D. Abrams (Eds.), *Group motivation: Social psychological perspectives* (pp. 173–190). London: Harvester-Wheatsheaf.

Hogg, M. A., & Abrams, D. (1999). Social identity and social cognition: Historical background and current trends. In D. Abrams & M. A. Hogg (Eds.), *Social identity and social cognition* (pp. 1–25). Oxford: Basil Blackwell.

Hogg, M. A., & Grieve, P. (in press). Social identity theory and the crisis of confidence in social psychology: A commentary and some research on uncertainty reduction. *Asian Journal of Social Psychology.*

Hogg, M. A., & Mullin, B. A. (1999). Joining groups to reduce uncertainty: Subjective uncertainy reduction and group identification. In D. Abrams & M. A. Hogg (Eds.), *Social identity and social cognition* (pp. 249–279). Oxford: Basil Blackwell.

Hogg, M. A., & Sunderland, J. (1991). Self-esteem and intergroup discrimination in the minimal group paradigm. *British Journal of Social Psychology, 30,* 51–62.

Holmes, J. G., & Rempel, J. K. (1989). Trust in close relationships. In C. Hendrick (Ed.), *Review of personality and social psychology: Close relationships* (Vol. 10, pp. 187–219). Newbury Park, CA: Sage.

Huber, G. L., & Roth, J. H. W. (1988, October). *Teachers' classroom activities and certainty/uncertainty orientation.* Paper presented at the conference of the International Study Association on Teacher Thinking, Nottingham, England.

Huber, G. L., Sorrentino, R. M., Davidson, M. A., Epplier, R., & Roth, J. W. H. (1992). Uncertainty orientation and cooperative learning: Individual differences within and across cultures. *Learning and Individual Differences, 4,* 1–24.

Janis, I. L. (1982). *Groupthink: Psychological studies of policy decisions and fiascos.* Boston: Houghton Mifflin.

Jetten, J., Spears, R., & Manstead, A. S. R. (1997). Distinctiveness threat and prototypicality: Combined effects on intergroup discrimination and collective self-esteem. *European Journal of Social Psychology, 27,* 635–657.

Johnson, D. W., Johnson, F. P., & Anderson, D. (1978). Students' cooperative, competitive, and individualistic attitudes, and attitudes toward schooling. *Journal of Psychology, 100,* 183–199.

Kagan, J. (1972). Motives and development. *Journal of Personality and Social Psychology, 22,* 51–66.

Kelman, H. C. (1961). Processes of attitude change. *Public Opinion Quarterly, 25,* 57–78.

Lemyre, L., & Smith, P. M. (1985). Intergroup discrimination and self-esteem in the minimal group paradigm. *Journal of Personality and Social Psychology, 49,* 660–670.

Lindeman, M. (1997). Ingroup bias, self-enhancement and group identification. *European Journal of Social Psychology, 27,* 337–355.

Mackie, D. M., Gastardo-Conaco, M. C., & Skelly, J. J. (1992). Knowledge of the advocated position and the processing of in-group and out-group persuasive messages. *Personality and Social Psychology Bulletin, 18,* 145–151.

Mackie, D. M., Worth, L. T., & Asuncion, A. G. (1990). Processing of persuasive in-group messages. *Journal of Personality and Social Psychology, 58*, 812–822.

McGarty, C., Turner, J. C., Oakes, P. J., & Haslam, S. A. (1993). The creation of uncertainty in the influence process: The roles of stimulus information and disagreement with similar others. *European Journal of Social Psychology, 23*, 17–38.

Mullin, B. A., & Hogg, M. A. (1998). Dimensions of subjective uncertainty in social identification and minimal intergroup discrimination. *British Journal of Social Psychology, 37*, 345–365.

Murray, S. L., & Holmes, J. G. (1993). Seeing virtues as faults: Negativity and the transformation of interpersonal narratives in close relationships. *Journal of Personality and Social Psychology, 65*, 707–722.

Owens, L. (1983, November). *An international comparison of the cooperative, competitive, and individualized learning preferences of students and teachers: Australia (Sydney) and the United States (Minneapolis).* Paper presented at the Annual Conference of the Australian Association for Research in Education, Canberra, Australia.

Pallak, S. R. (1983). Salience of a communicator's physical attractiveness and persuasion: A heuristic vs. systematic processing interpretation. *Social Cognition, 2*, 158–170.

Perreault, S., & Bourhis, R. Y. (1999). Ethnocentrism, social identification, and discrimination. *Personality and Social Psychology Bulletin, 25*, 92–103.

Petty, R. E., & Cacioppo, J. T. (1981). *Attitudes and persuasion: Classic and contemporary approaches.* Dubuque, IA: William C. Brown.

Petty, R. E., & Wegener, D. T. (1999). The elaboration likelihood model: Current status and controversies. In S. Chaiken & Y. Trope (Eds.), *Dual process theories in social psychology* (pp. 41–72). New York: Guilford Press.

Piaget, J. (1972). *The child's conception of the world.* Totowa, NJ: Littlefield, Adams.

Roney, C. J. R., & Sorrentino, R. M. (1995). Self-evaluation motives and uncertainty orientation: Asking the "who" question. *Personality and Social Psychology Bulletin, 21*, 1319–1329.

Rubin, M., & Hewstone, M. (1998). Social identity theory's self-esteem hypothesis: A review and some suggestions for clarification. *Personality and Social Psychology Review, 2*, 40–62.

Sorrentino, R. M. (1996). The role of conscious thought in a theory of motivation and cognition: The uncertainty orientation paradigm. In P. M. Gollwitzer & J. A. Bargh (Eds.), *The psychology of action: Linking cognition and motivation to behavior* (pp. 619–644). New York: Guilford Press.

Sorrentino R. M., Bobocel, D. R., Gitta, M. Z., Olson, J. M., & Hewitt, E. C. (1988). Uncertainty orientation and persuasion: Individual differences in the effects of personal relevant on social judgments. *Journal of Personality and Social Psychology, 55*, 357–371.

Sorrentino, R. M., & Hewitt, E. C. (1984). The uncertainty-reducing properties of achievement tasks revisited. *Journal of Personality and Social Psychology, 47*, 884–899.

Sorrentino, R. M., Hewitt, E. C., & Raso-Knott, P. (1992). Risk-taking in games of chance and skill: Informational and affective influences on choice behavior. *Journal of Personality and Social Psychology, 62*, 522–533.

Sorrentino, R. M., Holmes, J. G., Hanna, S. E., & Sharp, A. (1995). Uncertainty orientation and trust in close relationships: Individual differences in cognitive styles. *Journal of Personality and Social Psychology, 68*, 314–327.

Sorrentino, R. M., Raynor, J. O., Zubek, J. M., & Short, J. C. (1990). Personality functioning and change: Informational and affective influences on cognitive, moral, and social development. In E. T. Higgins & R. M. Sorrentino (Eds.), *Handbook of motivation and cognition: Foundations of social behavior* (pp. 193–223). New York: Guilford Press.

Sorrentino, R. M., & Roney, C. J. R. (2000). *The uncertain mind: Individual differences in facing the unknown.* London: Psychology Press.

Sorrentino, R. M., Roney, C. J. R., & Hanna, S. E. (1992). Attributions and cognitive orientations: Uncertainty orientation. In C. P. Smith (Ed.), *Motivation and personality handbook of thematic content analysis* (pp. 419–427). Cambridge: Cambridge University Press.

Sorrentino, R. M. & Short, J. C. (1986). Uncertainty orientation, motivation and cognition. In R. M. Sorrentino & E. T. Higgins (Eds.), *The handbook of motivation and cognition: Foundations of social behavior* (Vol. 1, pp. 379–403). New York: Guilford Press.

Sorrentino, R. M., Short, J. C., & Raynor, J. O. (1984). Uncertainty orientation: Implications for cognitive and motivational views of achievement behavior. *Journal of Personality and Social Psychology, 46*, 189–206.

Sorrentino, R. M., Walker, A. M., Hodson, G., & Roney, C. J. R. (in press). A theory of uncertainty orientation: A review and new developments. In A. Efklides, J. Kuhl, & R. M. Sorrentino (Eds.), *Trends and prospects in motivation research.* The Netherlands: Kluwer.

Tajfel, H. (1969). Cognitive aspects of prejudice. *Journal of Social Issues, 25*, 79–97.

Tajfel, H. (1972). Social categorization, English manuscript of "La categorisation social." In S. Moscovici (Ed.), *Introduction a la Psychologie Social* (Vol. 1). Paris: Larousse.

Tajfel, H., & Billig, M. (1974). Familiarity and categorization in intergroup behavior. *Journal of Experimental Social Psychology, 10*, 159–170.

Tajfel, H., Sheikh, A. A., & Gardner, R. C. (1964). Content of stereotypes and the inference of similarity between members of stereotyped groups. *Acta Psychologica, 22*, 191–201.

Tajfel, H., & Turner, J. C. (1979). An integrative thoery of intergroup conflict. In W. G. Austin & S. Worchel (Eds.), *The social psychology of intergroup relations* (pp. 33–47). Monterey, CA: Brooks/Cole.

Thibault, J., & Walker, R. (1975). *Procedural justice: A psychological analysis.* Hillsdale, NJ: Erlbaum.

Turner, J. C. (1978). Social categorization and social discrimination in the minimal group paradigm. In H. Tajfel (Ed.), *Differentiation between social groups* (pp. 101–140). London: Academic Press.

Turner, J. C. (1985). Social categorization and the self-concept: A social cognitive theory of group behavior. In E. J. Lawler (Ed.), *Advances in group processes: Theory and research* (Vol. 2, pp. 77–121). Greenwich, CT: JAI Press.

Turner, J. C., Hogg, M. A., Oakes, P. J., Reicher, S. D., & Wetherell, M. S. (1987). *Rediscovering the social group: A self-categorization theory.* Oxford: Basil Blackwell.

Van Knippenberg, D. (1999). Social identity and persuasion: Reconsidering the role of group membership. In D. Abrams & M. A. Hogg (Eds.), *Social identity and social cognition* (pp. 315–331). Oxford: Basil Blackwell.

Vygotsky, L. S. (1962). *Thought and language.* Cambridge, MA: MIT Press.

Weiner, B. (1972). *Theories of motivation and change: From mechanism to cognition.* Chicago: Markham.

Wilder, D. A. (1984). Predictions of belief homogeneity and similarity following social categorization. *British Journal of Social Psychology, 23,* 323–333.

PART III

The Social Mind in Personal Relationships and Interpersonal Behaviors

11. Perceiving, Feeling, and Wanting: Experiencing Prior Relationships in Present-Day Interpersonal Relations

SUSAN M. ANDERSEN AND KATHY R. BERENSON

Many theories hold that one's sense of who one is and one's motivations emerge in the context of interpersonal relations – in family, social networks, and culture. Early relationships with significant persons are particularly likely to influence the patterns of responding that people show in later interpersonal relations because these may provide a framework for later relations. A long history of clinical theory suggests that significant others from childhood – and perhaps from subsequent years as well – are important in self-definition, in working models of self and other, motivations, emotions, and interpersonal life (e.g., Bowlby, 1969; Freud, 1912/1958; Greenberg & Mitchell, 1983; Guidano & Liotti, 1983; Horney, 1939; Kelly, 1955; Ogilvie & Ashmore, 1991; Rogers, 1951; Safran & Segal, 1990; Sullivan, 1953). Whether the interpersonal patterns linked with representations of significant others are stable over time or evolve more continuously, such patterns should be linked with significant-other representations in memory and should consist in part of motivational material. Moreover, such motivational material should be activated and used – in relation to a new person – when a significant-other representation is activated and used. In our work, we have demonstrated this social-cognitive process of

Based on a paper presented at the Second Annual Sydney Symposium on Social Psychology, The Social Mind: Cognitive and Motivational Aspects of Interpersonal Behavior, Sydney, Australia, 1999. The research reported in this chapter was supported by a grant from the National Institute of Mental Health (RO1-MH48789). Special thanks to Noah Glassman, Serena Chen, Inga Reznik, and Michele Berk for their extensive and invaluable contributions. Address correspondence to Susan M. Andersen, Department of Psychology, New York University, 6 Washington Place, 4th Floor, New York, NY 10003. E-mail: andersen@psych.nyu.edu

231

transference in everyday social perception, such that representations of prior significant others have pervasive and wide-ranging influences on cognition, affect, and motivation (e.g., Andersen & Glassman, 1996; Andersen, Reznik, & Chen, 1997; Chen & Andersen, 1999). We review this work in the context of a broader conceptualization of motivation in interpersonal relations.

We begin with a detailed description of our social-cognitive model of transference and with a consideration of basic human motivations, as culled both from research literature and from personality theory, and how these basic motives may manifest themselves in transference. We then present a program of research establishing the process of transference, its antecedents, and the basic indices that measure it. Research on *preconscious* transient cueing in activating transference is also presented, highlighting the effortless nature of the process. Following this, we present studies demonstrating affect in transference, along with the basic motivations for *connection* and for *security*, and further delineate changes in behavior, the self-concept, self-evaluation, and self-regulation in transference. In particular, activation of a significant-other representation in transference activates idiographic *self-with-significant-other knowledge*, as well as normative interpersonal roles with the significant other and self-standards/self-discrepancies. The data show the reach of the transference process, and we conclude that our social-cognitive model of transference has implications for conceptualizing cognition, affect, and motivation in everyday interpersonal relations.

In our social cognitive framework, we define transference in terms of the activation and use of a significant-other representation in interpreting and responding to a new person. In most of our work, we have specifically focused on significant-other representations that are clearly positive or negative (on liked versus disliked significant-other representations; see McGuire & McGuire, this volume). When the overall evaluation and affect associated with a significant other are consistently positive (e.g., when the significant other is very well liked/loved and the self typically has positive feelings in the other's presence), this positive tone is predicted to result in positive responses in transference, as compared to transference responses based on a significant-other representation that is negatively evaluated and/or associated with negative feelings, and this has been demonstrated (e.g., Andersen & Baum, 1994; Andersen, Reznik, & Manzella, 1996). Of course, focus on representations with such a clear evaluation can be viewed as an oversimplification, given that affective and motivational components of relationships with significant others may quite normatively be complex and ambivalent. In fact, one could also argue that negative significant others are more aptly termed *ambivalent* because all significant others were once loved or highly valued (Thompson & Holmes, 1996). Still, a simple positive or negative evaluation does capture a basic quality of affective tone that we have been able to track in responses to a new person in transference. Work that examines more complex affective patterns in transference is also presented (Baum & Andersen, 1999; Reznik & Andersen, 1998). Each line of work supports and extends our social-cognitive model.

The Social-Cognitive Model of Transference

Our social-cognitive model of transference (Andersen & Glassman, 1996; Chen & Andersen, 1999) draws on social-construct theory (Bargh, 1997; Higgins, 1996a; Higgins & King, 1981; Sedikides & Skowronski, 1991; see also Bruner, 1957; Kelly, 1955) and is fairly consistent with connectionistic models as well (e.g., Read, 1984; Smith, 1995). Significant-other representations are essentially individual-person exemplars or *n*-of-one representations (depicting a specific individual rather than a generic category; Andersen, Lambert, & Dick, 1999; Carlston & Smith, 1996; Linville & Fisher, 1993; Smith & Zarate, 1992) that have special emotional significance (Andersen et al., 1997; Andersen, Glassman, & Gold, 1998). We assume that significant-other representations are linked to the self in memory by means of relational linkages, as many other models do, especially models that focus on relational schemas (Baldwin, 1992; Bugental, 1992). We emphasize, however, that these representations are individualized and idiographic because they are unique to the person being perceived and to the perceiver. Significant-other representations are also especially self-relevant, highly rich, distinctive, and accessible in memory. Nevertheless, they should be activated and used as are other social constructs and exemplars, and we have shown that this is the case (Andersen & Glassman, 1996; Chen & Andersen, 1999; for more on distinctiveness, see McGuire & McGuire, this volume).

We define *significant others* broadly as all individuals who have been deeply influential in one's life and in whom one is (or once was) emotionally invested, including members of one's family of origin (such as parents and siblings), as well as people encountered outside of family relations, either early on or later in life (such as a friend, spouse, coworker, or boss). Significant others from one's family of origin may be meta-representations of sorts that play a role in how knowledge of later significant relationships is perceived and structured in memory, but we have yet to examine this proposition and we assume that the basic process of transference is largely the same across significant-other representations.

Significant-other representations are readily used in interpersonal perception, both because of their chronic accessibility and because of transient contextual cueing (Andersen, Glassman, Chen, & Cole, 1995). Transient influences on activation may either involve cues presented *before* a new person is encountered (priming) or while the new person is encountered or learned about – that is, through applicability-based cues in the new person (Higgins, 1996a; see also Chen & Andersen, 1999; Chen, Andersen, & Hinkley, 1999). The research to be described employs applicability-based cues about a new person as a means of triggering transference in the laboratory because such cues seem to be an especially ecologically sensible analog for elements of a new person that might trigger transference in everyday life. When a new person is first encountered, readily observable characteristics (such as physical appearance or behavior) may figure prominently in initiating transference, but because covert aspects of significant others are important and relatively distinctive in the structure of significant-other representations (Andersen et al., 1998; see McGuire & McGuire, this volume), such qualities learned and/or inferred about a new person should also play a role in transference. The applicability-based cues we use to trigger transference in our experimental design are idiographically generated in advance and consist of whatever unique qualities the participant lists to describe the significant other (whether overt or covert). (On other idiographic methods, see Baumeister & Catanese; Cooper; McGuire & McGuire, this volume; on ipsative measures, see Fletcher & Simpson; Nezlek; Williams, Wheeler, & Marvey, this volume.)

As portrayed in Figure 11.1, we assume that mental representations of significant others are linked in memory with relational knowledge that reflects the self-with-the-significant-other (Andersen & Glassman, 1996; Andersen et al., 1997). When the significant-other representation is activated, those aspects of self linked to the significant other in the relationship are activated, along with considerable affective and motivational material. This model also fits well with the notion of the working self-concept (for a review, see Linville & Carlston, 1994) – in

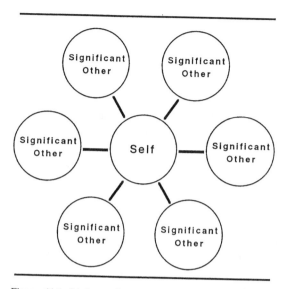

Figure 11.1. Linkages between the self and significant-other representations in memory.

which the self, too complex to be activated in its entirety at any one time, is constantly constructed anew as a function of context. We argue that what aspects of the self are activated depends in part on which (if any) significant-other representation is activated by cues in a new person (Chen & Andersen, 1999), highlighting the self in relation to specific significant others as another element to consider in the multiple selves people have. Considerable research suggests that multiple self-representations exist – based on social contexts (e.g., Deaux, 1991), motivations (e.g., Cantor, Markus, Niedenthal, & Nurius, 1986; Higgins, 1989), social roles (e.g., Linville, 1987; Markus & Nurius, 1986), relationships (e.g., Baldwin, 1992; Ogilvie & Ashmore, 1991), standards (e.g., Higgins, 1987), and situations (Mischel & Shoda, 1995), as well as present, actual, possible, future, or dreaded selves (e.g., Higgins, 1987, 1989; Markus & Kunda, 1986; Ogilvie & Ashmore, 1991; Showers, 1992). We view the self as multifaceted, composed of both individual and socially shared aspects and normatively quite context-bound. (On the context-bound self in narcissism, see Baumeister & Catanese; Rhodewalt, both this volume; on the self in response to norms, see Cooper, this volume; on the individual versus social or collective self, see Sedikides & Gaertner, this volume, who also distinguish collective from relational/familial selves; see, e.g., Brewer & Gardner, 1996. For other perspectives on the collective self, see Crano; Hogg; Kerr, this volume.)

We assume that motivations play an important role in characterizing the relational patterns that link the self with significant others, and in fact largely define motives in terms of the interpersonal needs and goals that individuals use to guide their behavior with significant others. Motivational knowledge linked with significant-other representations and with relationships should be represented in memory as social constructs are (e.g., Bargh & Gollwitzer, 1994) and should thus be activated when significant-other representations are activated in transference.

Motives in Transference: Assumptions about Basic Motivations

Most theories of personality developed in the 20th century assumed that particular motivations are central to how the self develops and functions and that a small set of human motivations may be basic. Those we propose are shown in Figure 11.2, and although we do not mean to suggest that this is the definitive list, we believe the literature supports this set of multiple motivations as operative in human behavior (see also Andersen et al., 1997; for related discussions see Baumeister & Catanese; Hogg; Kaplan & Wilke; Nezlek; Schütz; Tice & Faber; Williams et al., this volume).

One motive that regularly emerges as fundamental is the need for human *connection*, caring, warmth, tenderness, nurturance, or attach-

Connection

Security

Meaning

Competence/Control

Autonomy/Freedom

Figure 11.2. Basic human motivations.

ment (see Adler, 1927/1957; Bakan, 1966; Batson, 1990; Baumeister & Leary, 1995; Bowlby, 1969; Deci, 1995; Fairbairn, 1952; Greenberg & Mitchell, 1983; Guisinger & Blatt, 1994; Helgeson, 1994; Higgins, 1996b; Horney, 1939; McAdams, 1989; Mullahy, 1970; Rogers, 1951; Sullivan, 1953). Especially relevant to relationships with significant others, the motivation for connection has been central in our work to date (see also Fletcher & Simpson; Nezlek; Rhodewalt, this volume; on belonging and fitting in, see Crano; Hogg, & Wilke; Kaplan; Kerr; Schütz; Tice & Faber; Williams et al., all this volume). *Security* needs, which we think of as encompassing protection of self-esteem and self-enhancement in response to threat, have also been observed in transference, which comports well with the literature on motivated social cognition and self-bolstering processes (Baumeister & Jones, 1978; Epstein, 1973; Greenberg & Pyszczynski, 1985; Greenwald, 1980; Guidano & Liotti, 1983; Horney, 1939; Steele, 1988; Taylor & Brown, 1988; Taylor & Lobel, 1989; Tesser, 1988; on compensatory self-enhancement, see also Baumeister & Catanese; Cooper; Rhodewalt; Schütz; Sedikides & Gaertner; Tice & Faber, all this volume).

Other basic human motivations include the need for *meaning* (Frankl, 1959; Janoff-Bulman, 1992; Jung, 1933; Silver & Wortman, 1980; see also McGuire & McGuire and Williams et al., this volume; on meaning as uncertainty reduction, see Hogg; Sorrentino, Hodsany & Huber, this volume) and the need for *competence/control* (e.g., Abramson, Seligman, & Teasdale, 1978; Bakan, 1966; Bandura, 1986; Dweck & Licht, 1986; White, 1959; see also Nezlek, this volume; on being competent versus being liked, see Kaplan & Wilke; Schütz; Tice & Faber, all this volume) as well as the need for *autonomy/freedom* (e.g., Deci & Ryan, 1991; see Sedikides & Gaertner, this volume). Although we have yet to examine all of these basic motives in transference, we believe they are linked to significant-other representations and should thus emerge in new relationships when significant-other representations are activated and used (Andersen et al., 1997).

Initial Memory Confidence and Evaluation Findings Showing Transference

Our research utilizes an experimental manipulation of significant-other resemblance in a new person to trigger transference. Weeks in advance of this experiment, participants complete an idiographic stimulus-generation procedure by naming a significant other and describing him or her using complete sentences that refer to an equal number of positive and negative features. In the experiment, allegedly a different study, participants are exposed to descriptors of a new person that were or were not derived from their own significant other, and we assess the effects of this significant-other-resemblance manipulation by comparing participants in this condition with those in a no-resemblance control group. Each control participant is randomly yoked, without replacement, with a participant in the own-significant-other resemblance condition and encounters exactly the same descriptors about the new person as does this participant. Hence, the particular content of the stimulus descriptors is perfectly controlled across these conditions. Random assignment to these conditions enables causal conclusions about the effects of significant-other resemblance on inference, affect, and motivation, even though idiographic stimuli are used.

Representation-Derived Inference and Memory about a New Person

Significant-other representations are used in interpreting a new person such that significant-other derived inferences "go beyond the information given" (Bruner, 1957). We assess this in terms of *recognition-memory confidence for significant-other descriptors not presented about the new person* (Andersen & Cole, 1990), reflecting the tendency to fill in the blanks about the new person on the basis of the significant-other representation. Significant-other representations are especially chronically accessible, as indicated, which means that higher memory confidence derived from significant-other representations emerges – even when there is no significant-other resemblance in the new person – compared with the use of other representations, such as social categories (Andersen et al., 1995; Chen et al., 1999). Of course, increases in such memory confidence occur when there *is* significant-other resemblance in a new person, thereby triggering transference, as the results of our experimental manipulation demonstrate. Importantly, this memory confidence effect holds both among positively toned significant-other representations and among those that are negatively toned (see Andersen & Baum, 1994; Andersen et al., 1996; Baum & Andersen, 1999; Hinkley & Andersen, 1996), and global implicit theories about people generally cannot account for these findings (Andersen et al., 1995; Chen et al., 1999). This is our main index of transference.

Significant-Other Derived Evaluation of a New Person

Evaluation effects in transference indicate that people *come to like a new person* more when he or she resembles a positively toned rather than a negatively toned significant other, whereas no such effect occurs in the no-resemblance control condition (Andersen & Baum, 1994; Andersen et al., 1996; Baum & Andersen, 1999; Berk & Andersen, 1999; Reznik & Andersen, 1998). The general evaluation linked to the representation is applied to a new person, extending work on schema-triggered evaluation (e.g., Fiske & Pavelchak, 1986) to exemplars and importantly extending the literature on transference as well. *Significant-other derived evaluation* provides another basic index of transference, and provides one way of conceiving affective and motivational responses in transference.

Effortlessness in the Use of Significant-Other Representations

Triggering Transference Without Consciousness

Research on the *structure* of significant-other representations (Andersen & Cole, 1990, Studies 1 and 2; Andersen et al., 1998; see also McGuire & McGuire, this volume) and on the *cognitive processes* underlying their use in transference (e.g., Andersen & Glassman, 1996) suggests that transference should occur even in the absence of conscious awareness or cognitive effort because construct activation and use proceed this way. In meeting a new person who resembles a significant other, people may often be unaware of *seeing* relevant triggering cues in the new person that could trigger transference, and yet may make inferences about the new person deriving from the significant-other representation activated (Glassman & Andersen, 1999). Hence, transference should be triggered preconsciously, without effortful, strategic thinking – or subliminally.

To examine this issue, we presented participants subliminally with cues deriving from a significant other or from a yoked participant's significant other – in a modified transference experiment involving a computer task, allegedly with another person elsewhere sending self-descriptive messages through a linked computer. Only descriptors "irrelevant" to the participant's significant other were presented *supraliminally*, and random flashes on the left or right were subliminal text presentations in parafoveal vision (86 milliseconds followed by a pattern mask). Afterward, participants reported their inferences about the new person in a questionnaire that used some of their own significant-other features, and we assessed ratings of significant-other features *not* presented subliminally. The results of two studies showed that when participants were exposed subliminally to their own significant-other descriptors, they made more significant-other-derived inferences about the new person than when subliminally exposed to a yoked participant's significant-other features, going beyond the information given in the subliminal cues. (Self-generation effects in these findings were ruled out.) Hence, transference can be triggered preconsciously, and this is one element of automaticity (Bargh, 1997).

Automaticity as Effortlessness in the Use of Significant-Other Representations

We also have evidence for effortlessness in the use of significant-other representations (relative to other social constructs) in making simple judgments (Andersen et al., 1999). This latter research did not examine transference, but along with the subliminality data, the results support the possibility that the process of transference may under many circumstances proceed rather automatically. Of course, this does not imply that people are incapable of engaging in strategic, top-down processing that might enable them to short-circuit or redirect their responses (see Huguet, Galvaing, Dumas, & Monteil, this volume). Indeed, although we have not examined it empirically, the notion that one can consciously interrupt significant-other-based responses to a new person is important in clinical intervention for maladaptive transference patterns (Andersen & Berk, 1998). There are also likely to be individual differences in the degree to which significant-other representations are used automatically, such as certainty orientation (see Sorrentino et al., this volume), and these matters remain to be examined. Nonetheless, transference is not simply a matter of being consciously reminded of a significant other or of strategically deciding to use a significant-other representation to make inferences about a new person. The fact that significant-other representations can be triggered preconsciously and used with little cognitive effort speaks to just how pervasive and powerful past significant others may be in present relations.

Transference Evokes Interpersonal Connectedness Motivation, Expectancies, and Affect

When a significant-other representation is used in transference, this should lead motivations, expectancies, and affective responses typically experienced in relation to the significant other to be experienced with the new person. Activation of a positive significant-other representation should lead to responses in transference that parallel this overall tone. Relative to responses based on the activation of a significant other toward whom one feels a negative or very ambivalent evaluation, a positive transference should lead to motivations for closeness rather than distance, expectancies for acceptance rather than rejection, and the expression of positive rather than negative affect. Interestingly, although we examine affective responses as a function of the cognitive process of transference (the activation and use of a significant-other representation), it is also the case that affect cues influence judgments, broadly speaking (Forgas, this volume; see also Niedenthal, 1990), and may therefore contribute to transference. That is, stimulus cues conveying affect are likely to call to the fore significant-other representations sharing this affect, so although affective cues alone are unlikely to be sufficient to activate any one particular significant-other representation, they may well play a role in accentuating or attenuating transference effects triggered by featural cues, and this deserves more careful study.

Each of the studies described utilized a standard design in which participants were exposed – within their conscious awareness – to descriptors of a new person, who they believed they were about to meet, and then completed a variety of dependent measures. Our manipulation of significant-other resemblance (as described previously) made use of idiographic descriptions participants had provided of their own significant others in an earlier, allegedly unrelated, session. The features of the new person were also typically derived from a significant other identified as either positive or negative, thus varying the overall tone of the representation as well as significant-other resemblance. Regardless of the condition, however, the new person was characterized by equal numbers of positive and negative features, along with irrelevant fillers. Our central indices of transference – representation-derived memory confidence and/or significant-other derived evaluation – verified the occurrence of the phenomenon in each study to be presented and are not described further.

Significant-Other-Derived Motivation to Be Close in Transference

In the context of significant-other resemblance and transference, the desire to approach a new person emotionally should emerge as a reflection of the basic need for connection with the significant other and should vary with the overall positive versus negative tone of the representation. Examining this question directly, we asked participants in the transference experiment about their motivations to be close to the new person, and the results supported our hypothesis (Andersen et al., 1996). Participants reported that they were more motivated to approach the new person emotionally and not to distance from the person emotionally in the positive transference condition than in the negative transference condition; no such pattern occurred in the no-resemblance control condition. Hence, motivations pertaining to intimacy and connectedness between the self and the other do appear to be activated when the significant-other representation is activated in transference, and this evidence has been replicated (Berk & Andersen, 1999).

Significant-Other-Derived Expectancy of Being Accepted by the Other in Transference

Beliefs and expectancies about being accepted or rejected by a significant other should play a prominent role in transference. Contingencies for acceptance/rejection have multiple links to basic needs and may be fundamental in our relationships (e.g., Bandura, 1986; Higgins, 1989; on rejection sensitivity see Downey & Feldman, 1996; Downey, Khouri, & Feldman, 1997; on being liked versus respected, see Schütz; Tice & Faber; see also Kaplan & Wilke, all this volume). In one of these studies (Andersen et al., 1996) we asked participants to report on their expectancies about whether or not the new person would be likely to accept or reject them, predicting that less acceptance would be anticipated in transference when the relevant significant other has been harsh and rejecting. The results were consistent with this hypothesis. Participants expected to be more accepted by the new person who resembled their own positive versus negative significant other, a pattern that did not hold in the yoked-control condition.

Significant-Other-Derived Facial Affect in Transference

Immediate emotional responses in transference were also assessed. Participants' facial expressions while reading about the new person were covertly videotaped (Andersen et al., 1996), and judges rated the pleasantness of the facial affect expressed during the precise rating window while reading each of the descriptors (see Tesser, Millar, & Moore, 1988), with judges blind to condition and with adequate inter-judge reliability.

We predicted that facial affect in transference would reflect the overall tone of the representation, and this was confirmed by the evidence. When the new person resembled the participant's own positively toned significant other rather than the participant's own negatively toned significant other, participants expressed more pleasant facial affect while reading each feature, with no such effect occurring in the yoked-control condition. Hence, using this virtually instantaneous measure of transient affect, the data clearly showed significant-other-derived affect in transference as a function of the overall tone of the representation.

Facial Affect in Transference: Self-Serving Influences as Protection of the Other

In the same study (Andersen et al., 1996), facial affect was examined as a function of the valence of the individual descriptors read about the new person. This yielded another provocative finding. Participants responded with more *positive facial affect to negative descriptors* derived from their *positively toned significant other* than in any other condition. The positive overall tone clearly predicted positive facial affect in transference, especially when negative features of the positive significant other were presented.

One way of thinking about this is that it manifests needs for *connection* and for *security* in transference because negative featural cues derived from positive significant others threaten the positivity of the relationship and thus indirectly threaten the self. Hence, to protect the relationship and the self, compensatory enhancement of the other in highly positive affective responses occurred. This is intriguingly related to other research showing that people soften or neutralize negative features of their romantic partners (e.g., Holmes & Rempel, 1989; Murray & Holmes, 1993). Indeed, recalling a negative event in a relationship can result in even more positive evaluation of the significant other, because such events are viewed in terms of the overall store of positive feeling about the other, and perhaps because of a need to enhance the other in the face of a threat to one's overall positive regard for him or her. Compensatory self-enhancement (e.g., Greenberg & Pyszczynski, 1985; Greenwald, 1980) and compensatory relationship enhancement thus occur in transference. (For more on such processes, see Baumeister & Catanese; Cooper; Rhodewalt; Schütz; Sedikides & Gaertner; Tice & Faber, all this volume).

Transference Evokes Behavioral Confirmation of Overall Tone of Representation

On another level, explicit behavioral manifestations of transference should occur *in vivo* in an interpersonal encounter. That is, behavior deriving from the overall tone of the representation (Berk & Andersen, 1999) should emerge such that "social beliefs create social reality" – in the self-fulfilling prophecy or behavioral confirmation (e.g., Rosenthal, 1994; Snyder & Stukas, 1998). This hypothesis was tested in an experiment manipulating significant-other resemblance and overall representation tone. *After* being exposed to alleged descriptors of a new person, participants had a getting-acquainted telephone conversation with a randomly assigned naive stranger – the target (adapted from Andersen & Bem, 1981; Snyder, Tanke, & Berscheid, 1977). The target's contribution to the conversation was audiotaped and rated by judges, independently of perceiver behavior, in terms of how much positive and negative affect it conveyed, with adequate interjudge reliability. The results demonstrated behavioral confirmation in the transference condition in that the target's *behavior in the conversation* came to express the affect associated with the perceiver's significant other. No such effect occurred in the no-resemblance control condition. The data importantly extend prior work on transference by showing that it has measurable behavioral consequences.

Transference Evokes Change in the Working Self-Concept, Self-Evaluation, and Self-Enhancement Working Self-Concept: Change Toward the Self-with-Significant Other in Transference

When a significant-other representation is activated and used in relation to a new person, this activation should spread to the aspects of the self most linked with the significant other, resulting in changes in the *working self-concept* (Hinkley & Andersen, 1996). This should bring to mind the *self-when-with-the-significant-other* (Ogilvie & Ashmore, 1991) in the context of transference, and self-evaluation should also shift as the working self-concept shifts. Hence, when the activated significant-other representation is negatively toned, the shift in the working self-concept in transference would involve an infusion of negative self-features, which may pose a threat to the self and induce compensatory self-enhancement (e.g., Greenberg & Pyszczynski, 1985).

These hypotheses were examined using the same experimental design varying significant-other resemblance and overall tone. After learning about the new person, however, participants were asked to generate sentences to describe themselves "as they are now" – their working self-concept. Afterward, they classified each self-descriptor as positive or negative as an idiographic index of self-evaluation. At the pretest 2 weeks earlier, participants had described themselves as they are now in the same way, before describing a positively toned and a negatively toned significant other as usual, and also describing the *self they are when with* each significant other. Hence, baseline overlap between the features of the working self-concept and the self-with-the-significant-other at pretest was computed, so that this same overlap could be calculated based on descriptions of the working self-concept in the experiment, for an assessment of *change* in such *overlap* in the experiment. As predicted, the results showed a greater increase in overlap between the working self-concept in the experiment and the self-with-significant-other descriptors *when* the target resembled the participant's own significant other than when the target did not (covarying out pretest overlap scores). Thus transference leads to working self-concept change, with people becoming who they are when with the significant other in relating to the new person.

Self-Evaluation Deriving from the Significant-Other Representation

Changes in self-evaluation in transference should occur for working self-concept features *that changed* in the direction of the self-with-the-significant-other, reflecting the overall tone of the significant other, and the results supported this hypothesis. The self-evaluation in these critical working-self-concept descriptors – those newly overlapping with the self-with-significant-other – became more positive when the new person resembled the participant's own positively toned versus negatively toned significant other, controlling statistically for the same index of evaluation that was collected and calculated entirely at pretest. No such effect occurred in the no-resemblance control condition. Self-evaluation thus changed in transference in the direction of the overall positivity or negativity of the significant-other representation – when restricted to self-concept features changing in the direction of the self-with-the-significant-other.

Self-Serving Evaluation of Self in Transference: Protection of the Self

We also assessed changes in self-evaluation in transference more broadly – focusing on working self-concept features that did *not* shift toward the self-with-significant-other (those that were nonoverlapping), which were in the majority. The data showed pronounced self-enhancement in terms of highly positive self-evaluation in the negative transference condition and not in the no-resemblance control condition (again controlling for evaluation at pretest). The influx of negative self-features into the working self-concept in the negative transference condition (noted previously) presumably posed a threat to the self, thus provoking compensatory enhancement of aspects of the self not bound up with the significant other.

As with the compensatory effect that we described for facial affect, we conceptualize this as a self-regulatory process that derives from and reflects broader needs – in this case, the need for security – enabling recuperation from insults to the self. Although the two kinds of compensatory effects we have shown in transference are not directly comparable, both clearly show compensatory enhancement, as is common among individuals with average or high levels of self-esteem (see Baumeister & Jones, 1978; Greenberg & Pyszczynski, 1985; Steele, 1988; Taylor & Brown, 1988; Taylor & Lobel, 1989; Tesser, 1988; see also Baumeister & Catanese; Cooper; Rhodewalt; Schütz; Sedikides & Gaertner; Tice & Faber, this volume).

Transference Evokes Relational Roles, as Shown in Negative Affect in Response to a Role Violation

Relational roles are likely to influence affective and motivational responses in transference. Interpersonal roles are fundamental in relationships (see Fiske, 1992; Mills & Clark, 1993) and link significant others with the self in memory (e.g., Baldwin, 1992; Berscheid, 1994;

Bugental, 1992; Ogilvie & Ashmore, 1991; Sedikides, Olsen, & Reis, 1993). Hence, when a new person resembles a significant other, the significant other's chronic relational role should also be activated. Moreover, because a positive significant other's relational role is likely to be associated with expectancies for fulfillment of goals and positive affect (e.g., Martin, Tesser, & McIntosh, 1993; see also Oatley & Bolton, 1985), a role violation would make role-related goals seem unattainable and thus provoke negative affect (if not an opposing compensatory response).

This hypothesis was tested in an experiment focusing on positively toned significant others who were also authority figures (Baum & Andersen, 1999). In addition to our standard manipulation of significant-other resemblance, participants were told that the new person was either in an expert role (matching the significant other's role) or in a beginner role (as a role violation). The results confirmed that a role violation in the context of an otherwise positive transference led to increases in self-reported negative affect, as tapped by dysphoric, depressive mood. No such effect occurred in the control condition. An incongruent role in transference thus produced a dysphoric mood, presumably because it posed a threat to the role relationship, disrupting typical ways of behaving and typical expectations for positive outcomes. Although we do not know why compensatory responses were not observed in this study, we believe it may be because people have relatively little practice in handling role reversals with significant others (and their negative sequelae) in self-enhancing ways – unlike the more commonly experienced forms of threat to the self and/or relationship that we have studied.

Transference Evokes Self-Discrepancy from the Other's Standpoint and Predicted Affect and Motivation

Elaborations of self-discrepancy theory (e.g., Higgins 1989, 1996b) focus on motivated self-regulation and postulate two primary motives, nurturance and security. People seek nurturance from others by trying to elicit positive responses from them and seek security with others by trying to avoid or prevent negative responses, and individual differences are assumed to exist in the degree of focus on one or the other of these goals and associated self-regulatory strategies.

In self-discrepancy theory, parental representations are linked to self-discrepancies from the parent's standpoint when such discrepancies exist, and these discrepancies involve either the ideals that the parent holds, as wishes or hopes, or the "shoulds" or "oughts" the parent holds, as duties or obligations – and each is compared with the actual self. The theory predicts that activating self-discrepancies has complex affective and motivational consequences, as is supported by the evidence. For our purposes, activating a parental representation in transference should indirectly activate self-discrepancies from the parent's standpoint, resulting in dejection-related affect for ideal-discrepant individuals and agitation-related affect for ought-discrepant individuals, respectively (Reznik & Andersen, 1998). In terms of self-regulatory needs, it should also be associated with concerns about lack of nurturance and/or with seeking positive outcomes for ideal-discrepants, as well as with concerns about receiving criticism and/or with seeking to avoid negative outcomes for ought-discrepants. (For more on self-standards, see Cooper; on ideals, see Fletcher & Simpson; Schütz, all this volume)

Participants were preselected as having an ideal or ought self-discrepancy from a parent's standpoint (using the Selves Questionnaire; Higgins, Bond, Klein, & Strauman, 1986), with all parents positively toned, and learned about a new person who did or did not resemble this parent. Supporting our hypotheses, ideal-discrepants reported more depressed mood when the new person resembled their own parent rather than a yoked participant's; this did not occur for ought-discrepant participants. As a qualification on this effect, it occurred only when the experiment proceeded as stated, but not in an additional condition in which we explicitly primed the participant's self-standard with a generic statement about what the new person looks for in friendships. Although no self-reported agitation effect emerged for ought-discrepant participants, a clear-cut effect for self-reported *hostile mood* did emerge. That is, when the new person resembled the participant's own parent, ought-discrepant participants became more hostile and resentful than in the no-resemblance control condition, and no such effect occurred for ideal-discrepants. Participants with ought-discrepancies also reported being less calm in transference than in the no-resemblance control condition, whereas ideal-discrepants did not – although only after they no longer expected to interact with the new person. Everyone else had let his or her guard down at this stage and was relatively calm, except for ought-discrepant participants experiencing transference.

In spite of the unexplained variability in these findings, the weight of the evidence shows that activating a significant-other representation in transference indirectly activates self-discrepancies from the significant other's perspective, when they exist, so that both ideal-discrepants and ought-discrepants experience predictable and distinct affective consequences.

Concluding Comments

In summary, representations of significant others are highly emotionally laden, given their motivational relevance to the self. Our social-cognitive model of transference involves the activation and use of significant-other representations in relation to new people, and proposes that motivational and affective material is stored in memory with significant-other representations and triggered in transference. Transference can be accounted for by basic social-cognitive processing mechanisms, such as chronic accessibility and transient cues in a new person that "match" the significant other. This triggering process has been shown to occur outside of conscious awareness, that is, subliminally – evidence for how effortlessly significant-other representations can be used.

Based on this process, transference can be seen as a vehicle by which motivational responses to new persons may emerge. Individuals are motivated to approach a new person emotionally in transference based on how much they like or love the significant other. Reflecting basic needs for connection and security, transference also results in emotional changes and changes in self-evaluation in the working self-concept that parallel the overall tone of the significant-other representation, as well as compensatory enhancement. In particular, negative features of a positive significant other elicit especially positive facial expressions of affect in transference, protecting the positive view of the significant other. In addition, negative change in self-evaluation following activation of a negative significant-other representation is compensated for by an overall increase in positive self-evaluation, promoting recuperation from this threat to the self in transference. Self-regulatory strategies for maintaining connection and security that are presumably well practiced in relation to the significant other therefore emerge in transference in relation to a new person.

Along different lines, evidence on the indirect activation of normative relational knowledge – relevant to the pursuit of goals with the significant other – further maps out affective and self-regulatory patterns in transference. Data show that interpersonal roles are indirectly activated in transference, and role violation (in a positive transference) is disconcerting enough to lead to dysphoric mood, perhaps because it signals that desired positive outcomes are unlikely to occur. Finally, self-discrepancies (ideal and ought) from the standpoint of a parent are indirectly activated when such a parental representation is activated – resulting in predicted affective responses relevant to motivations for connection and security. That is, in transference, ideal-discrepant participants experience more depressed mood than do ought-discrepant participants, who experience more hostility or resentment and also less calm (although in each case with various limiting conditions). As understood in terms of the patterns of self-regulation delineated by self-discrepancy theory, this complex evidence provides further support for the role of connectedness (nurturance) needs and security needs in transference.

We view other basic motivations not yet examined in our work as also likely to be bound up with significant-other representations and to emerge in transference. Motivation for *meaning* seems quite relevant to transference because it is essentially a meaning-making process by which new people are interpreted in ways that feel sensible and deeply resonant with what is familiar and known. Indeed, people often find meaning in their lives through relationships with significant others, and connection to particular individuals has an influence on values and world views (e.g., Greenberg, Pyszczynski, Solomon, & Chatel, 1992). Motivation for *competence/control* is also worthy of examination, as its emergence in transference may have important consequences for how we view and utilize our capacity to be effective in new situations. Finally, motivation for *autonomy/freedom* is also likely be of the essence in transference, with elements of the struggle to be connected but not enmeshed in relation to a particular significant other influencing how free and authentic (rather than constrained by introjected standards) one feels in relation to a new person – a issue related to the nature of the true self (for an alternative view, see Tice & Faber, this volume). Future research should address these basic motivations, as well as broader social identities (e.g., identities shared or not shared with particular significant others) as they are relevant in transference.

A ubiquitous and normative coloring of present relationships by previous ones, transference is likely to have important implications for our choices of relationships and patterns in our current relations with friends, romantic partners, and other individuals, although we have thus far examined only initial perceptions (on ongoing relationships, see Fletcher & Simpson, this volume). Of course, the influence of transference on present relations may sometimes be problematic – such as when distortion leads us to neglect, misinterpret, or react inappropriately to real cues in the present interpersonal situation – but transference may also conceivably have positive effects, such as enhancing empathy and openness, because the resonance of the past is part of what makes present interpersonal relationships feel meaningful and desirable. In any event, cognition, affect, and motivation emerge in relation to new people as functions of the activation and use of significant-other representations, as we have shown, and a consideration of transference offers a useful vantage point for understanding human motivations in interpersonal life.

References

Abramson, L. Y., Seligman, M. E. P., & Teasdale, J. D. (1978). Learned helplessness in humans: Critique and reformation. *Journal of Abnormal Psychology, 87,* 49–74.

Adler, A. (1957). *Understanding human nature.* New York: Fawcett Premier. (Original work published in 1927).

Andersen, S. M., & Baum, A. B. (1994). Transference in interpersonal relations: Inferences and affect based on significant-other representations. *Journal of Personality, 62*(4), 460–497.

Andersen, S. M., & Bem, S. L. (1981). Sex typing and androgyny in dyadic interaction: Individual differences in responsiveness to physical attractiveness. *Journal of Personality and Social Psychology, 41,* 74–86.

Andersen, S. M., & Berk, M. S. (1998). Transference in everyday experience: Implications of experimental research for relevant clinical phenomena. *Review of General Psychology, 2,* 81–120.

Andersen, S. M., & Cole, S. W. (1990). "Do I know you?": The role of significant others in general social perception. *Journal of Personality and Social Psychology, 59,* 384–399.

Andersen, S. M., & Glassman, N. S. (1996). Responding to significant others when they are not there: Effects on interpersonal inference, motivation, and affect. In R. M. Sorrentino & E. T. Higgins (Eds.), *Handbook of motivation and cognition* (Vol. 3, pp. 262–321). New York: Guilford Press.

Andersen, S. M., Glassman, N. S., Chen, S., & Cole, S. W. (1995). Transference in social perception: The role of chronic accessibility in significant-other representations. *Journal of Personality and Social Psychology, 69,* 41–57.

Andersen, S. M., Glassman, N. S., & Gold, D. (1998). Mental representations of the self, significant others, and nonsignificant others: Structure and processing of private and public aspects. *Journal of Personality and Social Psychology, 75,* 845–861.

Andersen, S. M., Lambert, L., & Dick, W. (1999). *Processing efficiency in instance-based judgments about significant-other exemplars.* Unpublished manuscript, New York University.

Andersen, S. M., Reznik, I., & Chen, S. (1997). Self in relation to others: Cognitive and motivational underpinnings. In J. G. Snodgrass & R. L. Thompson (Eds.), *The self across psychology: Self-recognition, self-awareness, and the self-concept* (pp. 233–275). New York: New York Academy of Science.

Andersen, S. M., Reznik, I., & Manzella, L. M. (1996). Eliciting transient affect, motivation, and expectancies in transference: Significant-other representations and the self in social relations. *Journal of Personality and Social Psychology, 71,* 1108–1129.

Bakan, D. (1966). *The duality of human existence.* Chicago: Rand McNally.

Baldwin, M. W. (1992). Relational schemas and the processing of information. *Psychological Bulletin, 112,* 461–484.

Bandura, A. (1986). The explanatory and predictive scope of self-efficacy theory. Special issue: Self-efficacy theory in contemporary psychology. *Journal of Social and Clinical Psychology, 4*(3), 359–373.

Bargh, J. A. (1997). The automaticity of everyday life. In R. S. Wyer (Ed.), *Advances in social cognition* (Vol. 10, pp. 1–61). Hillsdale, NJ: Erlbaum.

Bargh, J. A., & Gollwitzer, P. M. (1994). Environmental control of goal-directed action: Automatic and strategic contingencies between situations and behavior. In W. D. Spaulding (Ed.), *Integrative views of motivation, cognition, and emotion: Nebraska Symposium on Motivation* (Vol. 41, pp. 71–124). Lincoln: University of Nebraska Press.

Batson, C. D. (1990). How social an animal?: The human capacity for caring. *American Psychologist, 45,* 336–346.

Baum, A., & Andersen, S. M. (1999). Interpersonal roles in transference: Transient mood states under the condition of significant-other activation. *Social Cognition, 17,* 161–185.

Baumeister, R. F., & Jones, E. E. (1978). When self-presentation is constrained by the target's knowledge: Consistency and compensation. *Journal of Personality and Social Psychology, 36,* 608–618.

Baumeister, R. F., & Leary, M. R. (1995). The need to belong: Desire for interpersonal attachments as a fundamental human motivation. *Psychological Bulletin, 117,* 497–529.

Berk, M. S., & Andersen, S. M. (1999). *Eliciting expected responses from new people based on prior relationships: Behavioral confirmation in transference.* Unpublished manuscript, New York University.

Berscheid, E. (1994). Interpersonal relationships. *Annual Review of Psychology, 45,* 79–129.

Bowlby, J. (1969). *Attachment and loss: Vol. 1. Attachment.* New York: Basic Books.

Brewer, M. B., & Gardner, W. (1996). Who is this "we"?: Levels of collective identity and self-representations. *Journal of Personality and Social Psychology, 36,* 608–618.

Bruner, J. S. (1957). Going beyond the information given. In H. E. Gruber, K. R. Hammond, & R. Jessor (Eds.), *Contemporary approaches to cognition* (pp. 41–60). Cambridge, MA: Harvard University Press.

Bugental, D. B. (1992). Affective and cognitive processes within threat-oriented family systems. In I. E. Sigel, A. McGillicuddy-de Lissi, & J. Goodnow (Eds.), *Parental belief systems: The psychological consequences for children* (2nd ed., pp. 219–248). Hillsdale, NJ: Erlbaum.

Cantor, N., Markus, H., Niedenthal, P., & Nurius, P. (1986). On motivation and self-concept. In R. M. Sorrentino & E. T. Higgins (Eds.), *Handbook of motivation and cognition: Foundations of social behavior* (pp. 96–121). New York: Guilford Press.

Carlston, D. E., & Smith, E. R. (1996). Principle of mental representation. In E. T. Higgins & A. W. Kruglanski (Eds.), *Social psychology: Handbook of basic principles* (pp. 184–210). New York: Guilford Press.

Chen, S., & Andersen, S. M. (1999). Relationships from the past in the present: Significant-other representations and transference in interpersonal life. In M. P. Zanna (Ed.), *Advances in Experimental Social Psychology* (Vol. 31, pp. 123–190). Mahwah, NJ: Erlbaum.

Chen, S., Andersen, S. M., & Hinkley, K. (1999). Triggering transference: Examining the role of applicability in the activation and use of significant-other representations in social perception. *Social Cognition, 17,* 332–365.

Deaux, K. (1991). Social identities: Thoughts on structure and change. In R. C. Curtis (Ed.), *The relational self: Theoretical convergencies in psychoanalysis and social psychology* (pp. 77–93). New York: Guilford Press.

Deci, E. L. (1995). *Why we do what we do.* New York: Putnam.

Deci, E. L., & Ryan, R. M. (1991). A motivational approach to self: Integration in personality. In R. Dienstbier (Ed.), *Nebraska symposium on motivation* (Vol. 38, pp. 237–288). Lincoln: University of Nebraska Press.

Downey, G., & Feldman, S. (1996). Implications of rejection sensitivity for intimate relationships. *Journal of Personality and Social Psychology, 70,* 1327–1343.

Downey, G., Khouri, H., & Feldman, S. (1997). Early interpersonal trauma and adult adjustment: The mediational role of rejection sensitivity. In D. Cicchetti & S. Toth (Eds.), *Rochester symposium on developmental psychopathology, Vol. VIII: The effects of trauma on the developmental process* (pp. 85–114). Rochester, NY: University of Rochester Press.

Dweck, C. S., & Licht, B. G. (1986). Learned helplessness and intellectual achievement. In J. Garber & M. E. P. Seligman (Eds.), *Human helplessness: Theory and applications* (pp. 197–222). New York: Academic Press.

Epstein, S. (1973). The self-concept revisited or a theory of a theory. *American Psychologist, 28,* 405–416.

Fairbairn, W. R. D. (1952). *Psychoanalytic studies of personality.* London: Tavistock.

Fiske, A. P. (1992). The four elementary forms of sociality: Framework for a unified theory of social relations. *Psychological Review, 99,* 689–723.

Fiske, S. T., & Pavelchak, M. (1986). Category-based versus piecemeal-based affective responses: Developments in schema-triggered affect. In R. M. Sorrentino & E. T. Higgins (Eds.), *Handbook of motivation and cognition* (Vol. 1, pp. 167–203). New York: Guilford Press.

Frankl, V. E. (1959). *Man's search for meaning.* Boston: Beacon Press.

Freud, S. (1958). The dynamics of transference. *Standard edition* (Vol. 12, pp. 99–108). London: Hogarth. (Original work published 1912.)

Glassman, N. S., & Andersen, S. M. (1999). Activating transference without consciousness: Using significant-other representations to go beyond subliminally given information. *Journal of Personality and Social Psychology, 77,* 1146–1162.

Greenberg, J., & Pyszczynski, T. (1985). Compensatory self-inflation: A response to the threat to self-regard of public failure. *Journal of Personality and Social Psychology, 49,* 273–280.

Greenberg, J., Pyszczynski, T., Solomon, S., & Chatel, D. (1992). Terror management and tolerance: Does mortality salience always intensify negative reactions to others who threaten one's world view? *Journal of Personality and Social Psychology, 49,* 273–280.

Greenberg, J. R., & Mitchell, S. A. (1983). *Object relations in psychoanalytic theory.* Cambridge, MA: Harvard University Press.

Greenwald, A. G. (1980). The totalitarian ego. *American Psychologist, 35,* 603–618.

Guidano, V. F., & Liotti, G. (1983). *Cognitive processes and emotional disorders.* New York: Guilford Press.

Guisinger, S., & Blatt, S. J. (1994). Individuality and relatedness: Evolution of a fundamental dialectic. *American Psychologist, 49,* 104–111.

Helgeson, V. S. (1994). Relation of agency and communion to well-being: Evidence and potential explanations. *Psychological Review, 116*(3), 412–428.

Higgins, E. T. (1987). Self-discrepancy theory: A theory relating self and affect. *Psychological Review, 94,* 319–340.

Higgins, E. T. (1989). Continuities and discontinuities in self-regulatory and self-evaluative processes: A developmental theory relating self and affect. *Journal of Personality, 57,* 407–444.

Higgins, E. T. (1996a). Knowledge activation: Accessibility, applicability, and salience. In E. T. Higgins & A. W. Kruglanski (Eds.), *Social psychology: Handbook of basic principles* (pp. 133–168). New York: Guilford Press.

Higgins, E. T. (1996b). Ideals, oughts, and regulatory focus: Affect and motivation from distinct pains and pleasures. In P. M. Gollwitzer & J. A. Bargh (Eds.), *The psychology of action: Linking cognition and motivation to behavior* (pp. 91–114). New York: Guilford Press.

Higgins, E. T., Bond, R. N., Klein, R., & Strauman, T. (1986). Self-discrepancies and emotional vulnerability: How magnitude, accessibility, and type of discrepancy influence affect. *Journal of Personality and Social Psychology, 51,* 5–15.

Higgins, E. T., & King, G. A. (1981). Accessibility of social constructs: Information processing consequences of individual and contextual variability. In N. Canto & J. F. Kihlstrom (Eds.), *Personality, cognition and social interaction* (pp. 69–121). Hillsdale, NJ: Erlbaum.

Hinkley, K., & Andersen, S. M. (1996). The working self-concept in transference: Significant-other activation and self-change. *Journal of Personality and Social Psychology, 71,* 1279–1295.

Holmes, J. C., & Rempel, J. K. (1989). Trust in close relationships. *Review of Personality and Social Psychology, 10,* 187–219.

Horney, K. (1939). *New ways in psychoanalysis.* New York: Norton.

Janoff-Bulman, R. (1992). *Shattered assumptions: Towards a new psychology of trauma.* New York: Free Press.

Jung, C. G. (1933). *Modern men in search of soul.* New York: Harcourt, Brace.

Kelly, G. A. (1955). *The psychology of personal constructs.* New York: Norton.

Linville, P. W. (1987). Self-complexity as a cognitive buffer against stress-related illness and depression. *Journal of Personality and Social Psychology, 52,* 663–767.

Linville, P. W., & Carlston, D. E. (1994). Social cognition of the self. In P. G. Devine, D. C. Hamilton, & T. M. Ostrom (Eds.), *Social cognition: Impact on social psychology* (pp. 143–193). New York: Academic Press.

Linville, P. W., & Fischer, G. W. (1993). Exemplar and abstraction models of perceived group variability. *Social Cognition, 11,* 92–125.

Markus, H., & Kunda, Z. (1986). Stability and malleability of the self concept. *Journal of Personality and Social Psychology, 51,* 858–866.

Markus, H., & Nurius, P. (1986). Possible selves. *American Psychologist, 41,* 954–969.

Martin, L. L., Tesser, A., & McIntosh, W. D. (1993). Wanting but not having: The effects of unattained goals on thoughts and feelings. In D. M. Wegner & J. W. Pennebaker (Eds.), *The handbook of mental control* (pp. 552–572). New York: Prentice-Hall.

McAdams, D. P. (1989). *Intimacy: The need to be close.* New York: Doubleday.

Mills, J., & Clark, M. S. (1993). Communal and exchange relationships: New research and old controversies. In R. Gilmour & R. Erber (Eds.), *Theoretical approaches to new relationships* (pp. 29–42). Hillsdale, NJ: Erlbaum.

Mischel, W., & Shoda, Y. (1995). A cognitive-affective system theory of personality: Reconceptualizing situations, dispositions, dynamics, and invariance in personality structure. *Psychological Review, 102,* 246–268.

Mullahy, P. (1970). *Psychoanalysis and interpersonal psychiatry. The contributions of Harry Stack Sullivan.* New York: Science House.

Murray, S., & Holmes, J. G. (1993). Seeing virtues in faults: Negativity and the transformation of interpersonal narratives in close relationships. *Journal of Personality and Social Psychology, 65,* 707–722.

Niedenthal, P. M. (1990). Implicit perception of affective information. *Journal of Experimental Social Psychology, 26,* 505–527.

Oatley, K., & Bolton, W. (1985). A social-cognitive theory of depression in reaction to life events. *Psychological Review, 92,* 372–388.

Ogilvie, D. M., & Ashmore, R. D. (1991). Self-with-other representation as a unit of analysis in self-concept research. In R. C. Curtis (Ed.), *The relational self: Theoretical convergencies in psychoanalysis and social psychology* (pp. 282–314). New York: Guilford Press.

Read, S. J. (1984). Analogical reasoning in social judgment: The importance of causal theories. *Journal of Personality and Social Psychology, 46,* 14–25.

Reznik, I., & Andersen, S. M. (1998). *Individual differences in transference: The role of self-discrepancy in affect and motivation.* Paper presented at the meeting of the American Psychological Society, Washington, DC.

Rogers, C. (1951). *Client-centered therapy.* Boston: Houghton Mifflin.

Rosenthal, R. (1994). Interpersonal expectancy effects: A 30-year perspective. *Current Directions in Psychological Science, 3,* 176–179.

Safran, J. D., & Segal, Z. V. (1990). *Interpersonal processes in cognitive therapy.* New York: Basic Books.

Sedikides, C., Olsen, N., & Reis, H. T. (1993). Relationships as natural categories. *Journal of Personality and Social Psychology, 64,* 71–82.

Sedikides, C., & Skowronski, J. J. (1991). The law of cognitive structure activation. *Psychological Inquiry, 2,* 169–184.

Showers, C. (1992). Compartmentalization of positive and negative self-knowledge: Keeping bad apples out of the bunch. *Journal of Personality and Social Psychology, 62,* 1036–1049.

Silver, R. C., & Wortman, C. B. (1980). Coping with undesirable life events. In J. Garber & M. E. P. Seligman (Eds.), *Human helplessness* (pp. 279–340). New York: Academic Press.

Smith, E. R. (1995). What do connectionism and social psychology offer each other? *Journal of Personality and Social Psychology, 70,* 893–912.

Smith, E. R., & Zarate, M. A. (1992). Exemplar-based model of social judgment. *Psychological Review, 99,* 3–21.

Snyder, M., & Stukas, A. A. (1998). Interpersonal processes: The interplay of cognitive, motivational, and behavioral activities in social interaction. *Annual Review of Psychology, 50,* 273–303.

Snyder, M., Tanke, E. D., & Berscheid, E. (1977). Social perception and interpersonal behavior. On the self-fulfilling nature of social stereotypes. *Journal of Personality and Social Psychology, 35,* 656–666.

Steele, C. M. (1988). The psychology of self-affirmation: Sustaining the integrity of the self. In L. Berkowitz (Ed.), *Advances in experimental social psychology* (Vol. 21, pp. 261–302). New York: Academic Press.

Sullivan, H. S. (1953). *The interpersonal theory of psychiatry.* New York: Norton.

Taylor, S. E., & Brown, J. D. (1988). Illusion and well-being: A social psychological perspective on mental health. *Psychological Bulletin, 103,* 193–210.

Taylor, S. E., & Lobel, M. (1989). Social comparison activity under threat: Downward evaluation and upward contrasts. *Psychological Review, 96,* 569–575.

Tesser, A. (1988). Toward a self-evaluation maintenance model of social behavior. In L. Berkowitz (Ed.), *Advances in experimental social psychology* (Vol. 21, pp. 181–227). New York: Academic Press.

Tesser, A., Millar, M., & Moore, J. (1988). Some affective consequences of social comparison and reflection processes: The pain and pleasure of being close. *Journal of Personality and Social Psychology, 54,* 49–61.

Thompson, M. M., & Holmes, J. G. (1996). Ambivalence in close relationships: Conflicted cognitions as a catalyst for change. In R. M. Sorrentino & E. T. Higgins (Eds.), *Handbook of motivation and cognition* (Vol. 3, pp. 497–530). New York: Guilford Press.

White, R. W. (1959). Motivation reconsidered: The concept of competence. *Psychological Review, 66,* 297–333.

12. Ideal Standards in Close Relationships

GARTH J. O. FLETCHER AND JEFFRY A. SIMPSON

How do people know whether they are in a good or a bad intimate relationship? On what basis do people decide whether to become more involved, live together, get married, or look for another mate? One answer to such questions is that judgments or decisions concerning a particular relationship should be based, at least in part, on the consistency between ideal standards, on the one hand, and perceptions of the current relationship, on the other. This idea is in common currency in folk wisdom, and it also has been formulated in academic circles, most famously by Thibaut and Kelley (1959) in terms of the contrast between what people believe they deserve in a relationship (*comparison level*) and the perceived level of rewards derived from their current relationship (*outcomes*). Our research and theoretical program over the last few years has confirmed that ideal standards are indeed pivotal knowledge structures in close relationship contexts. However, it has also suggested that any reasonable causal account of the underlying psychological processes is anything but simple and has raised many difficult but intriguing and important questions.

In this chapter, we review what we have learned so far about the structure and functions of ideal standards. In the first section, we present the latest incarnation of our model of ideal standards in relationships. We then summarize the results of a series of recent studies that have tested some basic tenets of this model. In the final section, we discuss some important unresolved issues regarding how

Correspondence should be addressed to Garth Fletcher, Department of Psychology, University of Canterbury, Christchurch, New Zealand (e-mail: g.fletcher@psyc.canterbury.ac.nz). The writing of this chapter was supported by a grant from the N.Z. Marsden Foundation (M1032) to both authors.

individuals establish and adjust their ideal standards over time, how relationship-discrepancy models are similar to and different from self-discrepancy models, and how the functioning of ideal standards can become complicated when the needs and expectations of both partners are considered.

A Model of Ideal Standards in Close Relationships

Structure and Content of Partner and Relationship Ideals

Relationship and partner ideals are key components of the social mind that people use to guide their interpersonal and motivational strategies. More specifically, according to our Ideals Standards Model (see Simpson, Fletcher, & Campbell, in press), partner and relationship ideals should operate as chronically accessible knowledge structures that probably predate – and may causally influence – important judgments and decisions in relationships (see Fletcher, Simpson, Thomas, & Giles, 1999). We further propose that relationship-based knowledge structures should involve three interlocking components: the self, the partner, and the relationship (see Baldwin, 1992; Fletcher & Thomas, 1996). Ideal standards, in particular, meld elements of all three categories. For example, a person's partner ideal of "handsome and warm" is a personally held ideal related to what the individual hopes and desires (the self), is a description of a hypothetical other (the partner), and represents an ideal in relation to a potential intimate relationship with the self (the relationship) (cf. Sedikides & Gaerther; Tice & Faber, this volume).

Ideal partner and ideal relationship standards could be stored and represented as separate, semi-independent constructs. However, ideal partner and ideal relationship categories are also likely to overlap because people should prefer ideal partners who can help them achieve their ideal relationships (see Fletcher et al., 1999). For example, individuals who believe that laughter and humor are important features of an ideal relationship should also value a sense of humor in their ideal mates, who in turn should be capable of creating a relationship filled with laughter and humor.

We also expected that the content of both partner and relationship ideals would revolve around three major categories: (a) warmth, commitment, or intimacy, (b) health, passion, and attractiveness, and (c) status and resources. Our expectations were derived from recent evolutionary models that suggest that each dimension represents a different route to obtaining a mate and promoting one's own reproductive fitness (see Buss & Schmitt, 1993; Gangestad & Simpson, in press). By being attentive to a partner's capacity for intimacy and commitment, for example, an individual should increase his or her chances of finding a cooperative, committed partner who is likely to be a devoted parent. By focusing on attractiveness and health, an individual is more likely to acquire a mate who is younger, healthier, and perhaps more fertile (especially in the case of men choosing women). And by considering a partner's resources and status, an individual should be more likely to obtain a mate who can ascend social hierarchies and form coalitions with other people who have – or can acquire – valued social status or other resources.

In effect, each ideal dimension reflects a possible solution to a specific barrier to successful reproduction. Different people favor different solutions and, hence, differentially weight each ideal dimension. Why don't people want it all in terms of their ideals and desire a partner who is incredibly attractive, rich, and warm? First, few people fit such a description. Second, most of us (if we were honest) would not be able to attract such persons even if they were available. Third, even if we succeeded in attracting such paragons, we might have difficulty holding on to them. In short, people must make trade-offs between these attributes when deciding whom to date or marry.

Functions and Flexibility of Ideal Standards

Our Ideals Standards Model also proposes that partner and relationship ideals should serve three functions: *evaluation, explanation,* and *regulation.* More specifically, the magnitude of discrepancies between ideal standards and perceptions of the current partner/relationship should be used by individuals to (a) estimate and evaluate the quality of their partners and relationships (e.g., to assess the appropriateness of potential or current partners/relationships), (b) explain and better understand what is happening in their relationships (e.g., to give causal accounts explaining relationship satisfaction, problems, or conflicts), and (c) regulate and make adjustments in their relationships (e.g., to predict and possibly control current partners/relationships).

The flexibility of ideal standards (i.e., the degree to which partners can fall below an ideal standard and still be considered acceptable) should also affect how partners and relationships are evaluated,

explained, and regulated. Flexibility beliefs might be stable and dispo-
sition-like, or they may be labile and sensitive to recent situational feedback (Campbell, Simpson, Kashy, & Fletcher, in press). A growing gap
between perceptions of the current partner and ideal standards, for
example, could be dealt with by simply adjusting one's latitude of
acceptance and rejection (i.e., temporarily settling for less to maintain
the relationship). Conversely, flexibility beliefs may be relatively stable,
given the evidence that the level of an individual's ideals is associated
with his or her self-perceptions (Murray, Holmes, & Griffin, 1996a).
According to this line of reasoning, individuals who see themselves
as highly physically attractive, for instance, should have high ideal
partner standards on this dimension, and they also should have a less
flexible range of acceptance on the same dimension. Thus, if a person
is very fit and highly attractive, he or she should be in a good position
to obtain a partner who also is highly attractive. Moreover, if the chosen
partner subsequently turns into a blob or a couch potato, then the individual is in a strong position to look for an alternative partner who
meets such exacting standards.

Enhancement Versus Accuracy in Relationships

We argue that two fundamental motives guide how individuals evaluate, explain, and regulate their relationships: (a) partner/relationship
enhancement or idealization motives and (b) accuracy motives. Both
motives can provide perceivers with an increase in knowledge or
certainty about their social world (see Sorrentino, Hodson, & Huber;
Hogg, this volume), but in very different ways. The emotional, cognitive, and behavioral consequences of discrepancies between ideals
and perceptions of the current partner or relationship should depend
(in part) on which motivational set tends to be predominant in a given
situation.

According to many self theorists, the self-enhancement motive is a
powerful force that leads people to view the social world through rose-
colored glasses, to exaggerate their own positive attributes and the
control they wield over social outcomes, and to be unduly optimistic
about future events (see Baumeister, 1998). Relationship theorists have
also proposed that people have a basic need to idealize and enhance
their romantic partners and relationships. Indeed, there is abundant
evidence that individuals often do perceive their partners and relationships in an excessively positive light (Murray et al., 1996a) and

that the tendency to idealize one's partner is associated with greater relationship satisfaction and lower rates of relationship dissolution (Murray, Holmes, & Griffin, 1996b).

It is not difficult to understand why people are motivated to idealize their partners and relationships. Individuals' self-concepts often are inextricably intertwined with the perceptions they have of their partners and relationships (Murray et al., 1996a). Thus, any self-serving bias or motive that is used to maintain optimistic, positive self-views should also be used to enhance views of the current partner and relationship, especially because the fate of the self and the partner/relationship frequently coincide. In addition, the costs associated with relationship conflict and dissolution should motivate most individuals to see the best in their partners and relationships when possible. From a rational standpoint, most people probably are aware that approximately 50% of marriages end in divorce, at least in Western countries (see Singh, Mathews, Clarke, Yannicos, & Smith, 1995). Despite this realization, the vast majority of men and women get married and have children at some point in their lives (Singh et al., 1995). Committing to a long-term relationship, therefore, requires a leap of faith and a level of confidence that may be difficult to justify on purely rational grounds. As a result, the psychological pressure to make charitable and positive judgments about one's partner and relationship needs to be strong to counteract these forces. This might explain the potency of the enhancement motive in most relationships.

In considering the hegemony of the relationship-enhancement motive, we are reminded of a quote by Thomas Huxley: "The great tragedy of Science [is] the slaying of a beautiful hypothesis by an ugly fact." In this case, the hypothesis is the presumed pervasiveness and dominance of the relationship-enhancement motive; the ugly fact is that the vast majority of romantic relationships eventually end. Apparently, the relationship-enhancement motive is either inoperative or is displaced by other basic motives in certain contexts. We contend that partner and relationship idealization processes will sometimes conflict with accuracy aims; namely, under conditions in which the *effective* prediction, explanation, and control of partners and relationships become paramount. Attempting to accurately understand and attribute motives and beliefs to others should be highly adaptive in certain situations (such as when deciding whether or not to start or remain in a relationship or when figuring out how to predict and control the behavior of others). Indeed, evolutionary pressures should have selected humans to ascertain and face the truth, no matter how bleak and depressing, in situations in which it was dangerous or extremely costly to do otherwise.

How can the coexistence and operation of these two motives be understood? We believe that, in many situations, the motive to bend reality in an enhancing fashion is likely to produce mild distortions that do not distort the truth enough to cause serious problems in most relationships. Moreover, the accuracy and enhancement motives may both operate, but under different conditions (Gollwitzer & Kinney, 1989). Some people, for example, may have cognitive styles that are better suited to achieving accuracy goals, whereas others may have styles that facilitate the enhancement of cherished views of themselves and their partners/relationships. In addition, relationship interactions that are threatening should increase the accessibility and power of esteem-maintenance goals, often subverting accurate attributions about the partner or the relationship (cf. Simpson, Ickes, & Blackstone, 1995). Different relationship stages or major life decision points should also be associated with systematic shifts in the salience and importance of the two motives. For example, when the need to make accurate, less biased judgments becomes critical in relationships (such as when individuals must decide whether or not to date someone, to get married, or to have a child), the accuracy motive should assume precedence. On the other hand, when couples are settled into a comfortable relationship maintenance phase, the enhancement motive should be ascendant.

Consequences of Discrepancies Between Ideals and Perceptions

According to our model, the consequences of large discrepancies between ideals and perceptions of the current partner/relationship should vary, depending on the accessibility and relative strength of relationship enhancement versus accuracy motives. As already noted, relationship enhancement and partner/relationship idealization processes should be dominant when the relationship is stable, has reached a relatively high level of commitment, or after major decisions have been made. When enhancement motives predominate, people should handle ideal-perception discrepancies (and the evaluations that stem from them) using cognitive strategies that involve (a) changing perceptions of the current partner/relationship so that they match one's ideal standards more closely, (b) changing one's ideal standards so that they match one's perceptions of the current partner/

relationship more closely, or (c) discounting the importance of ideal standards that one's partner is not likely to meet. We suspect that these processes typically occur automatically and largely outside of conscious awareness.

Many intriguing questions remain about the way in which cognitive idealization processes are likely to work. First, the extent of idealization might depend on the specific ideal standard under consideration. Previous research implies that individuals are most likely to idealize their partners on attributes that (a) are central to what they need or value in a mate (Stephan, Berscheid, & Walster, 1971), (b) are subjective or ambiguous (i.e., are difficult to verify because objective rules or standards for verification do not exist: Lambert & Wedell, 1991; Sedikides & Showronski, 1993), and (c) promote closeness and intimacy in the relationship (Levinger & Breedlove, 1966).

On the other hand, in situations that call for greater accuracy (e.g., when important relationship decisions must be made, when attractive alternative partners become available, or when difficult relationship problems emerge), moderate to large discrepancies should motivate most individuals to engage in more in-depth analysis and information processing about the partner or the relationship. One consequence of engaging in more systematic, in-depth processing might be that individuals will use current versus ideal discrepancies to explain their relationship problems more often (e.g., "My ideal partner is very warm, and you are cold and aloof, which explains why I am unhappy"). In-depth processing also may lead individuals to try to alter their own behavior, their partner's behavior, or both. If in-depth processing leads individuals to the conclusion that current-ideal discrepancies are important but cannot be reduced, individuals may leave the relationship, look for new partners, or seek solace in other activities (e.g., through job satisfaction).

Empirical Evidence for the Model

To date, much of our theoretical work remains at a speculative level. However, we are currently conducting a program of research that has tested some of the model's basic postulates. We next review three studies that have tested central components of our model.

Structure and Content of Partner and Relationship Ideals. To identify the structure and content of partner and relationship ideals, Fletcher et al.

(1999) conducted several studies. Adopting an inductive approach to identifying the ideals dimensions that people naturally possess, we asked men and women in Study 1 to list all the traits or characteristics that described their ideal romantic partners and their ideal romantic relationships. After removing redundant items, we created two extensive lists of attributes that described ideal partners and ideal relationships. In Study 2, another sample of men and women rated each item in terms of its importance for their *own* standards concerning ideal partners and ideal relationships. A factor analysis of the ideal partner items revealed the three factors we expected: (1) partner characteristics relevant to intimacy, warmth, trust, and loyalty (labeled Partner Warmth/Trustworthiness), (2) personality and appearance characteristics concerning how attractive, energetic, and healthy the partner was (labeled Partner Vitality/Attractiveness), and (3) characteristics relevant to the partner's social status and resources (labeled Partner Status/Resources). The relationship ideal items produced two factors: (1) the importance of intimacy, loyalty, and stability in a relationship (labeled Relationship Intimacy/Loyalty) and (2) the importance of excitement and passion in a relationship (labeled Relationship Passion). All five scales possessed good internal consistency and adequate test-retest reliability.

Study 3 tested the factor structure of the ideal partner and ideal relationship scales using confirmatory factor analysis (CFA). In a new sample of men and women who completed all of the ideals scales, two higher-order factors were identified (see Figure 12.1), which we labeled Warmth/Loyalty and Vitality/Status/Passion. As predicted, individuals who placed more importance on Passion than on Intimacy/Loyalty in their relationships desired ideal partners with attributes that would logically promote the development of such ideal relationships (e.g., partners who scored higher on the Partner Vitality/Attractiveness ideals scale). Further CFA tests revealed that this higher-order model produced a better fit than did other plausible models and, importantly, that a model in which all items loaded directly on the two higher-order factors fit poorly. Moreover, the factor structure replicated across different samples and across men and women. Intriguingly, these higher-order factors are similar to the two basic forms of love identified by Berscheid and Walster (1978): passionate love and companionate love.

Study 4 provided validation evidence for the ideals scales. Convergent validation tests, for example, indicated that individuals who had

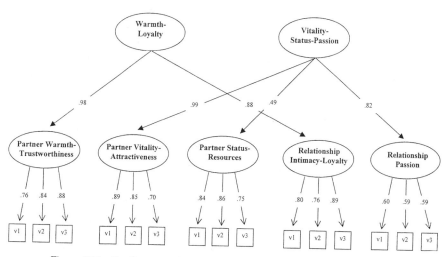

Figure 12.1. Confirmatory factor analysis of the ideal partner and relationships scales, with first-order and second-order latent factors (from Fletcher et al., 1999).

stronger beliefs about the importance of intimacy in successful relationships rated Partner Warmth/Trustworthiness and Relationship Intimacy/Loyalty ideals as relatively more important. Individuals who rated passion as a primary cause of relationship success, on the other hand, placed more emphasis on the Partner Vitality/Attractiveness and Relationship Passion ideals. Those who rated external factors (e.g., a nice house) as more important in influencing relationship success placed more weight on the Partner Status/Resources ideal. Individuals with a more unrestricted sociosexual orientation (i.e., those who were more willing to have sex without closeness and emotional bonding) rated the Partner Warmth/Trustworthiness and Relationship Intimacy/Loyalty ideals as *less* important than did individuals with a more restricted sociosexual orientation. Finally, individuals who were involved in more satisfying and longer-term relationships placed more emphasis on the Relationship Intimacy/Loyalty ideal. Discriminant validation tests confirmed that the ideals scales were not correlated with various response biases.

The final study tested the basic functional postulate that people should evaluate their current partners and relationships by comparing them against their ideal standards. According to our model, the more closely perceptions of the current partner/relationship match individuals' ideal standards, the more positively they should evaluate their relationship. To test this hypothesis, a new sample of men and women ranked the importance of various ideal attributes, along with their perceptions of their current partner/relationship, on items taken from the ideal partner and ideal relationship scales. As predicted, individuals who had smaller current-ideal discrepancies rated their relationships more favorably, even when the perceived difficulty of finding a good alternative partner/relationship was statistically controlled.

Changes in Ideal Standards Across Time. Although the Fletcher et al. (1999) studies provide initial support for our model, they were cross-sectional in design. To test and make stronger inferences about possible causal relations, cross-sectional designs are obviously problematic. Thus, Fletcher, Simpson, and Thomas (2000) conducted a longitudinal study. A large sample of individuals in newly formed dating relationships completed a battery of measures assessing perceptions of their current partner/relationship, the quality of their relationship, and their ideal standards once a month for 3 months. They then completed the same scales 9 months later (unless they had previously broken up with their partners). The first wave of measurement typically occurred 3 weeks after individuals had started dating someone.

Using cross-lagged analyses, we were able to test a crucial prediction from our model – that comparisons between ideals and perceptions of the current partner should, in fact, have a causal impact on relationship evaluations. We also tested a balance model, which proposes that ideals, current perceptions, and relationship evaluations all constrain one another equally. The cross-lagged analyses supported our causal hypothesis but refuted the balance model. Changes in ratings over time occurred in only one direction, with greater consistency between ideals and perceptions of the current partner/relationship (assessed at earlier times in the relationship) predicting more positive evaluations of the partner and the relationship over time, but not vice versa. Of course, because these analyses are correlational, third variables could be generating these effects. Nevertheless, the current evidence suggests that cognitive comparisons between ideal standards and perceptions of the current partner/relationship do influence the way in which partners and relationships are evaluated over time.

We also examined links between ideals and perceptions of the partner/relationship across time. As expected, more positive perceptions of the partner/relationship at earlier points in time predicted that more importance would be placed on similar ideal dimensions over time, but not the reverse. This finding may be attributable to the fact that ideals tend to be subjective, personally held standards that are similar to preferences. Consequently, ideals should be less constrained by reality than is true of perceptions of the partner and the relationship. For example, an individual may want to believe that his or her partner is loyal, considerate, and committed to the relationship, but this belief may be difficult to sustain in the face of incontrovertible evidence that the partner is interested in someone else.

Ideal Standards, Flexibility, and Relationship Quality. To determine how ideal standards and their flexibility jointly affect relationship evaluations, Campbell et al. (in press) had a large sample of individuals involved in dating relationships rate themselves and their ideal partners on all the items comprising the three ideal partner scales. Individuals also rated how flexible each of their ideals were (i.e., how far below each ideal standard a prospective partner could be and still remain a viable partner) and how closely their current partner matched their ideal standards on each scale. Individuals who rated themselves higher on each ideal scale had ideal standards that were less flexible. Corroborating past research (Fletcher et al., 2000), the quality of their relationships was higher if individuals' current partners more closely matched their ideal standards. However, this effect was moderated by the degree of flexibility individuals displayed on two ideals dimensions – warmth/trustworthiness and status/resources. For these dimensions, individuals who thought their partners more closely matched their ideals, and who had less flexible standards, reported the highest relationship quality.

The magnitude of current-ideal discrepancies not only should affect how individuals appraise and evaluate their relationships; such discrepancies also might affect how the partners of the individuals feel about the relationship. Thus, in a second study, Campbell et al. (in press) asked both members of a large sample of dating couples to report their ideal standards, how closely their partners matched their ideals, and their degree of flexibility on each ideal dimension. Smaller current-ideal discrepancies predicted a higher relationship quality, as reported by both members of the dyad (i.e., both the actor and the partner). In other words, individuals whose partners more closely matched their ideals reported that their relationships were better, as did the partners of these individuals. This partner effect suggests that individuals may sense how well they are living up to their partners' ideal standards. Over time, those who are faring poorly may feel threatened or insecure about the long-term status of the relationship or their position within it, which should lower their evaluations. Replicating the first study, individuals with partners who more closely matched their ideals, and who possessed less flexible standards, also reported the highest relationship quality (i.e., flexibility of ideals moderated the relation between current-ideal discrepancies and relationship quality).

Unresolved Questions and Issues

Several important questions remain concerning how individuals establish and adjust their ideal standards over time, the ways in which relationship discrepancies are similar to and different from self-discrepancies, and how dyad-level processes are likely to complicate the operation of ideal standards in relationships. In the final section, we address these issues, all of which require further research and theoretical development.

Establishment and Adjustment of Ideal Standards

Why do some individuals have high standards for their ideal partners and relationships, whereas others possess humble standards? At present, relatively little is known about what factors influence how individuals set and adjust their ideal standards. Certainly, experiences in relationships should substantially color and influence ideals, perhaps partly through the process of transference discussed by Andersen and Berenson (this volume). Supply and demand considerations also may affect the level of an individual's ideal standards. Persons who are in relatively short supply, for example, should be able to command more from prospective mates, slowly raising their own ideal standards. Those not in demand may gradually have to lower their standards (see Guttentag & Secord, 1983). Moreover, as we have seen, individuals with less flexible ideal standards tend to have higher ideals (Campbell et al., 1999). Being less flexible in terms of ideals may encourage individuals to aspire to loftier ideal standards, and vice versa.

Two variables, however, have particularly clear and theoretically important ties to the calibration of ideal standards. First, partners with more positive self-views (i.e., higher relationship-relevant self-esteem) tend to hold higher ideal standards (Murray et al., 1996a, 1996b). Second, partners who think they have more to offer others (i.e., those with higher self-perceived mate value) should have higher ideal standards, at least concerning their ideal partners (Regan, 1998). Indeed, recent research has documented that individuals who rate themselves higher on the three partner ideals scales (warmth/trustworthiness, vitality/attractiveness, and status/resources) tend to have higher ideal standards (Campbell et al., 1999).

Similarities and Differences Between Self-Discrepancy and Relationship-Discrepancy Processes

Several major theoretical perspectives posit that individuals use *actual-ideal* or *actual-ought* discrepancies to make important judgments and regulate their behavior, the most detailed and influential ones being those developed by Higgins (1987, 1989). We have adopted some of Higgins's theorizing in developing our Ideals Standards Model (see Simpson et al., in press). Nevertheless, we believe there are some important differences between the processes that are likely to govern self-based and relationship-based ideal standards.

First, there are specific categories of partner and relationship ideals that simply are not present in models of self ideals. Indeed, the three categories of partner ideals we have discovered we believe reflect specific and unique evolutionary adaptations that are likely to differ from those that may have generated self ideals.

Second, the cognitive, affective, and behavioral consequences of large current-ideal discrepancies are likely to be different in self-discrepancy versus relationship-discrepancy models. For example, individuals might react to large current-ideal discrepancies in relationships by leaving their relationship, by attempting to modify their partner's behavior, or by pursuing a different relationship. It is hard to see how these actions would resolve or reduce many self-ideal discrepancies (e.g., I am an introvert, but I wish I were an extrovert).

Third, a major difference between self-discrepancy models and relationship-discrepancy models is that two people are involved – and must be taken into account – in relationship-discrepancy models. When individuals' actual self-views are discrepant from their ideal standards, and changes in behavior could reduce these discrepancies, individuals typically have to focus only on altering their own actions. However, when individuals' perceptions of their current partners/relationships diverge from their ideal partner and relationship standards, behavior change is likely to involve not only the self but also the partner. This should complicate the operation and functioning of relationship discrepancies in significant ways. To date, only one study has examined how the ideal standards held by each partner in a relationship affect the relationship outcomes experienced by both partners. Campbell et al.'s (in press) finding that individuals with smaller current-ideal discrepancies have partners who also report being more satisfied with the relationship highlights the potential importance – as well as the potential complexity – involved in examining dyadic processes in the context of relationship ideals.

Dyad-Level Processes and Effects

As previously noted, relationship-discrepancy models, unlike self-discrepancy models, take on an added layer of complexity when the thoughts, feelings, perceptions, and behavior of the relationship partner are considered. Partners can influence or manipulate how individuals view themselves, the level of their ideal standards, what individuals expect from their partners, and even how they view their partners. For example, if individuals have large current-ideal discrepancies for which they think their partners are primarily responsible, such individuals by themselves may not be able to make the behavioral changes necessary to reduce these discrepancies. If a wife is unhappy about the lack of sexual activity in her marriage and blames her husband, the husband's steadfast refusal to have sex should sustain her discrepancies, perhaps regardless of what she says or does.

Moreover, in regulating their own discrepancies, individuals may have to take into account the magnitude and origins of their partners' discrepancies. There may be times when individuals find it difficult to reduce their own discrepancies because their partners refuse to alter their own behavior or because their partners might threaten to leave the relationship (or worse) if individuals try to reduce their own discrepancies. Consider, for example, how dyadic processes might influence what happens when an individual is motivated to be accurate and is highly committed to his or her relationship but is experiencing large, persistent current-ideal discrepancies that are partly due to the partner's undesirable actions (e.g., if one's partner is a classic narcissist; Rhodewalt, this volume). Initially, the individual might try to change his or her partner's behavior. However, if the partner simply will not or cannot change the undesirable behavior, the individual may be forced to shift away from purely behavioral strategies. At first, the individual may try to increase the flexibility of his or her ideal standards if possible. If this proves to be an ineffective solution but the individual remains committed to the relationship, he or she may shift away from an accuracy motivation set and begin using one or more of the enhancement-based perceptual strategies discussed earlier (such as lowering ideal standards, enhancing perceptions of the partner, or downplaying the importance of formerly valued ideal standards). If these cognitive strategies all fail, the individual eventually may decide to terminate the relationship.

Many intriguing questions remain about how dyad-level processes might influence the operation and use of ideal standards. We know very little, for instance, about how one partner's ideal standards are communicated or conveyed to the other partner, or what happens when one partner is motivated to be accurate in situations when the other partner is motivated to enhance the relationship. We also know almost nothing about whether possessing ideal standards that are similar to those held by one's partner facilitates relationship functioning and quality, or how partners might influence one another concerning the salience, importance, or amount of in-depth processing granted to ideal standards. Affective and emotional states are likely to play a pivotal role in alerting the individual to important events and in interpreting the meaning of current-ideal discrepancies (see Forgas, this volume). Indeed, the role of emotion and affect should play a major role in the use and regulation of current-ideal discrepancies in relationship contexts.

Conclusion

In this chapter, we have presented a new model and some supporting data that elucidates the content and structure of partner and relationship ideal standards, the basic functions that ideals serve, and how they may operate at the level of cognitive process. In addition, we have described the way in which current-ideal discrepancies are associated with how both partners in a relationship evaluate its quality. We have also outlined how two motivational sets – relationship enhancement versus accuracy – might be linked to ideals and related processes, and we have described the differences and similarities between ideals as they are likely to function in relation to the self and within dyadic relationships.

It is difficult to think of another domain in social life where the need to develop and use cognitive and motivational strategies is more obvious than in our most intimate interpersonal relationships. Hence, it is not surprising that laypeople develop general theories and knowledge structures of various kinds (including ideals), as well as local theories that deal with specific relationships. Understanding how these two levels of lay theory interact – especially with respect to ideal standards – promises to be informative about both basic social cognitive processes and interpersonal behavior.

References

Baldwin, M. W. (1992). Relational schemas and the processing of social information. *Psychological Bulletin, 112,* 461–484.

Baumeister, R. F. (1998). The self. In D. Gilbert, S. Fiske, & G. Lindzey (Eds.), *Handbook of social psychology* (pp. 680–740). New York: McGraw-Hill.

Berscheid, E., & Walster, E. H. (1978). *Interpersonal attraction* (2nd ed.). Reading, MA: Addison-Wesley.

Buss, D. M., & Schmitt, D. P. (1993). Sexual strategies theory: A contextual evolutionary analysis of human mating. *Psychological Review, 100,* 204–232.

Campbell, L. J., Simpson, J. A., Kashy, D. A., & Fletcher, G. J. O. (in press). *Personality and Social Psychology Bulletin.*

Fletcher, G. J. O., Simpson, J. A., & Thomas, G. (2000). *The role of ideals in early relationship development.* Unpublished manuscript, University of Canterbury, New Zealand.

Fletcher, G. J. O., Simpson, J. A., Thomas, G., & Giles, L. (1999). Ideals in intimate relationships. *Journal of Personality and Social Psychology, 76,* 72–89.

Fletcher, G. J. O., & Thomas, G. (1996). Lay theories in close relationships: Their structure and function. In G. J. O. Fletcher & J. Fitness (Eds.), *Knowledge structures in close relationships: A social psychological approach* (pp. 3–24). Mahwah, NJ: Erlbaum.

Gangestad, S. W., & Simpson, J. A. (in press). The evolution of human mating: Trade-offs and strategic pluralism. *Behavioral and Brain Sciences.*

Gollwitzer, P. M., & Kinney, R. F. (1989). Effects of deliberative and implemental mind-sets on illusion of control. *Journal of Personality and Social Psychology, 56,* 531–542.

Guttentag, M., & Secord, P. F. (1983). *Too many women? The sex ratio question.* Beverly Hills, CA: Sage.

Higgins, E. T. (1987). Self-discrepancy: A theory relating self and affect. *Psychological Review, 94,* 319–340.

Higgins, E. T. (1989). Self-discrepancy theory: What patterns of self-beliefs cause people to suffer? In L. Berkowitz (Ed.), *Advances in experimental social psychology* (Vol. 22, pp. 93–136). New York: Academic Press.

Kelley, H. H., & Thibaut, J. W. (1978). *Interpersonal relations: A theory of interdependence.* New York: Wiley.

Lambert, A. J., & Wedell, D. H. (1991). The self and social judgment: Effects of affective reaction and "own position" on judgments of unambiguous and ambiguous information about others. *Journal of Personality and Social Psychology, 61,* 884–897.

Levinger, G., & Breedlove, J. (1966). Interpersonal attraction and agreement: A study of marriage partners. *Journal of Personality and Social Psychology, 3,* 367–372.

Murray, S. L., Holmes, J. G., & Griffin, D. W. (1996a). The benefits of positive illusions: Idealization and the construction of satisfaction in close relationships. *Journal of Personality and Social Psychology, 70,* 79–98.

Murray, S. L., Holmes, J. G., & Griffin, D. W. (1996b). The self-fulfilling nature of positive illusions in romantic relationships: Love is not blind, but prescient. *Journal of Personality and Social Psychology, 71,* 1155–1180.

Regan, P. C. (1998). What if you can't get what you want? Willingness to compromise ideal mate selection standards as a function of sex, mate value, and relationship context. *Personality and Social Psychology Bulletin, 24,* 1294–1303.

Sedikides, C., & Showronski, J. J. (1993). The self in impression formation: Trait centrality and social perception. *Journal of Experimental Social Psychology, 29,* 347–357.

Simpson, J. A., Fletcher, G. J. O., & Campbell, L. J. (in press). The structure and functions of ideal standards in close relationships. In G. J. O. Fletcher & M. S. Clark (Eds.), *Blackwell handbook of social psychology: Interpersonal processes.* Oxford: Basil Blackwell.

Simpson, J. A., Ickes, W., & Blackstone, T. (1995). When the head protects the heart: Empathic accuracy in dating relationships. *Journal of Personality and Social Psychology, 69,* 629–641.

Singh, G. K., Mathews, T. J., Clarke, S. C., Yannicos, T., & Smith, B. L. (1995). Annual summary of births, marriages, divorces, and deaths: United States, 1994. *Monthly Vital Statistics Report* (Vol. 43, No. 13). Hyattsville, MD: National Center for Health Statistics.

Stephan, W., Berscheid, E., & Walster, E. (1971). Sexual arousal and heterosexual perception. *Journal of Personality and Social Psychology, 20,* 93–101.

Thibaut, J. W., & Kelley, H. H. (1959). *The social psychology of groups.* New York: Wiley.

13. Victims and Perpetrators Provide Discrepant Accounts: Motivated Cognitive Distortions about Interpersonal Transgressions

ROY F. BAUMEISTER AND KATHLEEN CATANESE

Many social interactions and situations are defined partly in terms of social roles. Hunter and prey, mentor and protégé, aspiring lover and reluctant object of affection, teacher and student, plaintiff and defendant, physician and patient, performer and evaluator – these examples indicate how roles provide structure for situations. Each person has a part to play, and the conflicting or complementary scripts for the roles provide the basis for the interaction. The roles also provide different perspectives on the action and increase the possibility that the interaction will be interpreted and recalled differently by the people who took part in it. The social mind is ineluctably immersed in situated interactions, and hence its cognitive processes are often subject to powerful motivations.

This chapter will focus on an especially powerful pair of situational roles, namely, victim and perpetrator. These roles are inherent in interpersonal transgressions: One person (the perpetrator) does something to harm or offend another person (the victim). The episode begins, perhaps, with some provocation or motive that leads the perpetrator to act in the offensive fashion. It ends with the victim either forgiving the perpetrator or holding a grudge; in some cases, it ends with the death of one or both of the participants.

The central theme of this chapter is that victim and perpetrator have different perspectives on the transgression episode that can often cause them to perceive, interpret, and remember it quite differently. These

Address for correspondence: Roy F. Baumeister, Department of Psychology, Case Western Reserve University, Cleveland, OH 44106, USA. Email: rfb2@po.cwru.edu differences reflect a gap in understanding between the two roles and seem likely to make reconciliation and other subsequent, positive interactions difficult. More generally, the implication is that interpersonal relations are made difficult not just by the traits of individual persons but also by situational structures that assign people to different roles that produce divergent perceptions. More broadly, the understanding of the social mind must acknowledge that different roles can produce vastly different outcomes and often vastly different understandings, depending on the perspective and role of the individual.

In this chapter, we shall cover several investigations that provided evidence of interpretive differences between victims and perpetrators. Our own research on this topic began with a collaboration with Arlene Stillwell and Sara Wotman (Baumeister, Stillwell, & Wotman, 1990). It approached the topic by asking a sample of college students to write a pair of stories each. The instruction for the victim story involved describing an incident in which someone did something to anger the subject. The instruction for the perpetrator story solicited an incident in which the subject did something to anger someone else. The order of the stories was counterbalanced, so that half of the people wrote the perpetrator story first, and the rest wrote the victim story first. Responses were kept anonymous to minimize self-presentational concerns (e.g., Tice & Faber, this volume). These stories were content-coded on a large number of dimensions, most of which involved the simple presence or absence of some feature (e.g., an apology or a reference to the present time). This investigation found no differences as a function of order of story (i.e., whether the victim or perpetrator story was written first). But the role difference produced many differences in the content of the stories. That is, victim stories differed systematically from perpetrator stories in many ways, and these differences will be the basis for much of what is covered in this chapter.

An important feature of that investigation was that every person was asked to furnish one story for each role. The differences between victim and perpetrator stories do not therefore signify that victims and perpetrators are different kinds of people. In this study, victims and perpetrators were the same people. The motivations and biases that produced the differences must be assumed to originate in the roles themselves.

Despite the advantages of having each person write both a victim and a perpetrator narrative, it is necessary to acknowledge a drawback that it entails. Baumeister et al. (1990) were not generally able to get the perpetrator and the victim from the same incident. This is a common problem in narrative research. For example, Vaughan (1987) collected detailed narrative accounts about divorce, but when she asked her research participants if she could contact their ex-partners, they almost universally refused, so she was left with only one side of each story.

With regard to the Baumeister et al. (1990) investigation, the most serious concern raised by the story-eliciting procedure is the possibility that victims and perpetrators selected different kinds of incidents to describe, so that differences in the stories reflect differences in the actual incidents, as opposed to motivated differences in the interpretation and narrative construction. The procedures of using standard instructions, limiting latitude of choice, and having the same people write both stories on the same occasion should have reduced some of this problem but would certainly not eliminate it. The authors did find that the stories were superficially similar in the kinds of incidents to which they referred, but that does not rule out the possibility that more subtle differences existed.

Perhaps the most encouraging results with regard to this potential problem are from subsequent studies. Mikula, Athenstaedt, Heschgl, and Heimgartner (1998) found similar results with a sample of romantic partners, such that both members reported on the same incident. Stillwell and Baumeister (1997) used a laboratory simulation to assign people randomly to roles in a standardized incident, and their results also converged with what the original study found. Thus, although the original investigation's findings cannot be unequivocally ascribed to interpretive differences rather than selection differences, the weight of evidence suggests that the biases operate more strongly on interpretation (including biased memory) than on biased selection of different kinds of events. This is consistent with ample other evidence that people are motivated to interpret and remember events in biased ways (see Rhodewalt, this volume).

Severity of Consequences

Although victim and perpetrator stories are often similar in regard to the types of incidents they describe, victims tend to present negative consequences as more severe and lasting than do perpetrators (Baumeister et al., 1990). Victims describe long-term damage to relationships following interpersonal transgressions. They also describe other problems or misfortunes that the transgression caused, including matters that continue to plague them in the present. Perpetrators, in contrast, tend to downplay such negative or lasting consequences. Indeed, perpetrator accounts are more likely than victim accounts to deny that there were lasting negative consequences.

Many people believe that anger can have positive, beneficial consequences, and researchers on anger have repeatedly found that people claim that anger can be constructive (e.g., Averill, 1982; Tavris, 1982). The investigation by Baumeister et al. (1990) failed to find much evidence of positive consequences, however. The stories people told about their major anger experiences did not contain much that was positive; in particular, positive consequences of the angry incident were almost entirely lacking.

The investigation did, however, include a category called *happy endings*, referring to stories that ended in a positive way. A story can have a happy ending without claiming or implying that the transgression had some positive consequence. If the conflict was resolved in a positive way, or even if the story affirmed that the erstwhile victim and perpetrator were now on good terms, the story was coded as having a happy ending. Baumeister et al. (1990) found that happy endings were more common in perpetrator than in victim accounts. Perpetrators are thus more likely than victims to report that things turned out well.

Converging evidence has been found in other contexts. Williams, Wheeler, and Harvey (this volume) have consistently found that the victims of ostracism report more severe and lasting harm than the ostracizers. Hansen (1987) devised a strategy for learning about infidelity without suffering from the difficulties that the low base rate of infidelity causes: He surveyed dating couples about any third-person (*extradyadic*) physical contact, including erotic kissing or petting. This enabled him to get fairly high base rates: A majority of both men and women had some experience with at least romantic kissing (by self or partner) of someone outside the relationship.

Consistent with the victim–perpetrator difference, the victims tended to see the transgression as worse than the perpetrators saw it. This was especially ironic insofar as the same people furnished accounts of the effects of both their own and their partners' minor acts of unfaithfulness. When people were asked whether the particular incident had "hurt a great deal" (the most severe response), relatively few people (9% of men, 14% of women) said their own transgressions had caused their partner that much pain. For their partner's transgressions, however, 45% of men and 30% of women said that such acts had hurt a great deal. Thus, they rated infidelity as much more severe and destructive when their partner did it than when they themselves did it.

More severe forms of sexual infidelity were studied by Spanier and Margolis (1983), who examined marital infidelity in relation to marital separation and divorce. Once again, victims tended to see the infidelity as worse than perpetrators. More precisely, respondents of both sexes said that their own infidelities were a result, rather than a cause, of the problems in the marriage, and so, in effect, they claimed that their own extramarital involvements did not damage the relationship. In contrast, respondents said that their partners' infidelities were a major, direct cause of the conflicts in (and eventual failure of) the marriage.

History offers many examples of similar discrepancies between victims and perpetrators, especially in connection with accounts of mass execution campaigns and other atrocities. Estimates of the number of persons killed in the Nazi Holocaust, the rape of Nanking, the former Yugoslavia, and Tibet, and similar tragedies, often diverge widely, depending on whether they are provided by the victims or the perpetrators.

Passing Moral Judgment

Another sphere in which perpetrator and victim accounts differ is in the moral culpability of the act. To victims, moral issues are clear and stark, and the transgression is often presented as an undeniable, even shocking, violation of moral standards. Baumeister et al. (1990) did not find perpetrator accounts to be the opposite in the sense of strong, clear assertions of moral innocence, except in a few cases. Rather, most perpetrators gave accounts that represented moral gray areas, such that they acknowledged some wrongdoing but also cited extenuating and mitigating circumstances, reciprocal causation (including causal instigation or provocation by the victim), and ambiguous or conflicting moral standards. Unlike the remorselessly evil bad guys portrayed in movies and popular entertainments, the perpetrators in this research sample presented morally complex figures.

Most people share the opinion that an act caused by external factors is less culpable than one that originates within the self, and even the legal system permits certain acts of violence or crime to be judged and punished less harshly if external factors mitigate their severity.

Perpetrator accounts were found to contain far more allusions to mitigating circumstances than victim accounts (68% to 20%) (Baumeister et al., 1990). This difference may in part reflect the actor-observer bias in attribution (Jones & Nisbett, 1971), according to which observers often fail to recognize the situational factors that may affect an actor's behavior and that are quite salient to the actor. The difference may also be motivated: Perpetrators highlight external causes because these causes reduce the severity of their offense, whereas victims downplay or ignore these external factors in order to present the transgression in a maximally bad light. Such motivations could reflect dissonance-reduction processes (Cooper, this volume).

Some acts may hurt or anger people even though the perpetrator has reason to believe that his or her actions are justified. Baumeister et al. (1990) coded for assertions that the acts were wholly or partly justified; these assertions were found in about half of the perpetrator narratives but in almost none (2%) of the victim narratives. Thus, as a group, perpetrator narratives were fairly complex and mixed in that they often acknowledged some wrongdoing but also appealed to partial justifications or extenuating circumstances. Victim accounts, in contrast, tended to be morally homogeneous and severe in that the perpetrator's acts were presented as without any moral justification or even mitigating circumstances. Consistent with this, victim accounts were several times more likely than perpetrator accounts to state that the perpetrator's actions were immoral.

Although we have emphasized the exonerating thrust of perpetrator narratives, it is important to note that perpetrators did blame themselves in many ways. Self-blame for the incident was far more common in perpetrator than victim incidents, and indeed, victims accepted almost none of the blame for the transgression. Perpetrator accounts often expressed regret over the incident, but victim accounts did not acknowledge that perpetrators felt any such regret.

Perhaps most revealing is the discrepancy in reports of apologies. Almost one-quarter of perpetrator accounts claimed that the perpetrator had apologized or tried to make amends to the victim. In contrast, almost none (4%) of the victim accounts acknowledged any such apology or restitution. One might think that an apology would be extremely salient to a victim because it provides proof that the perpetrator recognizes the misdeed. Yet apologies were largely absent from victims' accounts in the Baumeister et al. (1990) sample. This finding is consistent with the pattern that victims sought to portray the incident in the most negative light possible, whereas perpetrators provided morally complex and mixed accounts. Victims described unapologetic perpetrators, suggesting that these people performed their transgressions without scruple or remorse. Perpetrators claimed plenty of remorse and said they had tried to make up for what they had done.

Again, it is worth pointing out that these differences do not signify that victims and perpetrators are different kinds of people. Rather, the biases are in the roles. Victims and perpetrators were the same exact people in this study insofar as everyone furnished one story of each type.

Moving outside the laboratory, one can find similar discrepancies between victim and perpetrator accounts. It is well known that many convicted prisoners claimed to have been falsely accused and denied any wrongdoing, whereas, of course, their victims insisted otherwise (and did so convincingly enough to put the perpetrators in prison). To be sure, some of those denials may reflect a legal strategy of seeking to overturn one's conviction and gain freedom, so perpetrators who privately know themselves to be guilty might still claim innocence.

Other forms of evidence suggest, however, that even where no legal action or prosecution is involved, victims and perpetrators still have radically different views about what happened. Perhaps the most vivid evidence about such discrepancies concerns sexual coercion and rape. The most reliable data suggest that only about 3% of men report having forced women to engage in sexual activity, whereas 22% of women report having been forced (Laumann, Gagnon, Michael, & Michaels, 1994). These represent survey data, and few or none of the sexual assaults were reported to the police (see also other recent findings).

One might regard the 3% and 22% figures as plausible if a handful of men each coerced many different women, as in a pattern of serial rape. The data do not support this view, however (Laumann et al., 1994). The majority of women who report having been forced to engage in sexual activity against their will, however, report that they were forced by someone they were in love with or by a spouse or steady boyfriend. Many others fingered friends or casual acquaintances. Sexual coercion thus apparently occurs most often within established or incipient relationships, and this contradicts the view that a few serial rapists are responsible for the majority of such events.

Thus, apparently, there are many incidents in which a man and a woman who are romantically involved have some form of sexual contact that is subsequently regarded quite differently by the two of them. The woman may look back on the episode as involving force and going against her consent, whereas the man looks back on it without seeing force or coercion. Nor is this pattern based in some irreducible gender difference. Similar patterns and discrepancies are found with regard to women forcing men to engage in unwanted sexual activity, although these have received considerably less research attention (Anderson & Struckman-Johnson, 1998).

Insight into how these discrepant perceptions arise is furnished by Kanin's (1985) study of a large sample of men who admitted having engaged in date rape. In all cases, the coercive sexual activity occurred when the couple had been engaging in consensual sexual activity. Most commonly, the couple had engaged in heavy petting and oral sex; the woman wanted to stop there, but the man forced her to have intercourse. In Kanin's sample, the men admitted to having forced the women, but one may infer that in other cases, the woman's consent to participate in the petting and oral sex could be used by the man to disregard her reluctance to have intercourse. (Juries appear to have the same difficulty, incidentally, a fact that presents a considerable practical dilemma for the woman who desires to have physical contact that stops short of intercourse.) The perpetrator may therefore interpret the entire episode as consensual and hence justified, whereas the victim would be far more likely to believe that the perpetrator's actions were unjustified.

Time Span

Victims and perpetrators also differ in their treatment of time. Baumeister et al. (1990) found that victims used a relatively long time span, whereas perpetrators tended to use very brief time spans focusing simply on the incident. In a sense, perpetrator narratives tended to depict just the occasion of the transgression, and if they referred to later points in time, it was usually to deny that the transgression was relevant to subsequent events or to present circumstances. In contrast, victim accounts presented the transgression as woven into the context of prior and subsequent events.

The victims' accounts of transgressions often began well before the actual incident. They described previous circumstances that furnished a context and meaning. In a significant number of cases, they presented prior offenses by the perpetrator that led up to the transgression. These offenses are important because they depict the transgression as part of a pattern of repeated, multiple offenses. The perpetrators tended to describe single incidents, but many victims justified their anger by saying that they had put up with repeated problems and became angry only at the accumulated grievances.

Once again, there are parallels between the laboratory data and evidence about sexual transgressions. Spanier and Margolis (1983) found that people tended to describe their partners' infidelities as consisting of lasting, meaningful affairs in which the sexual misdeeds were part of a pattern of multiple transgressions and a meaningful external involvement. Although women described their own infidelities in the same way, men tended to describe their (men's) infidelities as one-time, relatively meaningless sexual encounters. Thus, for at least the men's infidelities, the perpetrators perceived and reported single incidents, whereas the victims alluded to multiple, accumulating misdeeds.

Although a simple coding of allusions to present time revealed no differences between victim and perpetrator accounts in the Baumeister et al. (1990) sample, further codings showed important differences in the way the transgression account invoked the present time. Victim accounts tended to describe lasting problems or relationship damage and to say that the transgression was often quite relevant to the present. Perpetrators, on the other hand, tended to deny that the transgression was relevant to the present, and their accounts contrasted the present with the transgression. This finding parallels research on ostracism, in which victims generally report more severe and lasting consequences than perpetrators (Williams et al., this volume).

One implication is that an important defense mechanism used by perpetrators is *temporal bracketing*, that is, marking the transgression off in time so as to separate it from the present. As already noted, many perpetrators acknowledged that they had done something wrong and bore some responsibility for the transgression. They coped by suggesting that their responsibility for the past transgression should not be used to judge them in the present. The perpetrator's motto may be characterized as "Let bygones be bygones." Victims, in contrast, say "Never forget."

Thus, victims see transgressions in a much longer time span than perpetrators. This is consistent with evidence that victims of traumas such as child sexual abuse and incest may continue to ruminate about past sufferings for years afterward (Silver, Boon, & Stones, 1983). Perpetrators, in contrast, are often reluctant to think back on the event and may quickly consign it to the category of ancient history that seems irrelevant to the present (e.g., Lifton, 1986; Sichrovsky, 1988).

One striking parallel to these findings can be found in histories of the Crusades (although similar patterns can be found with regard to the American Civil War, the Balkan and Yugoslavian conflicts, the Holocaust, and others). Western histories of the Crusades (e.g., Runciman, 1951–1954) present them as ancient events that produced both positive and negative consequences that have now at most a distant, indirect relevance to current events. In contrast, a recent history of the Crusades from the Arab perspective (Maalouf, 1987) concludes forcefully that current conflicts between the Middle East and the Western world have been crucially shaped by the acute historical griev-ance that the Arabs hold with regard to the Christian invasions and atrocities committed during the Crusades. Moreover, the lasting con-sequences are not nearly as mixed in the Arab perspective as in the European perspective, and the Arab world sees the consequences of the Crusades as predominantly negative.

Intentions of the Perpetrator

At the core of many moral issues is the question of what the per-petrator intended to happen. Intentional harm is generally judged far more culpable than unintentional harm. Not surprisingly, victims and perpetrators often differed sharply on how they characterized the perpetrator's intentions.

Victims were far more likely than perpetrators to characterize the perpetrator's intentions as deliberately hurtful or malicious (Baumeister et al., 1990). Thus, many victims regard perpetrators as having a clear, willful intent to cause harm, possibly deriving sadistic or other pleasure from hurting. Perpetrators do not, however, charac-terize themselves that way. Undoubtedly there are many reasons for this, among them the fact that viewing oneself as taking responsible action that leads to harmful consequences would generate considerable cognitive dissonance (Cooper, this volume).

Perpetrators were far more likely than victims to characterize their (the perpetrators') actions as impulsive or even as something they could not help. In fact, Baumeister et al. (1990) found that nearly a third of perpetrators, but no victims, described the perpetrator's actions as something that could not be helped. Thus, in the perpetrators' view, they were not seeking to do harm (as the victims often characterized them) but rather were forced by circumstances to do what they did or, at most, acted on the spur of the moment instead of in a planned, premeditated fashion.

An even more fundamental difference emerged when the stories were coded for whether they depicted any sort of reasonable, understandable motive or reason for acting on the perpetrator's part. Nearly all perpetrators described themselves as having some reason for doing what they did (i.e., the transgression). In contrast, about half of the victim accounts depicted the perpetrator as having had no valid reason. The perpetrator's acts were described by many victims as arbitrary, contradictory, incoherent, or senseless.

Thus, perpetrators generally regard themselves as having some meaningful reason for what they did, even though they often put some blame on themselves and regret their actions later. Victims, however, seem unable or unwilling to acknowledge the perpetrator's reasons, especially justifiable or understandable reasons. To victims, perpetrators either acted for no reason at all or at most out of a malicious, sadistic, and arbitrary wish to inflict harm. Clearly, these two views of perpetrator intentions are worlds apart, and reaching a mutual understanding to resolve the grievance is likely to be hampered by this gap in understanding.

There is one other pattern of perceived motivation that is relevant, even though it did not surface in that particular study. Baumeister (1997) remarked on the pattern that many victims perceive the acts of perpetrators as belonging to a broad evil conspiracy. Partly this is due to the magnitude gap: The gap between perpetrator and victim perceptions of magnitude is so large as to generate considerable dissonance (e.g., Cooper, this volume). Victims are reluctant to accept how minor or trivial their suffering may be from the perpetrators' perspective, so they shift their perceptions of perpetrators to emphasize the infliction of harm as central, widespread, and cooperative.

Several examples of such views may be cited. Many Jewish writers on the Nazi Holocaust have asserted that killing Jews was the primary, overriding goal of the Nazis, to the extent that all other goals were secondary (e.g., Goldhagen, 1996). When one realizes that the Nazis were trying to rebuild an economically and politically devastated country, introduce their own utopian social arrangement, conquer land for expansion, and carry on the largest war in world history, such an assumption is scarcely plausible, but undoubtedly it would be hard for victims to accept that the deaths of their friends and relatives were a relatively minor part of the overall plan. Similarly, many African Americans today perceive the acquired immune deficiency syndrome, the crack cocaine epidemic, and the sale of guns as part of a conspiracy by the white American society to eradicate black citizens, and many gang members even assert that the deadly violence between rival gangs of African American youth is actually instigated and controlled by the federal government as part of this effort (e.g., Shakur, 1993). The government's various efforts to curb violence and promote the well-being of African American citizens are not regarded as relevant counterevidence and can even be seen as a diversionary smoke screen. Yet another example is Brownmiller's (1975) assertion that all individual acts of rape are part of a grand conspiracy by all men to victimize all women. We shall return to this example later in this chapter in connection with our discussion of rape.

Who Is Accurate?

These findings show that victims and perpetrators differ sharply in the way they perceive and remember transgressions. It appears that when people move from one role to another, they adopt motivated biases that are rooted in each role, and a truthful, factual rendition of events is likely to suffer. The persistent discrepancies suggest that at least one of the two roles is sufficiently biased to distort the truth, but it is plausible that one of them is reasonably accurate. But which one?

Conventional wisdom holds that victims are more truthful and reliable than perpetrators. By definition, perpetrators are accused of wrongdoing, and so to preserve their good name, freedom of action, and other benefits, they would want to conceal evidence of misbehavior. Victims, in this view, have no incentive to alter the facts, so their accounts can be trusted. Historians, for example, often rely heavily on victim accounts because they assume that perpetrators lie and dissemble in order to reduce their appearance of guilt.

Yet it is plausible that the victim role holds motivations and biases too. Victims are widely regarded as being entitled to social support, tolerance, and even material restitution. A successful claim to be a victim may entitle someone to receive an assortment of benefits. Moreover, as the legal system makes clear, the magnitude of one's suffering and of the perpetrator's wrongdoing are directly related to the scope of benefits the victim deserves. In a lawsuit, for example, a large settlement award is quite unlikely if the victim claims not to have suffered much.

The difficulty of establishing relative degree of bias in the findings presented thus far is that there is no objective criterion of accuracy. Even if one can obtain accounts from the victim and the perpetrator in the same incident, it is difficult to know which one is closer to the truth. Some alternative procedure is needed in order to assess degrees of distortion.

To furnish an objective measure that could assess relative degree of distortion, Stillwell and Baumeister (1997) developed a procedure that assigned people to identify with either the victim or the perpetrator in a simulated transgression. All participants read a story in which one student promised to help another but later refused to help. There were various extenuating circumstances, including changes in the type of help needed and external interference. One-third of the participants were instructed to identify with the victim and then, after reading the story, to retell it in their own words in the first person (i.e., as if it had happened to them personally). One-third were instructed to identify with the perpetrator and retell the story as if they themselves had been the perpetrator. The rest read the story without identifying with either character and were instructed to retell the story in the third person (i.e., as if it had happened to someone else). By comparing the stories written by the subjects with the original, standard version of the story that everyone read, it was possible to assess precisely how many and what kinds of distortions were introduced.

The results indicated that both the victim and the perpetrator roles contain motivations that can bias memory. Victims and perpetrators made nearly identical numbers of errors on average (25 each). People who told the story in the third person, without identifying with either role, were significantly more accurate (mean of 17 errors).

Before we conclude that perpetrators are just as reliable as victims, it is necessary to acknowledge that the experiment by Stillwell and Baumeister (1997) was just a simulation, so there were no actual consequences hanging in the balance. In everyday life, perpetrators sometimes face the threat of prison, retaliation, a lawsuit, or other costs if they tell the truth about what they did, and these pressures may increase the number of distortions and lies in their accounts. Still, that study found ample evidence of distorted memory even in the complete absence of material consequences (and even if people were offered a financial inducement to tell the story accurately). Objective truth is elusive to both victims and perpetrators.

Although the victims and perpetrators distorted their stories to similar degrees, the nature and content of the distortions were quite different. Not surprisingly, victim accounts tended to maximizethe transgression, minimize any extenuating circumstances, emphasize the victim's suffering, and the like. In contrast, perpetrator accounts tended to minimize the transgression by assigning some responsibility to the victim, by noting extenuating circumstances, by downplaying the victim's suffering, and so forth.

The nature of the distortion was also examined according to three categories: deleting facts from the original story, adding new details that were not in the original story, and altering facts (e.g., putting "spin" on some piece of information to make it seem better or worse). By far the largest category involved deletions, although there were instances of both of the others. These results suggest that memory bias is most effective at altering a story by selectively deleting information that is unhelpful to the desired impression. Victims leave out information about mitigating circumstances to make the perpetrator's transgression seem worse than it was. Perpetrators leave out information about the victim's suffering to make the transgression seem less serious.

Language of Defense

In a recent article, Schütz and Baumeister (1999) examined the linguistic constructions of perpetrators by asking people to furnish first-person accounts of harming someone. These stories were compared with stories about helping someone, so this investigation did not study the language of victims. Still, these findings shed light on how perpetrators speak. As in the other work, each subject furnished one story of each type, so the differences reflect motivations inherent in situational roles.

Perpetrators of harm used multiple devices that seem designed to conceal or explain their guilt. Compared to narratives of helping someone, narratives of harming someone were "front-heavy": They contained longer introductions and shorter conclusions. Thus, they offered more information about the background, which could include mitigating circumstances, and less information about the consequences of their action. They also favored passive sentences such as "It turned out that . . ." that do not assign responsibility to any particular person and make the consequences seem unintended. A deconstructed style of speech was reflected in a tendency to use shorter sentences (especially toward the end of the story), thereby reducing meaningful connections among the events. Perpetrators also offered fewer details.

Narratives of harm described fewer emotions overall than narratives of helping. This pattern was found consistently across both situational roles and across both positive and negative emotions, with one exception: Perpetrators of harm were more likely to discuss their own negative emotions (as compared with people who described helping someone). By dwelling on their own distress and suffering, perpetrators may shift attention away from the victim's suffering and seek a sympathetic understanding that their actions may have been mitigated by their own problems. Consistent with this, the narratives about harm had significantly fewer allusions to the other person's thoughts than the narratives about helping.

Sexual Aggression

These insights into the perpetrator's style of thought, and particularly into discrepancies between victim and perpetrator thinking, may be applied to the issue of rape. We have been working to develop a new theoretical perspective on rape and sexual coercion (Baumeister, Catanese, & Wallace, 1999).

The very need for a new theory may well be grounded in victim–perpetrator differences. One of the most influential theories on rape was asserted by Brownmiller (1975) from a feminist standpoint. She asserted that rape occurs as part of a conspiracy by all men to intimidate and subjugate all women, and that the purpose of rape is power rather than sex. Although research on perpetrators has generally disconfirmed and discredited this theory (for reviews, see Palmer, 1988; Tedeschi & Felson, 1994), it may well have relevance for understanding victims' reactions. Thus, for example, victims may regard rape as having little or nothing to do with sex but much to do with power, even if perpetrators are guided primarily by sexual motives. Likewise, we noted earlier that victims often tend to view perpetrators as acting out of grand evil conspiracies, even if these theories often do not accurately fit the intentions and experiences of perpetrators. Rape victims (who are mainly women) may well perceive rape as part of a conspiracy by all men and feel that sexual coercion dramatizes female vulnerability to male aggression, but research on men does not show widespread support for rapists or suggest that all men are involved in any such conspiracy.

Our theory about the motivational processes that lead to rape does not seek to excuse rapists or blame victims, even if we do attempt to move beyond feminist assertions. In our view, the most important concerns and goals of anyone concerned with rape should be to prevent and alleviate the suffering of victims, and their views and perspectives deserve the utmost sympathy. Still, there is some utility in achieving an understanding of perpetrators. And, crucially, it is probably essential to set aside the victims' perspective in order to understand the perpetrators because (as the rest of this chapter has argued) victims and perpetrators have systematically different outlooks, so that empathizing with the victim is likely to impair one's capacity to understand the perpetrator. For example, it is possible that many victims may feel that rape is part of a conspiracy by all men to oppress all women, but empathizing with this view will clearly make it difficult to understand individual rapists who act on their own or who rape in deliberate defiance of the wishes of other men.

The theory we propose combines two lines of research in social psychology: reactance and narcissism. Reactance theory holds that people want to maintain their freedom and options (Brehm, 1966). When an option is removed, reactance ensues and can be manifested in three ways. First, the forbidden option becomes desired more intensely. Second, people want to perform the forbidden behavior. Third, people may aggress against whoever has reduced their freedom.

Applied to sex, this analysis assumes that (some) men desire sex but are sometimes refused or rejected by the women they desire. Reactance ensues, and all the behavioral consequences of reactance are relevant to rape: Wanting the forbidden sex all the more, trying to assert their freedom by having sex with the unavailable woman, and aggressing against the woman who denied them.

One problem with this theory is that it assumes that the man must in some sense expect to have sex with the woman initially, or regard himself as entitled to it, in order for the woman's rejection to be felt as a loss of his freedom. A partial solution to this problem is to focus on cases where the man does expect sex for some reason, such as (1) he has had sex with that woman previously even though she now refuses him, (2) they engaged in preliminary sexual activity, or (3) he believes she has consented to have sex with other men and will therefore accept him too. Research findings associate all these circumstances with an increased likelihood of rape (see Baumeister et al., 1999, for a review).

Still, it is necessary to look beyond reactance to provide a satisfactory account of rape that fits the available data. Narcissism theory is helpful here. Narcissists are defined in DSM-IV on the basis of having at least five of the following criteria: (1) a grandiose sense of self-importance, (2) fantasies of great success, power, brilliance, beauty, or ideal love, (3) a belief that one is special and unique and hence can only be understood by high-status people, (4) a quest for excessive admiration, (5) an unreasonable or exaggerated sense of entitlement, (6) interpersonal exploitation of others, (7) lacking empathy (unwilling to recognize or identify with others' feelings), (8) envying others or thinking that others envy him or her, and (9) arrogance or haughtiness (American Psychiatric Association, 1994).

The inflated sense of entitlement contributes to the man's expectation to have sex with the woman. Her refusal of him despite her having gone to bed with other men would be especially insulting to a narcissist, who regards himself as superior to other men, and narcissists respond to insults or derogation with elevated levels of aggression (Bushman & Baumeister, 1998).

The cognitive distortions of narcissism are conducive to the pattern of forcing the woman and then denying that he forced her, which appears to be the dominant pattern. (As already noted, Laumann et al., 1994, and most other investigators, have found that women perceive far more coercion of women than men perceive themselves as coercing women.) In particular, the narcissistic rapist is motivated in part by the desire to show off and brag to other men about a sexual conquest, and he gains more credit if she consents than if he forces her, so he should be inclined to downplay her resistance (at least afterward). His refusal of empathy makes him less deterred by the victim's suffering than the average man would be, as well as being less likely to acknowledge later that she did not consent. Many rapists claim afterward that their victims enjoyed the sex act and continued afterward to hold favorable opinions of the rapist, which suggests a remarkable degree of narcissistic distortion.

Also, the more desirable the woman, the more credit the narcissist gets, and so his selection of victims is likely to reflect a preference for sexually attractive women (which is confirmed by research findings, although contrary to the feminist view; see Tedeschi & Felson, 1994, for a review). The other side of this coin is that a dating partner who refuses to go all the way would cause the narcissist to lose face with his peer group, and so he is likely to force her. This too is found to be a very common pattern in rape.

Past theorizing about rape has debated whether the goal is to enjoy the forceful overpowering of the woman or the sexual reward. The former is contradicted by evidence that most rapists would prefer that the woman acquiesce without having to be forced (and many deny using force afterward). The latter is contradicted by the low rates of sexual pleasure reported by rapists. The present theory offers a different view of the goal of rape: The goal is to claim access to the woman symbolically. Penetration rather than orgasm is therefore the goal because penetration reasserts the lost freedom.

Conclusion

The study of the social mind is most directly concerned with cognitive and motivational processes in interpersonal settings. The present investigation has focused on two interpersonally complementary roles, namely, victim and perpetrator. Comparison of victim and perpetrator responses suggests that substantial amounts of motivated cognitions separate the two.

Victims and perpetrators participate in the same situation yet often come away with very different views of what happened. These differences appear to be rooted in situational roles and the accompanying motivations and cognitive processes rather than in trait differences between victims and perpetrators. In a series of studies, we have explored these systematic differences. Relative to perpetrators, victims tell stories in which (1) the victims were wholly innocent, (2) the perpetrators had no valid reason or justification for their actions, (3) severe and lasting negative consequences were caused, (4) mitigating or extenuating circumstances surrounding the perpetrator's actions are missing, (5) multiple offenses were involved, (6) the victim's reaction was either appropriate or highly restrained, and (7) the transgression is still seen as highly relevant to the present time. Despite traditional biases that assume that perpetrators lie to protect themselves whereas victims tell the unvarnished truth, two studies that matched role-based accounts with original information found that victims and perpetrators distorted information to an equal degree (not counting perjury to avoid punishment), and both distorted significantly more than a control group with no motivating role to play. Thus, both the victim and perpetrator roles contain biases that can distort interpretations and memories. An additional study examined linguistic biases in perpetrator accounts and found that perpetrators alter their speech patterns, such as by using shorter sentences, avoiding grammatical constructions that imply responsibility (e.g., "I decided . . ." vs. "before I knew it . . ."), featuring their own emotions rather than those of the victim, and presenting much more antecedent (background) material relative to consequence (aftermath) material.

Because victims and perpetrators think about, understand, and remember similar events in very different ways, it is difficult to resolve certain conflicts after the fact. These findings illuminate continuing problems in dealing with war crimes, racial oppression, and gender differences in perceptions of rape. More generally, they indicate that the cognitive and motivational processes in interpersonal settings can lead people to very different interpretations, thereby hampering interpersonal understanding and social harmony.

References

American Psychiatric Association (1994). *Diagnostic and statistical manual of the mental disorders* (4th ed.). Washington, DC: Author.

Anderson, P. B., & Struckman-Johnson, C. (Eds.). (1998). *Sexually aggressive women: Current perspectives and controversies.* New York: Guilford Press.

Averill, J. (1982). *Anger and aggression: An essay on emotion.* New York: Springer-Verlag.

Baumeister, R. F. (1997). *Evil: Inside human violence and cruelty.* New York: W. H. Freeman.

Baumeister, R. F., Catanese, K. R., & Wallace, H. M. (1999). Rape as narcissistic reactance. Manuscript in preparation.

Baumeister, R. F., Stillwell, A., & Wotman, S. R. (1990). Victim and perpetrator accounts of interpersonal conflict: Autobiographical narratives about anger. *Journal of Personality and Social Psychology, 59,* 994–1005.

Brehm, J. W. (1966). *A theory of psychological reactance.* New York: Academic Press.

Brownmiller, S. (1975). *Against our will: Men, women, and rape.* New York: Simon & Schuster.

Bushman, B. J., & Baumeister, R. F. (1998). Threatened egotism, narcissism, self-esteem, and direct and displaced aggression: Does self-love or self-hate lead to violence? *Journal of Personality and Social Psychology, 75,* 219–229.

Goldhagen, D. J. (1996). *Hitler's willing executioners.* New York: Knopf.

Hansen, G. L. (1987). Extradyadic relations during courtship. *Journal of Sex Research, 23,* 382–390.

Jones, E. E., & Nisbett, R. (1971). *The actor and the observer: Divergent perceptions of the causes of behavior.* Morristown, NJ: General Learning Press.

Kanin, E. J. (1985). Date rapists: Differential sexual socialization and relative deprivation. *Archives of Sexual Behavior, 6,* 67–76.

Laumann, E. O., Gagnon, J. H., Michael, R. T., & Michaels, S. (1994). *The social organization of sexuality: Sexual practices in the United States.* Chicago: University of Chicago Press.

Lifton, R. J. (1986). *The Nazi doctors: Medical killing and the psychology of genocide.* New York: Basic Books.

Maalouf, A. (1987). *The Crusades through Arab eyes.* New York: Schocken.

Mikula, G., Athenstaedt, U., Heschgl, S., & Heimgartner, A. (1998). Does it only depend on the point of view? Perspective-related differences in justice evaluations of negative incidents in personal relationships. *European Journal of Social Psychology, 28,* 931–962.

Palmer, C. T. (1988). Twelve reasons why rape is not sexually motivated: A skeptical examination. *Journal of Sex Research, 25,* 512–530.

Runciman, S. (1951–1954). *A history of the Crusades* (3 vols.) New York: Cambridge University Press.

Schütz, A., & Baumeister, R. F. (1999). The language of defense: Linguistic patterns in narratives of transgressions. *Journal of Language and Social Psychology.*

Shakur, S. (1993). *Monster: The autobiography of an L.A. gang member.* New York: Atlantic Monthly Press.

Sichrovsky, P. (1988). *Born guilty: Children of Nazi families.* New York: Basic Books.

Silver, R. L., Boon, C., & Stones, M. H. (1983). Searching for meaning in misfortune: Making sense of incest. *Journal of Social Issues, 39,* 81–102.

Spanier, G. P., & Margolis, R. L. (1983). Marital separation and extramarital sexual behavior. *Journal of Sex Research, 19,* 23–48.

Stillwell, A. M., & Baumeister, R. F. (1997). The construction of victim and perpetrator memories: Accuracy and distortion in role-based accounts. *Personality and Social Psychology Bulletin, 23,* 1157–1172.

Tavris, C. (1982). *Anger: The misunderstood emotion.* New York: Simon & Schuster.

Tedeschi, J. T., & Felson, R. B. (1994). *Violence, aggression, and coercive actions.* Washington, DC: American Psychological Association.

Vaughan, D. (1986). *Uncoupling.* New York: Oxford University Press.

14. Inside the Social Mind of the Ostracizer

KIPLING D. WILLIAMS, LADD WHEELER, AND
JOEL A. R. HARVEY

Introduction

You are having a fight about how much your partner is charging on your credit cards. The argument starts to heat up, and your partner starts to say some pretty nasty things about you. You stop arguing abruptly and say that you are not going to speak to your partner if those are the sorts of things that are going to be said. Your partner continues to argue, but you say nothing. More nasty insults are hurled; still, you act as though no one is there. You go about trying to behave as though you are alone, but your partner starts to get in your face, block your way, scream. Still you do nothing. Finally, in a desperate attempt to get you to show some sign of acknowledgment, your partner throws a marble ashtray at you, which strikes your head, sending you to the floor, bleeding and dazed.

This scenario, which actually happened in the mid-1980s between a well-known athlete and his wife, is an instance of the use of a form of ostracism at the interpersonal level. It gives us a glimpse into what might provoke it, how it is done, and what its consequences could be. Typically, this form of ostracism is known as the *silent treatment*, giving the *cold shoulder*, *sending to Coventry*, or any number of other euphemisms. Other forms of ostracism occur in small groups (Barner-Barry, 1986; Schachter, 1959), academic institutions ("time out" in

This research was funded by an "Australian Large Research Council Grant" (A79800071) and an ARC small grant ("Testing the Visibility Dimension of Ostracism Using an Event-Contingent Self-Recording Method") awarded to the first author. Portions of this chapter were presented at the Second Annual Sydney Symposium on Social Psychology. Correspondence concerning this article should be sent to: Kipling D. Williams, School of Psychology, University of New South Wales, Sydney NSW 2052, AUSTRALIA. *Email:* kip.williams@unsw.edu.au schools: Scholtz, McFarland, & Haynes, 1988; "silencing" in military academies: Davis, 1991), the workplace (Faulkner, 1995; Suziki, 1966, 1996), prisons (solitary confinement: Zippelius, 1986), religions (the use of *Meidung*, loosely translated as shunning, by the Amish: Gruter, 1986; excommunication in the Catholic Church: Zippelius, 1986), and in countries that exile (Woods, 1978; Zippelius, 1986). In fact, researchers even claim that animals use ostracism on members who in some way deviate from the group (Goodall, 1986; Kling, 1986; Lancaster, 1986; McGuire & Raleigh, 1986).

In this chapter, we will focus on the ostracizer. We will present a recent model (Williams, 1997) that attempts to envelop the literature and form new hypotheses to test. As will be obvious, up to now the literature has focused on targets of ostracism – individuals who are being ostracized – and how ostracism affects these individuals' cognition, emotions, behaviors, and physiological reactions. Admittedly, the model itself was originally constructed with the target as its focus. Nevertheless, after conducting over 30 experiments, surveys, and interviews, we have begun to appreciate the interconnections between the effects that ostracism has on its targets, and why and how it is used by *sources* (our relatively neutral term for those who ostracize). To this end, the remainder of this chapter will describe some recent research we have conducted on sources of ostracism, in which we make use of event-contingent records that sources fill out over a 2-week period. The participants carry these recording booklets, called the *Sydney Ostracism Record (SOR)*, with them at all times. Whenever they notice themselves ostracizing someone – anyone – they fill out the record, which contains a number of scales with room for open-ended descriptions of the event. The results of this research is largely descriptive at this point, although some provocative findings have emerged that allow us to understand the social mind of the ostracizer.

Let us begin by briefly presenting the model (from the perspective of the sources) and reviewing some of the research that it envelops or that has stemmed from it (for extensive reviews of ostracism research focusing on targets of ostracism, see Williams, 1997; Williams & Zadro, in press).

The Need for a Theoretical Model of Ostracism

Despite the fact that ostracism spans history, species, societies, and lifetimes (Gruter & Masters, 1986; Williams, 1997), empirical psychological research into this ubiquitous and powerful phenomenon is rather limited. Studies that have been conducted have documented the negative experience of ostracism, but they have varied in the way in which ostracism is operationally defined and tested as a construct. Moreover, such research has been limited to the target's perspective alone, failing to consider the experience of the source of ostracism. The different consequences that different forms of ostracism may have for both sources and targets have also been neglected.

Ostracism appears to be universally used and quite powerful, yet is not well understood. Much social psychological literature, in fact, seems to take it for granted. For example, we know that deviating from a group brings rejection and expulsion (Schachter, 1959); that we conform so as not to be excluded and rejected (Asch, 1956); that our behavior is facilitated by the presence of others, in part because we fear their potentially negative evaluations (Huguet, Galvaing, Dumas, & Monteil, this volume; Kerr, this volume), which can lead to our exclusion; and that we generally try to present ourselves in socially desirable ways so that we are not left out (Tice & Faber, this volume). But what do we know about what happens *when* we are ignored and excluded by others? We know considerably less. So, there seemed to be a need for programmatic research to be carried out. Based upon the existing literature and on the confluence of several theories, Williams constructed a model of ostracism to serve as a guide for such research. When ostracism is construed as a multidimensional construct, complexities of the phenomenon can be studied in isolation and in concert, with the aim of developing an integrated understanding. Moreover, providing clearer conceptual definitions of the different dimensions comprising ostracism allowed antecedents and consequences of ostracism to be examined in a comparative manner.

Williams (1997) put forth a temporally based need-threat model of ostracism and proposed that there are four taxonomic dimensions across which ostracism can vary.

Taxonomic Dimensions of Ostracism

Visibility

This dimension refers to whether or not the target is visible to the source. The dimension has three subcategories: physical, social, and cyber. *Physical ostracism* takes place if sources separate themselves physically from the target. If, however, an argument has taken place and the source individual decides to no longer acknowledge or interact with the target but remains in the same physical space, this is called *social ostracism*. Finally, the third subcategory of this dimension is *cyber ostracism*. This includes the failure to send or receive letters, telephone calls or e-mail messages within a reasonable time frame.

Motive

This dimension refers to the perceived or intended motive for the ostracism. This dimension contains five subcategories: not ostracism, role-prescribed, punitive, defensive, and oblivious. *Not ostracism* refers to the fact that some behaviors might appear to be ostracism at first glance, but either the source or the target decides that it really was not ostracism; hence no ostracism motive is attached to the behavior. This might seem rather strange, but our research suggests that not ostracism may be the most frequently considered motive because all types of ostracism (that occur for all other possible reasons) are ambiguous enough to make either sources or targets consider the not-ostracism option. Targets might ask themselves, "Was that ostracism, or was it just my paranoia?" Sources might wonder, "I hope they didn't take my lack of response to mean that I was ignoring them." It is this option, in fact, that appears to make ostracism particularly insidious because targets (especially) almost always have a certain amount of ambiguity attached to anything that might appear to be ostracism. This ambiguity, by itself, can be quite disconcerting and can motivate people to do any number of things to resolve it (Hogg, this volume; Sorrentino, Hodson, & Huber, this volume).

The second motive for ostracism is *role-prescribed* – ostracism that occurs because it is sanctioned or even encouraged by societal norms. This includes incidents such as not acknowledging individuals on public transport or those who are sharing the ride on the elevator. The third subcategory is *punitive* ostracism, which describes the motive to punish the target individuals for who they are or what they have done. This motive has been shown to be the primary motive for the silent treatment (which is also categorized as being primarily social ostracism) (Williams, Shore, & Grahe, 1998). The *defensive* motive, on the other hand, is a preemptive tactic, motivated in anticipation of disapproval or some other form of ego threat. In fact, one may preemptively use the silent treatment in anticipation of getting the silent treatment (Sommer, Williams, Ciarocco, & Baumeister, in press). Finally, there is the motive of *oblivious* ostracism, in which sources appear to be oblivious or unaware of the person that they are perceived to be ignoring. For targets, oblivious ostracism is hypothesized to be especially aversive because in addition to feeling ignored and excluded, the target feels unworthy of attention. In contrast, both punitive and defensive ostracism motives at least signal to the target that he or she is important enough to be consciously ignored by the source.

Quantity

The next dimension is the quantity of ostracism that is intended or perceived. The quantity of ostracism is a continuous variable that ranges from a just noticeable difference from normal levels of acknowledgment and interaction to behaviors that appear to signal total lack of awareness of the target. At an operational level, quantity refers to the degree to which eye contact is given, the number of utterances directed to the target, and the degree to which the verbal behavior lacks an affective component. If quantity of ostracism is low, then the act of ostracism becomes more ambiguous.

Causal Clarity

Two aspects combine to define causal clarity. Is ostracism occurring, and if so, why? Ostracism can occur unannounced and unanticipated. In these cases, the source may be relying on the ambiguity to (a) avoid having to apologize or even acknowledge that he or she is engaged in ostracism and (b) create more uncertainty in the target. With uncertainty comes a reduction in perceived control and a clear-cut means of coping with the ostracism.

Antecedents of Ostracism

Antecedents are what trigger the response of ostracism, as opposed to what might trigger other types of reactions. In our focus on the source, there could be characteristics of individuals that predispose them to rely on ostracism. Perhaps they do not like to confront others about problems but prefer to remain silent and elusive. Perhaps they become particularly frustrated or feel that they do not perform well in verbal (or physical) confrontations. Or maybe they hold their tongues and avert their eyes so that matters do not get worse, escalating to the point of saying things that cannot be taken back or harming the individual physically. There are probably numerous individual differences and experiences that might incline an individual (or a group) to use ostracism. At this point, little is known about these factors, and elucidating them is one of the aims of the program of research we begin to describe at the end of this chapter. Antecedents also include situational constraints (people might chose to ignore rather than confront while in the presence of others) and target factors (some individuals may be especially "ostracizable.")

Impact on Needs and Reactions Elicited

Williams (1997) postulated that there are four fundamental human needs that can be uniquely and simultaneously affected by ostracism. As mentioned earlier, these needs were originally proposed with the targets in mind. As such, the basic prediction was that ostracism deprived or threatened the needs for belonging, control, self-esteem, and a meaningful existence. There is already considerable evidence suggesting that each need is fundamental for the well-being of individuals. The need to belong has been well covered by Baumeister and Leary (1995). Essentially, humans need to feel a sense of belonging with at least a few important others. Without it, they suffer psychologically and physically. There is an abundance of theoretical perspectives and research showing that individuals need to have or at least perceive they have control to be effective, persistent, and successful (Bandura, 1995; Seligman, 1975; Skinner, 1996). Self-esteem enjoys a long and rich history of theory and research suggesting that not only is it a means to efficacious behavior, but for some theorists, that it is the primary goal (Greenberg et al., 1992; Marsh & Parker, 1984; Steele, 1988; Tesser, 1988). Finally, recent research argues compellingly that people need to perceive their existence as meaningful, and must buffer themselves from reminders of their insubstantial existence and eventual mortality (Greenberg et al., 1990).

How can ostracism uniquely and simultaneously threaten all four needs? When ostracized, targets are ignored and excluded. Almost by definition, they lose a sense of belonging with the source(s) who ostracize(s) them. Even with intense argument or physical confrontation, targets feel that they are connected to the source, albeit negatively.

Without that connection, belonging is severed. Control is deprived because, unlike the bilateral (yet negative) exchange that takes place in an argument or a physical fight, ostracism is unilateral. There is no give-and-take. No matter what the target says or does, there are no apparent consequences. The target has no control over what is happening. Self-esteem is threatened because, if ostracism is interpreted as punitive in nature, then it is inferred that to the sources, the targets are somehow bad or undesirable. This is a direct attack on one's self-esteem as seen through the eyes of others. Finally, there may be no better metaphor for a meaningless existence than for one to be completely and utterly ignored. In fact, in many cultures, ostracism is referred to as *social death* (Sweeting & Gilhooly, 1992), and carries the message that this is like what life would be like if the target were, in fact, dead.

Immediate reactions to ostracism are hypothesized to include negative affect and general hurt feelings. Research suggests that short-term threats to each of these needs result in attempts by the individual to regain, recover, or repair what was threatened or lost. Threats to belonging can be repaired by reminding oneself of other groups to which one belongs (Ko, 1994); loss of control is met with attempts to exert control (Pittman & Pittman, 1980; Williams & Lawson Williams, 1999; Wortman & Brehm, 1975); self-esteem threats are responded to by attempts to seek other forms of self-affirmation (Steele, 1988); and threats to a meaningful existence result in attempts to reinforce the buffer that separates self from mortality salience (Pyszczynski et al., 1996; Williams & Zadro, in press). Hence, short-term reactions to ostracism should trigger repair-type coping behaviors aimed at regaining that which was threatened.

Attempts to regain or repair threatened needs appear to have a limit, however, and after enduring repeated exposures to such threats, internalization of lost needs occurs. Long-term exposure to isolation may lead to alienation; loss of control, to helplessness; self-esteem threat, to depression; and reminders of death and a meaningless existence to despair and suicidal ideation. Long-term exposures to ostracism, therefore, are hypothesized to have these deleterious affects on targets.

Impact on Needs in Sources

Theory on the reactions of sources to the use of ostracism is not as clear. Most of our research on the effects of ostracism on sources has been exploratory. Initial findings suggest that some of the very needs that are threatened in targets are fortified in sources, particularly belonging and control. Zadro and Williams (1999) have shown that when two sources ostracize a target (compared to when they either include the target or argue with the target), they feel a stronger bond with each other. Sommer et al. (in press) showed through analyses of narratives that sources of punitive ostracism feel increased levels of control, and Williams et al. (1998) demonstrated that people rated the silent treatment as giving sources increased control. The research discussed in the second half of this chapter will further explore these possibilities in individuals' daily acts of ostracism.

Application of the Model Using a Variety of Methods

A variety of approaches, both quantitative and qualitative, have been used to test the model. We will first briefly present findings relating to targets of ostracism and will then concentrate in the remainder of this section on research investigating the psychological impact on the source of ostracism.

Target Research

Williams and Sommer (1997) used a ball-tossing paradigm to investigate the impact of social ostracism on targets. This paradigm involved participants being either included or ostracized in a seemingly spontaneous game of catch by two confederates. All participants were initially thrown the ball, with those in the ostracism condition subsequently being left only to watch the other two individuals throwing the ball to each other. Following the ball-tossing episode, participants were involved in a collective or coactive task in which they had to generate as many uses for an object as possible. If the need to belong had been threatened, it was hypothesized that participants would socially compensate (i.e., work harder) on the collective task as compared with the coactive task. For female participants, this hypothesis was supported: When ostracized, they worked harder on collective tasks compared with coactive tasks. Males, on the other hand, displayed social loafing behaviors when working collectively rather than coactively, regardless of whether they had been previously excluded or included. Both genders, however, showed signs of negative affect as a result of being ostracized.

Being ostracized in a conversation is another paradigm used to test predictions of the model. Similar to ball tossing, participants were excluded, this time by not being conversed with. Ezrakhovich et al. (1998) found that those ostracized for no apparent reason (i.e., causally unclear) worked harder on a subsequent group task, again perhaps in the attempt to regain a sense of belonging to the group.

Studies have also been conducted in cyberspace to reveal the aversive impact of ostracism on targets (Cheung, 1999; Croker, 1999; Lam, 1998; Tynan, 1999; Williams, Cheung, & Choi, in press). These studies revealed that those excluded in a virtual ball-toss game, or from chatroom conversations, perceived the exclusion and reacted negatively. In one study (Williams et al., in press), those who were ostracized in a virtual ball-toss game were even more likely to conform to incorrect perceptual judgments made by a new group.

Research has also been carried out on the impact of ostracism on the target's need for control. Williams and Lawson Williams (1999) used the ball-tossing paradigm to determine if participants reacted with a greater need for control when ostracized by two individuals appearing either as friends or as strangers. Findings revealed that for both males and females, those ostracized by two people perceived to be friends with each other (but strangers to the target) experienced a greater need for control.

Although these studies have provided us with detailed knowledge of the psychological effect of different forms of ostracism, they are still restricted to short-term incidents of ostracism. In order to investigate the long-term impact of ostracism, it was necessary to use to other approaches, specifically those of qualitative research. Discourse recorded from unstructured interviews carried out by Faulkner and Williams (1995) revealed that long-term ostracism can lead to feelings of helplessness, despair, lowered self-esteem, and depression, to name a few among many other negative emotional reactions. Further support for these findings came from structured cognitive interviews carried out by Zadro and Williams (1999). In order to obtain a more comprehensive account of this qualitative research, and of the other studies cited earlier, the reader should refer to Williams and Zadro (in press).

Source Research

Having provided a brief overview of the research pertaining to targets of ostracism, we will now concentrate on findings from studies including sources of ostracism in their design. Different methods have been used to tap the impact ostracism has on sources. A study conducted by Williams, Shore and Grahe (1998) used self-report narrative research to examine accounts of social ostracism. Participants had to list behaviors associated with either giving or receiving the silent treatment from a friend. After reporting these behaviors, participants were required to list the feelings associated with each behavior. Although for targets all four needs (belonging, control, self-esteem, and meaningful existence) were threatened, a different pattern emerged for sources. Their responses indicated that their need for control had been fortified, their need for belonging had been threatened, and there was an equal level of need threat and fortification for both self-esteem and meaningful existence.

A second study using narratives was conducted by Sommer et al. (in press). This research examined the moderating role of trait self-esteem on the source's use of the silent treatment. It was found that sources with low self-esteem used the silent treatment more in general and used it as a manipulative tactic rather than to indicate that they were disengaging from the target. High self-esteem individuals, on the other hand, were more likely than low self-esteem individuals to use ostracism in order to break ties with individuals they did not want to spend time with. Moreover, whereas targets experienced a threat to the feelings of belonging, control, self-esteem, and meaningful existence, sources experienced empowerment.

Experimental research has also been carried out taking the perspective of the source into account. Grahe and Williams (1998) induced pairs of participants ostensibly to volunteer to ostracize a third individual, thus allowing an examination of the impact of being excluded from a conversation on both sources and targets. Targets experienced aversive reactions to the incident, whereas some sources lowered their evaluations of targets.

Role-play studies involving the simulation of a train ride have also been conducted (Zadro & Williams, 1998b). This paradigm involved getting participants to play the role of train passengers, sitting three abreast in rows. They were given scenarios that they were to play out for the duration of a 5-minute ride. Those seated in the middle were designated targets, whereas those flanking the targets were sources. Sources were instructed to include, ignore, or argue with the target. Findings indicated that sources showed an increase in belonging in punitive episodes, although they reported feeling badly about themselves as a consequence of ostracizing.

Finally, a role-play study was carried out using the event-contingent self-report method (Williams, Bernieri, Faulkner, Gada-Jain, & Grahe, 2000). This study took place over a work week and involved one of five colleagues being randomly selected to be a target of ostracism for a day. Both sources and targets of ostracism completed diary entries describing their thoughts, feelings, and behaviors, and by the end of the week all participants had had the experience of being both a source and a target of ostracism. Findings revealed that being a source of ostracism, although effortful, resulted in feelings of empowerment, increased status, and a sense of belonging with sources.

In summary, a variety of studies have investigated the impact of ostracism on sources. Whereas targets suffer from threats to their needs, the same pattern does not emerge for sources. Evidence suggests that sources of ostracism may be empowered through their experience, increasing their feeling of control over the situation, and occasionally belongingness is strengthened.

The Sydney Ostracism Record (SOR)

We now set out to introduce you to a relatively new and innovative tool used to study ostracism as it occurs on a day-to-day basis. Although ongoing research is using this method to study targets, in this chapter we concentrate on the source of ostracism. The event-contingent self-report method, previously applied in other domains within social psychology (see Reis & Wheeler, 1991, for a review), was chosen in order to gain insight into the everyday routine ostracism that goes on from dusk to dawn. Participants were required to keep a structured diary over a 2-week period, entering each time they ostracized someone, ranging from more serious forms, such as employing the silent treatment, to less serious forms, such as failing to acknowledge the other person(s) in the elevator with them. Whereas previous studies have focused specifically on a particular dimension of ostracism, no study has looked at what generally occurs "out there," day in and day out. This approach is "concerned with the multitude of 'small events' that compose everyday activity and thought" (Reis & Wheeler, 1991, p. 270) and "requires a report from the participant every time an event meeting some predetermined definition occurs" (Reis & Wheeler, 1991, p. 281). The best-known example of this method is the Rochester Interaction Record (RIR)

(Pietromonaco & Barrett, 1997; Reis & Wheeler, 1991; Wheeler & Nezlek, 1977). Subsequent records include the Rochester Social Comparison Record, examining social comparison (Wheeler & Miyake, 1992); the Deception Record, examining lie telling (DePaulo, Kirkendol, Epstein, Wyer, & Hairfield, 1990); and the Iowa Communication Record, examining dyadic conversation (Duck, Rutt, Hurst, & Sterjc, 1991).

It is argued that the diary method is able to overcome the biases confronted by other types of research within this domain. For instance, self-report questionnaires are helpful in gaining an appreciation of what occurs during particular real-life instances. However, they suffer from a number of problems. The incident that is selected for recall may be the one that is most readily available to memory (selection bias), and the content of that incident may be distorted (recall of content). Moreover, several events occurring over time may be aggregated to form an overall global impression of the phenomena. Indeed, these descriptions are "best seen as personalized impressions of social activity that have been percolated, construed, and reframed through the various perceptual, cognitive and motivational processes" (Reis & Wheeler, 1991, p. 271). The event-contingent self-report method, on the other hand, attempts to confront these problems. It is argued that diary methods do not suffer to the same degree from selection bias, as participants are instructed to record and describe all incidents that they encounter. Secondly, distorted recall of content is minimized because records are completed as close in time to the incident as possible. Finally, with regard to aggregation, incidents are not aggregated personally but by computer analysis, thus solving this third identified problem.

Another method that is used to gain insight into everyday occurrence of a given behavior is behavioral observation. Although this method has important uses, much of what takes place in ostracism is not directly observable, and even if it were, each participant would have to forego all privacy and would require a full-time observer for us to obtain the desired 24-hour data.

The method thus chosen for this present research is the event-contingent self-report method. As stated by Reis and Wheeler (1991, p. 285), "although the hallmark of the RIR (Rochester Interaction Record) is its use of standardised, fixed format records, its content is intended to be flexible and responsive to the researcher's theoretical interests." This method was used to test day-to-day incidents of ostracism, with its structure derived from Williams's (1997) model of ostracism. A copy of the record is provided in Figure 14.1. As can be

Sydney Ostracism Record (SOR)

Date of incident ________ your code # ________

1. What time did the ostracism occur? Start ________ End ________
2. Whom did you ostracize (gender & initials)? M, F ____ M, F ____ M, F ____
   OR groups greater than three: # Males____ #Females____
3. What was your relationship to the person(s) you ostracized?
   (Place the initials of the individual(s) in the space provided. If initials unknown place a tick)
   Stranger ___ Acquaintance ___ Ordinary friend ___ Close friend ___ Relationship partner ___ Relative___
4. What was the status of the person(s) ostracized? Inferior to you ___ Your Equal ___ Superior ___
5. Were you the only one who ostracized this person? Yes___ (go to #7) No___
   If No, how many others were involved? ___ Were you all part of a group/team ___ or strangers to one another ___?
6. What was your relationship with the other person(s) who were also ostracising?
   (Place the initials of the individual(s) in the space provided. If initials unknown just place a tick).
   Stranger ___ Acquaintance ___ Ordinary friend ___ Close friend ___ Relationship partner ___ Relative___
7. What kind of ostracism was it? (Tick one option on each line.)
   V Social___ Cyber___ Physical___
   M Not ostracism___ Role-prescribed ___ Punitive ___ Defensive ___ Oblivious___
   Q Barely ___ Slight ___ Moderate ___ Substantial ___ Complete___
   C Totally unclear ___ Pretty unclear ___ Moderate ___ Pretty clear ___ Totally clear___
8. The reason I ostracized the individual(s) was primarily because of: Me___ Them ___ Situation___
9. Compared to how you felt prior to ostracising, how have your feelings changed as a result of ostracising?

Lower on Belonging	-3	-2	-1	0	+1	+2	+3	Higher on Belonging
Lower on Control	-3	-2	-1	0	+1	+2	+3	Higher on Control
Lower on Self-esteem	-3	-2	-1	0	+1	+2	+3	Higher on Self-esteem
Lower on Meaningful Existence	-3	-2	-1	0	+1	+2	+3	Higher on Meaningful Existence
Less Angry	-3	-2	-1	0	+1	+2	+3	More angry
Less Apologetic	-3	-2	-1	0	+1	+2	+3	More Apologetic

10. What happened? (*write on back of page*)
    Please describe the event. Where did it take place? If it is related to a previous ostracism or to ongoing ostracism, tell us about it. Current date/time: ________

Figure 14.1. Sydney Ostracism Record for sources of ostracism.

seen, it covers the major elements within the model, including the four dimensions, needs that may be affected, and moderators who may be in place. Moreover, it requires additional information, including the date, time, and duration of the incident, the gender of the target, the status of the target, the relationship to the target, whether the ostracism was directed against a group, and whether the source was part of the group. Finally, the record contains a section in which participants provide qualitative information on the incident itself. The information desired includes what actually happened, where the incident took place, whether this was the first incident of its kind, and further details on how it made the source feel. The time the record was completed must be entered to determine whether incidents were recorded soon after they took place. Furthermore, in order to facilitate timely completion, the SOR was made to be pocket-sized, allowing it to be carried about easily.

The Study

Sixty-one co-investigators took part in the study, 23 (37.7%) male and 38 (62.3%) female, with ages ranging from 17 to 56 ($M = 27$). The sample was diverse both in terms of occupational and martial status and in terms of religious and ethnic background.

Participants were drawn from the University of New South Wales and the Sydney Metropolitan Area; they had responded either to posters distributed on campus or to an advertisement placed in a local newspaper. They subsequently attended a $1\frac{1}{2}$-hour training session on how to complete the Sydney Ostracism Record (SOR), in groups ranging from five to ten people. Participants were introduced as co-investigators and were informed of the importance and value of the research that they would actively be involved in. A presentation was given describing each section of the SOR, with particular time and care taken to ensure that all individuals in the group understood fully how to make an entry in an accurate manner. In order to facilitate learning, numerous examples of different forms of ostracism were given and participants were encouraged to generate examples from their own life experiences. Moreover, written scenarios were compiled, conveying the different dimensions of the ostracism model, and participants had to code these accordingly. Reasons for their choices were also discussed in order to assess more fully their level of comprehension.

Participants were then instructed to complete the SOR over a 2-week period. Reis and Wheeler (1991) found that a time frame of less than a week or two may be "prejudiced by atypical days" (p. 286) and that a time period greater than 2 weeks "would probably tax subjects too generally" (p. 284). Within these 2 weeks, participants were required to return their completed records, preferably in person, every 2 to 3 days. This ensured that entries were completed as close to the incident of ostracism as possible and allowed any queries or concerns to be handled. Moreover, participants were encouraged to come in or telephone at any time during the work week in order to help develop a collaborative working relationship. Participants were each paid $80 after having completed the study.

Methodological Issues

Before we look at the data set itself, we will briefly address some of the methodological issues raised earlier in this section. Following the completion of the diary for 2 weeks, participants were asked to complete a short questionnaire providing details of their experience with the SOR. They were asked to indicate, on a 7-point Likert scale, how difficult it was to record incidents of ostracism, how accurate they perceived their records to be, and to what extent keeping the records interfered with their use of ostracism. Results indicated that participants found it fairly easy to keep the records, perceived their records to be accurate, and did not think that keeping the records interfered with their use of ostracism.

Participants were also asked to indicate on scales whether their accuracy in recording changed as the study progressed and whether their use of ostracism changed during the study as a result of keeping the records. Participants reported that their accuracy increased slightly over time and that their use of ostracism decreased slightly. These results are in line with those of previous studies using an event-contingent self-report method (Reis & Wheeler, 1991).

Data Set Descriptives

Over the 2-week period the total number of completed records obtained was 994, a little over 16 entries per participant. There were no overall sex differences in the submission of completed records. Males, however, were twice as likely to have ostracized males rather than females, whereas females ostracized males and females equally.

Considering the relationship of the source to the target, the majority of incidents were coded as involving ordinary friends, acquaintances, and strangers, as Table 14.1 shows.

Table 14.1. *Percentage of Incidents by Relationship of Source to Target*

Relationship of Source to Target	% of Incidents
Stranger	29
Acquaintance	25
Ordinary friend	25
Close friend	10
Relationship partner	5
Relative	7

The vast majority of these individuals were considered to be equal in status to the source of ostracism (78%), with 11% perceived as inferior and 11% perceived as superior. In the completed records, 22% of the incidents were classified as part of a group.

Turning now to the four dimensions of the model, most of the ostracism incidents (62%) were social in nature, 21% were physical, and 17% were cyber. Of the five motives, a fairly even distribution was evident, as Table 14.2 indicates.

Looking at the breakdown of the relationship of the target to the source is also of interest. Such a breakdown is provided in Table 14.3.

The most startling result is that incidents with partners are much more often punitive than incidents with other targets. As would be

Table 14.2. *Percentage of Incidents Rated According to Their Motive*

Motive	% of Incidents
Not ostracism	26
Role prescribed	20
Punitive	20
Defensive	15
Oblivious	18

Table 14.3. *Percentage of Incidents According to the Relationship Between Source and Target and the Motive for Ostracizing*

	Stranger (%)	Acquaintance (%)	Ordinary Friend (%)	Close Friend (%)	Partner (%)	Relative (%)
Not ostracism	19	27	34	34	27	24
Role-prescribed	32	17	15	20	4	18
Punitive	13	17	19	26	51	31
Defensive	11	20	17	8	16	15
Oblivious	25	19	15	12	2	12

expected, incidents with strangers are more likely to be role-prescribed than incidents with other targets.

Regarding the quantity of the ostracism within each episode, percentages revealed that ostracism tended to lean toward the low-quantity pole, as Table 14.4 shows.

On the dimension of causal clarity, the ambiguity of ostracism was revealed. As can be seen in Table 14.5, a third of all incidents were coded as being totally unclear.

Attributions for the incidents were evenly distributed across self (37%), target (30%), and situation (33%). Baumeister and Catanese (this volume) report that perpetrators often blame the victim or the situation. Our "perpetrators" to some extent followed form by deflecting the responsibility for 63% of the incidences, although they did own up to a fair number of them. As shown in the following discussion, punitive ostracism stood out from all others in being perceived as caused

Table 14.4. *Percentage of Incidents Rated According to Their Quantity*

Quantity	% of Incidents
Barely	23
Slightly	25
Moderately	23
Substantial	13
Complete	17

Table 14.5. *Percentage of Incidents Rated According to Their Causal Clarity*

Causal Clarity	% of Incidents
Totally unclear	33
Pretty unclear	22
Moderately unclear	20
Pretty clear	14
Totally clear	9

by the target (69%) rather than by the self (18%) or the situation (13%). Not ostracism and role-prescribed incidents, on the other hand, were attributed to the situation (47% and 53%, respectively) rather than to the target (9% and 14%, respectively).

Focusing now on the impact of needs, it was revealed that belonging decreased and control increased. These two findings are quite interesting. Previous research has also indicated that sources feel empowered as a result of using ostracism, although there have been inconsistent findings regarding belonging. Perhaps belonging is threatened particularly in dyadic situations when there is no one else to affiliate with, although we did not find this pattern in our data. We suspect that when participants were ranking their feeling of belonging, they may have been focusing on their relationship with the target. As Table 14.6 illustrates with respect to self-esteem, meaningful existence, anger, and the need to apologize, the majority of responses indicated that there was no change. Separate analyses remain to be conducted, however, looking at the change in each feeling in terms of the motive behind the ostracism.

As can be seen, the data cut across the different dimensions of the model, providing us with a complex set of responses to be analyzed. The situations in which ostracism manifests itself are also diverse, spanning a variety of social contexts. The responses on the back of each completed SOR capture this diversity in a qualitative manner, providing a contextual grounding of what is occurring on a day-to-day basis. Table 14.7 provides some examples taken from the 994 completed records.

Table 14.6. *Percent Change after Employing Ostracism*

Need	Increase (%)	No Change (%)	Decrease (%)
Belonging	12	49	39
Self-esteem	24	51	25
Control	39	39	22
Meaningful existence	18	66	17
Anger	21	60	19
Apology	27	48	25

Table 14.7. *Samples of Episodes and How They Were Categorized*

"I was sitting on the lounge with my partner. I was quiet and content. I was totally engrossed in a current affairs issue on TV and I didn't hear him talking to me at all." (Social and Not Ostracism)

"I was doing a day's work for a firm I had worked for a few years ago. My boss approached me with a mistake I had made. I had incorrectly written a docket. He was very angry and yelled at me in front of other people in the shop. This upset me so much I collected my bags and walked out." (Physical and Defensive)

"I went for lunch with my close friend at a Chinatown restaurant. I ignored the waitress who served us food because I'm engaged in the conversation with my friend. I think that's alright because I'm the customer. I've the right not to acknowledge the presence of the waitress. I feel at ease and great that she has given us a good service" (Social and Role-Prescribed)

"This person I refer to here is a relative. She has never been worthy of my attention. I have ignored her on many occasions. She works in a place where, unfortunately, I am forced to visit because of my work. She has an ego bigger than UNSW." (Social and Oblivious)

"My best friend asked me to ring him but later I got really angry with him and after we'd had an argument I didn't call him." (Cyber and Punitive)

Preliminary Results

Although these descriptive results provide us with a global perspective of what is occurring in frequency from day to day, it is obviously necessary to conduct analyses for hypothesis testing. The results of such analyses documented in this subsection are preliminary and are thus limited.

One-sample *t*-tests on each motive were conducted to test whether the source's feelings changed as a result of the different forms of ostracism. Sources had to indicate the extent to which their feelings had changed as a result of the ostracism, ranging from −3 to +3, with a negative number always indicating a decrease in the feeling following ostracism. Because each individual had multiple responses, means were calculated for each individual, and subsequent analyses were carried out using these individual mean scores. These means and standard deviations are reported in Table 14.8.

Table 14.8. *Means and Standard Deviations of Feelings on Each Motive*

	Belonging	Control	Self-Esteem	Meaningful Existence	Anger	Apology
Not ostracism	−.41*	.10	−.1	−.04	−.17*	.31*
	(.65)	(.75)	(.72)	(.61)	(.63)	(.88)
Role-prescribed	−.21	.43**	.15	.18	−.08	−.04
	(.88)	(.91)	(.72)	(.70)	(.90)	(.90)
Punitive	−.33*	.59**	.40*	.21	.56**	−.67**
	(.96)	(1.18)	(1.04)	(.99)	(1.04)	(.88)
Defensive	−.75**	.20	−.20	0.07	.19*	.02
	(1.02)	(1.18)	(1.18)	(.99)	(.58)	(1.0)
Oblivious	−.73**	.51*	.19	.1	.06	−.25
	(1.0)	(1.1)	(.97)	(.63)	(1.0)	(1.1)

* $p < .05$.
** $p < .001$.

The feeling of belonging was significantly reduced as a function of all recorded motives except for role prescribed. The feeling of control was increased when ostracism was used for all motives except defensive and not ostracism. Self-esteem was increased only when the motive was punitive. Participants' reports of meaningful existence were unaffected by motives.

Regarding belonging, our results are consistent with those of Williams, Shore, and Grahe (1998), who also reported a decrease in belonging, but they are incongruent with the results of Zadro and Williams (1998b) and Williams et al. (2000), both of whom reported an increased sense of belonging. The latter two studies, however, involved cosources; thus belonging may have increased with the other source(s) but not necessarily toward the target of ostracism. Further analyses should separate incidents that have occurred as part of a group from those that have taken place singly. Analysis reveals that 22% of incidents took place along with cosources, and future studies should consider these incidents in their own right.

For control, the significant results of this study are consistent with those of previous source research (Sommer et al., in press; Williams &

Lawson Williams, 1999; Williams et al., 2000). Participants in previous studies felt empowered by having used ostracism; this finding also holds in the present research for punitive, role-prescribed, and defensive ostracism.

Our finding that self-esteem increases when the motive is punitive is, on the face of it, inconsistent with the findings of Zadro and Williams (1998b), who found that those in the punitive condition of the role-played train ride experienced a threat to their self-esteem rather than fortification. This difference is probably a peculiarity of the role play studies in that those participants are asked to ostracize another individual for a reason that they do not genuinely feel. Presumably, in the research reported here, the acts of ostracism are real and participants' desire to punish is genuine. Under these conditions of apparent justification, we would not expect participants' self esteem to decline.

Other Feelings

Anger was decreased when the motive was not ostracism, but it was increased for defensive and punitive motives. Apparently, ostracizing by itself does not repair the mood and, according to these findings, only serves to exacerbate anger. Did sources feel like apologizing for their ostracism? Yes, they did when they reported that the incident was not ostracism (perhaps to clarify a potential misinterpretation?), but not when their motive was punitive.

Differences Between Motives

A final set of analyses was also carried out on specific pairs of motives. For example, compared to the defensive motive, reporting a punitive motive was associated with higher increases in self-esteem and anger and a reduced inclination to apologize. Thus sources felt angrier, unrepentant, and, at the same time, better about themselves after ostracizing someone to punish that person than when they ostracized in order to deflect some form of ego threat themselves. Participants also reported more threats to belonging and a greater increase in anger after reporting a punitive motive compared to an oblivious motive. The comparisons between punitive and role-prescribed motives revealed that punitive ostracism resulted in relatively higher increases in anger.

It was also of interest to look at the differences between role-prescribed and not ostracism. Both motives are hypothesized to have the least impact on targets (when targets decide that they had misperceived something else as ostracism or when they decide that it was done because the norms of the situation called for it). What effect should it have on sources? Perhaps thinking that another individual may have interpreted something the source did (or did not do) as ostracism, when the source did not intend to use ostracism, would be a concern for sources, whereas when the motive was perceived by the source to be role-prescribed, sources were not concerned. In line with this way of thinking, not ostracism results in a lower feeling of control (sources felt frustrated because of the potential miscommunication?), lower self-esteem, and an increased need to apologize. This pattern yielded an interesting dynamic not previously considered. When sources recognize a behavior they emit as potentially communicating ostracism when they do not consider it to be ostracism themselves, they react negatively and desire to apologize. Perhaps, though, this was more likely to occur in our participants because the concept of ostracism was made salient and they recognized its potential impact on targets.

Summary

Despite the fact that these results are preliminary in nature, and further analyses using Hierarchical Linear Modeling (HLM) are required, they still reveal the complexities involved when assessing the impact of ostracism on sources. It is evident that different needs are affected in different ways, depending on the motive behind the ostracism. Different processes appear to be going on, and rather than seeing all needs as being uniformly fortified for sources of ostracism, these results indicate that it is necessary to understand the motives for using ostracism before we can assess its probable impact on that person's needs and feelings.

Future Directions in Research

In this final section we will take a brief look at the future, putting forward proposals for further research in this area. Firstly, regarding the SOR, in order to determine the differential impact of different forms of ostracism, more sophisticated analyses are required. Moreover, the qualitative responses detailed on the back of each SOR will be analyzed and will provide useful insights into the variety of situations and contexts in which ostracism occurs. A second study is also underway in which we adapted the format of the SOR for targets of ostracism. Participants are now recording every time they are targets of ostracism over a 2-week period. We are receiving about the same number of entries as we got from sources. These results can then be analyzed in their own right and in a comparative manner against the SOR source data.

Looking more generally toward future research, studies on the potential moderators of ostracism are necessary. Attachment style (Hazan & Shaver, 1987) is currently being tested as an important variable that may moderate the impact of ostracism on a particular target. An attachment scale was also administered to those involved in the SOR study for sources, and analyses will be conducted.

Finally, it would be beneficial to look at the potentially spiraling effect of defensive ostracism. From the target's perspective, defensive ostracism may occur when a target of ostracism becomes a source as a reaction against ostracism. This may lead to the source's becoming a target once again, producing a self-perpetuating ostracism effect. Although this chapter has focused primarily on sources as opposed to targets of ostracism, the dynamic interplay between target and source must be studied in order to reveal the complex intertwining of factors inherent within each episode.

There are other, perhaps more practical uses for the SOR in future research. Because our sources indicated (a) that they felt that they ostracized less often over the 2-week period than usual and (b) that they felt particularly bad about having others misperceive what they did as ostracism, perhaps an instrument like the SOR can be useful in reducing the frequency of strategic ostracism within relationships. Current research by Zadro and Williams (in progress) involves interviews with long-term targets and sources of ostracism, of the silent treatment, in particular. Some sources are quite repentant and would like nothing more than to stop using the silent treatment, but they claim that they cannot stop. They recognize the difficulty that their targets have when faced with the silent treatment, and they enjoy the temporary increase in control that they experience. However, they also report that, over time, the control they enjoy over the other person gradually shifts to the feeling of being controlled themselves by the silent treatment. They feel that in order not to lose face, they have no other choice than to continue its use, even through it continues for months or years, often beyond the point where they can recall its initial impetus and beyond the point of being able to repair their relationship. Perhaps one way to reduce their reliance on the silent treatment would be to have them keep a record, such as the SOR, to make salient to them not only the frequency of its use, but also its consequences for themselves and their loved ones. In the example with which we opened this chapter, such an intervention may have been welcomed. That particular incident of ostracism led to a physical assault, charges, an arrest, and lifelong damage to the ccuple's reputation.

The potential for further research and application in the area of ostracism is vast. Many questions remain unanswered, with many theoretical constructs requiring examination. Through the process of research triangulation, continuing to use a variety of tools, it is hoped that meaningful results will continue to be produced. What is essential, however, is that research progress in a manner that views ostracism as a highly complex, contextual, potentially reciprocal and living process, rather than an unidirectional procedure performed on an unresponsive object.

References

Asch, S. E. (1956). Studies of independence and conformity. A minority of one against a unanimous majority. *Psychological Monographs, 70*, (Whole No. 416).

Bandura, A. (1995). *Self-efficacy in changing societies*. New York: Cambridge University Press.

Barner-Barry, C. (1986). Rob: Children's tacit use of peer ostracism to control aggressive behavior. *Ethology and Sociobiology, 7*, 281–293.

Baumeister, R. F., & Leary, M. R. (1995). The need to belong: Desire for interpersonal attachments as a fundamental human motivation. *Psychological Bulletin, 117*, 497–529.

Cheung, C. (1999). *Ostracizing clients on the Internet: The effects of not responding to electronic mail inquiries*. Unpublished masters thesis, University of New South Wales, Sydney, Australia.

Croker, V. M. (1999). *Target's reactions during ostracism in face-to-face and computer-mediated interactions: Does computer-mediated communication foster virtual courage?* Unpublished manuscript, University of New South Wales.

Davis, B. O. (1991). *Benjamin O'Davis, Jr., American: An autobiography*. Washington, DC: Smithsonian Institution Press.

DePaulo, B. M., Kirkendol, S. E., Epstein, J. E., Wyer, M., & Hairfield, J. (1990). *Everyday lies*. Unpublished manuscript, University of Virginia, Charlottesville.

Duck, S., Rutt, D. J., Hurst, M. H., & Strejc, H. (1991). Some evident truth about conversation in everyday relationships: All communications are not created equal. *Human Communication Research, 18*, 228–267.

Ezrakhovich, A., Kerr, A., Cheung, S., Elliot, K., Jerrems, A., & Williams, K. D. (1998, April). *Effects of norm violation and ostracism on working with the group*.

Paper presented at the meeting of the Society of Australasian Social Psychologists, Christchurch, NZ.

Faulkner, S. L., & Williams, K. D. (1995, May). *The causes and consequences of social ostracism: A qualitative analysis.* Paper presented at the meeting of the Midwestern Psychological Association, Chicago.

Goodall, J. (1986). Social rejection, exclusion, and shunning among the Gombe chimpanzees. *Ethology and Sociobiology, 7,* 227–236.

Grahe, J., & Williams, K. D. (1998, April). *A conversation paradigm to study sources and targets.* Paper presented at the meeting of the Midwestern Psychological Association, Chicago.

Greenberg, J., Pyszczynski, T., Solomon, S., Rosenblatt, A., Veeder, M., Kirkland, S., & Lyon, D. (1990). Evidence for terror management theory II: The effects of mortality salience on reactions to those who threaten or bolster the cultural worldview. *Journal of Personality and Social Psychology, 58,* 308–318.

Greenberg, J., Solomon, S., Pyszczynski, T., Rosenblatt, A., Burling, J., Lyon, D., Simon, L., & Pinel, E. (1992). Why do people need self-esteem? Converging evidence that self-esteem serves an anxiety-buffering function. *Journal of Personality and Social Psychology, 63,* 913–922.

Gruter, M. (1986). Ostracism on trial: The limits of individual rights. *Ethology and Sociobiology, 7,* 271–279.

Gruter, M., & Masters, R. D. (1986). Ostracism as a social and biological phenomenon: An introduction. *Ethology and Sociobiology, 7,* 149–158.

Hazan, C., & Shaver, P. (1987). Conceptualizing romantic love as an attachment process. *Journal of Personality and Social Psychology, 52,* 511–524.

Kling, A. S. (1986). Neurological correlates of social behavior. *Ethology and Sociobiology, 7,* 215–225.

Ko, T. (1994). *Social ostracism and social identity.* Unpublished master's thesis, University of Toledo, Toledo, Ohio.

Lam, A. (1998). *The effects of cyber ostracism and group membership on self-esteem: Does it matter who's ostracising me?* Unpublished manuscript, University of New South Wales.

Lancaster, J. B. (1986). Primate social behavior and ostracism. *Ethology and Sociobiology, 7,* 215–225.

Marsh, H. W., & Parker, J. W. (1984). Determinants of student self-concept: Is it better to be a relatively large fish in a small pond even if you don't learn to swim as well? *Journal of Personality and Social Psychology, 47,* 213–231.

McGuire, M. T., & Raleigh, M. J. (1986). Behavioral and physiological correlates of ostracism. *Ethology and Sociobiology, 7,* 187–200.

Pietromonaco, P. R., & Barrett, L. F. (1997). Working models of attachment and daily social interactions. *Journal of Personality and Social Psychology, 73,* 1409–1423.

Pittman, T. S., & Pittman, N. L. (1980). Deprivation of control and the attribution process. *Journal of Personality and Social Psychology, 39,* 377–389.

Pyszczynski, T., Wicklund, R. A., Floresku, S., Koch, H., Gauch, G., Solomon, S., & Greenberg, J. (1996). Whistling in the dark: Exaggerated consensus estimates in response to incidental reminders of mortality. *Psychological Science, 6*, 332–336.

Reis, H. T., & Wheeler, L. (1991). Studying social interaction with the Rochester Interaction Record. In M. P. Zanna (Ed.), *Advances in experimental social psychology* (Vol. 24, pp. 270–312). New York: Academic Press.

Schachter, S. (1959). *The psychology of affiliation.* Stanford, CA: Stanford University Press.

Scholz, D., McFarland, B., & Haynes, M. (1988). Time-out in schools. *Behavior Problems Bulletin, 2*, 12–16.

Seligman, M. E. P. (1975). *Helplessness: On depression, development, and death.* San Francisco: W. H. Freeman.

Skinner, E. A. (1996). A guide to constructs of control. *Journal of Personality and Social Psychology, 71*, 549–570.

Sommer, K. L., Williams, K. D., Ciarocco, N. J., & Baumeister, R. F. (in press). When silence speaks louder than words: Explorations into interpersonal and intrapsychic consequences of social ostracism. *Basic and Applied Social Psychology.*

Steele, C. M. (1988). The psychology of self-affirmation: Sustaining the integrity of the self. In L. Berkowitz (Ed.), *Advances in experimental social psychology* (Vol. 21, pp. 261–302). New York: Academic Press.

Suziki, N. (1966). Middle-aged and older Japanese employees in Japanese corporations: Their plight during the process of major historic change in employment. *Journal of Management Development, 15*, 7–15.

Suziki, N. (1996). Redundant employees who turn up for work everyday. *Japanese Management Today, http://www.mcb.co.uk/apmforum/japan/hrm-art4.htm.*

Sweeting, N., & Gilhooly, M. L. M. (1992). Doctor, am I dead? A review of social death in modern societies. *Omega, 24*, 254–269.

Tesser, A. (1988). Toward a self-evaluation maintenance model of social behavior. In L. Berkowitz (Ed.), *Advances in experimental social psychology* (Vol. 21, pp. 181–227). New York: Academic Press.

Tynan, D. (1999). *Controlling the uncontrollable: The effects of cyber ostracism and causal clarity on the illusion of control.* Unpublished manuscript, University of New South Wales.

Wheeler, L., & Miyake, K. (1992). Social comparison in everyday life. *Journal of Personality and Social Psychology, 62*, 760–773.

Wheeler, L., & Nezlek, J. (1977). Sex differences in social participation. *Journal of Personality and Social Psychology, 35*, 742–754.

Williams, K. D. (1997). Social ostracism. In R. Kowalski (Ed.), *Aversive interpersonal behaviors* (pp. 133–170). New York: Plenum.

Williams, K. D., Bernieri, F., Faulkner, S., Grahe, J., & Geda-Jain, N. (2000). The Scarlet Letter Study: Five days of social ostracism. *Journal of Personal and Interpersonal Loss, 5*, 19–63.

Williams, K. D., Cheung, C., & Choi, W. (1998, October). *Cyberostracism: Being ignored in cyberspace.* Paper presented at the meeting of the Society of Experimental Social Psychology, Lexington, KY.

Williams, K. D., & Lawson Williams, H. (1999). *Effects of social ostracism on need for control.* Unpublished manuscript, University of New South Wales.

Williams, K. D., Shore, W. J., & Grahe, J. E. (1998). The silent treatment: Perceptions of its behaviors and associated feelings. *Group Processes and Intergroup Relations, 1,* 117–141.

Williams, K. D., & Sommer, K. L. (1997). Social ostracism by one's coworkers: Does rejection lead to loafing or compensation? *Personality and Social Psychology Bulletin, 23,* 693–706.

Williams, K. D., & Zadro, L. (in press). Ostracism: On being ignored, excluded and rejected. In M. Leary (Ed.), *Interpersonal rejection.* New York: Oxford University Press.

Woods, D. (1978). *Biko.* New York: Paddington Press.

Wortman, C. B., & Brehm, J. W. (1975). Responses to uncontrollable outcomes: An integration of reactance theory and the learned helplessness model. In L. Berkowitz (Ed.), *Advances in experimental social psychology* (Vol. 8, pp. 277–336). New York: Academic Press.

Zadro, L., & Williams, K. D. (1998a). *Structured interviews with long-term sources and targets of the silent treatment.* Unpublished manuscript, University of New South Wales.

Zadro, L., & Williams, K. D. (1998b, April). *Take the "O" train: Oblivious versus punitive ostracism.* Paper presented at the meeting of the Society of Australasian Social Psychologists, Christchurch, NZ.

Zippelius, R. (1986). Exclusion and shunning as legal and social sanctions. *Ethology and Sociobiology, 7,* 159–166.

PART IV

The Social Mind of Groups: Group Representations and Group Behavior

15. Self-Categorization and Subjective Uncertainty Resolution: Cognitive and Motivational Facets of Social Identity and Group Membership

MICHAEL A. HOGG

Originating in the early 1970s, social identity theory has developed within social psychology as an influential social-cognitive-motivational perspective on the relationship between self-concept and group phenomena. Commentators have attributed to it an important role in the recent revival of interest among social psychologists in group processes (e.g., Abrams & Hogg, 1998; Hogg & Abrams, 1999; Hogg & Grieve, 1999; Moreland, Hogg, & Hains, 1994; Operario & Fiske, 1999). However, social psychologists who now study groups focus more on cognitive self-definitional aspects, cognitive-perceptual processes, and intergroup dimensions than did their forebears during the 1950s' heyday of group research, who focused more on interpersonal behavior among people in small face-to-face groups, a shift in emphasis that clearly reflects social identity concerns and the influence of social cognition. Although historically social identity theory was a vehicle for the establishment of a European social psychology (e.g., Tajfel, 1984) that was distinct from American social psychology and latterly social cognition, recent years have witnessed a growing symbiosis between social identity and social cognition (e.g., Abrams & Hogg, 1999).

One way in which social identity theory has tended to differ from more social cognitive perspectives is in terms of motivational emphasis. Social identity theory placed significant explanatory weight on people's motivation for self-esteem and self-enhancement as reflected

Address for correspondence: Michael A. Hogg, School of Psychology, University of Queensland, Brisbane, QLD 4072, Australia. Email: m.hogg@psy.uq.edu.au in group members' striving for positive social identity and positive intergroup distinctiveness, an analysis called the *self-esteem hypothesis* (e.g., Abrams & Hogg, 1988). During the early and mid-1980s, some social identity theorists focused more closely on the role of the social categorization process in social identity contexts, producing *self-categorization theory* (Turner, 1985; Turner, Hogg, Oakes, Reicher, & Wetherell, 1987). This change in emphasis largely removed motivation from the social identity agenda and focused instead on cognitive processes. Indeed, Farr (1996) went so far as to remark that self-categorization theory was the influence of social cognition on social identity theory. However, this change in emphasis contains the components of a new motivational emphasis in social identity theory, an epistemic motivation to reduce subjective uncertainty (Hogg, in press-a, in press-b; Hogg & Abrams, 1993; Hogg & Mullin, 1999).

In this chapter I describe social identity theory and self-categorization theory from a motivational perspective in order to prepare the ground for a description of how subjective uncertainty reduction may motivate social identity processes and how such processes are very well suited to subjective uncertainty reduction. I also mention some direct tests of this idea, some indirect support for it, and some of the wide range of implications that the model has for social identity explanations of group processes and intergroup relations.

Social Identity and the Self-Concept

Tajfel first introduced the notion of social identity in 1972 to capture how self is conceptualized in intergroup contexts, that is, how a system of social categorizations "creates and defines an individual's *own* place in society" (Tajfel, 1972, p. 293). He defined social identity as "the individual's knowledge that he belongs to certain social groups together with some emotional and value significance to him of this group membership" (Tajfel, 1972, p. 292). He believed that since "all groups in society live in the midst of other groups" (Tajfel, 1972, pp. 293–294), the positive aspects of social identity (those aspects from which "some satisfaction" is derived) and the social value of a specific group membership (e.g., its social status and the social valence of its attributes) "only acquire meaning in relation to, or in comparison with, other groups" (Tajfel, 1972, p. 294). Tajfel claimed that it is "this comparative perspective that links social categorization with social identity" (Tajfel, 1972, p. 294). Social identity rests on social comparison processes.

Although he drew on Festinger's (1954a) original version of social comparison theory, Tajfel viewed social comparison as more fundamental and as having a different form in intergroup contexts (see Hogg, in press-b; Turner, 1975).

Tajfel believed that groups and thus social identity acquire meaning because ingroups are different from outgroups; logically, it cannot be otherwise because it is differentiation that delineates categories. Thus intergroup comparisons aim to evaluate or confirm differences: "social comparisons between groups are focussed on the establishment of distinctiveness between one's own and other groups" (Tajfel, 1972, p. 296). Furthermore, because social identity is self-evaluative and derives its evaluation from the evaluative properties of one's own group relative to other groups, the intergroup social comparison process strives to accentuate differences that evaluatively favor the ingroup; that is, it strives to achieve evaluatively positive intergroup differentiation.

It is clear from Tajfel's analysis that although self-evaluation is a motive for intergroup comparisons (rendering the ingroup distinct from the outgroup and thus validating social identity), self-enhancement, through evaluatively positive social identity, is also a very important, perhaps more important, motive. Turner (1975) clarifies this: "An individual's need for positively valued identity requires that where an intergroup comparison can be made in terms of a dimension whose poles have a clear value differential, then his own group must differentiate itself relative to other groups on that dimension towards the positively valued pole" (p. 8). The idea that social identity processes are motivated by a striving for positive social identity through positive distinctiveness underpins social identity theory's well-known analysis of intergroup relations (Tajfel & Turner, 1979; also see Ellemers, 1993; Hogg & Abrams, 1988).

Self-Enhancement and Self-Esteem

Turner (1975) notes that "the important comparative dimensions for social identity . . . are value laden. . . . [T]he individual's need to evaluate himself in society is more correctly expressed as a need to make a favourable or positive evaluation of himself in society" (p. 9). For social identity theory, the principal motivation for intergroup social comparisons is self-enhancement, a motivational emphasis that has an interpersonal parallel in downward comparison theory (e.g., Wills, 1981, 1991).

In his subsequent research, Turner takes this idea one stage further (see Hogg & Abrams, 1990) by predicating a striving for favorable evaluation of self in society on a fundamental need for self-esteem. For example, Turner states that "those aspects of an individual's self-concept, and hence self-esteem, which are anchored in his social category memberships can be referred to as his perceived social identity" (Turner, 1978, p. 105), and considers the "need for positive self-esteem" (Turner, 1982, p. 33) to be a fundamental human motivation that, under conditions of heightened social identity salience, is satisfied by relatively positive evaluation of one's own group (Turner, Brown, & Tajfel, 1979). Turner has stated: "I do assume that there is a need for positive self-esteem, not as an axiom, but on the basis of extensive research (into, for example, social comparison, cognitive dissonance, interpersonal attraction, self-presentation, defensive attribution, and so on)" (1981, p. 133).

The implication is that social identity processes as a whole – not just intergroup comparisons, but the entire range of group behaviors associated with social identity, including group membership itself – are motivated by a striving for self-enhancement. This implication was elaborated by Abrams and Hogg (1988; Hogg & Abrams, 1988, 1990, 1993), who postulated the existence of a self-esteem hypothesis in social identity theory: Lowered self-esteem motivates social identification and intergroup behavior, and social identification elevates self-esteem. The idea that group membership and belonging may be motivated by self-enhancement concerns is well established in social psychology; for example, Baumeister and Leary (1995) nominate belonging as a fundamental human need because belonging mediates liking, positive regard, and self-esteem (see Tice & Faber, this volume).

Reviews of research on the self-esteem hypothesis reveal inconsistent and unreliable findings that suggest a distinction between individual- and group membership-based self-esteem, and also suggest that the relationship between self-esteem and group behavior may be affected by other variables, such as the extremity of self-esteem, the degree to which people identify with the group, and the extent to which groups and their members may feel threatened (see Abrams & Hogg, 1988; Hogg & Abrams, 1990, 1993; Hogg & Mullin, 1999; Long & Spears, 1997; Rubin & Hewstone, 1998). Crocker and her colleagues, largely taking Wills's (1981) downward comparison theory as their departure point (e.g., Crocker, Thompson, McGraw, & Ingerman, 1987; Luhtanen & Crocker, 1991), have explored self-esteem processes in intergroup behavior extensively, and have developed a collective self-esteem scale that many researchers, particularly in the United States, employ as a measure of social identity. Social identity has largely become transformed into collective self-esteem (e.g., Crocker, Blaine & Luhtanen, 1993; Crocker & Luhtanen, 1990; Luhtanen & Crocker, 1992).

Generally, the causes and consequences of varying self-esteem are complex (see Schütz, this volume). For example, Markus and Kitayama (1991) distinguish between the independent and the interdependent self-concept (roughly paralleling personal and social identity in social identity theory), and Schütz (this volume) shows that although people generally identify the independent self as the primary source of self-esteem (cf. Sedikides's argument for the primacy of the individual self: Gaertner, Sedikides, & Graetz, 1999; Sedikides & Gaertner, this volume), high self-esteem individuals place greater emphasis on the self as it is derived from comparisons with others. Schütz goes on to show that the comparative basis of high self-esteem people's self-concept often means that such people are socially disruptive; rather than extending self-liking to liking for others, such people derogate others in order to feel good themselves (also see Leary, Tambor, Terdal, & Downs, 1995). If groups provide a readily available social comparative context, then high self-esteem people who make intragroup comparisons will disrupt intragroup cohesion due to their derogation of other members. Furthermore, if high self-esteem is a contextual product of intergroup comparisons that provide positive distinctiveness and positive social identity, then contextual high self-esteem may have a similar effect. These ideas may qualify the social identity and self-categorization theory notion that positive distinctiveness increases group solidarity and depersonalized social attraction for other ingroup members (e.g., Hogg, 1992, 1993) and may raise further questions about the exact motivational role of self-esteem in social identity.

Self-Categorization and Prototypical Depersonalization

Although social identity theory grew out of Tajfel's earlier work on social categorization and social perception (e.g., Tajfel, 1959, 1969), much of the research emphasis shifted, as we have just seen, toward intergroup relations, positive distinctiveness, and self-enhancement processes underpinned by self-esteem motivation. However, during the early 1980s, the social categorization dimension was reexplored and developed by Turner and his students and was published as self-categorization theory (Turner, 1985; Turner et al., 1987). Self-categorization theory grows out of Tajfel's and Turner's earlier ideas on social identity, and can thus be viewed as a development of that theory or, perhaps more accurately, as part of a social identity perspective on the relationship between self and group behavior (e.g., Abrams & Hogg, in press; Hogg, 1996, in press c; Hogg & Abrams, 1988, 1999; Hogg & McGarty, 1990; Hogg, Terry, & White, 1995). Social categorization depersonalizes perception in terms of ingroup or outgroup prototypes that are formed according to the principle of meta-contrast (maximization of the ratio of perceived intergroup to intragroup differences). Social categorization of self (i.e., self-categorization) likewise depersonalizes self-perception, but it goes further in transforming self-conception and assimilating all aspects of one's attitudes, feelings, and behaviors to the ingroup prototype. Depersonalization is the "basic process underlying group phenomena" (Turner, 1985, p. 99). For self-categorization theory, prototypes are context-specific fuzzy sets that define and prescribe attitudes, feelings, and behaviors that characterize one group and distinguish it from other groups. *Depersonalization* refers simply to a change in self-conceptualization and the basis of the perception of others; it does not have the negative connotations of terms such as *deindividuation* or *dehumanization* (cf., Reicher, Spears, & Postmes, 1995).

Although "self-categorization theory is . . . about the structure and functioning of the social self-concept (that based on social comparison and relevant to social interaction)" (Turner, 1985, pp. 93–94) with the aim "to explain the social psychological basis of group phenomena, i.e. to identify the mechanisms by which individuals become unified into a psychological group" (Turner & Oakes, 1986, pp. 240–241), the motivational role of self-esteem in intergroup comparisons is no longer emphasized, as it was in social identity theory. Self-categorization theory has tended to focus on cognitive process rather than motivation: For example, research on salience has dealt mainly with category accessibility and fit (e.g., Oakes, 1987), research on stereotyping has mainly dealt with contextual variability (e.g., Oakes, Haslam, & Turner, 1994), research on cohesion has focused mainly on prototypicality and depersonalization (e.g., Hogg, 1992, 1993), and research on conformity and polarization has dealt mainly with meta-contrast and prototypicality (e.g., Turner, 1991).

In the context of the present volume, there are some interesting parallels between self-categorization theory's explanation of group membership-based depersonalization and Andersen's social cognitive model of interpersonal transference (Andersen & Berenson, this volume; Chen & Andersen, 1999). Andersen explains that people form exemplar-type cognitive representations of interpersonally significant others (e.g., parents, lovers) that are stored in memory (cf. prototypes of social groups). The representation can be triggered (automatically or more deliberately; cf. salience) by encountering a new person who somehow resembles the significant other (cf. social categorization), and this leads to a "transference" of the contents of the representation to the new person, who becomes imbued with the properties of the relevant significant other (cf. prototype-based depersonalization). Andersen also believes that *connection* (defined in terms of intimacy, tenderness, and belonging) is a basic human need and that representations of significant others encompass the need for connection. Thus transference engages a process of connection with the new person (e.g., Andersen, Reznik, & Manzella, 1996). The motivation to affiliate is a consequence of transference.

Subjective Uncertainty Reduction

Although self-categorization theory appears to have little to say about motivation, its focus on social categorization and meta-contrast still involves social comparison processes. It is the self-enhancement aspect of social comparison that is played down. Instead there is an implicit shift of motivational emphasis to Festinger's original belief that there is a "motivation to know that one's opinions are correct and to know precisely what one is and is not capable of doing" (Festinger, 1954b, p. 217). In other words, the motivation for self-evaluation, an epistemic motivation, rather than or in addition to self-enhancement, may have a role in group membership/social identity processes. It is this idea that forms the basis for the motivational model of social identity processes described here (for full details, see Hogg, in press-a; also see Hogg, in press-b; Hogg & Abrams, 1993; Hogg & Mullin, 1999). The self-categorization process is well suited to satisfy people's striving to reduce uncertainty. Uncertainty reduction motivates social identity processes and group behaviors.

Motivational Status of Uncertainty Reduction

People have a fundamental need to feel certain about their world and their place within it. Subjective certainty renders existence meaningful and thus gives one confidence in how to behave and what to expect from one's physical and social environment. Uncertainty about one's attitudes, beliefs, feelings, and perceptions, as well as about oneself and other people, is aversive (e.g., Fiske & Taylor, 1991; Lopes, 1987; Sorrentino & Roney, 1986) because it is ultimately associated with reduced control over one's life. Thus, uncertainty motivates behavior that reduces subjective uncertainty.

The search for certainty is closer to Bartlett's (1932) notion of a search for meaning than to James's (1890) argument that people try to simplify their experiences. This is not to say that people don't try to simplify their experiences, but rather that any simplification that occurs is associated with a more fundamental search for certainty. An overly simplified world view would be so crudely textured that it would be functionally meaningless and would therefore not provide subjective certainty. People do not strive for certainty about all aspects of life, but only those that are subjectively important. Consistent with the cognitive miser and cognitive tactician models of social cognition (Fiske & Taylor, 1991), people would be expected to expend cognitive effort in reducing uncertainty only when the reduction of uncertainty really matters.

Subjective uncertainty is produced by contextual factors that challenge people's certainty about their cognitions, perceptions, feelings and behaviors, and, ultimately, their certainty about and confidence in their sense of self. Self-certainty can be undermined because self is the critical organizing principle, referent point, or integrative framework for diverse perceptions, feelings, and behaviors. The locus of uncertainty is to be found overwhelmingly in the social context, and therefore anyone is prone to uncertainty. However, biographical factors may have some influence on people's orientation toward uncertainty and the reduction of uncertainty.

Epistemic motives related to uncertainty have a high profile in social psychology. For example, they appear in the recent explosion of research on the self and on self-motives (e.g., Banaji & Prentice, 1994; Sedikides & Strube, 1995; Swann & Schroeder, 1995), which considers the quest for self-definition to be a persistent and central feature of human existence (Gaertner et al., 1999; Sedikides & Gaertner, this volume). Festinger (1954a, 1954b) believed that knowing one is correct (cf. uncertainty reduction) is a critical human motivation that drives people to make interpersonal social comparisons with individual others when nonsocial means are unavailable. Communication researchers believe that people communicate to reduce uncertainty and that effective communication itself requires interpersonal certainty (e.g., Berger, 1987; Berger & Bradac, 1982; Gudykunst & Shapiro, 1996; Gudykunst, Yang, & Nishida, 1985). Self-presentation researchers believe that although impression management is an important motive in self-presentation (e.g., Baumeister, 1982), another important motive is self-construction; we present ourselves publicly to others in order to confirm who we are (Tice, 1992; Tice & Faber, this volume). Self-construction represents internalized self-conceptual change on the basis of other people's commitment to the publicly presented behavior (Schlenker, Dlugolecki, & Doherty, 1994; Tice, 1992), and the self-presentation process that produces this outcome need not be deliberate; it can be automatic (Paulhus, 1993; Tice, Butler, Muraven, & Stillwell, 1995).

Many social psychologists study individual differences in uncertainty-related motives: for example, Adorno, Frenkel-Brunswik, Levinson, and Sanford's (1950) description of the authoritarian personality, Rokeach's (1948, 1960) notion of a dogmatic or closed-minded personality, and Kruglanski and others' research on need for structure, and need for closure, and fear of invalidity (e.g., Kruglanski, 1989; Kruglanski & Webster, 1996; Neuberg & Newson, 1993; Thompson, Naccarato, & Parker, in press; Thompson & Zanna, 1995; Webster & Kruglanski, 1994). Of particular relevance, in the context of this book, is Sorrentino's work on uncertainty orientation (e.g., Brouwers & Sorrentino, 1993; King & Sorrentino, 1988; Roney & Sorrentino, 1995; Sorrentino, Holmes, Hanna, & Sharp, 1995; Sorrentino & Short, 1986; see Sorrentino, Hodson, & Huber, this volume). Sorrentino differentiates between (a) uncertainty-oriented people, who seek out information that may raise uncertainty in order to resolve uncertainty ("need to know" or scientific types) and (b) certainty-oriented people who avoid uncertainty if they can and, when confronted with uncertainty, defer to others or use heuristics to resolve uncertainty quickly.

There are also other constructs that identify individual differences in the complexity and number of explanations people have of other people (attributional complexity: Fletcher, Danilovics, Fernandez, Peterson, & Reeder, 1986), individual differences in how much people like to think deeply about things (need for cognition: Cacioppo & Petty, 1982), and individual differences in the complexity of people's cognitive processes and representations (cognitive complexity: Crockett, 1965). People also differ in self-concept clarity (the extent to which self-beliefs are clearly and confidently defined, internally consistent, and stable: e.g., Campbell, 1990; Campbell et al., 1996), self-complexity (the number of different or independent dimensions that underlie self-conception: e.g., Linville, 1987), and compartmentalization of the self (e.g., Showers, 1992).

From the perspective of social identity theory, personality and individual difference conceptualizations of uncertainty should be treated cautiously. The theory is certainly not intended to trace group behaviors such as discrimination and prejudice to personality (cf., Billig, 1976). Rather, social contextual factors influence uncertainty, the resolution of uncertainty, and the way in which such resolution is expressed. If predispositions have a role to play, it is a relatively minor role, and it is tightly constrained by the social context. Individual differences may be better understood as a function of enduring social contexts rather than personality differences; uncertain times produce uncertain people. For example, if we take Sorrentino's distinction between uncertainty-oriented (UO) and certainty-oriented (CO) people (Sorrentino, Hodson, & Huber, this volume), we would suggest that (a) although UOs and COs may approach uncertainty in different ways, they are both motivated by a need to resolve uncertainty, and (b) although some people may be UO in almost all contexts and others may be CO in almost all contexts, many, perhaps most, people's uncertainty orientation will depend on relatively enduring or transitory contextual factors (cf. a similar argument concerning authoritarianism and prejudice: Minard, 1952; Pettigrew, 1958). In keeping with social identity theory's emphasis on social contextual determination of behavior, the uncertainty reduction model described here focuses on uncertainty as a product of the social comparative context.

Reducing Subjective Uncertainty by Self-Categorization

People can probably reduce subjective uncertainty in many different ways. For example, according to social comparison theory, physical reality checks are the first port of call. If physical reality checks are impossible, people make interpersonal comparisons with interpersonally similar others. The idea I propose here is that another very powerful way to reduce subjective uncertainty is through self-categorization, and indeed, that uncertainty reduction is a core motive for social identity processes, perhaps an even more fundamental motive than self-enhancement.

Social identity theory does make some reference to motivations related to uncertainty reduction. Tajfel (1969) refers to the notion of a "search for coherence." Predicated on his belief that intergroup contexts are in a constant "flux of social change," he believed that people need to understand the causes of these changes. People satisfy this need for coherence through causal attribution processes that construct explanations that equip people to deal with a changed situation and "preserve the integrity of the self image"(Tajfel, 1969, p. 92). "This need to preserve the integrity of the self-image is the only motivational assumption that we need to make in order to understand the direction that the search for coherence will take" (Tajfel, 1969, p. 92). Self-categorization theory, although more firmly grounded in the notion that epistemic considerations motivate social comparison, has tended to focus more on the social influence dimension. Uncertainty arises when we discover that we disagree in our beliefs, attitudes, feelings, and behaviors with "similar" others, who can be defined as people we categorize as members of the same group as ourselves. Uncertainty is reduced when similar others agree with us or when we agree with similar others (e.g., Abrams, 1996; Abrams, Wetherell, Cochrane, Hogg, & Turner, 1990; Turner, 1985, 1991). Social agreements and disagreements map out the contours of social groups, and thus socially derived certainty resides in group membership within intergroup contexts, not in interindividual comparisons with similar others.

The process of self-categorization that is responsible for social identification and group membership-based behaviors itself reduces subjective uncertainty. Social categorization constructs contextually relevant ingroup and outgroup prototypes on the basis of the meta-contrast principle. Such prototypes capture meaningful similarities within and differences between groups, and the categorization process further accentuates prototypical similarities within groups and differences between groups. The perceptual field is rendered more clear and meaningful, and less complex and perplexing; it is brought clearly into focus in subjectively meaningful ways. Social categorization of self (self-categorization) depersonalizes self in terms of the ingroup prototype. Self is contextually transformed so that self-conceptualization, attitudes, feelings, and behaviors are governed by the ingroup prototype, a prototype that is both descriptive and prescriptive. This process also provides an ingroup social comparative context containing similar others (physically or cognitively present) who all appear to validate one's self-concept and associated cognitions and behaviors. Thus, uncertainty about self-conceptualization, attitudes, feelings, perceptions, and so forth is reduced. The process of self-categorization reduces uncertainty, and in a more enduring sense, people may join (identify with) groups because they reduce uncertainty.

The focus of uncertainty needs to be subjectively important in that context (something that matters in one context may not matter in another context) for uncertainty to motivate people to try to reduce uncertainty. It is very likely that contextually important uncertainties are those that relate to self-conception; they represent uncertainty about things that define the self, and therefore one's cognitions and actions. Resolution of important uncertainties may almost necessarily imply self-conceptual realignment rather than, or in addition to, simply acquiring knowledge. The self-categorization process is ideally suited to this need.

The mechanism of uncertainty reduction is assimilation of self to the ingroup prototype. Therefore, properties of the prototype, the ingroup defined by the prototype, and the wider intergroup context that generates the prototype all have important effects on self-categorization-based uncertainty reduction. Self-categorization is more effective in reducing uncertainty if people have a concentrated, clearly focused, and relatively unambiguous prototype. If the prototype is prescriptively unclear and dissensual, then it is only of limited use in regulating cognition and behavior in unambiguous ways that confer subjective certainty. Indeed, if people cannot form a prototype at all, then self-categorization does not reduce uncertainty, and people will pursue other means or other self-categorizations to reduce uncertainty. The prototype should also be relevant to the dimension of uncertainty. It should embrace properties that address the specific dimension of uncertainty, or it should be sufficiently relevant to the self-concept to inform the dimension of uncertainty. To reduce uncertainty, people will identify more readily with groups that are relevant to aspects of self-conceptualization that are challenged by the specific contextual uncertainty being experienced.

Typically, clearly focused prototypes are best provided by homogeneous, consensual groups that are high in entitativity (e.g., Campbell, 1958; also see Brewer & Harasty, 1996; Hamilton & Sherman, 1996; Hamilton, Sherman, & Lickel, 1998; Sherman, Hamilton, & Lewis, 1999) and that are located in a crystallized intergroup context where intergroup relations are stable and clearly delineated. Indeed, in seeking uncertainty reduction, people probably pay as much attention to clarity

of social structural differentiation among groups as to ingroup prototype clarity itself, although the latter is probably the most direct source
of self-definitional information. In any case, according to the meta-
contrast principle, prototype formation depends on both intergroup
differentiation and intragroup homogenization.

Prototypes are dynamic representations, and due to their critical role
in uncertainty reduction, it is very likely that under conditions of
uncertainty people pay very close attention to prototypicality. Under
these conditions, prototype-relevant information will be processed systematically via a central processing route rather than heuristically via
a peripheral route (e.g., Eagly & Chaiken, 1993; Petty & Wegener, 1998).
People will do cognitive work on prototypes in order to construct them
in ways that maximize their uncertainty reduction properties. Thus,
systematic processing of prototype information will be more evident
when individuals or groups confront greater uncertainty – for example,
minority groups or majority groups faced by growing challenges to
their hegemony.

Some Implications of Uncertainty Reduction Through Self-Categorization

One implication of the role of prototype clarity in uncertainty reduction is that extreme, and possibly chronic, uncertainty about subjectively critical matters, such as the self-concept itself, may motivate
people to join extreme groups that are orthodox (very clear prototypes)
and distinct from other groups, or may motivate people to make groups
to which they already belong more extreme and more orthodox. The
psychology of extremism may hinge on uncertainty reduction through
self-categorization. In this way, self-categorization may help explain
why and how uncertainty is implicated in many large-scale social
structural phenomena.

For example, sociologically oriented commentators have observed
that the stable identities of 100 years ago had been replaced by the 1950s
by a more atomistic, individual-oriented status society that "did not
promote [a] feeling of identification or collective involvement" (Nisbet,
1959, p. 17). This has produced a characteristic postmodern paradox that
people with today's less structured self yearn for community and the
collective affiliations of times past (e.g., Barber, 1995; Bashevkin, 1991;
Dunn, 1998; Gergen, 1991; McNeil, 1986; Naisbett, 1984), a yearning that
may be reflected in contemporary religious fundamentalism, ethnic and

racial revival, and the reemergence of nationalism and "new" racism (e.g., Barker, 1981; Billig, 1991; Hogg & Hornsey, 1998). People are striving to construct a more certain sense of self in society.

Staub (1989) suggests that extreme and enduring uncertainty, due to socioeconomic crises or natural disasters, may be a powerful motivational factor in the subsequent emergence of group violence and genocide. Less extreme but in a similar vein, uncertainty has been proposed as a significant motivation for people to join extremist political parties (e.g., Billig, 1991; Hogg & Hornsey, 1998; Hogg & Reid, 1998) and "totalist" groups such as cults (e.g., Curtis & Curtis, 1993; Galanter, 1989). Marris (1996) places uncertainty reduction at the motivational core of intergroup relations. He argues that intergroup relations consist of a struggle to offload uncertainty onto other groups and thus construct a hierarchy of uncertainty with desirable high-status groups characterized by low uncertainty.

System justification theory (Jost, 1995; Jost & Banaji, 1994) suggests that it can sometimes be more important for people to perceive a stable system of intergroup relations than to engage in a struggle for self-enhancement. Uncertainty is aversive, and people try to justify rather than challenge an existing status quo. Jost and associates argue that this idea is consistent with a number of other notions, such as failure to perceive injustice (Crosby, 1982), the just world hypothesis (Lerner, 1980), institutional loyalty (Tyler, 1990), stereotypic rationalization (Hoffman & Hurst, 1989), hierarchy enhancement (Pratto, Sidanius, Stallworth, & Malle, 1994), false consciousness (Jost, 1995), and legitimacy of inequality (Major, 1994).

Finally, pronounced uncertainty may produce hierarchical groups with all-powerful leaders. This may happen because extreme uncertainty generates concrete and consensual prototypes coupled with strong ingroup identification. Together these processes imbue prototypical members with leadership charisma and very high status, and psychologically these processes differentiate them from the group and thus allow them to exercise power in autocratic ways (see the social identity theory of leadership presented in Hogg, in press-d; also see Hains, Hogg, & Duck, 1997; Hogg, 1996; Hogg, Hains, & Mason, 1998).

Empirical Matters

There are at least three types of support for the model presented here. First, support for the idea that uncertainty may motivate behavior comes from the literature on uncertainty and uncertainty-related motivations cited earlier on. Second, support for the idea that group phenomena, particularly large-scale societal-level phenomena, are influenced by subjective uncertainty comes from the literature on extremism and related topics just cited, to which can be added cross-cultural research by Hofstede (1980, 1983). Hofstede (1980) identified four key motivational dimensions in international organizational contexts, among which were individualism-collectivism (people's tendency to define themselves in terms of personal choices and achievements or by the character of the collective groups to which they are more or less permanently attached) and uncertainty avoidance (people's tendency to focus on planning and the creation of stability as a way of dealing with life's uncertainties). In a subsequent study of 53 countries and regions, Hofstede (1983) found that cross-cultural variability in collectivism was positively associated with cross-cultural variability in uncertainty avoidance.

The third type of support is the most important because it comes from direct empirical tests of the uncertainty reduction model described here. A series of eight minimal group-type laboratory experiments has now been conducted (Grieve & Hogg, 1999; Hogg & Grieve, 1999; Hogg & Mullin, 1998; Mullin & Hogg, 1998, 1999; see Hogg & Mullin's 1999 overview of some of these studies). The general paradigm is one in which (a) contextual subjective uncertainty and/or type of uncertainty is manipulated, (b) participants are explicitly categorized or not (or category salience is manipulated), and/or (c) prototypical properties of the category are manipulated. The key dependent measures are self-report measures of group identification and behavioral measures of resource allocations. Together these studies show quite robustly that (a) people who are explicitly categorized self-categorize and thus identify with the category, express group attitudes, and engage in group behaviors only when they are categorized under conditions of subjective uncertainty, and (b) this effect is most pronounced when the dimension of subjective uncertainty is subjectively important and when the category is relevant to the dimension of uncertainty. Research by Sedikides and his colleagues on the motivational primacy of different selves (Gaertner et al., 1999; Sedikides & Gaertner, this volume) provides additional indirect evidence for the subjective uncertainty model. Threat to the individual self (viewed by Sedikides and colleagues as a source of uncertainty) caused participants to identify with an available group that made the collective self salient.

Other aspects of the model remain to be fully tested, but they do have some indicative preliminary support. For example, (a) an experiment has shown that people categorized under uncertainty who were prevented from forming a group prototype did not self-categorize (Hogg & Schuit, 1998); (b) an experiment has shown that people categorized under uncertainty identify with higher- and lower-status groups equally – resolution of self-conceptual uncertainty can be motivationally more important than self-enhancement (Reid & Hogg, 2000); (c) experiments and questionnaire studies have shown that greater uncertainty, particularly self-conceptual uncertainty, was associated with identification with groups that had clear, distinctive prototypes (Jetten, Hogg, & Mullin, in press; Sussman & Hogg, 1998); and (d) a questionnaire study has shown that support for extremist political groups was more evident among people who felt most uncertain (Hogg & Reid, 1998).

Finally, Sorrentino and colleagues have recently related their theory of uncertainty orientation to our own uncertainty reduction theory of social identity and self-categorization processes (see Sorrentino et al., this volume). They believe that the theories are compatible but that the latter is more relevant to CO than to UO people; COs seek rapid, heuristic resolution of uncertainty, and this is provided by consensual high-entitativity groups and their prototypes, whereas UOs seek information to gradually resolve uncertainty. Sorrentino and colleagues (this volume) report a replication of the work of Mullin and Hogg (1998) in which the predictions under uncertainty reduction theory are indeed stronger for COs than for UOs. Although this finding is intriguing, Sorrentino and colleagues' reading of social identity theory is unusual. They separate social identity processes that they feel relate to group belonging, and thus to CO people, from self-categorization processes that they feel relate to information about the self-concept and thus to UOs. They then link uncertainty reduction to social identity and group belonging, and thus to CO people. In fact, as described at the beginning of this chapter, self-categorization is the process underlying and responsible for social identity processes including collective self-definition, conformity, ethnocentrism, belonging, social attraction, and so forth. Uncertainty reduction is a motive for self-categorization and all its concomitants, and is thus relevant to both COs and UOs. However, it is possible that enduring or transient social contexts that elevate self-conceptual uncertainty and direct people toward CO-type resolution strategies may produce identification with highly consensual and possibly extremist categories, whereas contexts that elevate self-conceptual uncertainty and direct people toward UO-type resolution strategies may produce identification with less consensual and more internally diverse categories. Clearly, more work remains to be done to relate uncertainty orientation to uncertainty reduction as a social identity motivation.

Concluding Comments

Although it is a social-cognitive theory of group processes, intergroup relations, and the self-concept, social identity theory rested heavily on motivational processes, specifically self-enhancement and self-esteem, which produce a striving in group contexts for positive social identity through positive intergroup distinctiveness. This motivational emphasis was not pursued by self-categorization theory, which focused on antecedents and consequences of the social categorization process, particularly as it related to the self. In this chapter I have developed the epistemic motive that is implicitly associated with self-categorization into a model of how subjective uncertainty reduction motivates social identity processes and is satisfied by self-categorization.

People strive to be certain about their perceptions, attitudes, feelings, behaviors, and self-concept, particularly on important dimensions that relate to self-conception. Certainty is adaptive; it renders the world and one's place within it meaningful and predictable and enables successful goal-oriented action. Uncertainty can be reduced in different ways, of which self-categorization as a group member is particularly effective. Self-categorization is particularly effective because self is assimilated to a consensual prototype that prescribes perceptions, attitudes, feelings, and behaviors and furnishes social support for such prototype-consistent behaviors. Groups with clearly defined and highly consensual prototypes are particularly effective at reducing uncertainty, which may help to explain extremism, group homogeneity, and the emergence of hierarchical and authoritarian power and leadership structures in some groups.

Although uncertainty reduction may be an important motivation in social identity contexts, it undoubtably works in conjunction with the self-enhancement and self-esteem motives that promote positive distinctiveness. Some commentaries suggest that self-esteem, although important, may be less fundamental than forms of self-conceptual certainty. For example, Jost (1995; Jost & Banaji, 1994) believes that uncertainty reduction and the maintenance of stability may be stronger group motives than self-enhancement, and others suggest that the pursuit of self-esteem is indulged only after one has developed a certain self-concept (e.g., Sedikides & Strube, 1995; Taylor, Neter, & Wayment, 1995); self-esteem is related to, or even contingent on, self-certainty (e.g., Banaji & Prentice, 1994; Baumgardner, 1990; Brown, Collins, & Schmidt, 1988; Campbell, 1990; Gibbons & McCoy, 1991).

That self-enhancement flows from uncertainty reduction makes sense from a social identity perspective. Because reduction of uncertainty is adaptive, people will feel good about themselves and thus experience elevated self-esteem. Self-enhancement is a plausible consequence of uncertainty reduction. However, this is a generalized social self-enhancement that extends to embrace the group, its prototype, and its members, because self and group are psychologically fused and because the group and its members validate one's cognitions and behaviors (Hogg, 1987, 1992, 1993). In this way, the satisfaction achieved by uncertainty reduction may generate ethnocentrism, depersonalized social attraction for other group members, and, paradoxically, a degree of satisfaction with stable social structural relations among groups (cf. Jost & Banaji's 1994 notion of system justification).

In real intergroup contexts, both motivations probably operate with differing urgency, depending on the specific nature of the intergroup context. Under some circumstances, a group may feel primarily that its distinctiveness is threatened (the motivation to reduce uncertainty is aroused), and under other circumstances primarily that its evaluative positivity is under threat (the motivation to enhance self-esteem is aroused); see Brewer's optimal distinctiveness theory (e.g., Brewer, 1991, 1993). It is possible that slightly different outcomes may emerge from these two scenarios. For example, distinctiveness threat would encourage symmetrical rejection of evaluatively positive and negative ingroup deviants because the main aim would be to obtain a distinct prototype within a homogeneous and consensual group. In contrast, positivity threat would encourage asymmetrical rejection of deviants. Negative deviants would be rejected more than positive deviants because, positive deviants would reflect relatively more positively on the valence of the ingroup prototype and thus ultimately on self-esteem. This idea remains to be explored.

In conclusion, direct tests of the uncertainty reduction model provide some support for its main tenets, but future research is need to explore its wider implications and to explore the relationship between uncertainty reduction and self-enhancement motivations in social identity processes.

References

Abrams, D. (1996). Social identity, self as structure and self as process. In W. P. Robinson (Ed.), *Social groups and identities: Developing the legacy of Henri Tajfel* (pp. 143–167). Oxford: Butterworth-Heinemann.

Abrams, D., & Hogg, M. A. (1988). Comments on the motivational status of self-esteem in social identity and intergroup discrimination. *European Journal of Social Psychology, 18*, 317–334.

Abrams, D., & Hogg, M. A. (1998). Prospects for research in group processes and intergroup relations. *Group Processes and Intergroup Relations, 1*, 7–20.

Abrams, D., & Hogg, M. A. (Eds.). (1999). *Social identity and social cognition.* Oxford: Basil Blackwell.

Abrams, D., & Hogg, M. A. (in press). Collective identity: Group membership and self-conception. In M. A. Hogg & R. S. Tindale (Eds.), *Blackwell handbook of social psychology: Group processes.* Oxford: Basil Blackwell.

Abrams, D., Wetherell, M. S., Cochrane, S., Hogg, M. A., & Turner, J. C. (1990). Knowing what to think by knowing who you are: Self-categorization and the nature of norm formation, conformity, and group polarization. *British Journal of Social Psychology, 29*, 97–119.

Adorno, T. W., Frenkel-Brunswick, E., Levinson, D. J., & Sanford, R. N. (1950). *The authoritarian personality.* New York: Harper.

Andersen, S. M., Reznik, I., & Manzella, L. M. (1996). Eliciting transient affect, motivation, and expectancies in transference: Significant-other representation and the self in social relations. *Journal of Personality and Social Psychology, 71*, 1108–1129.

Banaji, M. R., & Prentice, D. J. (1994). The self in social contexts. *Annual Review of Psychology, 45*, 297–332.

Barber, B. R. (1995). *Jihad vs. McWorld.* New York: Random House.

Barker, M. (1981). *The new racism.* London: Junction Books.

Bartlett, F. C. (1932). *Remembering.* Cambridge: Cambridge University Press.

Bashevkin, S. B. (1991). *True patriot love: The politics of Canadian nationalism.* Toronto: Oxford University Press.

Baumeister, R. F. (1982). A self-presentational view of social phenomena. *Psychological Bulletin, 91*, 3–26.

Baumeister, R. F., & Leary, M. R. (1995). The need to belong: Desire for interpersonal attachments as a fundamental human motivation. *Psychological Bulletin, 117*, 497–529.

Baumgardner, A. H. (1990). To know oneself is to like oneself: Self-certainty and self-affect. *Journal of Personality and Social Psychology, 58*, 1062–1072.

Berger, C. R. (1987). Communicating under uncertainty. In M. E. Roloff & G. R. Miller (Eds.), *Interpersonal processes: New directions in communication research* (pp. 39–62). Newbury Park, CA: Sage.

Berger, C. R., & Bradac, J. J. (1982). *Language and social knowledge: Uncertainty in interpersonal relations.* London: Edward Arnold.

Billig, M. (1976). *Social psychology and intergroup relations.* London: Academic Press.

Billig, M. (1991). *Ideology and opinions.* London: Sage.

Brewer, M. B. (1991). The social self: On being the same and different at the same time. *Personality and Social Psychology Bulletin, 17,* 475–482.

Brewer, M. B. (1993). The role of distinctiveness in social identity and group behaviour. In M. A. Hogg & D. Abrams (Eds.), *Group motivation: Social psychological perspectives* (pp. 1–16). London: Harvester Wheatsheaf.

Brewer, M. B., & Harasty, A. S. (1996). Seeing groups as entities: The role of perceiver motivation. In E. T. Higgins & R. M. Sorrentino (Eds.), *Handbook of motivation and cognition, Vol. 3: The interpersonal context* (pp. 347–370). New York: Guilford Press.

Brouwers, M. C., & Sorrentino, R. M. (1993). Uncertainty orientation and protection motivation theory: The role of individual differences in health compliance. *Journal of Personality and Social Psychology, 65,* 102–112.

Brown, J., Collins, R. L., & Schmidt, G. W. (1988). Self-esteem and direct vs. indirect forms of self-enhancement. *Journal of Personality and Social Psychology, 55,* 445–453.

Cacioppo, J. T., & Petty, R. E. (1982). The need for cognition. *Journal of Personality and Social Psychology, 42,* 116–131.

Campbell, D. T. (1958). Common fate, similarity, and other indices of the status of aggregates of persons as social entities. *Behavioral Science, 3,* 14–25.

Campbell, J. D. (1990). Self-esteem and the clarity of the self-concept. *Journal of Personality and Social Psychology, 59,* 538–549.

Campbell, J. D., Trapnell, P. D., Heine, S. J., Katz, I. M., Lavalle, L. F., & Lehman, D. R. (1996). Self-concept clarity: Measurement, personality correlates, and cultural boundaries. *Journal of Personality and Social Psychology, 70,* 141–156.

Chen, S., & Andersen, S. M. (1999). Relationships from the past in the present: Significant-other representations and transference in interpersonal life. In M. P. Zanna (Ed.), *Advances in Experimental Social Psychology* (Vol. 31, pp. 123–190). Mahwah, NJ: Erlbaum.

Crocker, J., Blaine, B., & Luhtanen, R. (1993). Prejudice, intergroup behaviour and self-esteem: Enhancement and protection motives. In M. A. Hogg & D. Abrams (Eds.), *Group motivation: Social psychological perspectives* (pp. 52–67). Hemel Hempstead, UK: Harvester Wheatsheaf.

Crocker, J., & Luhtanen, R. (1990). Collective self-esteem and ingroup bias. *Journal of Personality and Social Psychology, 58,* 60–67.

Crocker, J., Thompson, L. J., McGraw, K. M., & Ingerman, C. (1987). Downward comparison, prejudice, and evaluations of others: Effects of self-esteem and threat. *Journal of Personality and Social Psychology, 52,* 907–916.

Crockett, W. H. (1965). Cognitive complexity and impression formation. In B. A. Maher (Ed.), *Progress in experimental personality research* (Vol. 2, pp. 47–90). New York: Academic Press.

Crosby, F. J. (1982). *Relative deprivation and working women.* New York: Oxford University Press.

Curtis, J. M., & Curtis, M. J. (1993). Factors related to susceptibility and recruitment by cults. *Psychological Reports, 73,* 451–460.

Dunn, R. G. (1998). *Identity crises: A social critique of postmodernity.* Minneapolis: University of Minnesota Press.

Eagly, A. H., & Chaiken, S. (1993). *The psychology of attitudes.* San Diego, CA: Harcourt Brace Jovanovich.

Ellemers, N. (1993). The influence of socio-structural variables on identity enhancement strategies. *European Review of Social Psychology, 4,* 27–57.

Farr, R. M. (1996). *The roots of modern social psychology: 1872–1954.* Oxford: Basil Blackwell.

Festinger, L. (1954a). A theory of social comparison processes. *Human Relations, 7,* 117–140.

Festinger, L. (1954b). Motivation leading to social behavior. In M. R. Jones (Ed.), *Nebraska symposium on motivation* (Vol. 2, pp. 121–218). Lincoln: University of Nebraska Press.

Fiske, S. T., & Taylor, S. E. (1991). *Social cognition* (2nd ed.). New York: McGraw-Hill.

Fletcher, G. J. O., Danilovics, P., Fernandez, G., Peterson, D., & Reeder, G. D. (1986). Attributional complexity: An individual differences measure. *Journal of Personality and Social Psychology, 51,* 875–884.

Gaertner, L., Sedikides, C., & Graetz, K. (1999). In search of self-definition: Motivational primacy of the individual self, motivational primacy of the collective self, or contextual primacy? *Journal of Personality and Social Psychology, 76,* 5–18.

Galanter, M. (Ed.). (1989). *Cults and new religious movements.* Washington, DC: American Psychiatric Association.

Gergen, K. J. (1991). *The saturated self: Dilemmas of identity in contemporary life.* New York: Basic Books.

Gibbons, F. X., & McCoy, B. (1991). Self-esteem, similarity and reactions to active vs. passive downward comparison. *Journal of Personality and Social Psychology, 60,* 414–424.

Grieve, P., & Hogg, M. A. (1999). Subjective uncertainty and intergroup discrimination in the minimal group situation. *Personality and Social Psychology Bulletin, 25,* 926–960.

Gudykunst, W. B., & Shapiro, R. B. (1996). Communication in everyday interpersonal and intergroup encounters. *International Journal of Intercultural Relations, 20,* 19–46.

Gudykunst, W. B., Yang, S. M., & Nishida, T. (1985). A cross-cultural test of uncertainty reduction theory: Comparisons of acquaintance, friend, and dating relationships in Japan, Korea, and the United States. *Human Communication Research, 11,* 407–455.

Hains, S. C., Hogg, M. A., & Duck, J. M. (1997). Self-categorization and leadership: Effects of group prototypicality and leader stereotypicality. *Personality and Social Psychology Bulletin, 23,* 1087–1100.

Hamilton, D. L., & Sherman, S. J. (1996). Perceiving persons and groups. *Psychological Review, 103,* 336–355.

Hamilton, D. L., Sherman, S. J., & Lickel, B. (1998). Perceiving social groups: The importance of the entitativity continuum. In C. Sedikides, J. Schopler, &

C. A. Insko (Eds.), *Intergroup cognition and intergroup behavior* (pp. 47–74). Mahwah, NJ: Erlbaum.

Hoffman, C., & Hurst, N. (1989). Gender stereotypes: Perception or rationalization? *Journal of Personality and Social Psychology, 58,* 197–208.

Hofstede, G. (1980). *Culture's consequence: International differences in work-related values.* Beverly Hills, CA: Sage.

Hofstede, G. (1983). Dimensions of national cultures in 50 countries and three regions. In J. Deregowski, S. Dzuirawiec, & R. Annis (Eds.), *Expiscations in cross-cultural psychology.* Lisse, the Netherlands: Swets & Zeitlinger.

Hogg, M. A. (1987). Social identity and group cohesiveness. In J. C. Turner, M. A. Hogg, P. J. Oakes, S. D. Reicher, & M. S. Wetherell (Eds.), *Rediscovering the social group: A self-categorization theory* (pp. 89–116). Oxford and New York: Basil Blackwell.

Hogg, M. A. (1992). *The social psychology of group cohesiveness: From attraction to social identity.* Hemel Hempstead, UK: Harvester Wheatsheaf and New York: New York University Press.

Hogg, M. A. (1993). Group cohesiveness: A critical review and some new directions. *European Review of Social Psychology, 4,* 85–111.

Hogg, M. A. (1996). Intragroup processes, group structure and social identity. In W. P. Robinson (Ed.), *Social groups and identities: Developing the legacy of Henri Tajfel* (pp. 65–93). Oxford: Butterworth-Heinemann.

Hogg, M. A. (in press-a). Uncertainty reduction, self-categorization, and social identification. *European Review of Social Psychology.*

Hogg, M. A. (in press-b). Social identity and social comparison. In J. Suls & L. Wheeler (Eds.), *Handbook of social comparison: Theory and research.* New York: Plenum.

Hogg, M. A. (in press-c). Social categorization, depersonalization and group behavior. In M. A. Hogg & R. S. Tindale (Eds.), *Blackwell handbook of social psychology: Group processes.* Oxford: Basil Blackwell.

Hogg, M. A. (in press-d). A social identity theory of leadership. *Personality and Social Psychology Review.*

Hogg, M. A., & Abrams, D. (1988). *Social identifications: A social psychology of intergroup relations and group processes.* London: Routledge.

Hogg, M. A., & Abrams, D. (1990). Social motivation, self-esteem and social identity. In D. Abrams & M. A. Hogg (Eds.), *Social identity theory: Constructive and critical advances* (pp. 28–47). London: Harvester Wheatsheaf and New York: Springer-Verlag.

Hogg, M. A., & Abrams, D. (1993). Towards a single-process uncertainty-reduction model of social motivation in groups. In M. A. Hogg & D. Abrams (Eds.), *Group motivation: Social psychological perspectives* (pp. 173–190). London: Harvester-Wheatsheaf and New York: Prentice-Hall.

Hogg, M. A., & Abrams, D. (1999). Social identity and social cognition: Historical background and current trends. In D. Abrams & M. A. Hogg (Eds.), *Social identity and social cognition* (pp. 1–25). Oxford: Basil Blackwell.

Hogg, M. A., & Grieve, P. (1999). Social identity theory and the crisis of confidence in social psychology: A commentary, and some research on uncertainty reduction. *Asian Journal of Social Psychology, 2,* 43–57.

Hogg, M. A., Hains, S. C., & Mason, I. (1998). Identification and leadership in small groups: Salience, frame of reference, and leader stereotypicality effects on leader evaluations. *Journal of Personality and Social Psychology, 75,* 1248–1263.

Hogg, M. A., & Hornsey, M. J. (1998). *Pauline Hanson's one nation: A social psychological analysis.* Manuscript submitted for publication.

Hogg, M. A., & McGarty, C. (1990). Self-categorization and social identity. In D. Abrams & M. A. Hogg (Eds.), *Social identity theory: Constructive and critical advances* (pp. 10–27). Hemel Hempstead, UK: Harvester Wheatsheaf and New York: Springer-Verlag.

Hogg, M. A., & Mullin, B.-A. (1998). *Reducing subjective uncertainty by group identification: The role of group relevance.* Manuscript submitted for publication.

Hogg, M. A., & Mullin, B.-A. (1999). Joining groups to reduce uncertainty: Subjective uncertainty reduction and group identification. In D. Abrams & M. A. Hogg (Eds.), *Social identity and social cognition* (pp. 249–279). Oxford: Basil Blackwell.

Hogg, M. A., & Reid, S. (1998). *Uncertainty, social identification and extremism in Australia.* Unpublished manuscript, University of Queensland.

Hogg, M. A., & Schuit, R. (1998). *The role of prototype construction in uncertainty reduction through self-categorization.* Unpublished manuscript, University of Queensland.

Hogg, M. A., Terry, D. J., & White, K. M. (1995). A tale of two theories: A critical comparison of identity theory with social identity theory. *Social Psychology Quarterly, 58,* 255–269.

James, W. (1890). *The principles of psychology.* New York: Holt, Rinehart, & Winston.

Jetten, J., Hogg, M. A., & Mullin, B.-A. (in press). Ingroup variability and motivation to reduce subjective uncertainty. *Group Dynamics: Theory, Research, and Practice.*

Jost, J. T. (1995). Negative illusions: Conceptual clarification and psychological evidence concerning false consciousness. *Political Psychology, 16,* 397–424.

Jost, J. T., & Banaji, M. R. (1994). The role of stereotyping in system-justification and the production of false consciousness. *British Journal of Social Psychology, 33,* 1–27.

King, G. A., & Sorrentino, R. M. (1988). Uncertainty orientation and the relationship between individual accessible constructs and person memory. *Social Cognition, 6,* 128–149.

Kruglanski, A. W. (1989). *Lay epistemics and human knowledge: Cognitive and motivational bases.* New York: Plenum.

Kruglanski, A. W., & Webster, D. M. (1996). Motivated closing of the mind: "Seizing" and "freezing." *Psychological Review, 103,* 263–283.

Leary, M. R., Tambor, E. S., Terdal, S. K., & Downs, D. L. (1995). Self-esteem as an interpersonal monitor: The sociometer hypothesis. *Journal of Personality and Social Psychology, 68,* 518–530.

Lerner, M. J. (1980). *The belief in a just world: A fundamental delusion.* New York: Plenum.

Linville, P. W. (1987). Self-complexity as a buffer against stress-related illness and depression. *Journal of Personality and Social Psychology, 52,* 663–676.

Long, M. K., & Spears, R. (1997). The self-esteem hypothesis revisited: Differentiation and the disaffected. In R. Spears, P. J. Oakes, N. Ellemers, & S. A. Haslam (Eds.), *The social psychology of stereotyping and group life* (pp. 296–317). Oxford: Basil Blackwell.

Lopes, L. L. (1987). Between hope and fear: The psychology of risk. *Advances in Experimental Psychology, 20,* 255–295.

Luhtanen, R., & Crocker, J. (1991). Self-esteem and intergroup comparisons: Toward a theory of collective self-esteem. In J. Suls & T. A. Wills (Eds.), *Social comparison: Contemporary theory and research* (pp. 211–234). Hillsdale, NJ: Erlbaum.

Luhtanen, R., & Crocker, J. (1992). A collective self-esteem scale: Self-evaluation of one's social identity. *Personality and Social Psychology Bulletin, 18,* 302–318.

Major, B. (1994). From social inequality to personal entitlement: The role of social comparisons, legitimacy appraisals, and group memberships. *Advances in Experimental Social Psychology, 26,* 293–355.

Markus, H. R., & Kitayama, S. (1991). Cultures and the self: Implications for cognitions, emotion and motivation. *Psychological Review, 98,* 224–253.

Marris, P. (1996). *The politics of uncertainty: Attachment in private and public life.* London: Routledge.

McNeil, W. H. (1986). *Polyethnicity and national unity in world history.* Toronto: University of Toronto Press.

Minard, R. D. (1952). Race relations in the Pocahontas coal field. *Journal of Social Issues, 8,* 29–44.

Moreland, R. L., Hogg, M. A., & Hains, S. C. (1994). Back to the future: Social psychological research on groups. *Journal of Experimental Social Psychology, 30*(6), 527–555.

Mullin, B.-A., & Hogg, M. A. (1998). Dimensions of subjective uncertainty in social identification and minimal intergroup discrimination. *British Journal of Social Psychology, 37,* 345–365.

Mullin, B.-A., & Hogg, M. A. (1999). Motivations for group membership: The role of subjective importance and uncertainty reduction. *Basic and Applied Social Psychology, 21,* 91–102.

Naisbitt, J. (1984). *Megatrends: Ten new directions transforming our lives.* New York: Warner.

Neuberg, S. L., & Newson, J. T. (1993). Personal need for structure: Individual differences in the desire for simpler structure. *Journal of Personality and Social Psychology. 65,* 113–131.

Nisbet, R. (1959). The decline and fall of social class. *Pacific Sociological Review, 2,* 11–17.

Oakes, P. J. (1987). The salience of social categories. In J. C. Turner, M. A. Hogg, P. J. Oakes, S. D. Reicher, & M. S. Wetherell (Eds.), *Rediscovering the social group: A self-categorization theory* (pp. 117–141). Oxford and New York: Basil Blackwell.

Oakes, P. J., Haslam, S. A., & Turner, J. C. (1994). *Stereotyping and social reality.* Oxford: Basil Blackwell.

Operario, D., & Fiske, S. T. (1999). Integrating social identity and social cognition: A framework for bridging diverse perspectives. In D. Abrams & M. A. Hogg (Eds.), *Social identity and social cognition* (pp. 26–54). Oxford: Basil Blackwell.

Paulhus, D. L. (1993). Bypassing the will: The automatization of affirmations. In D. M. Wegner & J. W. Pennebaker (Eds.), *Handbook of mental control* (pp. 573–587). Englewood Cliffs, NJ: Prentice-Hall.

Pettigrew, T. F. (1958). Personality and sociocultural factors in intergroup attitudes: A cross-national comparison. *Journal of Conflict Resolution, 2,* 29–42.

Petty, R. E., & Wegener, D. T. (1998). Attitude change: Multiple roles for persuasion. In D. T. Gilbert, S. T. Fiske, & G. Lindzey (Eds.), *The handbook of social psychology* (4th ed., Vol. 1, pp. 323–390). New York: McGraw-Hill.

Pratto, F., Sidanius, J., Stallworth, L. M., & Malle, B. F. (1994). Social dominance orientation: A personality variable predicting social and political attitudes. *Journal of Personality and Social Psychology, 67,* 741–763.

Reicher, S. D., Spears, R., & Postmes, T. (1995). A social identity model of deindividuation phenomena. *European Review of Social Psychology, 6,* 161–198.

Reid, S., & Hogg, M. A. (2000). *When status doesn't matter: Self-categorization to reduce subjective uncertainty.* Manuscript submitted for publication, University of Queensland.

Rokeach, M. (1948). Generalized mental rigidity as a factor in ethnocentrism. *Journal of Abnormal Social Psychology, 43,* 259–278.

Rokeach, M. (1960). *The open and closed mind.* New York: Basic Books.

Roney, J. R., & Sorrentino, R. M. (1995). Self-evaluation motives and uncertainty orientation: Asking the "who" question. *Personality and Social Psychology Bulletin, 21,* 1319–1329.

Rubin, M., & Hewstone, M. (1998). Social identity theory's self-esteem hypothesis: A review and some suggestions for clarification. *Personality and Social Psychology Review, 2,* 40–62.

Schlenker, B. R., Dlugolecki, D. W., & Doherty, K. (1994). The impact of self-presentations on self-appraisals and behavior: The roles of commitment and biased scanning. *Personality and Social Psychology Bulletin, 20,* 20–33.

Sedikides, C., & Strube, M. J. (1995). The multiply motivated self. *Personality and Social Psychology Bulletin, 21*(12), 1330–1335.

Sherman, S. J., Hamilton, D. L., & Lewis, A. C. (1999). Perceived entitativity and the social identity value of group memberships. In D. Abrams & M. A. Hogg (Eds.), *Social identity and social cognition* (pp. 80–110). Oxford: Basil Blackwell.

Showers, C. (1992). Compartmentalization of positive and negative self-knowledge: Keeping bad apples out of the bunch. *Journal of Personality and Social Psychology, 62,* 1036–1049.

Sorrentino, R. M., Holmes, J. G., Hanna, S. E., & Sharp, A. (1995). Uncertainty orientation and trust in close relationships: Individual differences in cognitive styles. *Journal of Personality and Social Psychology, 68,* 314–327.

Sorrentino, R. M., & Roney, C. J. R. (1986). Uncertainty orientation, achievement-related motivation and task diagnosticity as determinants of task performance. *Social Cognition, 4*, 420–436.

Sorrentino, R. M., & Short, J. C. (1986). Uncertainty orientation, motivation and cognition. In R. M. Sorrentino & E. T. Higgins (Eds.), *The handbook of motivation and cognition: Foundations of social behavior* (Vol. 1, pp. 379–403). New York: Guilford Press.

Staub, E. (1989). *The roots of evil: The psychological and cultural origins of genocide and other forms of group violence.* New York: Cambridge University Press.

Sussman, K., & Hogg, M. A. (1998). *Uncertainty, prototype clarity and group identification: A survey of campus groups.* Unpublished manuscript, Princeton University and the University of Queensland.

Swann, W. B., & Schroeder, D. G. (1995). The search for beauty and truth: A framework for understanding reactions to evaluations. *Personality and Social Psychology Bulletin, 21*, 1307–1318.

Tajfel, H. (1959). Quantitative judgement in social perception. *British Journal of Psychology, 50*, 16–29.

Tajfel, H. (1969). Cognitive aspects of prejudice. *Journal of Social Issues, 25*, 79–97.

Tajfel, H. (1972). Social categorization. English translation of "La catégorisation sociale." In S. Moscovici (Ed.), *Introduction à la Psychologie Sociale* (Vol. 1, pp. 272–302). Paris: Larousse.

Tajfel, H. (Ed.). (1984). *The social dimension: European developments in social psychology.* Cambridge: Cambridge University Press.

Tajfel, H., & Turner, J. C. (1979). An integrative theory of intergroup conflict. In W. G. Austin & S. Worchel (Eds.), *The social psychology of intergroup relations* (pp. 33–47). Monterey, CA: Brooks/Cole.

Taylor, S. E., Neter, E., & Wayment, H. A. (1995). Self-evaluation processes. *Personality and Social Psychology Bulletin, 21*, 1278–1287.

Thompson, M. M., Naccarato, M. E., & Parker, K. H. (in press). The personal need for structure and personal need for invalidity scales: Histroical perspectives, current applications and future directions. In G. B. Moskowitz (Ed.), *Cognitive social psychology.* Mahwah, NJ: Erlbaum.

Thompson, M. M., & Zanna, M. P. (1995). The conflict individual: Personality-based and domain-specific antecedents of ambivalent social attitudes. *Journal of Personality, 63*, 259–288.

Tice D. M. (1992). Self-presentation and self-concept change: The looking-glass self as magnifying glass. *Journal of Personality and Social Psychology, 63*, 435–451.

Tice, D. M., Butler, J. L., Muraven, M. B., & Stillwell, A. M. (1995). When modesty prevails: Differential favorability of self-presentation to friends and strangers. *Journal of Personality and Social Psychology, 69*, 1120–1138.

Turner, J. C. (1975). Social comparison and social identity: Some prospects for intergroup behaviour. *European Journal of Social Psychology, 5*, 5–34.

Turner, J. C. (1978). Social categorization and social discrimination in the minimal group paradigm. In H. Tajfel (Ed.), *Differentiation between social groups: Studies in the social psychology of intergroup relations* (pp. 101–140). London: Academic Press.

Turner, J. C. (1981). Redefining the social group: A reply to the commentaries. *Cahiers de Psychologie Cognitive, 1*, 131–138.

Turner, J. C. (1982). Towards a cognitive redefinition of the social group. In H. Tajfel (Ed.), *Social identity and intergroup relations* (pp. 15–40). Cambridge: Cambridge University Press.

Turner, J. C. (1985). Social categorization and the self-concept: A social cognitive theory of group behavior. In E. J. Lawler (Ed.), *Advances in group processes: Theory and research* (Vol. 2, pp. 77–122). Greenwich, CT: JAI Press.

Turner, J. C. (1991). *Social influence*. Milton Keynes, UK: Open University Press.

Turner, J. C., Brown, R. J., & Tajfel, H. (1979). Social comparison and group interest in ingroup favouritism. *European Journal of Social Psychology, 9*, 187–204.

Turner, J. C., Hogg, M. A., Oakes, P. J., Reicher, S. D., & Wetherell, M. S. (1987). *Rediscovering the social group: A self-categorization theory*. Oxford: Basil Blackwell.

Turner, J. C., & Oakes, P. J. (1986). The significance of the social identity concept for social psychology with reference to individualism, interactionism and social influence. *British Journal of Social Psychology, 25*, 237–252.

Tyler, T. R. (1990). *Why people obey the law*. New Haven, CT: Yale University Press.

Webster, D. M., & Kruglanski, A. (1994). Individual differences in need for cognitive closure. *Journal of Personality and Social Psychology, 67*, 1049–1062.

Wills, T. A. (1981). Downward comparison principles in social psychology. *Psychological Bulletin, 90*, 245–271.

Wills, T. A. (1991). Similarity and self-esteem in downward comparison. In J. Suls & T. A. Wills (Eds.), *Social comparison: Contemporary theory and research* (pp. 51–78). Hillsdale, NJ: Erlbaum.

16. Motivation Gains in Performance Groups: Aspects and Prospects

NORBERT L. KERR

The title of the symposium for which this work was prepared is "The Social Mind – Cognitive and Motivational Factors in Interpersonal Behavior." This contribution will focus on one aspect of social motivation, itself a rather complex notion in modern social psychology (Gollwitzer & Brandstätter, 1995). I'll focus on an older and much simpler conception of social motivation – how hard one is willing to work at a group task. To distinguish the latter, let's refer to it as the study of *group motivation* (or, perhaps more precisely, *group member motivation*). My proximal goals in this chapter are (a) to discuss the prospects for identifying and understanding instances of *group motivation gains* (by which I mean levels of effort in group performance contexts that exceed those observed in comparable individual performance contexts) and (b) to describe some of the work on this topic that my colleagues and I have been doing. My distal goal is to encourage interest in and sustained research attention to group motivation gains.

Group Motivation: Historical Trends

I have just suggested that this is an old conception of social motivation, and so it is. As experimental social psychology begins its second century, it is interesting to note that the first questions addressed by the field's pioneers focused on how task motivation was different in settings that were less or more "groupy". Whether one gives the honor to Triplett's (1897) classic study of social facilitation or to the group size studies of Ringelmann (1913; research carried out earlier than Triplett's

Address for correspondence: Norbert L. Kerr, Department of Psychology, Michigan State University, East Lansing, MI 48824, USA. Email: kerr@pilot.msu.edu but published later; cf. Kravitz & Martin, 1986), the first systematic empirical investigations of scientific social psychology were concerned with the comparison of individual versus group task performance. This probably reflected the clear relevance of this contrast to applied as well as basic social psychological research.

Progress in this general area has tended to follow a pattern: (a) early studies documenting effects of interest; (b) a long period of inactivity; (c) a theoretical insight rekindling interest; and (d) a period of sustained activity and progress. Work on social facilitation is illustrative. Triplett's early work was followed by many other studies (e.g., Allport, 1924; Dashiell, 1930; Pessin, 1933) establishing that the presence of a passive audience or of coactors performing the same task had reliable effects on individual performance (a facilitory effect in some cases, an inhibitory effect in others) (see Cottrell, 1972, for a review). When no clear pattern could be discerned or imposed on the data, interest waned. It took Zajonc's (1965) brilliant application of Hull-Spence learning theory to the problem to bring order to the old data, to suggest new provocative questions, and to stimulate and guide a new generation of scholars in their reexamination of the old question (e.g., Baron, 1986; Bond & Titus, 1983; Cottrell, 1972; also see the chapter by Huguet, Galvaing, Dumas, & Monteil in this volume).

Similarly, it was Steiner's (1972) book, *Group Process and Productivity*, that provided the theoretical insights that rekindled and redirected research on task motivation in cooperative groups. Steiner showed that simple comparisons of individual and group performance are rarely very illuminating, and that we are likely to learn much more of value by comparing actual group performance with the potential productivity of groups (usually estimated with models that assume *no* motivational differences between individuals and groups and assume optimal use and combination of group member resources). He argued further that one cannot make this comparison without carefully analyzing just what a group's task permits and prescribes from its members, and he proposed what has proven to be a very useful taxonomy of task demands to assist in such analyses.

Group Motivation Losses: Phenomena and Theory

Just as the early social facilitation literature gave Zajonc's theory something interesting to explain, Ringelmann's (1913) early and nearly forgotten study of the effects of group size on rope-pulling performance offered Ingham, Levinger, and others, Steiner's colleagues at the University of Massachusetts, a vehicle for applying Steiner's ideas. In their classic study, Ingham, Levinger, Graves, and Peckham (1974) showed that at least part of the decline in per capita performance with group size originally observed by Ringelmann could be attributed to a decline in group member motivation (a result replicated and extended by Latané, Williams, & Harkins's initial paper on social loafing in 1979).

So, although social psychology has been interested in group motivation for over a century, it has really been in the last quarter of that century, since the publication of Ingham et al.'s (1974) paper, that substantial progress has been made. And what that generation (my generation, since I got my Ph.D. in the same year that their paper was published) has learned in those 25 years has been that there are a number of group task contexts and psychological processes that lead group members to show what Steiner (1972) called *group motivation losses* or what Latané et al. (1979) termed *social loafing* – lower task motivation in the group than in the individual performance context (for overviews, see Baron, Kerr, & Miller, 1992; Karau & Williams, 1993; Shepperd, 1993). We have learned, for example, that group members are likely to reduce their efforts when (a) their individual contributions cannot be identified and evaluated as easily in the group context as when they work individually (Kerr & Bruun, 1981; Williams, Harkins, & Latané, 1981), (b) individual group members see their efforts as dispensable for group success (e.g., Harkins & Petty, 1982; Kerr & Bruun, 1983), or (c) a group member believes that working hard would result in "playing the sucker," that is, doing more than his or her fair share of the group's work (Kerr, 1983).

Accompanying all the new empirical work on group motivation losses has been theoretical work to organize it. In 1993, James Shepperd, as well as Steve Karau and Kip Williams independently published papers that analyzed and integrated the group motivation loss literature using the same basic theoretical approach – namely, expectancy-value or instrumentality models (e.g., Porter & Lawler, 1968; Vroom, 1964). These models hold that one's choice of effort level is governed by how instrumental that level of effort is for achieving an outcome, weighted by the value placed on that outcome (summed, typically, across all possible outcomes).[1] Unlike early learn-

---

[1] There are many theoretical variations on this basic theme. Some models (e.g., Vroom, 1964) distinguish between the contingency between an action and an outcome, on the

ing models of group motivation (e.g., that of Zajonc, 1965), these models emphasize the role of cognition for the *social mind*. From these models' perspective, the Ringelmann (1913) effect can be understood as stemming from the decreased risk of identification and evaluation of one's contribution at certain group tasks (cf. Williams et al., 1981). That is, in these group performance contexts, high effort is not as instrumental in obtaining a valued outcome (viz., a positive evaluation by others or oneself, or, conversely, avoiding the disvalued outcome of a negative evaluation) as it would be if one were working individually.

Group Motivation Gains

There is nothing in the structure of these theoretical models that limits their application to instances of group motivation loss. That is, at least in principle, it is quite possible either that high effort is more instrumental or that the salient outcomes are valued more in the group performance context than in the individual performance context (or both), in which case we would expect to see higher levels of effort in groups. In the remainder of this chapter, I will focus on this relatively neglected but important possibility – that there are interesting group contexts within which group members will have *higher* task motivation than they do as individuals (i.e., that there are replicable *group motivation gains* as well as group motivation losses).

If motivation gains are as easily conceived as motivation losses, why is there so much focused research demonstrating the latter and far less documenting the former? I think there are several reasons. The first is attentional: Research attention tends to follow provocative findings or theories. It was research demonstrating motivation losses (Ingham et al., 1974; Latané et al., 1979; Ringelmann, 1913) that initially captured the attention and emulation of a number of scholars of group processes.

one hand, and between the outcome and a salient reward or punishment, on the other hand. Other models (e.g., Karau & Williams, 1991) distinguish between the expectancy that one can achieve a certain level of performance (much akin to perceived self-efficacy; Bandura, 1986) and the expectancy that this performance will produce a particular valued (or disvalued) outcome. Still others (e.g., Kerr, 1983) introduce the notion of *dispensabilty of effort*, focusing on the difference in the probability of obtaining valued outcomes (e.g., group success) with or without high task effort. These different models might use somewhat different terminology than we have used here (e.g., some might use the term *expectancy* where we use *instrumentality*). Although such distinctions may be useful for certain purposes, the generic I × V model outlined in the text is sufficient for our present purposes.

Until recently, there were no comparable empirical demonstrations of provocative motivation gain phenomena.

Second, there is an inherent asymmetry in the choice to decrease versus to increase one's task effort. Whenever exerting task effort is costly, there is always an incentive to reduce one's effort whenever it is safe or sensible to do so; there is no such inherent incentive to increase one's (costly) effort.

Third, there are likely to be social norms and roles that constrain extreme levels of motivation. For example, Roethlisberger and Dixon (1939) documented antiproduction norms among industrial workers; those who worked too hard were censured ("dinged") by their fellow workers. More recently, Steele (e.g., 1997) has described a "disidentified student role" (particularly in certain ethnic and racial subcultures) that proscribes investing too much energy in academic activities (lest one be identified with other stigmatizing roles – "nerd," "Uncle Tom"). Much has been written (e.g., Orne, 1962) about the role of the *good subject* and the (sometimes pathological; e.g., Milgram, 1974; Orne & Evens, 1965) willingness of experimental subjects to be cooperative. I suspect, though, that one element of the modern good subject role is not to try too hard. This is partly because there is always a risk that the experiment may not turn out to be what it seems, and one can end up looking foolish by throwing oneself wholeheartedly into the experimental task. And, I suspect, this is partly because many of our experimental participants are either involuntary or nonvoluntary, and giving less than one's best effort is often one's only means of protest. I suspect that the roles that limit motivation losses are more likely to arise in natural groups outside the laboratory, whereas various antiproduction norms/roles may plague the intrepid motivation-gain hunter inside the lab (where most of us social psychologists seek our prey).

A fourth and related problem is methodological. Under typical laboratory conditions, individual motivation is already likely to be nearly maximal (i.e., near the level at which subjects [Ss] are willing to exert themselves, even if not near their true performance limits). Individual performers are exhorted to "do their best." Usually, their performance is closely monitored and subject to evaluation by the experimenter and (potentially) by others (Harkins & Szymanski, 1988). And in some instances, good individual performance is also rewarded tangibly. If individual controls are already working as hard as they can (or at least are willing), we would not expect group contexts to induce gains in task motivation. So, at least one challenge for discovering and analyzing group motivation gains is to develop paradigms within which they can occur and be detected.

Group Motivation Gains: Preliminary Findings and Research Directions

Despite these roadblocks, there is growing evidence that there are reliable group motivation gain mechanisms. I'd like to describe three such mechanisms and some of the work that my colleagues and I have done (and are currently doing) to document and better understand them. I'll organize my presentation around a generic instrumentality model – the same basic model that has helped bring order to the group motivation loss literature. In its simplest form,

Effort = Instrumentality of effort × Value of outcome(s) obtained through effort

or

$$E = I \times V$$

One mechanism will focus on altering the value of an effort-contingent outcome, a second on altering the instrumentality of effort, and a third on altering both.

Value-Mediated Motivation Gains

One category of potential group motivation gains is group performance settings where the same effort-contingent outcomes are valued more by group members than by individuals or where there are unique highly valued outcomes available to group members (and, perhaps, to coactors) that are simply unavailable to individual performers. There are a number of promising motivation gain candidates that could fit into this category, including the motivating effect of interpersonal (e.g., Stroebe, Diehl, & Abakoumkin, 1996, Exps. 2–4) and intergroup (e.g., Erev, Bornstein, & Galili, 1993) competition and the special rewards of succeeding in a highly cohesive group (Karau & Williams, 1997). However, I would like to illustrate this category with some completed work from my lab on group sex composition and member motivation.

Group Sex Composition and Member Motivation. This was a program of research that began with one objective and ended up pursuing another.

The original intent was not to identify a motivation gain, but rather to document a particular kind of motivation loss – reducing one's efforts to conform to role requirements. Specifically, I was intrigued by reports (e.g., Feather & Simon, 1975) that women sometimes had to under-achieve to meet the role expectations of their male coworkers and supervisors. This speculation, along with some interesting confirma-tory evidence from nonperformance contexts (e.g., Zanna & Pack, 1975), led Megan Sullaway and I to do our first study on group sex-composition.

KERR AND SULLAWAY (1983). Subjects worked at a simple motor task (pumping air with a sphygmograph bulb) task under one of three conditions: (a) individual performance, (b) same-sex dyads, and (c) opposite-sex dyads. In the latter two conditions, the task demands were additive – the dyad score would be the simple sum of dyad members' scores. In all conditions, Ss worked in separate cubicles, eliminating the nuisance effects of mere presence, distraction, or modeling. Explicit incentives for performance were (per capita) constant across conditions.

Contrary to our underachieving-female expectation, both males and females worked significantly harder with an opposite-sex partner than either with a same-sex partner or individually. The latter two condi-tions did not differ significantly. The latter finding, along with the fact that the anonymity of one's performance score had no effect, tended to rule out simple social comparison and interpersonal competition as the source of the observed motivation gain. However, several expla-nations still were possible. There might have been greater cohesiveness, increased self-awareness, or greater drive in the mixed-sex groups. To narrow the range of viable explanations, we conducted a follow-up study.

KERR AND MACCOUN (1984). Again we contrasted individuals, same-sex dyads, and opposite-sex dyads. However, in this study we used a novel task – hitting buttons on a custom-made keyboard in a fixed sequence as rapidly as possible. With this task, we could manipu-late perceived partner ability in the dyad conditions. All Ss were led to believe that their own practice trial performance was about average. Ss in the dyad conditions were also led to believe that their partner was either above, at, or below average in ability. The motivation gain effect we had observed in Kerr and Sullaway (1983) was replicated only in the condition in which Ss were led to believe that they had performed less well than their partner during practice trials. This pattern of data disconfirmed certain possible explanations – namely, enhanced drive, cohesiveness, or self-awareness with an opposite-sex partner. We concluded that when their competence was in question, Ss placed a higher value on demonstrating their competence to an opposite-sex partner than to a same-sex partner. These results show that concerns with self-evaluation in performance contexts can be highly motivating (Breckler & Greenwald, 1986; Harkins & Syzmanski, 1988, 1989) and that aspects of the group, such as the identity of other group members, can intensify such evaluative concerns enough under some conditions to produce significant group motivation gain effects.

Instrumentality-Mediated Motivation Gains

When one works alone, performance must, of necessity, hinge only on one's own efforts. When one works with others, the contingency between individual member effort and group performance can become much more complicated. Free-riding work (e.g., Harkins & Petty, 1982; Kerr & Bruun, 1983) identifies some of the group contexts within which group performance conditions lower the instrumentality of high effort and encourage motivation losses. However, there are also some situations in which one's efforts are more instrumental in the group context, potentially leading to group motivation gains.

The best evidence for this possibility is Williams and Karau's (1991; Karau & Williams, 1997) work on *social compensation*, which occurs when "individuals increase their efforts on collective tasks to compensate for the anticipated poor performance of other group members" (Karau & Williams, 1997, p. 158). In a series of experiments, Williams and Karau have compared sets of coactors with cooperative groups working at an idea generation task (introduced by Harkins & Petty, 1982) that stressed quantity (not quality) of ideas. In the collective condition, the idea generation task was additive and "information-reducing," that is, individual group members' contributions could not be identified. Earlier work (Williams et al., 1981) has shown that the latter conditions can prompt social loafing. However, Williams and Karau added two features that distinguished their experiment from most prior social loafing studies. The first was the value group members placed on group success (or, in their terminology, how *meaningful* the task was). In their generic procedure, Williams and Karau told their Ss that performance at the idea generation task was highly correlated with intelligence. Hence, poor group performance at the idea generation task would mark the group (and its members) as low in intelligence, clearly a stigmatizing outcome. The second was the expectation of one's partner's performance. In the key conditions, Ss expected rather poor performance from their partners, either because (a) the confederate-partner asserted low ability (Karau & Williams, 1997, Exp. 2; Williams & Karau, 1991, Exp. 3), (b) the confederate-partner asserted the intention to exert little effort (Williams & Karau, 1991, Exp. 2), or (c) the S was chronically mistrustful of others (Williams & Karau, 1991, Exp. 1). Under all of these conditions, the S should value group success highly and should see himself or herself as indispensable for that group success. And, as their analysis predicted, Williams and Karau (1991; Williams & Karau, 1997) found higher levels of performance in the collective condition than in the corresponding coactive condition (i.e., with the same expectation of the coactor's performance). Moreover, as their instrumentality analysis suggested, reducing the value Ss placed on group success (or, as they put it, the meaningfulness of the task) eliminated this social compensation motivation gain effect (Williams & Karau, 1991, Exp. 3).

Social Stigma and Social Compensation. In our own lab, we have recently completed a series of experiments extending Williams and Karau's findings. In their first experiment, Williams and Karau (1991) assumed that Ss with low interpersonal trust would expect the worst from coworkers and subsequently would socially compensate for them. In our studies, we reversed this logic: We presumed that Ss would socially compensate when they doubted their partner's capability, and so we used the social compensation paradigm to probe Ss' expectations about their partners (or, alternatively, the content of the representation that would be activated upon learning that one had a particular type of partner; see Andersen and Berenson's chapter in this volume). Specifically, in the first two studies, we focused on physically handicapped partners.

PHYSICAL HANDICAP AS A MASTER STATUS. We were interested in determining whether possession of a serious physical handicap (viz., being paraplegic) would lead Ss to presume a general task incapacity, even when there was no direct evidence of incapacity at the task at hand. That is, does physical handicap define a *master status* (Frable, 1993; Goffman, 1963), such that everything about a handicapped person is understood in terms of his or her master status condition? In the first study (Swanson, Messé, & Kerr, 1999, Exp. 1), the same confederate either walked into the lab or came in a wheel chair. Ss worked at one of two tasks: (a) a cognitive task (the idea generation task used by Williams & Karau, 1991) or (b) a physical task (paper folding). For neither task was being in the wheelchair a handicap (indeed, if anything, the strength required to handle a wheelchair should have enhanced the ability to perform the physical task). Several incentives were provided to make the task important and meaningful to Ss. Ss either worked cooperatively in a dyad with the confederate, worked next to the confederate in a coaction condition, or (in an extension of Williams and Karau's procedure) worked individually.

For the physical task, coworking Ss showed a social-compensation motivation gain (relative to either coactors or individuals) when their partner was physically handicapped but not when he or she was non-handicapped. This supported the notion that physical handicap implied a more general physical incapacity to our Ss. On the other hand, there were limits to the master status of such a handicap. Partner handicap status did not affect performance at the cognitive task; that is, Ss did not work harder in an attempt to compensate for a presumed cognitive incapacity of their physically handicapped partner.

However, there were aspects of the methods of Experiment 1 that made the latter finding inconclusive (e.g., the idea generation task may not have been as effort sensitive). To further explore whether physical handicap implied cognitive incapability, another experiment was done (Swanson et al., 1999, Exp. 2) in which all Ss performed the same simple task (viz., vowel cancellation). For half of the Ss, it was alleged that performance hinged primarily on physical factors (e.g., hand–eye coordination); for the rest, it was alleged that performance hinged primarily on cognitive skills. To place a high value on group success in both cases, it was alleged that task performance was correlated with desirable general intellectual or physical skills. Furthermore, there were additional incentives (cash for good performance, an extra experimental task for any dyad that couldn't reach a vaguely described criterion). In this experiment, we found social compensation with a handicapped partner for *both* task framings. Thus, we found evidence that Ss presume both general physical incapacity and mental incapacity for persons with serious (but task-irrelevant) physical handicaps, leading them to socially compensate for a handicapped partner. It remains to be seen what other combinations of other group member characteristics and task demands trigger this kind of stereotype-based social compensation.

SOCIAL COMPENSATION AS A (NON)BOGUS-PIPELINE? Our findings concerning physical handicaps suggested that the social compensation paradigm might offer another means of unobtrusively measuring sensitive stereotyped beliefs (e.g., racial stereotyped beliefs). A number of such techniques have been developed, ranging from the bogus pipeline (Roese & Jamieson, 1993) to implicit attitudes tests (Banaji & Greenwald, 1995; see Hilton & von Hipple, 1996, for a general overview). In our third preliminary study (Swanson et al., 1999, Exp. 3), instead of varying the handicap of the coworker or coactor, we varied the race of Ss' partners (Black vs. White) for White Ss. We again varied the task framing (cognitive vs. physical abilities stressed). Here, we did find a motivation gain with a Black (but not a White) partner when the task ostensibly required physical abilities but *not* when (the same) task ostensibly required cognitive abilities. Interestingly, Ss working on the cognitive (but not the physical) task reported their Black partner to be significantly less capable than their White partner. In fact, when asked whether they could, through their own efforts, compensate for any poor performance by their partner, they were most pessimistic when paired with a Black partner working at the cognitive task. We speculated that this was why no social compensation was observed with a Black partner in the cognitive task framing of our Exp. 3; Ss may have seen the required level of compensation as beyond their capabilities.

Joint Instrumentality and Value Mediation of Motivation Gains

Finally, in a few group work settings, both values (of existing or new outcomes) and instrumentalities combine to encourage high effort. A promising candidate for such a setting is the one discovered by Otto Köhler in the 1920s. I noted earlier that sustained research on group motivation losses was stimulated by the rediscovery of a long-ignored result: Steiner's (1972) and Ingham et al.'s (1974) rediscovery of Ringlemann's early findings. Witte's (1989) rediscovery of Köhler's (1926, 1927) long-ignored findings could serve a similar function for the study of group motivation gains. In the studies of most direct interest to us, Köhler asked male rowing club members to perform a simple motor task either as individuals or in dyads. In the individual condition, the rower held a bar connected to a 41-kg weight through a series of pulleys. His task was to do standing bicep curls as long as possible, paced by a metronome with a 2-second interval. In the dyad condition, the weight was doubled (to 82 kg), and one member of the dyad gripped either side of the bar.

Köhler was most interested in the effects of group ability composition on group performance. His key finding for his dyads was that when there was either very little discrepancy in the abilities of the dyad members or a very large discrepancy, the dyads did worse than the average member, whereas for moderate levels of discrepancy, the dyads did better than the average member. Köhler (and Witte) took the latter result as evidence for a group motivation gain. Köhler reported qualitatively similar results for performance triads working at the lifting task and for dyads at a wheel-turning task.[2]

Serving as a discussant in a Society of Experimental Social Psychology symposium at which Wolfgang Stroebe unveiled his own plans for looking into the Köhler effect, I (Kerr, 1990) proposed an explanation for the effect derived from the general instrumentality approach. This explanation held that the conjunctive nature of the task makes the performance of the less capable member crucial for the group's success. At such a task, as soon as one member quits, the other must soon quit as well. Hence, the less capable member is likely to see his or her efforts as particularly indispensable for the group's success. Moreover, the group's success/failure may not be the only (or, perhaps, even the most important) effort-contingent outcome for the less capable dyad member in Köhler's paradigm. There may also be highly salient interpersonal evaluations at stake (see Tice & Faber's chapter in this volume). When one person in the dyad quits at Köhler's task, he or she (a) compels the partner to quit before the partner must or wants to quit and (b) is likely to be seen as personally responsible for the fact that both the partner and the group do no better. Both of these judgments

---

[2] Actually, as Stroebe et al. (1996) have noted, Köhler used an inappropriate baseline of dyad potential productivity. His lifting task was really what Steiner (1972) termed a *conjunctive* task, one at which the group can do no better than its least capable member. Remember that in Köhler's studies, twice as much iron is being pumped by the dyad as by an individual. As soon as either dyad member stops, the task for the remaining (partially spent) partner immediately becomes twice as difficult – making it effectively impossible for the stronger partner to continue. Thus, if dyad members simply worked exactly as hard in the dyad as they did individually (no motivation loss or gain), the dyad should perform only as well as the weaker member, not as well as the average of the two individual dyad members. Using the proper baseline, though, doesn't really alter the thrust of Köhler's findings.

are likely to be aversive and stigmatizing, especially for people like Köhler's rowers, for whom doing well at the task and gaining the esteem of fellow club members were important. They might even anticipate some degree of social exclusion or ostracism for contributing to an early group failure (see Williams, Wheeler, & Harvey's chapter in this volume).

How does the instrumentality explanation account for Köhler's nonlinear function? As follows: When dyad members' abilities are nearly equal, they both want to quit at the same time, so neither is seen as holding back the other (or the group). (Even a little coordination loss would account for the small process loss observed by Köhler for minimal discrepancies.) When the discrepancy is very large, it should become clearly apparent to the less capable member (from one another's apparent level of fatigue or perhaps from foreknowledge of one's partner's strength) that there is no way that he or she could match the performance of the much more capable partner, and so he or she gives up. But when the difference in ability is moderate, we suspect that the less capable member can entertain hopes of matching the stronger partner, lift for lift, and he or she should therefore persist as long as possible (to improve the group's performance and to avoid the stigmas marking the person to quit first).

Replicating the Köhler Effect. In a recently published chapter, Stroebe et al. (1996) reported five attempts to replicate the Köhler effect. The first experiment used Köhler's original lifting task. It was successful: Dyads did better than their average member (Köhler's inappropriate baseline) and their less capable member (the appropriate baseline) when there was a moderate discrepancy in abilities. However, this study also confirmed a serious problem with the lifting task: It is altogether too taxing and too hazardous. Stroebe et al. reported that "Most of our subjects suffered from intense muscle pain after the first [individual] session and were rather unwilling to participate in the second [group] phase of the experiment" (Stroebe et al., 1996, p. 52). Although cash inducements prompted enough Ss to return to enable dyad versus individual comparisons, Stroebe et al. recognized that Köhler's experimental task, acceptable to athletes in the 1920s, is probably not acceptable to student subjects (or committees charged with protecting the welfare of human subjects) in the 1990s and that a different laboratory task would be required to study the Köhler effect. In our own preliminary work, we have reasoned that the next step in exploring the Köhler effect would be to develop an efficient and safe experimental paradigm that both avoids these drawbacks and replicates the effect.

A task used by Ruess (1992) (developed and described by Stroebe et al., 1996) was our starting point. The S's task was to sit in a chair, attach a 1-kg weight to one arm, and then hold that arm horizontally as long as possible. The arm was held above a string, 1 m above the floor, connected at either end to a stand. The end of a trial occurred when the arm was lowered and broke the string. In the dyad condition, two participants held their arms above a single string.

Ruess's task appeared to incorporate many task features that are methodologically or theoretically essential. In particular, it was a simple physical persistence task for which effort and performance should be monotonically related (one can't "try too hard"). Most important, although it may pose the risks of mild fatigue and muscular soreness, the Ruess task did not pose the substantial risks of serious injury or exhaustion implicit in the Köhler lifting task. Further, practically no coordination was required in dyads performing this task, minimizing the probability of coordination losses (i.e., suboptimal levels of performance due to incoordination rather than lowered motivation).

The Ruess task had several other potentially important similarities with Köhler's original studies. For example, for Ruess's task, (a) experimental participants were in one another's presence and could observe one another's performance; (b) there seemed to be substantial between-individual variability in ability (hence, it should be possible to compose dyads with a wide range of ability discrepancies); and (c) because the trial ended whenever either dyad member's arm hit the string, the task demands were conjunctive (a crucial task feature, according to our instrumentality explanation).

Other such features could be attained through simple modifications of Ruess's task. The physical yoking of dyad members present in Köhler's studies could be achieved by having dyads grasp a single weighted bar instead of having each member attach a weight to his or her wrist. Individuals could hold a bar weighing half as much as the dyad's bar. It appears that Ruess's participants held their arms a relatively short distance over the string. This arrangement reduces the chance that group members (e.g., the less capable member) could tell when one member was approaching his or her limit in time to do anything with this knowledge (e.g., decide not to quit just yet). To better approximate Köhler's conditions, we decided to have participants (both individuals and dyads) hold their bar several inches (viz., 10 inches or about 25 cm) above the trip wire. With this arrangement, as soon as either dyad member started getting fatigued and his or her arm started to drop, it would be immediately evident to both members (through the slope of the bar), and they could get this information well before the trial ended (i.e., before the weaker member's arm dropped all the way to the trip wire).

It was also important to make sure that our Ss were not operating at or near their true performance limits and, hence, might not leave dyads room to show motivation gains. We developed an instructional device to reduce this risk. Consistent with the requirements imposed by our Institutional Review Board (human Ss committee), participants were told that although they were always to do their best, they were each to decide individually how long they could persist before the resultant muscular soreness and fatigue became uncomfortable enough to end a trial. This instruction, besides safeguarding the health and welfare of the participants, sets the operative performance ceiling at the individual's level of initial discomfort, which is likely to be well below the individual's true performance ceiling.

Finally, we wanted to create a task performance situation in which our participants, like Köhler's, cared about doing well at the task and about their groups. Pilot work with the modified Ruess task led us to develop the following cover story. The experiment was described as a study of the relative persistence of males versus females. It was noted that such comparisons are meaningful only if the task was of equal difficulty for males and females. Then it was explained (correctly) that the weights of the bars used by males and females in our experiment had been chosen to equalize the mean performance scores for males and females. There was an explicit cash incentive for maximizing individual and group task performance, but in addition, it was explained that a special bonus would be paid if, on average, one's own sex did better overall than the opposite sex. Although this "battle of the sexes" procedure was unlikely to completely reproduce the levels of task importance and group identification of Köhler's rowers, it was designed to approximate these features more closely.

Guido Hertel, Larry Messé, and I recently attempted to replicate the Köhler effect using the modified Ruess task (Hertel, Kerr, & Messé, 1999, Exp. 1). Participants performed the task both individually and in same-sex dyads, with both their dominant and nondominant arms (counterbalanced orders), always in the presence of the experimenter and another (and silent) observer (another same-sex session participant). There were always six Ss in each session, comprising a superordinate "session group." Each second that an individual or a dyad persisted in the task added one point to the session group's total score. After the entire experiment was over, Ss were (accurately) told that one session group would be randomly selected and each member would receive 5 cents for every point in his or her session group's score, plus a 15% bonus if the mean performance for the member's sex was better than the corresponding mean for the opposite sex. (It turned out, however, that there were no reliable sex differences.)

Analyses of dyad performance data revealed a significant ($p < .001$) overall motivation gain: On average, dyads performed 14.25 seconds longer than their weaker member performed individually (an increase of about 10% over the no-motivation-gain performance baseline). As in Ruess's (1992) study, we found (a) only a positive linear (and no nonlinear) relationship between the discrepancy of dyad members' abilities and the group's motivation gain, but (b) this moderation effect could confidently be attributed to a regression-to-the-mean artifact. The clear implication is that for our version of the Köhler task, working in the dyad did have a motivation-enhancing effect on the less capable member, but it was constant across dyads with members who were equal, moderately unequal, or extremely unequal in ability (as indexed by individual performance).

Explaining the Köhler Effect: Preliminary Results. In a subsequent study (Hertel et al., 1999, Exp. 2), we competitively tested our favored instrumentality explanation for the Köhler effect against a leading alternative explanation – Stroebe, Diehl, Abakoumkin, and Arnscheid's (1990) goal comparison explanation. Stroebe et al. suggest that when there is no clear standard of good performance, group members engage in social comparison of one another's level of performance to decide on reasonable performance goals. They go on to suggest that when task accomplishment is important or valued by group members, there will be an upward bias in this social comparison process; that is, those performing less well should set goals closer to the performance levels of the most capable group members. Stroebe et al. plausibly argue that the weight-lifting task used by Köhler's rowers was an important training activity for the club. Thus, the less capable members should have set higher goals in the dyad conditions, producing genuine motivation gains by the less capable dyad members at Köhler's conjunctive group task.[3]

To test these explanations competitively, we compared the performance of dyads to that of individual controls under both conjunctive and additive task demand conditions (Steiner, 1972). All participants first performed an individual trial and then a group trial under one of these two task demand conditions. The conjunctive task version was very similar to the task requirements of the study described previously; the trial was over when one of the dyad members quit the task and hit the flexiglass bar. In the additive task demand condition, a dyad trial was not over when one member quit. The other member could continue as long as possible and thereby earn more points for the team.

According to the instrumentality explanation, motivation gains should have occurred only in the conjunctive condition because it is only in this condition that the weaker member was indispensable for dyadic performance, may have been seen as responsible for group/partner failure, and may have set limits on the stronger member's performance. However, the processes of social comparison and goal-setting could operate equally well under both additive and conjunctive task demand conditions. Hence, the goal-setting explanation predicted that motivation gains by the weaker dyad member should have occurred only in both the conjunctive and additive conditions. Moreover, because this explanation held that the weaker member tries to match the performance of the stronger member, it also predicted that motivation gains should increase as the discrepancy in members' abilities increases (only limited, perhaps, by some giving up at very high discrepancy levels).

The results of the study were clear. There was a significant overall motivation gain (of 45.7 seconds, $p < .001$) in the conjunctive condition but no comparable gain in the additive condition (i.e., using the first member to quit to index the dyad's performance). Further (after correcting for regression artifacts), there was no evidence of an association between the discrepancy in members' abilities and level of motivation of the dyads in either of the two experimental conditions. Moreover, consistent with some informal observations made by Köhler, we found

---

[3] Köhler's curvilinear function was explained by suggesting that no adjustment of goals is necessary when dyad members perform at the same level (very low discrepancy) and that the weaker member will not accept his or her partner's level of performance as a reachable goal when there is a very high discrepancy in ability.

that the enhanced motivation of the weaker members in the conjunctive condition was accompanied by subjective judgments that their input was more important, and that they were working harder but nevertheless were enjoying themselves more and experiencing no more stress (than corresponding weaker partners in the additive condition). The latter findings raise the possibility that the positive affect that results from successfully pushing oneself to match more capable partners' efforts may contribute independently to the Köhler effect (see Forgas's chapter in this volume). Thus, the available evidence makes it unlikely that the Köhler motivation gain effect is due to weaker members setting higher goals, trying to match the performance levels of stronger members through a process of social comparison.

Concluding Thoughts

Earlier I suggested that progress in the area of group motivation (and, I suspect, many other areas in our field) has tended to follow a particular cycle of initial empirical work → inactivity → theoretical work → renewed activity. In the case of the Köhler motivation gain, this pattern seems to be quite descriptive; for the other motivation gains I've discussed, it is also fairly descriptive (although in the case of social compensation, some of the original empirical work [Williams & Karau, 1991] has closely coincided with the needed theoretical developments [Karau & Williams, 1993; Shepperd, 1993]). Regardless of how closely work on group motivation gains has followed the early stages of this proposed pattern, it is my conviction that the empirical and theoretical foundation has now been laid for the proposed fourth stage of sustained, programmatic, and highly productive research. We have seen our field pass through this stage in work on group motivation losses over the last 25 years. I hope I have convinced you that in the next 25 years our field can be equally successful in identifying and understanding powerful motivation gain mechanisms, with the promise of substantially improving the performance of work groups and teams.

References

Allport, F. H. (1924). *Social psychology*. Boston: Houghton.
Banaji, M. R., & Greenwald, A. G. (1995). Implicit gender stereotyping in judgments of fame. *Journal of Personality and Social Psychology, 68*, 181–198.
Bandura, A. (1986) *Social foundations of thought and action: A social cognitive theory*. Englewood Cliffs, NJ: Prentice-Hall.

Baron, R. S. (1986). Distraction-conflict theory: Progress and problems. In L. Berkowitz (Ed.), *Advances in experimental social psychology* (Vol. 19, pp. 1–40). New York: Academic Press.

Baron, R. S., Kerr, N. L., & Miller, N. (1992). *Group process, group decision, group action.* Pacific Grove, CA: Brooks/Cole.

Bond, C. F., & Titus, L. J. (1983). Social facilitation: A meta-analysis of 241 studies. *Psychological Bulletin, 94,* 265–292.

Breckler, S. J., & Greenwald, A. G. (1986). Motivational facets of the self. In R. M. Sorrentino & E. T. Higgins (Eds.), *Handbook of motivation and cognition* (Vol. 1, pp. 145–164). New York: Guilford Press.

Cottrell, N. B. (1972). Social facilitation. In C. McClintock (Ed.), *Experimental social psychology* (pp. 185–236). New York: Holt, Rinehart, & Winston.

Dashiell, J. F. (1930). An experimental analysis of some group effects. *Journal of Abnormal and Social Psychology, 25,* 190–199.

Erev, I., Bornstein, G., & Galili, R. (1993). Constructive intragroup competition as a solution to the free rider problem: A field experiment. *Journal of Experimental Social Psychology, 29,* 463–478.

Feather, N. T., & Simon, J. G. (1975). Reactions to male and female success and failure in sex linked occupations. *Journal of Personality and Social Psychology, 31,* 20–31.

Frable, D. (1993). Being and feeling unique: Statistical deviance and psychological marginality. *Journal of Personality, 61,* 86–110.

Gollwitzer, P. M., & Brandstätter, V. (1995). Motivation. In A. Manstead & M. Heswtone (Eds.), *The Blackwell encyclopedia of social psychology* (pp. 397–403). Oxford: Basil Blackwell.

Goffman, E. (1963). *Stigma: Notes on the management of spoiled identity.* Englewood Cliffs, NJ: Prentice-Hall.

Harkins, S. G., & Petty, R. E. (1982). Effects of task difficulty and task-uniqueness on social loafing. *Journal of Personality and Social Psychology, 43,* 1214–1229.

Harkins, S. G., & Szymanski, K. (1988). Social loafing and self evaluation with an objective standard. *Journal of Experimental Social Psychology, 24,* 354–365.

Harkins, S. G., & Szymanski, K. (1989). Social loafing and group evaluation. *Journal of Personality and Social Psychology, 56,* 934–941.

Hertel, G., Kerr, N. L., & Messé, L. A. (1999). *Motivation gains in task groups: Paradigmatic and theoretical developments on the Köhler effect.* Unpublished manuscript.

Hilton, J. L., & von Hipple, W. (1996). Stereotypes. *Annual Review of Psychology, 47,* 237–271.

Ingham, A. G., Levinger, G., Graves, J., & Peckham, V. (1974). The Ringelmann effect: Studies of group size and group performance. *Journal of Personality and Social Psychology, 10,* 371–384.

Karau, S. J., & Williams, K. D. (1993). Social loafing: A meta-analytic review and theoretical integration. *Journal of Personality and Social Psychology, 65,* 681–706.

Karau, S. J., & Williams, K. D. (1997). The effects of group cohesiveness on social loafing and social compensation. *Group Dynamics: Theory, Research, and Practice, 1,* 156–168.

Kerr, N. L. (1983). Motivation losses in task-performing groups: A social dilemma analysis. *Journal of Personality and Social Psychology, 45,* 819–828.

Kerr, N. L. (1990). *Reflections on group productivity.* Discussant in the Symposium "Group Performance" (W. Stroebe, Chair), annual convention of the Society of Experimental Social Psychology, Buffalo, NY, October 11–13.

Kerr, N. L., & Bruun, S. (1981). Ringelman revisited: Alternative explanations for the social loafing effect. *Personality and Social Psychology Bulletin, 7,* 224–231.

Kerr, N. L., & Bruun, S. (1983). The dispensability of member effort and group motivation losses: Free rider effects. *Journal of Personality and Social Psychology, 44,* 78–94.

Kerr, N. L., & MacCoun, R. (1984). Sex composition of groups and member motivation II: Effects of relative member ability. *Basic and Applied Social Psychology, 1984, 5,* 255–271.

Kerr, N. L., & Sullaway, M. E. (1983). Group sex composition and member motivation. *Sex Roles, 9,* 403–417.

Köhler, O. (1926). Kraftleistungen bei Einzel- und Gruppenabeit [Physical performance in individual and group situations]. *Industrielle Psychotechnik, 3,* 274–282.

Köhler, O. (1927). Über den Gruppenwirkungsgrad der menschlichen Körperarbeit und die Bedingung optimaler Kollektivkraftreaktion [On group efficiency of physical labor and the conditions of optimal collective performance]. *Industrielle Psychotechnik, 4,* 209–226.

Kravitz, D. A., & Martin, B. (1986). Ringelmann rediscovered: The original article. *Journal of Personality and Social Psychology, 50,* 936–941.

Latané, B., Williams, K., & Harkins, S. (1979). Many hands make light the work: The causes and consequences of social loafing. *Journal of Personality and Social Psychology, 37,* 822–832.

Milgram, S. (1974). *Obedience to authority.* New York: Harper & Row.

Orne, M. (1962). On the social psychology of the psychological experiment. *American Psychologist, 17,* 776–783.

Orne, M., & Evans, F. J. (1965). Social control in the psychological experiment: Antisocial behavior and hypnosis. *Journal of Personality and Social Psychology, 1,* 189–200.

Pessin, J. (1933). The comparative effects of social and mechanical stimulation on memorizing. *American Journal of Psychology, 45,* 263–270.

Porter, L. W., & Lawyer, E. E. (1968). *Managerial attitudes and performance.* Homewood, IL: Dorsey.

Ringelmann, M. (1913). Research on animate sources of power: The work of man. *Annales de l'Institut National Agronomique, 2e serie, tome XII,* 1–40.

Roese, N. J., & Jamieson, D. W. (1993). Twenty years of bogus pipeline research: A critical review and meta-analysis. *Psychological Bulletin, 114,* 363–375.

Roethlisberger, F. J., & Dixon, W. J. (1939). *Management and the worker.* Cambridge, MA: Harvard University Press.

Ruess, M. (1992). *Auddauerleistung in Dyaden: Eine Untersuchung zum Köhler-Effekt* [Persistence in dyads: A study of the Köhler effect]. Unpublished diploma thesis, University of Tübingen, Tübingen, Germany.

Shepperd, J. A. (1993). Productivity loss in performance groups: A motivation analysis. *Psychological Bulletin, 113*, 67–81.

Steele, C. (1997). A threat in the air: How stereotypes shape intellectual identity and performance. *American Psychologist, 52*, 613–629.

Steiner, I. D. (1972). *Group process and productivity.* New York: Academic Press.

Stroebe, W., Diehl, M., & Abakoumkin, G. (1996). Social compensation and the Köhler effect: Toward a theoretical explanation of motivation gains in group productivity. In E. Witte & J. Davis (Eds.), *Understanding group behavior: Consensual action by small groups* (Vol. 2, pp. 37–65). Mahwah, NJ: Erlbaum.

Stroebe, W., Diehl, M., Abakoumkin, G., & Arnscheid, R. (1990). *The Köhler effect: Motivation gains in group performance.* Paper presented at the annual meeting of the Society of Experimental Social Psychology, Buffalo, NY, October 11–13.

Swanson, D., Messé, L. A., & Kerr, N. L. (1999). *Social stigma and social compensation.* Unpublished manuscript, Michigan State University.

Triplett, N. (1897). The dynamogenic factors in pacemaking and competition. *American Journal of Psychology, 9*, 507–533.

Vroom, V. H. (1964). *Work and motivation.* New York: Wiley.

Williams, K. D., Harkins, S., & Latané, B. (1981). Identifiability as a deterrent to social loafing: Two cheering experiments. *Journal of Personality and Social Psychology, 40*, 303–311.

Williams, K. D., & Karau, S. J. (1991). Social loafing and social compensation: The effects of expectations of co-worker performance. *Journal of Personality and Social Psychology, 61*, 570–581.

Witte, E. H. (1989). Köhler rediscovered: The anti-Ringelmann effect. *European Journal of Social Psychology, 19*, 147–154.

Zajonc, R. (1965) Social facilitation. *Science, 149*, 269–274.

Zanna, M. P., & Pack, S. J. (1975). On the self-fulfilling nature of apparent sex differences in behavior. *Journal of Experimental Social Psychology, 11*, 583–591.

17. The Social Influence of Automatic Responding: Controlling the Uncontrollable

PASCAL HUGUET, MARIE P. GALVAING,
FLORENCE DUMAS, AND JEAN-M. MONTEIL

The situations in which human beings perceive, manipulate, and interpret information have traditionally been neglected by cognitive psychologists and cognitive scientists in general. According to Levine, Resnick, and Higgins (1993), the recognition of the importance of domain-specific knowledge led cognitive psychologists to take a first step toward the inclusion of social factors as part of cognition. This first step, however, did not specifically involve social factors but "did highlight how particular, how *situated* or contextualized, cognition always is" (Levine et al., 1993, p. 586). For example, the use of abstract problem materials to study reasoning processes in the 1950s and 1960s has fallen out of favor, and psychologists have become much more interested in *pragmatic influences* or the use of real-world knowledge (see Evans, 1993). Although this orientation is obviously interesting for social psychologists, it is insufficient to capture the social dimension of cognition in its full complexity. As noted by Levine et al. (1993), it is necessary to attend not only to knowledge elements but also to the conditions of their use, that is, the situations in which cognition takes place. Most experimentalists are aware that cognitive psychological experiments always take place in a social context and can be influenced by social factors. They conceive of these factors as *minor in the understanding of cognition*, however.

In contrast with this widespread conception of social factors in the cognitive literature, our purpose here is to show that cognition is better

Correspondence concerning this chapter should be addressed to Pascal Huguet, Laboratoire de Psychologie Sociale de la Cognition, ESA CNRS 6024, 34 Avenue Carnot, 63037 Clermont-Ferrand, FRANCE, or requested through the Internet: huguet@srvpsy.univ-bpclermont.fr understood when we take into account the social conditions under which individuals engage in various cognitive activities. Specifically, it is argued that what has been thought to be invariant automatic processing in the literature on the Stroop effect is in fact controllable, in particular social presence situations, suggesting indeed that more can be learned about cognition when it is studied in its social context. As such, the present chapter focuses on a specific aspect of the *social mind*, that is, the way the presence of other people affects cognitive responses that have been well established in psychology. Forgas (this volume) defined the social mind as a composite of affective, cognitive, and motivational reactions to social situations. In line with this definition, our chapter suggests that the way individuals respond to the presence of others can help capture key aspects of the social mind (see also Kerr, this volume) and, simultaneously, can be a source of significant advances in understanding primitive operations of cognition that are traditionally examined outside of social psychology.

As noted in Chapter 1 of this book, social psychology has neglected the study of interpersonal relations in the past two or three decades. Increasingly focused on the mental lives of individuals, our scientific field has been dominated by a social-cognitive paradigm, *social cognition*, intended to understand how individuals process information about their social world (Devine, Hamilton, & Ostrom, 1994; Fiske & Taylor, 1991). Although the studies briefly described in this chapter investigate the social mind from the perspective of a *social dimension of cognition*, they do not fall under the classical social cognition framework. A basic assumption in this framework is that individuals in their social context – the classic focus of social psychology – are virtually always engaged in some form of information processing. We agree. As in cognitive psychology, however, the situations in which information processing takes place have been and still are neglected in theory and research on social cognition. From this perspective, it is mainly the fact that cognition applies to social objects that makes cognition "social." As suggested earlier, we believe that the social dimension of cognition also refers to the fact that *potentially all cognitive processes depend on the social context in which they occur, regardless of whether these processes involve social or nonsocial objects.* Human beings are consistently faced with the presence of others, engage in strategic social interactions and comparisons, belong to social groups, and are the object of myriad categorizations. In our opinion, it is this continuous social reality that truly defines the social nature of cognition (see Monteil & Huguet, 1999).

Of particular interest here, the real, implied, or imagined presence of other people is one of the most prominent features of the social context of cognition, and interest in the way this presence affects cognitive performances has a long history in social psychology. Under the label *social facilitation* (Zajonc, 1965), it has been found that audiences and coactors affect individual performance, sometimes facilitating and sometimes impeding it (see Bond & Titus, 1983; Geen, 1991; Guerin, 1993, for reviews; see also Kerr, this volume, for a discussion of other group performance phenomena). In this area, it is generally assumed that automatic or dominant response tendencies are facilitated by the presence of others. Social presence, Zajonc (1965) reasoned, enhances the individual's dominant response tendency (via an increase in drive/arousal) and, therefore, facilitates or inhibits performance, depending on whether this tendency leads toward correct or incorrect responses. Consistent with this reasoning, Bond and Titus's (1983) meta-analysis of 241 social facilitation studies found that social presence (1) increases the speed of well-learned, simple task performance but decreases the speed of complex task performance and (2) impairs complex performance accuracy and slightly facilitates simple performance accuracy. Zajonc's (1965) account is still well accepted today. In contrast with this account, however, our findings in the context of the Stroop task reveal that social facilitation can also be due to the inhibition (not facilitation) of the individual's dominant response tendency, a phenomenon that supports an alternative, attentional view of social facilitation–inhibition (SFI) effects.

Social Presence Effects in the Stroop Task

Our current investigation of SFI effects is part of a larger project on the social regulation of cognitive functioning and performance (Monteil & Huguet, 1999) and is rooted in Baron's (1986) extensive paper on social facilitation. In this paper, Baron suggested a completely different explanation (relative to Zajonc) of the interactive effect of social presence and task complexity on performance. The key idea is that social presence, when it is distracting, threatens the organism with cognitive overload, a phenomenon that may itself lead to a restriction in attention focus (see also Cohen, 1978). Attention focusing can indeed produce just the task effects usually viewed as evidence of drive: facilitation of performance (by screening out nonessential stimuli) when the task is simple or requires attention to a small number of central cues and inhibition of performance (by neglecting certain crucial stimuli) when the task is more complex or demands attention to a wide range of cues (see Huguet, Galvaing, Monteil, & Dumas, 1999, for further arguments). Several studies (Bruning, Capage, Kosuh, Young, & Young, 1968; Geen, 1976) support the claim that social presence can trigger this form of attention focusing. These studies did not clearly differentiate the dominant response and cue utilization perspectives, however (see Huguet, Galvaing, et al., 1999).

According to Baron (1986), one strategy for differentiating the two perspectives is to focus on poorly learned tasks that involve only a few key stimuli. Here the attention-focusing perspective predicts that social presence should facilitate performance, whereas the drive-dominant response perspective predicts impairment. The standard Stroop task (Stroop, 1935) is especially appropriate to test such competing predictions (as suggested by Baron). In this task, individuals are required to identify the ink color in which words and control signs are printed. Typically, the time needed to identify the ink colors of incongruent words (the word *Red* printed in green, for example) is greater than the time needed to name the ink colors of control signs (+++ printed in green), a robust effect called *Stroop interference*. This interference is the classic example of a task in which a relatively automatic, unintended cognitive process (word reading) conflicts with a relatively controlled, intended cognitive process (color naming). As such, it has been the subject of several hundred research projects over the past half century (MacLeod, 1991).

As noted by Besner, Stolz, and Boutilier (1997), the many variants of the Stroop task have been explored theoretically, empirically, and computationally by cognitive and developmental psychologists, psycholinguists, neuropsychologists, and cognitive scientists in more than 500 papers over the past 60 years. A core assumption of virtually all the theoretical accounts is that skilled readers process the irrelevant word without consciousness or intent. Reading the word is said to be automatic in the sense that readers cannot refrain from accessing the meaning of the word despite explicit instructions not to do so. As Anderson (1995, p. 100) put it: "Reading is such an automatic process that it is difficult to inhibit and it will interfere with processing other information about the word." Apparently, even knowing about the Stroop effect is not protection (Reisberg, 1997), a point suggesting that the processes underlying this effect are not open to control.

To the extent that word reading is the dominant but incorrect response tendency in the Stroop task, Zajonc's solution predicts that social presence should increase response latencies on the incongruent words and, therefore, *increase* Stroop interference.[1] Consistent with this prediction, arousal has been associated with increased Stroop interference in past research. Hochman (1967, 1969) found that increased arousal due to time pressure led to more interference in the Stroop task. Pallak, Pittman, Heller, and Munson (1975) found that arousal induced by the threat of an electric shock also increased Stroop interference.

Conversely, if social presence is associated with a reduction in cue utilization, it should improve response latencies on the incongruent words and *reduce* Stroop interference. Narrowing one's focus should indeed allow one to screen out the incorrect semantic cues and focus exclusively on the letter color cues. Consistent with this prediction, Baron (1986) noted that distraction has been associated with decreased Stroop interference in past research. Results in the Stroop literature even seem to indicate that Stroop interference decreases in coactive situations. In MacKinnon, Geiselman, and Woodward's (1985) Study 1, participants performed the Stroop task alone or in the presence of a coactor competing for one extra credit. Those working coactively were successful in inhibiting Stroop interference, whereas those working alone were not. In Study 2, this effect was accompanied by a significant reduction in memory recognition for the Stroop list words, exactly as one would expect if social presence really did cause attention to focus. Because coaction covaried with a desired reward in these studies, however, its causal role in attention focusing remains unclear.

As noted earlier in this chapter, our findings in the context of the Stroop task also support a cue utilization view of SFI effects. These findings do not lead to the conclusion that distraction necessarily mediates attention focusing in the presence of others, however.

Evidence in the Audience Paradigm

Four experiments (including three pilot studies) were conducted using the audience paradigm to test whether the presence of others affects Stroop interference (see Huguet, Galvaing, et al., 1999). In these

---

[1] Some might claim that color naming rather than word reading is the dominant response tendency in the Stroop task on which the error rate is generally low (an error consisted in selecting the response "red" for the word *Red* printed in blue ink, for example). However, this would imply ignoring the fact that word reading is a dominant tendency at an early stage before response output. As such, word reading should be enhanced by the presence of others.

experiments, it was assumed that audiences can have effects on individuals, regardless of any directional influences. Examples of these influences are the distribution of reinforcements, punishments, and feedback cues; the supplying of information; and the setting of norms and standards with which the participant feels obligated to comply. There is indeed evidence for the existence of *mere presence* (Zajonc, 1980) or passive audience effects, especially when there is some uncertainty about the behavior of the person present (Guerin, 1986). According to Guerin (1986), this uncertainty is especially high when the person present is a stranger and is not coacting, when he or she is sitting close to the individuals, doing nothing (compared with when individuals can see that the audience is engaged in a predictable activity), and when the audience cannot be monitored by the individuals. The pilot studies tested whether social presence affects Stroop interference in these different conditions.

In the pilot work, participants (all females) were faced with a computer version of the Stroop task[2] alone and then had to perform the task in the presence of a same-sex confederate (social presence varied within subjects). In Study 1, the confederate sat opposite the participants, on the edge of their peripheral vision, and never looked at them (e.g., read a book). In Study 2, the confederate sat behind the participants and thus remained invisible. In Study 3, the confederate sat opposite the participants, as in Study 1, but watched them 60% of the time. As in previous research on mere presence (Guerin, 1983), the confederate was positioned in various ways so as not to see the task. In Study 1 and Study 3, the confederate could not see the computer and therefore was unable to determine whether the participants had given correct or incorrect responses. In Study 2, the participant's body blocked the screen. Several criteria were also satisfied regarding the concept of mere presence. Most notably, the confederate was supposedly naive about the nature of the experimental task, her presence was clearly incidental, there was no obvious emphasis on evaluation by the instructions or by the task, and participants were truly alone in the

---

[2] A computer-keypress version of the task was systematically used in our investigation. Whereas an oral version was possible in the audience paradigm, it was not possible in the coaction paradigm, in which the confederate's and coactor's oral responses could interfere with each other. Consequently, before performing the Stroop task, participants were always faced with training sessions in which only color-neutral words (e.g., *Table*) were used as a means of learning the correct response keys. Participants had no difficulty learning these keys correctly during the training sessions.

Alone condition and not with the experimenter partially concealed (the experimenter left the room during all Stroop trials in both the Alone and social conditions).

Finally, in these preliminary experiments, the Stroop list consisted of color words such as *Blue, Green, Red,* or *Yellow,* which were presented in the center of a light gray computer screen. Each word was randomly generated several times by the computer in a color that conflicted with its meaning. Colored plus signs varying in length (+++ vs. ++++) were used as control patches. Participants were instructed to select "as quickly as possible" (while minimizing errors) the key corresponding to one of the four colors in which the words was generated. Latencies were measured in milliseconds.

Consistent with the Stroop literature, the main effect of Item Type was significant in each study (with a large effect size), indicating the systematic emergence of a Stroop interference (about 100 milliseconds on average).[3] As expected, however, participants identified the letter color cues of incongruent color words *more rapidly* when they worked in the presence of a relatively unpredictable (Attentive or Invisible) audience than when they worked alone or in the presence of a predictable (Inattentive) audience. Taken together, our preliminary findings were consistent with a distraction/cue utilization view of social facilitation: Attention that, in isolation, could be allocated to competing cues (the words) was consumed in monitoring relatively unpredictable audiences. Due to the lack of distraction data, however, we could not decide whether our findings were due to distraction rather than to something else. Measures of distraction were therefore included in another study (see later), in which participants were also faced with a recognition memory test of the words on the Stroop list. Several studies (see MacLeod, 1991) have shown that a significant component of Stroop interference can be localized before response output, at an earlier stage where the degree of semantic processing can be altered. This alteration in the critical audience conditions would heighten our confidence that semantic meaning is more effectively screened out, as one would expect if the presence of unpredictable others really does cause attention to focus.

---

[3] In the pilot studies, as in the other studies reported in this chapter, more errors were generally made for the incongruent words than for the control signs, providing further evidence for the strength of word reading at an early stage before response output.

In this new study (Huguet, Galvaing, et al., 1999, Study 1), participants were faced with the Stroop task Alone, in the presence of an Inattentive-Busy, Invisible, or relatively Attentive Audience (with a same-sex confederate in each condition), as previously. Social presence now varied between subjects. Likewise, the Stroop list consisted of color words and color-related words (because of the use of a recognition task) generated in one of the four target colors, excluding congruent colors. Colored plus signs varying in length were used as control patches. Once the Stroop session was ended, participants were asked to rate the extent to which (1) they felt they had thought about something other than the task while performing it (internal distraction) and (2) they spent some time away from the task – turning their head or body – during the Stroop session (external distraction). At the end of the experiment, participants were asked to recognize the words previously generated by the computer.

Consistent with our preliminary findings, participants working in the presence of an Attentive or Invisible Audience identified the letter color cues of the incongruent color words *more rapidly* than those working Alone (see Figure 17.1). As expected, participants' recognition memory of the Stroop list words was especially low in the critical audience conditions, suggesting that attention affected Stroop interference at an early stage where the degree of semantic processing could be altered (latencies on the Incongruent Words correlated positively with recognition performance). Taken together, these findings provided further evidence that the mere presence of others can be associated with a reduction in cue utilization, at least when this presence is relatively unpredictable. An important question in this study was whether the degree of uncertainty in the behavior of the person present affected self-reports of distraction. It did not. Furthermore, the level of reported distraction was extremely low in each condition. Thus, although these new findings supported the distraction/cue-utilization perspective, there was no evidence in our data that distraction increased in the critical audience conditions.

Of course, the lack of audience effects on self-reports of distraction is not necessarily surprising. Individuals may be unable to report reliably on their attention allocation strategies, especially when self-reports are made retrospectively (see Nisbett & Wilson, 1977). However, although doubts have been raised as to the validity of direct verbal measures of distraction (e.g., how distracted were you during the task?; see Baron, 1986, p. 14), indirect measures such as those used here have been found

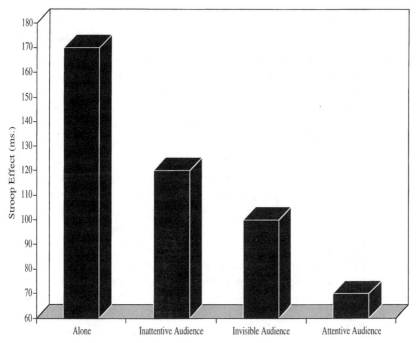

Figure 17.1. The effect of work condition (audience presence) on Stroop interference.

to be sensitive to social presence manipulations. Sanders, Baron, and Moore (1978), for example, used self-reports of attention (asking participants where they directed their attention) to assess distraction and found it to be higher in coaction conditions where SFI occurred. Thus, it seems that distraction did not play a significant role in our findings.

Evidence in the Coaction Paradigm

The coaction paradigm is especially appropriate to examine the role of socially induced distraction in the context of the Stroop task. Competitive pressures are indeed high in most coaction situations. As suggested by Baron (1986), these pressures typically force the individuals to attend to their coactor(s) to gain social comparison information about their relative performance (see also Sanders et al., 1978). If distraction explains the previous audience effects, the effect arising from the comparison checks on one's coactor(s) should cause attention to focus regardless of whether social comparison is downward, lateral, or upward. Put differently, when coaction is associated with forced social comparison, it should consistently facilitate Stroop performance. In previous studies (Seta, 1982; Seta, Seta, & Donalson, 1991), however, coaction facilitated performance only when participants engaged in slightly upward social comparison. No effects were found when forced social comparison was either downward or strongly upward. Although the role of distraction was not investigated in these studies, it seems that the motivation to do better in the presence of others, not distraction per se, explained the performance effects. If the motivation to do better than others plays a crucial role in coaction effects (i.e., if distraction is not the key process), we reasoned, Stroop interference should decrease only when participants engage in slightly upward (and maybe lateral) comparison with the person present.

In a coaction study (Huguet, Galvaing, et al., 1999, Study 2) participants performed the last training session (see footnote 2) either alone or in the presence of a same-sex confederate coactor who worked either slower, similarly, or faster than themselves on the task. In the first and third coaction conditions, the confederate completed the task 40 seconds later versus earlier (on average) than the participants. In the second coaction condition (similar speed), he or she ended the task at the same time as the participants. Participants were forced to compare themselves with the confederate, and those faced with a Slower or Faster Coactor could readily attribute the difference in performance speed to a difference in ability. The Stroop task (designed as before) was then performed, and the confederate behaved as in the last training session (e.g., worked either slower than, similarly to, or faster than participants). As previously, the experimenter left the room in both the Alone and social conditions in all sessions (including the training sessions). Finally, participants were asked to recognize the words previously generated by the computer, as in the previous study.

Consistent with the expectations, participants who engaged in upward social comparison identified the letter color cues of the incongruent color words *more quickly* than those in the three other conditions (see Figure 17.2).[4] Participants' recognition memory of the Stroop list words was especially low in this critical condition, suggesting (once

---

[4] In the lateral comparison condition, the interference did not decrease because of faster latencies on the Incongruent Words (unlike what happened in the Upward Comparison condition). It decreased because of slower latencies on the Control Signs.

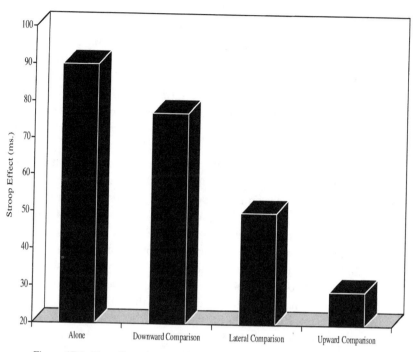

Figure 17.2. The effect of work condition (coaction) on Stroop interference.

more) that attention affected Stroop interference at an early stage before response output (latencies on the Incongruent Words correlated positively with recognition performance). This finding could not be easily explained by an increase in distraction. All participants working co-actively were accurate in their ratings of relative performance speed, a phenomenon that implies that some attention was allocated to the confederate in each coaction condition. To the extent that this allocation of attention was similar in its intensity regardless of the direction of social comparison, distraction does not appear to be the cause of the present findings.

Consistent with the results of previous coaction studies (Seta, 1982; Seta et al., 1991), it seems that participants faced with slightly upward social comparison expended more effort on the task, perhaps as a means of achieving success. As suggested by Seta (1982), only slightly upward social comparison elevates the level of performance that is necessary in order to achieve success and/or avoid failure (e.g., the performance goal or standard). From this perspective, the fact that Stroop interference decreased in participants who engaged in upward social comparison is even more interesting. This implies that word reading did not become weaker simply as the result of distraction but also because it was *actively inhibited* by the participants. Our suggestion is that participants who compared upward engaged consciously or strategically in attention focusing as a means of preventing further self-threatening comparison.

New evidence for a strategic inhibition of word reading comes from another study (Dumas & Huguet, 1999), which tested whether reduced Stroop interference can also be associated with the necessity to maintain a self-enhancing social comparison. If there is a motivational component in the Stroop effect, we reasoned, this effect should also decrease when participants are faced with downward comparison but believe that a special effort is needed on the Stroop task in order to maintain the superiority of the self. In this new study, confederate co-actors behaved as if they did or did not do their best in the training session (see Wheeler, Martin, & Suls, 1997, for more information about this factor). In the first condition, participants who compared downward during training could believe that they should still respond faster than the coactor on the Stroop task without much effort. In the second condition, participants faced with downward comparison during training could feel that a special effort was needed on the Stroop task because of a possible change in the coactor's level of effort that could threaten their relative standing. In these two conditions, participants who experienced upward comparison could increase their effort to prevent further self-threatening comparison. As expected, in the condition where coactors did their best, the time needed to identify the color of the incongruent words was shorter for participants who compared upward than for those who compared downward. This difference did not occur in the condition where the coactors did not do their best (i.e., where participants' relative standing could change). In this critical condition, both groups of participants were successful at inhibiting word reading (see Figure 17.3). Thus, under specific conditions, upward and downward social comparison can both optimize cognitive functioning in the context of the Stroop task.

As revealed by other recent findings (Huguet & Dumas, 1999), real coaction is not necessary for social comparison effects to occur. In this last study, participants were simply informed about how they per-

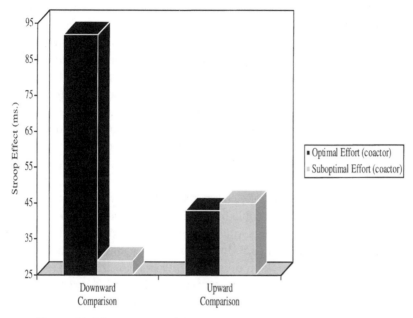

Figure 17.3. The interaction of social comparison × coactor's effort.

formed in comparison with previous participants on the last training session. Downward, lateral, and upward social comparisons were induced. Participants in the control group received no comparison information. The pattern of results was approximately the same as in Huguet et al.'s Study 2. Once again, participants faced with an upward social comparison were especially successful at inhibiting word reading (see also Huguet, Charbonnier, & Monteil, 1999; Huguet & Monteil, 1995, for other social comparison effects on individual performance). Collins (1996) argued that upward social comparison only sometimes results in more negative self-evaluations and is in fact frequently self-enhancing. Our findings show that upward comparison can also lead to better performance, even when this requires the inhibition of a powerful automatic, unintended cognitive process.

Concluding Comments

Over the past 60 years, investigators in the domain of the Stroop task have suggested that when they must identify the ink colors of incongruent color words, individuals cannot refrain from accessing the meaning of words despite explicit instructions not to do so. Although this automatic response tendency is dominant only at an early stage, before response output, it is indeed a source of considerable interference that increase response latencies on incongruent words. Our central question was whether this interference increases (as predicted by the classic view of social facilitation) or decreases (as predicted by an alternative cue utilization view) in audience and coaction situations.

Overall, the present results provide strong support for the cue utilization view of SFI effects. Automatic word reading was indeed inhibited in audience situations in which the behavior of the person present was relatively unpredictable, compared with situations in which this behavior was more predictable or in which participants worked alone. Likewise, word reading was inhibited in coactive situations that forced participants to engage in slightly upward (and sometimes downward) comparison with the person present, compared to situations in which participants worked alone. In most cases, this inhibition was associated with a reduction in recognition memory of the words in the Stroop list, an effect that attests to the strength of the focusing phenomenon.

The reduction in cue utilization facilitated performance in the present studies. This is not always the case, however. As suggested by Bruning et al. (1968) and Geen (1976), attention focusing can also inhibit performance when the task demands attention to a wide range of cues. There is therefore some reason to believe that the reduction in cue utilization is a valuable mechanism for explaining both social facilitation and social inhibition effects. This alternative view of SFI effects has been recently clarified (see Huguet, Galvaing et al., 1999).

Our findings also demonstrate the power of social situations over what has been thought to be invariant automatic processing in the Stroop literature. Interestingly, or perhaps unfortunately, the impact that the presence of others may have on Stroop interference, as well as on other cognitive phenomena, is generally neglected by cognitive psychologists. In the Stroop literature, both the place where the experimenter stands and how he or she behaves during Stroop performance are never reported by authors. This does not promote a clear interpretation of their findings, especially when the results of different Stroop studies are compared. As shown by our results, even subtle differences in testing arrangements can change performance in the Stroop task. This point, however, is less important than the general conclusion to be drawn regarding the Stroop literature: Our findings are inconsistent with the widespread view reiterated in this literature that lexical and semantic analyses of single words are uncontrollable in the sense that they cannot be prevented. Instead, it seems that it is possible to prevent the computation of semantics, a point suggesting that mental processes operating outside awareness are not necessarily inevitable (see also Besner et al., 1997 for a similar argument).

This is an important conclusion. For example, Andersen and Berenson (this volume) reported evidence showing the nonconscious activation of significant-other representations and hence of transference in social perception. They also have evidence that in a simple judgment task, significant-other representations are used more efficiently (one type of automaticity) than are various other representations. Based on our findings, it seems that Andersen and Berenson's evidence does not necessarily imply that people are incapable of engaging in top-down strategic processing that might enable them to short-circuit or redirect their responses.

In the Stroop literature, there is ample reason to believe that a significant amount of semantic processing can be controlled by elements of the task. As noted by MacLeod (1991), if the to-be-named color and the to-be-ignored words are presented in separate spatial locations or if the color cues are presented 300 to 500 milliseconds before the words (by manipulating Stimulus Onset Asynchrony), Stroop interference will be reduced compared to the standard, integrated version of the task. Our findings tell us a completely different story, however. In the present studies, the color and word cues overlapped perfectly over time and space. Although this should have made very unlikely any disruption of automatic verbal processing, this disruption generally occurred in the critical social conditions. Thus, automatic verbal processing can not only be controlled by elements of the task, but it can also depend on the social context in which cognition takes place.

The idea that automatic effects in the Stroop paradigm can be altered and overcome by attention is not really new. Logan and Zbrodoff (1979), for example, showed that when a cue provided advance information about whether the upcoming trial was congruent or incongruent, response time on cued trials was faster than on uncued trials. Such results can be taken as evidence that attentional-allocation policy is a critical element in the Stroop task (see MacLeod, 1991). As suggested by Logan (1980), however, the boundary conditions of attentional effects are well established neither in the Stroop paradigm nor in other major paradigms of cognitive psychology. The present findings indicate that these conditions must also be understood in relation to basic features of the social context in which human performance occurs. And the fact that more can be learned about cognition when it is studied in social situations is certainly interesting for cognitive psychologists. To the extent that cognitive processes elicited by nonsocial and social stimuli are not completely interchangeable, cognitive theories will be incomplete until they address elemental and contextual social factors and processes (see also Monteil & Huguet, 1999).

In conclusion, the present findings provide evidence that even relatively simple social situations can regulate human cognitive functioning. Future research is needed to understand exactly how this regulation operates. As such, however, our findings offer new reasons to "pay constant attention to the social environment of cognition" (Simon, 1990, p. 16): How people experience their social world, or what they come to believe about it, can play a significant role in determining primitive operations of cognition.

References

Anderson, J. (1995). *Cognitive psychology and its implications.* New York: Freeman.

Baron, R. S. (1986). Distraction-conflict theory: Progress and problems. In L. Berkowitz (Ed.), *Advances in experimental social psychology* (pp. 1–40). New York: Academic Press.

Besner, D., Stolz, J. A., & Boutilier, C. (1997). The Stroop effect and the myth of automaticity. *Psychonomic Bulletin and Review, 4,* 221–225.

Bond, C. F., & Titus, L. J. (1983). Social facilitation: A meta-analysis of 241 studies. *Psychological Bulletin, 94,* 265–292.

Bruning, J. L., Capage, J. E., Kosuh, J. F., Young, P. F., & Young, W. E. (1968). Socially induced drive and range of cue utilization. *Journal of Personality and Social Psychology, 9,* 242–244.

Cohen, S. (1978). Environmental load and the allocation of attention. In A. Baum, J. E. Singer, & S. Valins (Eds.), *Advances in environmental psychology* (pp. 1–29). Hillsdale, NJ: Erlbaum.

Collins, R. (1996). For better or worse: The impact of upward social comparison on self-evaluations. *Psychological Bulletin, 119,* 51–69.

Devine, P. G., Hamilton, D. L., & Ostrom, T. M. (1994). *Social cognition: Impact on social psychology.* San Diego, CA: Academic Press.

Dumas, F., & Huguet, P. (1999, July). *Upward and downward social comparison both can optimize cognitive functioning in the Stroop task.* Poster presented at the 12th general meeting of the European Association of Experimental Social Psychology, Oxford, UK.

Evans, J. (1993). On the relation between cognitive psychology and social cognition. In M. F. Pichevin, M. C. Hurtig, & M. Piolat (Eds.), *Studies on the self and social cognition* (pp. 220–230). London: World Scientific.

Fiske, S. T., & Taylor, S. E. (1991). *Social cognition.* Singapore: McGraw-Hill.

Geen, R. G. (1976). Test anxiety, observation, and range of cue utilization. *British Journal of Clinical and Social Psychology, 15*, 253–259.

Geen, R. G. (1991). Social motivation. *Annual Review of Psychology, 42*, 377–399.

Guerin, B. (1983). Social facilitation and social monitoring: A test of three models. *Bristish Journal of Social Psychology, 22*, 203–214.

Guerin, B. (1986). Mere presence effects in humans: A review. *Journal of Experimental Social Psychology, 22*, 38–77.

Guerin, B. (1993). *Social facilitation.* Cambridge: Cambridge University Press.

Hochman, S. H. (1967). The effect of stress on Stroop color word performance. *Psychonomic Science, 9*, 475–476.

Hochman, S. H. (1969). Stress and response competition in children's color word performance. *Perceptual and Motor Skills, 28*, 115–118.

Huguet, P., Charbonnier, E., & Monteil, J. M. (1999). Productivity loss in performance groups: People who see themselves as average do not engage in social loafing. *Group Dynamics: Theory, Research, and Practice, 3*, 118–131.

Huguet, P., & Dumas, F. (1999). *Upward social comparison leads to better performance: Evidence in the context of the Stroop task.* Unpublished manuscript.

Huguet, P., Galvaing, M. P., Monteil, J. M., & Dumas, F. (1999). Social presence effects in the Stroop task: Further evidence for an attentional view of social facilitation. *Journal of Personality and Social Psychology, 77*, 1011–1025.

Huguet, P., & Monteil, J. M. (1995). The influence of social comparison with less fortunate others on task performance: The role of gender motivations or appropriate norms. *Sex Roles, 33*, 753–765.

Levine, J. M., Resnick, L. B., & Higgins, E. T. (1993). Social foundations of cognition. *Annual Review of Psychology, 44*, 585–612.

Logan, G. D. (1980). Attention and automaticity in Stroop and priming tasks: Theory and data. *Cognitive Psychology, 12*, 523–553.

Logan, G. D., & Zbrodoff, N. J. (1979). When it helps to be misled: Facilitative effects of increasing the frequency of conflicting stimuli in a Stroop-like task. *Memory and Cognition, 7*, 166–174.

MacKinnon, D. P., Geiselman, R. E., & Woodward, J. A. (1985). The effects of effort on Stroop interference. *Acta Psychologica, 58*, 225–235.

MacLeod, C. M. (1991). Half a century of research on the Stroop effect: An integrative review. *Psychological Bulletin, 109*, 163–203.

Monteil, J. M., & Huguet, P. (1999). *Social context and cognitive performance: Towards a social psychology of cognition.* London: Psychology Press.

Nisbett, R. E., & Wilson, T. D. (1977). Telling more than we can know: Verbal reports on mental processes. *Psychological Review, 84*, 231–259.

Pallack, M. S., Pittman, T. S., Heller, J. F., & Munson, P. (1975). The effect of arousal on Stroop color-word task performance. *Bulletin of the Psychonomic Society, 6*, 248–250.

Reisberg, D. (1997). *Cognition: Exploring the science of mind.* New York: Norton.

Sanders, G. S., Baron, R. S., & Moore, D. L. (1978). Distraction and social comparison as mediators of social facilitation effects. *Journal of Experimental Social Psychology, 14*, 291–303.

Seta, J. J. (1982). The impact of comparison processes on coactors' task performance. *Journal of Personality and Social Psychology, 42*, 281–291.

Seta, J. J., Seta, C. E., & Donalson, S. (1991). The impact of comparison processes on coactors' frustration and willingness to expend effort. *Personality and Social Psychology Bulletin, 17,* 560–568.

Simon, H. (1990). Invariants of human behavior. *Annual Review of Psychology, 41,* 1–19.

Stroop, J. R. (1935). Studies of interference in serial-verbal reaction. *Journal of Experimental Psychology, 18,* 643–662.

Wheeler, L., Martin, R., & Suls, J. (1997). The proxy model of social comparison for self-assesment of ability. *Personality and Social Psychology Review, 1,* 54–61.

Zajonc, R. B. (1965). Social facilitation. *Science, 149,* 269–274.

Zajonc, R. B. (1980). Compresence. In P. B. Paulus (Ed.), *Psychology of group influence* (pp. 35–60). Hillsdale, NJ: Erlbaum.

18. Directed Social Influence

WILLIAM D. CRANO

The story of social influence began auspiciously with Triplett's (1897) demonstration that the mere presence of coactors in a competitive context exerted a powerful influence on behavior. Triplett's results usually are attributed to social facilitation, a phenomenon still studied, especially in connection with questions concerning the impact of new technologies on productivity (Aiello & Kolb, 1995; Aiello & Svec, 1993). Allied to research on the incidental presence of coactors is the issue of *directed social influence*, which is concerned with the persuasive impact of socially supplied information that is intended instrumentally to shape or change a target's beliefs and actions. Directed social influence is a central feature of social psychology. It provides the link between the group and the individual, compliance and conversion, and cognitive processing, beliefs, and actions. In short, directed social influence affords a portal into the social mind, the focus of this volume. The foundational presupposition of this chapter is that we can come to a better understanding of the social mind by analyzing the interaction of the cognitive and motivational processes that play so important a role in directed social influence.

The importance social psychology attaches to the social mind in general, and directed social influence in particular, can be inferred from its history. Although its ardor has varied over the years, the field's preoccupation with social influence has been continuous; its evaluation

This research was supported by a grant (R01 DA12578) from the National Institute on Drug Abuse. I am grateful for this organization's support. I also appreciate the careful and constructive editorial reaction of Joseph Forgas to an earlier draft of this chapter. Address for correspondence: William D. Crano, Department of Psychology, Claremont Graduate University, 123 E. 8th Street, Claremont, CA 91711, USA. Email: william.crano@cgu.edu

389

may be inferred by the preeminence of those who have labored on its understanding. Of the great names in the history of the field – Allport, Asch, Campbell, Festinger, Hovland, McGuire, Moscovici, Jones, Kelley, Sherif – all have devoted time and talent to understanding social influence. A brief consideration of some of the early studies in the field amply demonstrates why researchers of this stature would dedicate so much to this issue.

Sherif's Autokinetic Series

Muzafer Sherif's work provides a link between the incidental social influence effects of Triplett (1897) and the more intentional (directed) influence concerns of today's social psychology. Sherif's contributions are readily and recurrently apparent but nowhere more evident than in his autokinetic research series (Sherif, 1935, 1936). These studies capitalized on a well-established but poorly understood perceptual shortcoming to investigate norm formation, a theme to which Sherif returned in his classic Robbers Cave experiment (Sherif, Harvey, White, Hood, & Sherif, 1961). In Sherif's (1936) initial autokinetic study, participants over a series of judgment trials estimated the distance of an illusory movement of a (motionless) pinpoint of light in an otherwise darkened room. There was nothing social in this study. All participants were studied in isolation, with no attempt to influence them. Why would Sherif, a social psychologist, conduct such research? Because he anticipated that participants' *patterns* of judgments would be highly similar, and he was right. Although the average judgment varied from person to person, people's judgment patterns were comparable. Participants' initial responses were characterized by enormous variation. However, as perceivers gained task experience, within-subject oscillations in judged movement abated. The results suggest that individuals, working on their own, had formed a framework within which the illusion was constrained. They had, in the early trials, defined the outer boundaries of the light movement. On succeeding trials, they progressively narrowed the range of the light's illusory transit.

Owing to the manner in which the study was conducted, it is apparent that participants had made their judgments on the basis of information directly perceived. Past experience probably was not a factor, nor was socially supplied information, insofar as participants were studied in isolation. Suppose, however, that another person supplied information to the perceiver about the illusion. It stands to reason that adding socially supplied information might accelerate the norm for- mation process. If participants had individually developed a structure with which to organize their perception of the illusion, would not the same structuring process be expedited when the perceptions of others were made available? Triplett's work suggests that it would be. If his nondirective actors influenced one another, would not the more focused (if not purposively prescriptive) perceptions of other players have an even more profound effect on perceptions? To test this pos- sibility, Sherif (1936) designed a study in which two participants responded in concert on each of a series of autokinetic trials. As in the first study, their assignment was to estimate the light's movement. The result? Participants influenced one another. After an initial period of wide oscillations, participants reduced the variability of their individual responses and moved to a judgmental accommodation. In short order, the paired respondents were reporting estimates that were bounded within a relatively narrow response channel. This is an extraordinary result insofar as the participants were reporting on a pure illusion. More impressively, a third study suggested that this accommodation process was not the result of simple compliance, in which the second-responding participant mimicked the report of the first to maintain a noncontentious atmosphere. In this study, response partners were split after their initial interaction and reassigned to new response groups. Sherif believed that each pair of participants formed a group response norm in their original interaction. He did not expect that assigning them to new groups after this norm formation process would affect their subsequent judgments; over the short term, they would continue to respond as they had at the end of the initial inter- action. However, if the participants had merely acquiesced to the implicit demands of their response partners, if their initial judgments represented nothing more than simple assent, then a similar form of compliant accommodation would occur in the second session as well. As Sherif conjectured, such a pattern did not occur. Participants main- tained the norm they had formed during their initial trials and strongly resisted their new partners' information.

Sherif's study series strongly suggests that subjects had learned, and this learning had affected either their eyesight or the way they inter- preted the light's movement. This conclusion was supported by follow- up research completed three decades after the initial studies. In the long-delayed extension, Hood and Sherif (1962) paired a naive partic- ipant with a confederate in an autokinetic task. In the first phase, the confederate made a series of judgments while the participant simply observed. The judgments were either consistently high or consistently low. Afterward, the participant made an independent series of judgments after the confederate had been removed from the scene. The naive participants were strongly influenced by the confederate. Estimates of those paired with the high-responding confederate were significantly greater than those paired with the low-responding one. Interpersonal social pressure is not a good explanation of this result. Participants were under no pressure to adopt the confederate's norm. Indeed, by the time they had begun to respond, the confederate had been removed. If simple acquiescence to pressure is not a reasonable explanation of Hood and Sherif's (1962) results, then how are they to be interpreted? Sherif suggested an answer to this question that relied on a more rational conception of the social mind, a view of people as data-cognizant information processors who use others' insights and behaviors to decide upon the proper course of action. This reliance would be especially useful on unusual, novel, or ambiguous judgments.

Asch's Line Judging Research

Hood and Sherif's (1962) arguments were made at a time when Asch's (1951, 1952, 1955, 1956) research had stimulated widespread attention. Asch's findings did not appear amenable to Sherif's desire (or Asch's, for that matter – see Campbell, 1990) to characterize the social mind as a rational, information-processing organ. The Asch line judgment series is so well established that its description is superfluous, but some features of his approach deserve emphasis. In Asch's study, participants were shown three lines and asked which of them matched a stimulus line that also was presented. When studied in isolation, for all practical purposes participants' perceptions proved perfect. The task was so simple, the correct answer so inescapable, that no mistakes were made. As in Sherif's series, Asch's initial investigation was a preliminary to a more important study. It was a perceptual rather than a social psychological exercise, necessary to establish unequivocally that the judgments asked of participants were so transparent that any deviations from the obvious represented something more than simple misperception.

Such deviations made Asch a household name in social psychology. He found that naive participants often made egregious errors when responding after two or more trained confederates had unwaveringly given the wrong answer on specified judgment trials. Two noteworthy findings emerge from this research. First, social influence was evident only when the entire cadre was unanimously erroneous. Second, enlarging the size of the majority beyond three had little incremental effect. Apparently, the compliance-inducing consequence of a unanimous peer group quickly reaches asymptote.

Failure to discover a group size effect is not compatible with an information-processing orientation. Clearly, if 15 people report a perception at odds with one's own, the combined weight of their views should be accorded greater weight than that of 3 – if the rational weighing of multiple inputs represents the process by which judgments are made under uncertainty (Campbell, 1961, 1963; Crano, 1970). The simplicity of Asch's task, the near inevitability of correct responses under noninfluenced conditions, argued against an optimistic, Rousseau–like view of the noble information processor. A darker, more cynical view is suggested in which people are seen as easily swayed by the dictates of a brutish majority, who influence reports of even basic perceptual judgments by mere surveillance and the implied threat of ostracism, castigation, or punishment. Milgram (1974) was later to expand on this theme in an equally renowned series of studies.

Later studies provide insight into the lack of fit between the two research series. For example, Insko, Smith, Alicke, Wade, and Taylor (1985) found that majority size did affect judgments in a color-naming task; further, its effect was augmented when respondents were led to believe that a verifiable (as correct or incorrect) judgment was possible. Insko et al.'s (1985) verifiability manipulation is important. It might have suggested that even apparently simple judgments were subject to validity tests. The mindset of participants in this study must have been very different from that of Asch's subjects, many of whom admitted in poststudy interviews that the correct answer was obvious, but they had not reported their perceptions accurately. Other research also produced findings at odds with Asch's proposition that majority size was irrelevant (e.g., Gerard, Wilhelmy, & Conolley, 1968; Kumar, 1983), and contemporary social influence models all assume, and make allowance for, size effects in influence (Latané & Wolfe, 1981; Tanford & Penrod, 1984).

The field's response to this complexity was admirable and suggests the importance it attaches to social influence. Early on, for example, Festinger (1953) highlighted the theoretical distinction between public compliance and private acceptance. Contemporaneously, Deutsch and Gerard (1955) made the distinction between normative and informational social influence, and Kelman's (1958) operational differentiation of compliance, identification, and internalization followed only 2 years later. These approaches all were developed, at least in part, to make sense of the variation in the results of Sherif and Asch. The problem with all of these attempts at organization and synthesis is that none unequivocally specified in psychologically compelling terms the conditions that called forth the distinct processes. The answer they developed to the central question "Under which conditions will one process (compliance or acceptance; informational or normative influence; compliance, identification, or internalization) occur" was incomplete or incorrect. It usually was couched in terms of variations in source qualities. As the work of many of the contributors to this volume clearly suggests, such main effects explanations almost inevitably fall short as satisfying theoretical positions (see Hogg, Kerr, or Kaplan & Wilke, all this volume). Source expertise, competence, skill, attractiveness, ability, trustworthiness, and the like make for strong influence effects, which sometimes persist. Brute force – number, surveillance, strong social pressure – also makes for influence, but the effects often do not persist, nor do they follow a pattern that suggests learning or cogent integration of information.

The major problem with all of the explanatory devices is that their predictions sometimes are reversed: Expert sources sometimes produce short-lived (or no) change, and brute force effects sometimes persist. How? The answer seems to lie in the interaction of source and task characteristics. This is a problem if the explanatory model follows a main effects tack, an orientation that succeeded in prior research not because of its predictive validity, but rather because investigators were expeditious in their choice of research contexts. In many common conformity settings, the proper answers to the questions posed are so obvious as to be inescapable. In these situations, normative social influence is adequate because there is no room for information-based variance. Such a description characterizes Asch's line judgment task if we believe his control group results. If influence occurs in such a context, it will be norm-based, and a univariate theoretical model will capture the necessary variance. There is no need to worry about informational social influence in these settings or in the interaction of source, context, and message. Such knowledge is largely superfluous. However, main effects approaches do not work well in social influence contexts involving questions whose answers are less obvious. In these circumstances, attention shifts to a consideration of factors that come into play in determining the extent of the compliant response and its persistence. This focus requires a return to Festinger's (1953) distinction of public compliance and private acceptance and to the recurrent question of the factors that stimulate these responses.

Interactive Approaches

Contemporary theorizing in persuasion is obviously motivated by this question. The dual process model of Petty and Cacioppo (1986a, 1986b), the elaboration likelihood model (ELM), is a good example of an approach that attempts to stipulate the conditions under which short-term compliance or long-term acceptance occurs (see also Chaiken, 1987). The ELM owes a great debt to the pioneering studies of Hovland and his colleagues (Hovland, Janis, & Kelley, 1953), who in organizing their work were guided by Lasswell's (1948) mantra, "Who says what to whom, how, and under which circumstances?", a formula meant to capture the central features of attitude change. Lasswell's is a good incantation that has served us well for 50 years. However, it does admit to a serious shortcoming because it can be taken to suggest that the various parts of the blueprint can be studied in isolation rather than as interconnected parts of a whole. Further, because it admits to a view of persuasion as a solitary intrapersonal phenomenon, the importance of interpersonal interaction in influence may be diminished.

Such tendencies seem ill advised. By focusing solely on internal cognitive states, we lose sight of the fact that the social group may serve as an important moderator, and sometimes originator, of change pressures (Turner, 1991). This is not to suggest that progress has not been made. Over the years, we have identified many factors that affect people's tendencies to weigh socially supplied inputs relative to independent perceptions. These factors have to do with the qualities of the person or group that is laying on the influence, the personal qualities of the target, and the social psychological contexts (external and internal) in which the information is conveyed and in which the behavior occurs. We still have far to go in developing a comprehensive system, but on the whole, the movement of our conceptualizing is in the right direction. Contemporary dual process approaches are considerably more complex than their forebears, and the complexity makes sense. They are grounded on reasonable interpretations of regularities in the literature, and they foster prediction of complex variations in the data that are commonly observed and reproducible.

An Apparent Regression to a Unidimensional Approach

Although the general movement toward a more multifactored, interactive conceptualization of social influence is a consistent feature of contemporary theory and research, there is an apparent exception to this trend. That exception is found in the work of Moscovici, whose theory of majority and minority influence is at least partly responsible for the revitalization of social psychology's interest in social influence. Moscovici's model focuses almost entirely on source and target characteristics. It devotes little direct attention to context, message, or their interaction (Moscovici, 1980, 1985a, 1985b; Moscovici, Lage, & Naffrechoux, 1969; Moscovici & Personnaz, 1980, 1991). Moscovici assumes that majorities and minorities instigate different change processes. Disagreement with the (ingroup) majority causes targets to focus on the negative interpersonal ramifications of deviance. These negative features promote movement in the direction of the majority, but the movement is motivated by the need to avoid censure; it is not the result of processing and accepting the message. The majority persuades because it can punish. In Festinger's (1953) terms, public compliance, not conversion or private belief change, characterizes responses to majority influence.

Minorities prevail in entirely different ways. By virtue of the unexpectedness of their position, minorities motivate (ingroup) targets to understand why they hold their deviant view. In gaining this understanding, targets must process and comprehend the message. This process, akin to elaboration, is the basis of minority influence. Nemeth (1987) suggests that the processes of divergent thinking may form the basis of the minority effect, and De Dreu and De Vries (1996) support her reasoning.

As considerable research has shown, direct minority influence is rare. Moscovici hypothesized that majority group members are reluctant to be identified with the minority, so his theory assumes that minority influence, should it occur, will be delayed, or that its effects will be seen on attitudes associated with, but not identical to, the focus of persuasion. Pérez and Mugny (1987, 1990) have supplied interesting evidence of the changes in attitudes that are associated with, but not identical to, the thrust of the minority's arguments. Moscovici's focus on influence sources specifically designated as being of majority and minority status explicitly obligates researchers to consider the social group as an essential component in the social influence equation. Even more than his concern with the power of minorities (vs. the more common emphasis on majority influence), this feature of his work takes a truly original stance. His insistence on the centrality of the group ties his work to developments in social identity theory (e.g., Abrams & Hogg, 1990; Hogg & Abrams, 1988; Tajfel & Turner, 1986), a developing and increasingly important feature of contemporary social psychology. Contrary to the prevailing winds, Moscovici was not particularly concerned with the internal cognitive processes of individuals under persuasive stress, another common theme of mainline social research, especially mainline North American social research. His work provides a useful corrective to an excessively intraindividualistic orientation that had come to characterize much of the field. It is important not to overcorrect, however. Concentrating on the relevance of the social group in persuasion does not negate the need to understand the cognitive processes involved in minority (and majority) influence. Considering both group and social cognition is necessary, for in combination they lead to a more complete understanding of the social mind, at least as it unfolds in persuasion. This suggests that persuasion researchers should carefully delineate the features of the influence agent while simultaneously attending to the cognitive processes activated by these features. In general, this dual focus is not characteristic of contemporary research. Rarely are defining aspects of the minority (or majority) specified in other than a gross numeric sense (but see Wood, Pool, Leck, & Purvis, 1996). This is an important lapse. Without such information, the relevance of the minority or majority to the target's self-definition is moot, and the predictive contribution of social identity theory is attenuated or lost. Similarly, measuring the cognitive processes activated in response to a counterattitudinal communication is not common, although Baker and Petty (1994) and De Dreu and De Vries (1993, 1996) supply good examples of how this can be done.

The Leniency Contract

Neglect of group features and cognitive responses when developing a predictive framework for minority (and majority) influence is in part responsible for earlier annoyances in the research literature. As shown by Wood, Lundgren, Ouellette, Busceme, and Blackstone (1994), the basic tenets of Moscovici's model have been generally supported, but they are far from uniformly supported, and the model provides little insight into the reasons behind predictive failures. With majority sources, for example, we often find immediate short-term change, as predicted. However, some (e.g., Baker & Petty, 1994; Crano & Chen, 1998; Mackie, 1987) have found persistent majority effects. Similarly, minorities are theorized to stimulate delayed or indirect changes. Sometimes these expectations are confirmed, but as the meta-analysis of Wood and her colleagues (1994) has shown, they often are not. What's more, the theory does not specify when indirect or delayed focal change, or both, are expected to occur. The theoretical base of minority influence research is not sufficiently developed to digest this rich diversity of results. However, the literatures of social influence, social identity, and small groups concerned with interpersonal relations may be combined to develop a model that provides provocative and potentially critical insights. The leniency contract represents an attempt to do just this. It was developed to lend greater predictive specificity to the analysis of minority influence. In broad detail, the model is in general agreement with the predictive outcomes of Moscovici. This is as it should be, as his model has met with a good degree of success. However, the leniency approach brings to bear considerations of social influence, social identity theory, small group research, and ELM-based reasoning in developing a model with a strong social psychological basis for predicting majority- and minority-inspired persuasion effects. The potential advantage of this theoretically catholic approach is not only that it results in a more accurate predictive device, but it also provides a means of investigating and ultimately eliminating predictive failures when they occur.

The initial assumption of the contract is that the targets of persuasive attacks consider the self-relevance of the issue under debate before deciding upon a response. Relevance is judged in terms of the implications of compliance or resistance for the target's place maintenance in the social group. The leniency model assumes that social identity concerns (Tajfel, 1982; Tajfel & Turner, 1986) become prominent as a consequence of the mere specification of the source as being of majority or minority status. Unlike earlier research on source credibility (e.g., Hovland et al., 1953), this form of source characterization renders the context interpersonal and thus relevant to considerations of self-identity. A majority source represents the prevailing opinion on an issue within an identifiable assemblage of individuals. If the source is a consequential feature of the target's self-definition, then deviations from it will prove threatening if the issue is relevant to group concerns. If the target deems the issue irrelevant to the group, the majority will have no persuasive effect.

When a source is characterized as being in the minority, it is by definition deviant with respect to the larger group (Crano & Hannula-Bral, 1994). The importance of this depiction is that it suggests an association or connection between target and group that is of consequence for the target. Depicting a source as of minority or majority status not only describes features of the source, but also suggests a relationship with the target vis-à-vis the group on an issue or characteristic of potential importance. If this were not the case, the classification as majority (or minority) could not be expected to have much impact. A counterattitudinal communication from a majority thus represents a relational threat, which jeopardizes the target's association with a potentially important source of self-identity. Such threats are ignored at great peril. Reactions can take many forms, but at a minimum, we would expect the target to *consider* the issue that is the origin of contention with the identity source. In reflecting on the ramifications of a target's considering a source's message, the leniency contract (Alvaro & Crano, 1996, 1997; Crano, 1994; Crano & Alvaro, 1998a, 1998b; Crano & Chen, 1998) suggests that reactions may well vary as a function of source status and the relevance of the issue for membership in the group the source represents. For example, if the issue under discussion is not one on which the majority is seen as a legitimate authority, its impact will be attenuated; pressure will be judged inappropriate, and the group will lose stature in the eyes of the target. If the issue is relevant to group concerns – as, for example, a consideration of comprehensive examinations or tuition would be for a group of students of the same university – the majority is seen as having a legitimate stake. In this circumstance, its message will be examined carefully. If it is weak and unpersuasive, Petty and Cacioppo (1986a, 1986b) suggest that the majority might have an impact, but it will be short-lived. If the message is strongly argued, it may have both immediate and long-term effects (e.g., Baker & Petty, 1994; Crano & Chen, 1998; De Dreu & De Vries, 1993, 1996; Mackie, 1987). Thus, depending upon the relevance and strength of its message, a majority may have no effect, a short-lived consequence, or a lasting impact on beliefs and consequent behavior (Crano, 1997; Sivacek & Crano, 1982). This complex predictive pattern is not a feature of any other current theory of majority influence.

The model also provides a theoretical explication of minority influence that accounts for both the delayed focal change and the indirect change effects that have been associated with minority sources (Wood, et al., 1994). The leniency contract assumes that uneasiness or perceptions of threat do not arise in targets that find themselves at odds with the counterattitudinal pronouncements of an ingroup minority. However, when presenting their deviant views, ingroup (opinion) minorities are expected to receive courteous and polite treatment from the majority group. Owing to concerns with group maintenance, cohesion, and stability, ingroup minorities are not derogated for propounding their beliefs unless their position is perceived as a threat to the continued existence of the group. The model holds that on issues of less critical moment, their message is elaborated with little counterargument or source derogation. This would seem to create the ideal format for persuasion. From considerable research, we know that attitude change is enhanced if a target actively elaborates a strong message, fails to counterargue, and does not derogate the source. This is precisely the formula suggested by the leniency contract in prescribing the majority's presumed response to ingroup deviants – at least when the issue is not central to the viability of the group. Such open-minded and poorly defended elaboration would be expected to result in continuous change of the majority's position and continual group instability, yet we know from considerable research that a majority's position often is quite persistent. How can the theoretical claims of the leniency model be sustained?

To answer this question, we must consider one additional feature of the leniency contract. Like all contracts, the leniency contract specifies a quid pro quo. In recompense for the open-minded elaboration of the minority's appeal, the model posits a cost, and that cost is paid in terms of an implicit understanding that no change will ensue from the persuasive interchange. This implicit agreement is a pivotal feature of the contract. It allows the majority to maintain its central core beliefs, values, and aspirations while assuaging or at a minimum not alienating significant ingroup minorities. Leniency fosters and sustains the group. It allows for considerable attitudinal variation on all issues but those that threaten the viability of the group. Research on intragroup relations suggests that such apparent beneficence is a common feature of cohesive groups. The leniency model supplies the mechanism by which the group can tolerate some degree of freedom of expression while simultaneously protecting and maintaining the status quo. On the surface, such a complex process would appear to offer the best of all possible worlds, except for those members who, as minority voices, are truly intent on changing the character of the majority.

Although the contractual feature of the leniency model accounts for stability of established groups, it also offers the means by which minorities effect change. The implicit agreement that majority group members will not change as a result of open-minded elaboration of the minority's position does not offset the fact that strong change pressures have been introduced as a result of undefended message elaboration. How is this pressure diffused? The leniency model suggests that beliefs in close cognitive proximity to the critical issue are put at risk as a result of the target's lenient response. The focal belief is strongly defended. By the terms of the contract, it will not change; however, related beliefs are unprotected. The change pressure experienced as a result of the lenient response is diffused by spreading activation to these related beliefs, which may be easy prey for attitude change (Anderson, 1983). This process suggests a means by which indirect attitude change, a consistent feature of minority influence, comes about. The model also suggests a mechanism for delayed focal change, another consistent feature of the literature.

If we assume that attitudes are connected in some way, then when an attitude is changed, those attitudes that are contiguous in cognitive space will be put under pressure to change. Thus, indirect attitude change would prompt delayed focal change if (1) the focal attitude were cognitively proximal to the newly changed indirect attitude and (2) the indirect change was sufficient to destabilize the overall belief structure. Crano and Chen (1998) confirmed this prediction: When a minority source induced major indirect attitude change, subsequent (delayed) change on the focal issue occurred, especially when the indirect change was a result of a strongly argued focal message.

The leniency model thus accounts for both indirect, minority-induced attitude change and delayed focal change. It provides a theoretically plausible explanation of the ways in which minorities and majorities persuade while simultaneously accounting for prior results. The leniency contract is in accord with a changing emphasis in social influence research, a return to the recognition of the important role of the group in social influence. Over the years, social influence had departed from its roots as an interpersonal process. The simultaneous consideration of group identity, intergroup process, persuasion, belief structure, and message elaboration, central building blocks of the leniency contract, combines to create a predictive model of considerable depth and predictive potential. Certainly the leniency contract appeals to recent results in social cognition, but it also acknowledges the importance of intergroup processes in providing a better and more precise account of the ways in which social influence occurs. With continual development, it is conceivable that this general approach will provide a mechanism by which both the internal and external architecture of social influence, the group and social cognition, articulate to determine the success or failure of attempts at social influence.

References

Abrams, D., & Hogg, M. A. (Eds.). (1990). *Social identity theory: Constructive and critical advances.* New York: Harvester Wheatsheaf.

Aiello, J. R., & Kolb, K. J. (1995). Electronic performance monitoring and social context: Impact on productivity and stress. *Journal of Applied Psychology, 80,* 339–353.

Aiello, J. R., & Svec, C. M. (1993). Computer monitoring of work performance: Extending the social facilitation framework to electronic presence. *Journal of Applied Social Psychology, 23,* 537–548.

Alvaro, E. M., & Crano, W. D. (1996). Cognitive responses to minority or majority-based communications: Factors that underlie minority influence. *British Journal of Social Psychology, 35,* 105–121.

Alvaro, E. M., & Crano, W. D. (1997). Indirect minority influence: Evidence for leniency in source evaluation and counterargumentation. *Journal of Personality and Social Psychology, 72,* 949–964.

Anderson, J. R. (1983). *The architecture of cognition.* Cambridge, MA: Harvard University Press.

Asch, S. E. (1951). Effects of group pressure on the modification and distortion of judgments. In H. Guetzkow (Ed.), *Groups, leadership, and men* (pp. 177–190). Pittsburgh: Carnegie Press.

Asch, S. E. (1952). *Social psychology.* Englewood Cliffs, NJ: Prentice-Hall.

Asch, S. E. (1955). Opinions and social pressure. *Scientific American, 193,* 31–35.

Asch, S. E. (1956). Studies of independence and conformity: A minority of one against a unanimous majority. *Psychological Monographs, 70*(9) (Whole No. 416).

Baker, S. M., & Petty, R. E. (1994). Majority and minority influence: Source advocacy as a determinant of message scrutiny. *Journal of Personality and Social Psychology, 67,* 4–19.

Campbell, D. T. (1961). Conformity in psychology's theories of acquired behavioral dispositions. In I. A. Berg & B. M. Bass (Eds.), *Conformity and deviation* (pp. 101–140). New York: Harper.

Campbell, D. T. (1963). Social attitudes and other acquired behavioral dispositions. In S. Koch (Ed.), *Psychology: A study of a science, Vol. 6: Investigations of man as socius* (pp. 94–172). New York: McGraw-Hill.

Campbell, D. T. (1990). Asch's moral epistemology for socially shared knowledge. In I. Rock (Ed.), *The legacy of Solomon Asch: Essays in cognition and social psychology* (pp. 39–52). Hillsdale, NJ: Erlbaum.

Chaiken, S. (1987). The heuristic model of persuasion. In M. P. Zanna, J. M. Olson, & C. P. Herman (Eds.), *Social influence: The Ontario Symposium* (Vol. 5, pp. 3–39). Hillsdale, NJ: Erlbaum.

Crano, W. D. (1970). Effects of sex, response order, and expertise in conformity: A dispositional approach. *Sociometry, 33,* 239–252.

Crano, W. D. (1994). Context, comparison, and change: Methodological and theoretical contributions to a theory of minority (and majority) influence. In S. Moscovici, A. Mucchi-Faina, & A. Maass (Eds.), *Minority influence* (pp. 17–46). Chicago: Nelson-Hall.

Crano, W. D. (1997). Vested interest, symbolic politics, and attitude–behavior consistency. *Journal of Personality and Social Psychology, 72,* 485–491.

Crano, W. D., & Alvaro, E. M. (1998a). Indirect minority influence: The leniency contract revisited. *Group Process and Intergroup Relations, 1,* 99–115.

Crano, W. D., & Alvaro, E. M. (1998b). The context/comparison model of social influence: Mechanisms, structure, and linkages that underlie indirect attitude change. In W. Stroebe & M. Hewstone (Eds.), *European review of social psychology* (Vol. 8, pp. 175–202). Chichester, UK: Wiley.

Crano, W. D., & Chen, X. (1998). The leniency contract and persistence of majority and minority influence. *Journal of Personality and Social Psychology, 74,* 1437–1450.

Crano, W. D., & Hannula-Bral, K. A. (1994). Context/categorization model of social influence: Minority and majority influence in the formation of a novel response norm. *Journal of Experimental Social Psychology, 30,* 247–276.

De Dreu, C. K. W., & De Vries, N. K. (1993). Numerical support, information processing, and attitude change. *European Journal of Social Psychology, 23,* 647–662.

De Dreu, C. K. W., & De Vries (1996). Differential processing and attitude change following majority and minority arguments. *British Journal of Social Psychology, 35,* 77–90.

Deutsch, M., & Gerard, H. B. (1955). A study of normative and informational social influence upon individual judgment. *Journal of Abnormal and Social Psychology, 51,* 629–636.

Festinger, L. (1953). An analysis of compliance behavior. In M. Sherif & M. O. Wilson (Eds.), *Group relations at the crossroads* (pp. 232–256). New York: Harper.

Festinger, L. (1954). A theory of social comparison processes. *Human Relations, 7,* 117–140.

Gerard, H. B., Wilhelmy, R. A., & Conolley, E. S. (1968). Conformity and group size. *Journal of Personality and Social Psychology, 8,* 79–82.

Gorenflo, D. W., & Crano, W. D. (1989). Judgmental subjectivity/objectivity and locus of choice in social comparison. *Journal of Personality and Social Psychology, 57,* 605–614.

Hogg, M. A., & Abrams, D. (1988). *Social identifications*. London: Routledge.

Hood, W. R., & Sherif, M. (1962). Verbal report and judgment of an unstructured stimulus. *Journal of Psychology, 54,* 121–130.

Hovland, C. I., Janis, I. L., & Kelley, H. H. (1953). *Communication and persuasion.* New Haven, CT: Yale University Press.

Insko, C. A., Smith, R. H., Alicke, M. D., Wade, J., & Taylor, S. (1985). Conformity and group size: The concern with being right and the concern with being liked. *Personality and Social Psychology Bulletin, 11,* 41–50.

Kelman, H. C. (1958). Compliance, identification, and internalization: Three processes of attitude change. *Journal of Conflict Resolution, 2,* 51–60.

Kumar, J. (1983). Conformity behavior as a function of confederates' age and size of confederate group. *Personalty Study and Group Behavior, 3,* 69–73.

Lasswell, H. D. (1948). The structure and function of communication in society. In L. Bryson (Ed.), *Communication of ideas* (pp. 37–51). New York: Harper & Row.

Latané, B., & Wolfe, S. (1981). The social impact of majorities and minorities. *Psychological Review, 88,* 438–453.

Mackie, D. M. (1987). Systematic and nonsystematic processing of majority and minority persuasive communications. *Journal of Personality and Social Psychology, 53,* 41–52.

Milgram, S. (1974). *Obedience to authority.* New York: Harper & Row.

Moscovici, S. (1980). Toward a theory of conversion behavior. In L. Berkowitz (Ed.), *Advances in experimental social psychology* (Vol. 13, pp. 209–239). New York: Academic Press.

Moscovici, S. (1985a). Innovation and minority influence. In S. Moscovici, G. Mugny, & E. Van Avermaet (Eds.), *Perspectives on minority influence* (pp. 9–52). Cambridge: Cambridge University Press.

Moscovici, S. (1985b). Social influence and conformity. In G. Lindzey & E. Aronson (Eds.), *The handbook of social psychology* (Vol. 2, 3rd ed., pp. 347–412). New York: Random House.

Moscovici, S., Lage, E., & Naffrechoux, M. (1969). "Sleeper effect" and/or minority effect? Theoretical and experimental study of delayed social influence. *Cahier de Psychologie Cognitive, 1981,* 199–221.

Moscovici, S., & Personnaz, B. (1980). Studies in social influence V: Minority influence and conversion behavior in a perceptual task. *Journal of Experimental Social Psychology, 16,* 270–282.

Moscovici, S., & Personnaz, B. (1991). Studies in social influence: VI. Is Lenin orange or red? Imagery and social influence. *European Journal of Social Psychology, 21,* 101–118.

Nemeth, C. (1987). Differential contributions of majority and minority influence. *Psychological Review, 93,* 1–10.

Pérez, J. A., & Mugny, G. (1987). Paradoxical effects of categorization in minority influence: When being an out-group is an advantage. *European Journal of Social Psychology, 17,* 157–169.

Pérez, J. A., & Mugny, G. (1990). Minority influence: Manifest discrimination and latent influence. In D. Abrams & M. Hogg (Eds.), *Social identity theory: Constructive and critical advances* (pp. 78–102). London: Harvester Wheatsheaf.

Petty, R. E., & Cacioppo, J. T. (1986a). *Communication and persuasion: Central and peripheral routes to attitude change.* New York: Springer-Verlag.

Petty, R. E., & Cacioppo, J. T. (1986b). The elaboration likelihood model of persuasion. In L. Berkowitz (Ed.), *Advances in experimental social psychology* (Vol. 19, pp. 123–205). New York: Academic Press.

Sherif, M. (1935). A study of some social factors in perception. *Archives of Psychology, 27*(187), 1–60.

Sherif, M. (1936). *The psychology of social norms.* New York: Harper & Row.

Sherif, M., Harvey, O. J., White, B. J., Hood, W. R., & Sherif, C. W. (1961). *Intergroup conflict and cooperation: The Robbers Cave experiment.* Norman: University of Oklahoma Book Exchange.

Sivacek, J., & Crano, W. D. (1982). Vested interest as a moderator of attitude–behavior consistency. *Journal of Personality and Social Psychology, 43,* 210–221.

Tajfel, H. (1982). *Social identity and intergroup relations.* Cambridge: Cambridge University Press.

Tajfel, H., & Turner, J. T. (1986). The social identity theory of intergroup behavior. In S. Worchel & W. Austin (Eds.), *Psychology of intergroup relations* (pp. 7–24). Chicago: Nelson-Hall.

Tanford, S., & Penrod, S. (1984). Social influence model: A formal integration of research on majority and minority influence. *Psychological Bulletin, 95,* 189–225.

Triplet, N. (1897). The dynamogenic factors in pacemaking and competition. *American Journal of Psychology, 9,* 507–533.

Turner, J. C. (1991). *Social influence.* Milton Keynes, UK: Open University Press.

Wood, W., Lundgren, S., Ouellette, J. A., Busceme, S., & Blackstone, T. (1994). Minority influence: A meta-analytic review of social influence processes. *Psychological Bulletin, 115,* 323–345.

Wood, W., Pool, G. J., Leck, K., & Purvis, D. (1996). Self-definition, defensive processing, and influence: The normative impact of majority and minority groups. *Journal of Personality and Social Psychology, 71,* 1181–1193.

19. Cognitive and Social Motivation in Group Decision Making

MARTIN F. KAPLAN AND HENK WILKE

Introduction

Group decision making is an ideal context for studying cognitive and social motives in interpersonal behavior. A group of people is convened to solve a task or come to a decision on an issue with alternative solutions. This engages *cognitive* motives, the most obvious being to reach some sort of consensus regarding the most accurate and useful decision. Although this is true in any decision-making context, the fact that a *group* of people must achieve consensus also engages *social* motives, that is, the solution must be acceptable to most if not all members. This chapter will examine the interplay of cognitive and social motives in determining group decision processes. Unless all members have identical outcome preferences prior to deliberation, there will be initial conflict, with the potential of factions being formed. The process questions are, how does the group resolve the conflict, and to what degree is the conflict cognitive (e.g., disagreement about the most factually correct solution) or social (e.g., disagreement with reference group norms regarding the most preferred or satisfying solution)?

One impetus to the current interest in group process was the discovery that group discussion produces more extreme solutions in both groups and individuals than individual prediscussion preferences: the *group polarization* phenomenon (Stoner, 1961). This produced a torrid controversy over whether changes wrought by discussion were due to normative or informational processes (see, e.g., Kaplan, 1989; Lamm & Myers, 1978; Pruitt, 1971). The underlying issue was whether members

Address for correspondence: Martin F. Kaplan, Department of Psychology, California State University at Channel Islands, One University Drive, Camarillo CA, 93012, USA. Email: martin.kaplan@csun.edu were influenced by the normative preferences of group members (and, by extension, of distal referent groups) or by shared facts about the issue (see the subsequent discussion for a full definition of normative and informational influence). The general conclusion to this controversy has been that both processes are relevant to within-group influence, their relative dominance depending on task and situational conditions (Kaplan, 1989). But the important residue of this controversy is the sharpening of distinctions between influence based on the impact of the social context, that is, the group and its normative preferences, and influence based on the cognitive context, or demonstrable facts about the decision task.

A second impetus to renewed interest in the nature of group processes is the emergence of a European viewpoint that centers on social relationship motives (Moscovici, 1992; Tajfel & Turner, 1986; Turner, Hogg, Oakes, Reicher, & Wetherall, 1987, see also Hogg, this volume), acting as a counterbalance to the more cognitive view that had permeated North American treatments. Increased attention to the social context of decisions, according to our view, recasts the earlier duality of informational and normative group processes into a broader duality of two complementary motivational forces that govern group decision making: cognitive and social motives. The former is driven largely by concerns for *accurate, task-relevant* solutions, whereas the latter is driven by group-centered needs to maintain *relationships and identity* by achieving mutually *satisfying* solutions. Put simply, groups must deal with the task and its cognitive demands, and also with intragroup relationships, with their implications for social rewards, member welfare, and social identity.

The remainder of this chapter explores the conditions that produce cognitive (task) and social (relationship) motives and, in turn, the consequences of these motives for group processes and productivity. The interplay of cognitive and social motives will be illustrated with regard to generating diverse ideas and reasoning about them in depth, as captured in normative and informational processes.

Sources of Cognitive and Social Motives

Broadly speaking, what motives might be engaged when groups make decisions? *Cognitive* motives would include the extrinsic need to produce a factually accurate solution or a decision that would be instrumental to the goals of the organization. In addition, there is the intrinsic need to know and understand the nature of reality (Kaplan, 1989). Related to the intrinsic need to make sense of our world is the need for closure, to reach definitive answers to questions (Kruglanski, 1989). Finally, we are motivated to test the adequacy of our own behavior, thoughts, and judgments by seeking information in the real world (Deutsch & Gerard, 1955; Festinger, 1954). And so, whether to satisfy the demand for accurate and/or useful solutions, to test one's views of reality, to understand the world, or just to reach closure, task groups will be motivated to seek, evaluate, and reason systematically about relevant information.

Social motives may be more diverse (see Kaplan, 1989). There are, of course, obvious social rewards to be gained by interaction with a group, such as praise, acceptance, and enhancement of one's self-presentation (see, e.g., Tice & Faber, this volume, for evidence of the need to make a positive impression on others). Groups may also be motivated to maintain cohesion and harmony. Congenial, cohesive groups are poised to engage more members in discussion and sample more preferences and relevant information, and will thus function better as a unit in future tasks. Another social motive is the personal welfare of comembers, which requires attending to others' needs and solution preferences, whether instrumental to task accuracy or not (Wood, 1987; Wood & Carten, 1986). Concern for group dynamics and the members' solution preferences can also derive from cognitive motivation; for example, when factual information needed either for accuracy or for testing the adequacy of one's beliefs is lacking (i.e., an information-poor environment), people may seek consensual validation by comparing their beliefs to those of others (Festinger, 1954).

Finally, groups serve to provide us with our social identity, that is, a portion of our identity derives from how we categorize ourselves by reference to the groups to which we belong (Moscovici, 1976, 1992; Turner & Oakes, 1989). As Andersen and Berenson (this volume) show, our stored representations of others affect our ongoing cognitions, including those about ourselves. The distinction between our *collective self*, which is the product of our group identifications and stored representations of others' appraisals, and our *individual self* is beyond the scope of this chapter, but it is clear that both are important to our self-definition, and nurturance of both is a prime motive (see Sedikides & Gaertner, this volume). Thus, an important social motive in within-group influence is to maintain our social identity by finding common ground with our groups on decision issues. Witness, for example, the deleterious effects of ostracism. Williams, Wheeler, and Harvey (this volume) suggest that ostracism threatens fundamental needs such as belongingness and self-esteem. In our analysis, avoidance of ostracism as a consequence of disagreeing with a valued group would be a powerful motive for group consensus because of its implications for belongingness and maintaining one's self-identity and esteem.

Cognitive and social motives may conflict in task groups, as will be elaborated later. But they also can interact in the sense of affecting one another. Uncertainty about reality may enhance dependence on relevant others (see also Hogg, this volume), provoking social comparisons to evaluate our abilities and beliefs and thereby reducing uncertainty (Festinger, 1954). Conversely, social interaction can affect cognition. Group activity enhances collaborative memory, that is, it augments individual memories (Clark & Stephenson, 1989). Moreover, deep involvement in a cohesive ingroup can override the motivation to consider information and alternative solutions realistically, leading to groupthink (Janis, 1972). Finally, Levine, Resnick, and Higgins (1993) argue that the individual contributions of members aggregate to form a new, socially shared cognition based on social motivations such as facilitating communication, maintaining group distinctiveness, and facilitating member identity.

It should not be thought that this duality of cognitive and social motives is limited to intragroup behavior. This volume provides ample evidence of the centrality of these broad motives to other forms of interpersonal interactions. Tice and Faber and Schütz posit that being competent and being liked are the major goals that drive self-presentation and self-esteem, respectively. Similarly, Andersen and Berenson include among their fundamental human motivations *connectedness/relatedness* and *competence*. The former encompasses both intimacy and belongingness, the latter, task mastery. Moreover, Hogg asserts that self-categorization – a basis for differentiating *between* groups – is driven by the motive to enhance self-esteem by identifying with a positively valued group and the motive to reduce cognitive uncertainty. Finally, Nezlek, extrapolating from studies of socioemotional and agentic leader orientation, suggests that interpersonal behavior in everyday life is governed by both the social-emotional need to belong, and the cognitive need to understand, predict, and control one's world. *In short, the motivational basis of the varied sorts of interpersonal activities addressed in this volume can be characterized by concerns for one's relation to relevant groups, and for adequacy in dealing with life's tasks.*

Conditions That Elicit Cognitive and Social Processes: Informational and Normative Influence

The prime concern attending cognitive motives is to produce the most accurate and useful solution to the question that is posed to the group, that is, to focus on competency for task demands. The prime concern for social motives is to produce the most satisfying solution, that is, to focus on the preferences and sensibilities of group members. What sorts of processes would be instrumental to satisfying each set of motives? The distinction between informational and normative influence, first posed in understanding conformity processes (Deutsch & Gerard, 1955) and later extended to group decision processes (e.g., Burnstein & Vinokur, 1973; Pruitt, 1971), maps well onto the duality of concern for tasks versus groups (Kaplan, 1989; Kaplan & Miller, 1983). *Informational influence* is defined as influence to accept information from others as evidence about reality. This implies a cognitive strategy that would be instrumental for accuracy demands in a task. *Normative influence* refers to influence to conform to the expectations of others. This strategy involves seeking and considering the preferences of others, and is instrumental to meeting the social motive of finding the most satisfying solution by reaching convergence of preferences.

Any conditions that engage cognitive motives, that is, concern for the task, should result in decision processes that reflect informational influence. Similarly, conditions that induce social motives, or a concern for the group, should enhance the use and effectiveness of normative influence. Two examples of such conditions, group interactive goal and personal orientation, will be briefly discussed, and a third, group task, will then be treated in more detail.

Interactive goal refers to the group's beliefs regarding the purpose of their interaction, that is, the goal of the discussion and decision (Thibaut & Strickland, 1956). *Group goals* accent harmony and cohesion, centering on socioemotional relations. *Task goals* emphasize the resolution of the task and the need to reach the most factually correct decision. This distinction fits the essential difference between social and cognitive motives very well. Conditions that produce one or the other interactive goal include instructions with regard to both how the "good" decision group should function and the composition of the group, that is, whether the group is in long- or short-term interaction (Kaplan, 1989). Groups instructed that the ideal is to seek harmony, cohesion, and mutual satisfaction are more influenced by normative argumentation, whereas those instructed that ideal groups should focus on the task are changed more by informational influence (Rugs & Kaplan, 1993). Moreover, group members who anticipate dealing with a topic under a group goal report less satisfaction if they are told they will be limited to using informational rather than normative arguments. Conversely, groups who are given a task set report less satisfaction if the anticipated discussion will employ normative rather than informational content (Kaplan, Schaefer, & Zinkewicz, 1994). Finally, a group goal leads to earlier initial ballots than a task goal, implying that it is more desirable to know and discuss members' preferences and internal norms given the former goal (Kaplan & Kickul, 1996). *In sum, groups with social goals prefer and are impacted more by normative influence, and seek out the preferential norms of members earlier, compared to those with task goals.*

Individual members may adopt a personal orientation closely related to group interactive goals (Bales & Slater, 1955; Fiedler, 1972; Piliavin & Martin, 1978; Stodgill, 1974). A *socioemotional orientation* is characterized by concern for harmony, cohesiveness, and the welfare of others. An *agentic orientation* centers on achieving factually correct solutions by adhering to task demands. It is easy to see how this distinction parallels the dichotomy of group and task goals, and it should therefore be related to the facilitation of, respectively, normative and informational influence (Kaplan, 1989). Wood and Karten (1986), for example, report that females, who tend to be more socioemotionally oriented than males, engage in more group-oriented discussion than males, whereas the roles are reversed with regard to discussion of task or informational matters.

The Importance of the Group Task

The Type of Task

Perhaps the most salient factor that focuses the group on either social or cognitive concerns is the type of decision facing the group. All *group* tasks may be described on a dimension running from *intellective tasks,* which have a demonstrably correct solution within a consensual conceptual system, to *judgmental tasks,* for which solutions are based mainly on social consensus (Laughlin & Ellis, 1986; McGrath, 1984). The former includes tasks for which a correct solution exists (although it is not essential that complete, relevant information is available) such as "Which car is most economical to own?" In such tasks, the definition of terms is not in question (people agree on what is meant by *miles per gallon*) but the solution depends on acquiring facts. The latter include behavioral, ethical, and aesthetic judgments that are matters of preference rather than demonstrable facts, for example, "Which car is more attractive?" Intellective tasks demand a correct solution, and marshaling facts is most instrumental, whereas judgmental tasks implicate a preferred solution, requiring appeal to norms and group consensus, because there is no demonstrably correct answer. Individual decision makers have no recourse to preference consensus within a local group, but, of course, they can refer to consensus from salient reference groups. Thus, informational influence would be more relevant to intellective tasks, and normative influence would be more useful for judgmental tasks.

Consistent with our reasoning, intellective issues elicit more informational and less normative influence than judgmental issues (Kaplan & Martin, 1999; Kaplan & Miller, 1987). When members are asked to choose issues to be discussed in anticipated group decisions, they prefer informational over normative issues when the task is intellective and the reverse when the task is judgmental (Kaplan et al., 1994). Also, members of groups that have decided a judgmental issue under a majority rule (and have therefore engaged in more normative than informational influence) report less satisfaction with the decision than groups deciding the same issue under a unanimity rule (Kaplan & Miller, 1987). Because judgmental tasks cannot be validated by reference to demonstrable solutions but are matters of normative consensus, decisions by less than unanimous consensus are disturbing.

In conclusion, group tasks can engage either social or cognitive motives to varying degrees, which in turn produce, respectively, normative or informational processes. This distinction between motives and their resultant processes is critical to our analysis with regard to the quality of discussion and productivity in groups.

Interdependence of Group Members: Effectance and Fairness

The distinction between intellective and judgmental tasks is based on their inherent content, referring to the cognitive motive to be competent and the normative motive to seek consensus. However, tasks may also differ in their effective means used to reach a group solution. Steiner (1972) analyzed how members' contributions combine to solve the task effectively in terms of a taxonomy of group tasks based in large part on the specific interdependence of group members. For additive tasks such as pulling a rope or stuffing envelopes, individual contributions are added together. For disjunctive tasks, which involve "yes-no" or "either-or" answers such as math problems or physical tasks (Steiner, 1972), the task solution is provided by the most able group member. In conjunctive tasks, such as climbing a mountain as a group, the performance of the group depends on that of the least able member. Regarding mutual interdependence, in additive tasks *each* member's contribution to the group task counts, whereas in disjunctive and conjunctive tasks, group success depends on the efforts and abilities of the most or least able member, respectively.

There is ample evidence that group members' efforts on physical tasks may be understood from their motivation to strive for an effective task contribution, that is, to reach the task goal. For example, in Kerr and Bruun's experiment (1983), members of different-sized groups received information about their relative abilities. Each group had one member with a high ability score and one member with a low ability score, both randomly assigned to ability positions. Task demands provided either additive, conjunctive, or disjunctive task instructions. Kerr reasoned that in a disjunctive task, in which only the best member's performance matters, less able members would lower their efforts because their efforts would be dispensable. In contrast, in a conjunctive task, in which the least able group member's performance matters, high-ability group members should reduce their efforts. As predicted, member ability had opposite effects on the disjunctive and conjunctive tasks. When only the best individual score counted, the low-ability member performed less well, but when the group score was defined by the worst individual score, the high-ability member worked less hard. These motivational effects reflected the extent to which group members reported themselves dispensable (see also Harkins and Petty, 1982). Another instance of effectance can be found in Williams and Karau (1991), who looked at effort rather than ability. When an anonymous coworker expended high effort, participants reduced their own effort, but when the coworker expended low effort, participants compensated by increasing their efforts.

In addition to evidence of an effectance motive that focuses group members on task requirements, there is evidence that members are led by normative considerations while expending effort. Kerr (1986, 1995) found evidence for fairness considerations, that is, members do their fair share when others also do so, but they perform at a lower level when they know that others underperform. For example, group members with a capable but unproductive partner reduce their efforts compared with when their partner does make a strong effort (Kerr, 1983). The fairness motive implicitly encourages group members to match the contributions of fellow members.

Given the support for the task-related effectance motive in some studies and the support for the norm-related fairness motive in others, we ask: When are task-related motives (such as effectance) or group-related motives (such as fairness) more salient?

Highlighted Experiment I: Task Effects on Effectance and
Fairness Motives

Groenenboom, Wilke, and Wit (in press) recently argued that support for the effectance motive, that is, the tendency to produce as much as is necessary to meet the requirements of the group task, has been demonstrated predominantly in studies in which group members received only information about how much was actually necessary to achieve group success. In contrast, in studies that support the fairness motive, members received only information about the relative contributions of others rather than about the task requirements. Note here the recurring distinction between conditions that focus a group on the task versus the group (see the section "Conditions that Elicit Cognitive and Social Processes: Informational and Normative Influence"). This study investigated when task/efficiency versus fairness/normative considerations would be more salient in affecting members' contributions to the task. Members of a dyad were provided with information about how much effort was necessary to accomplish a physical group task and how much the other member already had accomplished. They were told that the other group member had performed either at a high or a low level. The task was presented as either additive or disjunctive. The additive task required a dyad to depress a button 150 times in 5 minutes collectively. The disjunctive task was also to depress the button 150 times in 5 minutes, but only one member had to meet the criterion. The authors predicted and showed (Experiment 1) that when the task was additive, participants were more ready to match the task performance of the other group member, that is, they performed more (less) when the other performed more (less). However, when the task was disjunctive, participants were led more by effectance, that is, they performed more when the other group member performed less and the reverse. This finding was explained by the idea that for additive tasks a sense of commonality is emphasized, which fosters group identification (see Turner, 1991). For disjunctive tasks, the fact that success is dependent merely on the contribution of one of the group members weakens the sense of identity and focuses attention on task success, which presumably leads to greater salience of the task effectance motive.

In sum, the extent to which one's task efforts will be effective or needed to achieve the required group product is more salient in disjunctive tasks. The extent to which one is focused on matching the efforts of one's fellow group members is more salient in additive tasks.

Whereas in Experiment 1 Groenenboom et al. (in press) demonstrated that task demands (Steiner, 1972) affected the relative salience of task versus fairness motives, in Experiment 2 it was shown that when members anticipated future task interaction with the same cohort, they were led more by the fairness motive, that is, they tended to match the performance of the other group members, performing more (less) when the other performed more (less). However, if they were aware that they were to work only once with a specific group member at a task and did not anticipate doing so for the next round, they performed more when the other performed less and the reverse. Groenenboom et al. argued that with anticipated future interaction, group members are more concerned about social relations, whereas without anticipation of future interaction, members tend to focus more on the task itself. This implicates once again the distinction between group and task interactive goals discussed earlier. Note that the second experiment involved an additive task only, so that the elicitation of a fairness motive does not depend entirely on the additive nature of the task, but also on whether the task invokes interdependence and thus concern for the group. When members were assured that they would have no further interaction with their cohorts, they were guided more by effectance.

This last point is underscored by research reported by Williams and Karau (1991) in which members loafed when working with a high-effort coworker and compensated when working with a low-effort coworker, that is, they found evidence for effectance in an additive task. Note that, unlike Groenenboom et al., Williams and Karau did not have a set criterion for performance, but instead asked participants to produce as many ideas as possible in the time period. This would emphasize task completion motives over group relationship motives. Thus, when future interdependence is expected (Groenenboom et al., Experiment 2), a fairness motive is invoked, and members will match the effort of cohorts. But when productivity is emphasized (Gronenboom et al., the disjunctive condition, Williams & Karau), effectance is invoked, and members will reverse the effort of coactors, that is, loaf when others work hard and compensate when others loaf.

These results show that normative considerations are invoked when a task is presented as an additive (we-) task and one is concerned about groupness in the future. In this case, one is more inclined to focus on social stimuli and match one's performance to those of other group members. On the other hand, task considerations (i.e., effectance motives) are more salient when the task focuses attention on the performance of only one of the group members (as with disjunctive task instructions), when one does not anticipate future interaction and when cumulative productivity is stressed (as in Williams & Karau). Members are concerned with the task, and either compensate for a low-performing other or perform at a lower level when the other's efforts are clearly sufficient to achieve group success. In accordance with Katz and Kahn's (1978) argument that both group maintenance and group productivity are major goals in task-performing groups, it is shown that task interdependence and anticipation of future interaction affect the relative salience of normative (fairness) and task (effectance) influence. Thus, this research indicates that task interdependence and the interdependence of group members may provide group members with cues about how much they should produce. Some cues, such as disjunctive task interdependence and anticipation of no future interaction, focus attention on the task itself, invoking a task effectance motive. Other cues, such as additive task interdependence and anticipation of future interaction, focus attention more on social norms such as fairness.

Task-Induced Motives and Creative Versus Conventional Idea Generation

We demonstrated the relevance of the distinction between informational and normative influence for group tasks that have, respectively, intellective and judgmental characteristics. Then we showed that, due to the task or interpersonal interdependence, groups may focus to varying extents on effectance or fairness considerations. For effectance, information about the *task* is most salient, whereas for fairness, the performance of other *group members* functions as a normative anchor, again implicating the importance of cognitive and social motives that are invoked by the nature of the task.

In the following discussion, we suggest that some tasks, and the cognitive motives they invoke, may give rise to in-depth processing that focuses the group on the task in a way that may lead to ideas that are creative. On the other hand, other tasks may give rise to superficial group processing when members adhere to the shared ideas of other group members in a way opposite to creativity, that is, conventional thinking. To generate creative ideas in the group, and thereby enhance productivity, it is necessary to sample ideas in *breadth* and then consider them in *depth*. That is, to take advantage of their greater amount and range of information, groups must sample the unique relevant information possessed by individual members and then elaborate fully on this information. We will first review the relevant literature regarding emergence of information that is unshared by all members and then discuss the contributions of minority and majority factions. We will show that recipients of minority influence are more inclined to process information in depth, which leads to more creative ideas, and that recipients of majority influence are more inclined to conform to others, a focus that facilitates the generation of conventional ideas.

Information Sampling During Group Discussion

Group decisions may introduce a conflict between cognitive processing and normative processing of information. On the one hand, to obtain the best possible solution to the task, cognitive processing demands that no arguments from a collective pool of arguments should be neglected. On the other hand, group unison is better served when members focus on arguments they have in common, that is, normative processing requires that group members focus on arguments they have in common and neglect arguments they do not share. Different motives may dictate different patterns and breadth of information sharing.

Normative influence stems from the group's desire to agree, to reach a consensus, and to reduce conflict. Informational influence originates in the desire to gather the information necessary to perform the group task. In a group in which each member has the same pieces of information, both motives coincide, because by exchanging or discussing all information, group members can achieve unity while making optimal use of all information. But what will happen when some information is not shared by all group members?

Seminal research by Stasser and his collaborators (e.g., Stasser, 1992; Stasser, Taylor, & Hannah, 1989; Stewart & Stasser, 1998) suggests that normative processing of information dominates at the expense of optimal solutions. Stasser and Titus (1985, 1987) argue that when group members discuss choice alternatives, they sample from an information pool that is based on the previous experience of group members. Because group members may differ in their experiences, not all information may be available to all group members before discussion. In that case, items of information that are not shared by all group members have a lower likelihood of discussion than items that are shared by all group members. For example, Stasser et al. (1989) found that overall, groups discussed 45% of the shared information but only 18% of the unshared information, and discussions were less likely to return to initially unshared than to shared pieces of information.

When both shared and unshared information favors the same optimal solution to the task, neglecting to discuss unique or unshared information is not always detrimental for the quality of the group solution. However, the sampling advantage of shared over unshared information may also lead to what Stasser and Stewart (1992) termed *hidden profiles*. A hidden profile occurs when the collective profile of information available to the group favors one decision alternative (e.g., B) but the pattern of information actually discussed favors another alternative (e.g., A). Imagine a group that has the choice between two alternatives, A and B. The three group members share three items of information supporting A and one item supporting B. In addition, each group member has one unique (unshared) item favoring B. Each individual profile of information supports solution A, that is, three pieces of information pro-A and two pieces of information pro-B. However, the collective hidden profile contains three pro-A but four pro-B items, so that from a collective task perspective, alternative B should be chosen. However, due to the tendency to underuse unshared information, it is likely that alternative A will be selected as the group solution. Stasser and Titus (1985) found that when all information was shared, 83% of participants chose option B, the one favored by the collective task information, whereas when only common information was shared, only 18% chose the option that had the most favorable collective information.

In the previous section, we demonstrated that informational processes are relatively stronger for intellective tasks and normative processes for judgmental tasks. Similarly, Stasser and Stewart (1992) suggest that the way members perceive the group task affects the patterning of communication of shared and unshared information. When told that the task had a correct solution (*solve set*), members introduced more unshared information than when they believed that preferences and values (*judge set*) were involved. That is, when group members believe that there is no correct solution, normative processes are dominant. However, if members believe that there is a demonstrably correct answer, information processes are dominant. Thus, focusing on a correct solution for the task may counteract the sampling of shared information and ineffective decision making. Similarly, Stasser, Stewart, and Wittenbaum (1995) demonstrated that when all unshared items were assigned to one group member, the number of unshared items discussed increased when it was announced that one group member had additional information. Moreover, announcing that the one group member had additional (unshared) information enhanced the chance of a correct solution (see also Stewart & Stasser, 1998). In short, these results suggest that informational influence may be strengthened and normative influence weakened by stressing the problem-solving nature of the task and by emphasizing that some members may have unique ideas.

In addition to *framing* a task as either judgmental or intellective, the task's *nature* may counteract consensus seeking. Davis (1973, 1982; see also Laughlin & Ellis, 1986) looked at a priori preferences before group discussion. In agreement with the notion of consensus-seeking (normative influence), he found for judgment tasks that when a majority of group members favored a specific solution before discussion, that solution was likely to become the group's solution. However, for tasks having a correct solution such as Eureka tasks, it was sufficient for one group member to propose the ultimate group solution.

In conclusion, when groups focus on the task as having a correct solution, informational influence prevails. In contrast, when the task is perceived as judgmental, unshared information is underused, leading to ineffective decision making due to stronger pressures to uniformity (Festinger, 1950) or normative processing. Thus, as shown earlier in the discussion of informational and normative influence, the amount of task-relevant information discussed is increased by cognitively driven task goals and reduced by socially driven normative goals.

In-Depth and Superficial Processing of Information

To this point, we have seen how cognitive motives for effectance can be invoked by certain tasks and, in turn, will lead to the group's focus on the task and to greater use of unshared information, that is, to broader sampling of information. Another way of viewing the potentially salutary effect of focusing on the task rather than on group consensus is to distinguish between eliciting creative versus conventional information (see Wilke & Kaplan, in press, for more on this distinction). As shown, a task effectance motive promotes the use of creative ideas (i.e., information that is previously unshared by all members), whereas a group consensus motive such as fairness favors discussion of conventional ideas (i.e., those shared by all members). We now address group composition as it affects the creativity/conventionality of ideas generated and the depth of idea processing.

Moscovici (1980) was the first to contrast systematically the influence processes of majority and minority factions in disagreeing groups. He proposed that majorities foster social validation, whereby members compare their opinions with those of the majority, with little attention to the task or issue. Minorities, conversely, promote active thought about the issue. Taken a step further, majorities facilitate conventional, consensus-oriented ideas and discussion, whereas minorities facilitate creative, task-oriented discussion. In support of the view that majority influence centers on group concerns whereas minority influence centers on the task, recipients of majority disagreement during discussion report more interpersonal conflict, whereas recipients of minority influence report increasing cognitive conflict (Moscovici, 1985; Nemeth, Mayseless, Sherman, & Brown, 1990). Different faction membership appears to produce different motives regarding conflict. However, the difference between factions due to whether their focus is interpersonal (group) or cognitive (task) does not translate in a simple manner into *number* of thoughts produced; recipients of majority arguments generate as many thoughts as do recipients of minority arguments (Maass & Clark, 1983). Instead, it is the *nature* of the thoughts that differs. Minority influence produces more novel ideas in recipients (Maass & Clark, 1983) and leads to more divergent or creative thinking, whereas majority influence produces convergent or conventional thinking (Nemeth, 1986). This accords with Moscovici's (1980) contention that majority disagreement leads to interpersonal conflict, and therefore a group consensus goal, but minority disagreement leads to cognitive conflict, and therefore attention to the issue.

When the concept of information breadth is replaced by that of conventional/shared versus creative/novel information, we see that conventional idea generation is more likely when tasks or faction membership fosters interpersonal motives such as group consensus and reduction of social conflict, and creative idea generation is more likely when tasks or faction membership promotes task motivation, such as effectance and reduction of cognitive conflict. To be sure, it is just as possible to focus in breadth on normative, conventional arguments as on task-relevant, creative arguments (e.g., Maass & Clark, 1983). The critical distinction is that group productivity requires divergence of task-relevant information beyond the conventional and normative (Nemeth, 1986).

Group productivity also requires thinking about elicited arguments in depth, that is, elaborating on emergent facts. In summarizing the work up to that point, Nemeth (1986) concluded that recipients of minority messages engage in thought that goes beyond the received messages, that is, they engage in more careful thought and elaboration. Recipients of majority messages reflect more narrowly on the majority's position without considering alternative ideas. Although messages attributed to majorities are recalled better than those of minorities, suggesting that the former are being carefully processed (Mackie, 1987), this does not preclude the more divergent thought attending minority influence that would reflect a greater propensity to consider alternatives, form inferences, and in general elaborate beyond the information given (Nemeth, 1986). More recently, Crano and Chen (1998; see also Crano's chapter, this volume) refined the distinction between careful thought about arguments given by majorities versus elaborated thought that goes beyond arguments from minorities. They reported that recipients of majority influence process more information about the *focal* topic, but recipients of minority influence generate more thought about a *related* topic. Thus, majority influence promotes greater depth of processing about the focal task, which implies a concern for processing information consistent with the majority's position in the service of achieving consensus. Crano (this volume) further suggests that majority messages will be systematically elaborated (presumably by minorities) only if the influence topic is relevant to the basis of group identity. This elaboration is what leads to greater processing and effect of (strong) majority messages. Conversely, minority influence promotes greater depth of processing in the sense of thinking about related, relevant topics. This, Crano suggests, is due to a norm to listen to, and elaborate on, messages from minorities in order to foster cohesion. Unless the argument for the focal issue is particularly strong (and, presumably, the issue is intellective), the majority's attitude toward the focal issue will not change, but associated beliefs may change in the service of the cohesion norm.

Note that research on the depth of thought produced by minority and majority factions has been conducted within a persuasion paradigm whereby persuasive arguments are attributed to one or the other faction and effects are observed on the arguments generated by responding recipients. It remains to be seen whether, *in intact decision-making groups,* minorities and majorities *process* ideas in more or less depth and *present* their arguments to the opposing faction in more or less depth.

Highlighted Experiment II: How Factions Influence Intact Groups

In a recent study, Kaplan and Martin (1999) composed 16 mock jury groups of majority and minority factions in terms of their power. Majority factions consisted of two graduate psychology or law students who were trained in the university's Student Judicial Code and methods, and who had participated in multiple "trials." Minority factions were three students from introductory psychology courses, naive to Student Judicial practices, who served in only one trial. Groups decided guilt and punishment for students accused of Judicial Code violations. Each group adjudicated two cases, one of which presented a primarily intellective issue (e.g., property destruction) and the other a judgmental issue (e.g., harassment). The cases had been extensively pretested to ensure their characterization. Deliberation was conducted to consensus. Discussion was videotaped and coded for total number of assertions by factions and number of normative or informational statements by factions. The majority faction, or trained members, discussed the judgmental cases more actively and were more normative in their influence than the minority, adjusting for faction size. On the other hand, the minority faction engaged in more informational than normative influence. Thus, in intact groups, minorities (defined here by relative power) are more prone to informational influence and majorities to normative influence.

Influence over the final group decision was indexed by correlations between the initial verdicts of faction members and the final group decision. In keeping with its greater use of normative influence and greater per-member activity in judgmental cases, the trained faction was more influential in determining the verdicts in judgmental cases. The two factions were, however, equally influential in determining the verdicts in intellective cases. Thus, majorities appear to wield greater social power, which promotes greater use of normative argumentation, and greater influence in judgmental matters, which typically invoke social motives. Minorities in intact groups resort to informational argumentation and can therefore hold their own on intellective issues.

Conclusions

In this chapter we have shown that members of problem-solving groups are involved in a delicate interplay of two motivations: the motivation to produce an optimal group product (i.e., to be correct) and the motivation to act in unison with the other group members (i.e., to go along). The same competence and social-relational motivations figure prominently in other domains addressed in this volume. These cognitively and socially driven motivations give rise respectively to informational and normative influence processes in groups.

The first theme of this chapter is that there are antecedent conditions that may weaken or enhance informational in favor of normative processes, and the reverse. Our review of separate domains of the literature shows that factors such as goal-setting (task vs. group interactive goals), task type (degree of intellective vs. judgmental tasks), members' task interdependence (disjunctive vs. additive tasks), and the likelihood of future interaction may affect the balance between informational and normative processes.

The second major theme is the consequences of normative and informational influence for problem-solving groups. It is argued that for productivity in such groups, it is necessary that ideas be sampled in breadth, and that subsequently ideas and arguments must be considered in depth. It is shown that due to normative influence, arguments commonly known to members are exchanged, neglecting unique information at the expense of group productivity. Normative influence may inhibit the processing of information in breadth. However, these negative consequences of normative influence may be counteracted by task focusing (see also Wilke & Kaplan, in press, for similar arguments concerning brainstorming and creativity).

Lastly, regarding group composition, it is argued that in groups having majority and minority factions, recipients of minority influence are more inclined to process task information in depth, thus promoting more creative ideas. Recipients of majority influence, in the service of consensus, conform more to the ideas of others, leading to the generation of conventional ideas. Although minimally investigated so far, by logical inference it may be suggested that in factionated groups, inducing greater emphasis on the task (i.e., increasing task motivation and subsequent informational influence) might generate more unique arguments (information processing in breadth) and more attention to the influence of minorities. This would enhance processing of task-relevant information in depth compared with factionated groups in which the usual normative processes prevail.

References

Bales. R. F., & Slater, P. (1955). Role differentiation in small decision making groups. In T. Parsons & R. F. Bales (Eds.), *Family, socialization, and interaction process* (pp. 259–306). New York: Free Press.

Baron, R. S., & Roper, G. (1976). Reaffirmation of social comparison views of choice shifts: Averaging and extremity effects in an autokinetic situation. *Journal of Personality and Social Psychology, 33,* 521–530.

Burnstein, E., & Vinokur, A. (1973). Testing two classes of theories about group-induced shifts in individual choice. *Journal of Experimental Social Psychology, 9,* 123–137.

Chaiken, S. (1987). The heuristic model of persuasion. In M. P. Zanna, J. M. Olson, & C. P. Herman (Eds.), *Social influence: The Ontario symposium* (Vol. 5, pp. 3–39). Hillsdale, NJ: Erlbaum.

Clark, N. K., & Stephenson, G. M. (1989). Group remembering. In P. Paulus (Ed.), *Psychology of group influence* (2nd ed., pp. 357–391). Hillsdale, NJ: Erlbaum.

Crano, W. D., & Chen, X. (1998). The leniency contract and persistence of majority and minority influence. *Journal of Personality and Social Psychology, 74*(6), 1437–1450.

Davis, J. H. (1973). Group decision and social interaction: A theory of social decision schemes. *Psychological Review, 80,* 97–125.

Davis, J. H. (1982). Social interaction as a combinatorial process in group decision. In H. Brandstätter, J. H. Davis, & G. Stocker-Kreichgauer (Eds.), *Group decision making* (pp. 27–58). London: Academic Press.

Deutsch, M., & Gerard, H. B. (1955). A study of normative and informational social influences upon individual judgment. *Journal of Abnormal and Social Psychology, 51,* 629–636.

Festinger, L. (1950). Informal social communication. *Psychological Review, 57,* 271–282.

Festinger, L. (1954). A theory of social comparison processes. *Human Relations, 7*, 117–140.

Fiedler, F. E. (1972). Personality, motivational system, and the behavior of high- and low-LPC persons. *Human Relations, 24*, 391–412.

Groenenboom, A. C. W. J., Wilke, H. A. M., & Wit, A. P. (in press). Efficiency and fairness trade-offs in collective performance. *Journal of Experimental Social Psychology.*

Harkins, S. G., & Petty, R. E. (1982). Social loafing: Allocation of effort or taking it easy. *Journal of Experimental Social Psychology, 16*, 457–465.

Janis, I. L. (1972). *Victims of groupthink.* Boston: Houghton Mifflin.

Kaplan, M. F. (1989). Task, situational, and personal determinants of influence processes in group decision making. In E. J. Lawler & B. Markovsky (Eds.), *Advances in group processes* (pp. 87–105). Greenwich, CT: JAI Press.

Kaplan, M. F., & Kickul, J. (1996, May). *Timing of first public ballot and jury deliberation style.* Paper presented at the meeting of the Midwestern Psychological Association, Chicago.

Kaplan, M. F., & Martin, A. M. (1999). Effects of differential status of group members on process and outcome of deliberation. *Group Processes and Interpersonal Relations, 2*, 347–364.

Kaplan, M. F., & Miller, C. E. (1977). Discussion polarization effects in a modified jury decision paradigm: Informational influences. *Sociometry, 40*, 262–271.

Kaplan, M. F., & Miller, C. E. (1983). Group discussion and judgment. In P. Paulus (Ed.), *Basic group processes* (pp. 65–94). New York: Springer-Verlag.

Kaplan, M. F., & Miller, C. E. (1987). Group decision making and normative versus informational influence: Effects of type of issue and assigned decision rule. *Journal of Personality and Social Psychology, 53*(2), 306–313.

Kaplan, M. F., Schaefer, E. G., & Zinkiewicz, L. (1994). Member preference for discussion content in anticipated group decisions: Effects of type of issue and group interactive goal. *Basic and Applied Social Psychology, 15*, 489–508.

Katz, D., & Kahn, R. L. (1978). *The social psychology of organizations* (2nd ed.). New York: Wiley.

Kerr, N. L. (1983). Motivation losses in small groups: A social dilemma analysis. *Journal of Personality and Social Psychology, 45*, 819–828.

Kerr, N. L. (1986) Motivational choices in task groups: A paradigm for social dilemma research. In H. Wilke, D. Messick, & C. Rutte (Eds.), *Experimental social dilemmas* (pp. 1–27). Frankfurt am Main: Lang GmbH.

Kerr, N. L. (1992). Efficacy as a causal and moderating variable in social dilemmas. In W. Liebrand, D. Messick, & H. Wilke (Eds.), *A social psychological approach to social dilemmas* (pp. 59–88). New York: Pergamon Press.

Kerr, N. L. (1995). Norms in social dilemmas. In D. A. Schroeder (Ed.), *Social dilemmas: Perspective on individuals and groups* (pp. 31–48). Westport, CT: Praeger.

Kerr, N. L., & Bruun, S. E. (1983). Dispensability of member effort and group motivation losses: Free-rider effects. *Journal of Personality and Social Psychology, 44*, 78–94.

Kruglanski, A. W. (1989). *Lay epistemics and human knowledge: Cognitive and motivational bases.* New York: Plenum.

Lamm, H., & Myers, D. G. (1978). Group-induced polarization of attitudes and behavior. In L. Berkowitz (Ed.), *Advances in experimental social psychology,* (Vol. 11, pp. 145–195). New York: Academic Press.

Laughlin, P. R., & Ellis, A. L. (1986). Demonstrability and social combination processes on mathematical intellective tasks. *Journal of Experimental Social Psychology, 22,* 177–189.

Levine, J. M. (1980). Reaction to opinion deviance in small groups. In P. B. Paulus (Ed.), *Psychology of group influence* (pp. 375–429). Hillsdale, NJ: Erlbaum.

Levine, J. M., Resnick, L. B., & Higgins, E. T. (1993). Social foundations of cognition. *Annual Review of Psychology* (Vol. 44, pp. 585–612). Palo Alto, CA: Annual Reviews.

Maass, A., & Clark, R. D., III (1983). Internalization versus compliance: Differential processes underlying minority influence and conformity. *European Journal of Social Psychology, 13,* 197–215.

Mackie, D. M. (1987). Systematic and nonsystematic processing of majority and minority persuasive communications. *Journal of Personality and Social Psychology, 53*(1), 41–52.

McGrath, J. E. (1984). *Groups: Interaction and performance.* Englewood Cliffs, NJ: Prentice-Hall.

Moscovici, S. (1976). *Social influence and social change.* London: Academic Press.

Moscovici, S. (1980). Towards a theory of conversion behavior. In L. Berkowitz (Ed.), *Advances in experimental social psychology* (Vol. 13, pp. 209–239). New York: Academic Press.

Moscovici, S. (1985). Innovation and minority influence. In S. Moscovici, G. Mugny, & E. Van Avermaet (Eds.), *Perspectives on minority influence* (pp. 9–52). Cambridge: Cambridge University Press.

Moscovici, S. (1992). The discovery of group polarization. In D. Granberg & G. Sarup (Eds.), *Social judgment and intergroup relations* (pp. 107–127). New York: Springer-Verlag.

Nemeth, C. J. (1985). Dissent, group process, and creativity: The contribution of minority influence. In E. Lawler (Ed.), *Advances in group processes* (Vol. 2, pp. 57–75). Greenwich, CT: JAI Press.

Nemeth, C. J. (1986). Differential contributions of majority and minority influence. *Psychological Review, 93,* 23–32.

Nemeth, C. J., Mayseless, O., Sherman, J., & Brown, Y. (1990). Exposure to dissent and recall of information. *Journal of Personality and Social Psychology, 58,* 429–437.

Piliavin, J. A., & Martin, R. R. (1978). The effects of the sex composition of groups on style of social interaction. *Sex Roles, 4,* 281–296.

Pruitt, D. G. (1971). Conclusion: Toward an understanding of choices shifts in group discussion. *Journal of Personality and Social Psychology, 20,* 495–510.

Rugs, D., & Kaplan, M. F. (1993). Effectiveness of informational and normative influence in group decision making depends on group interactive goal. *British Journal of Social Psychology, 32,* 147–158.

Stasser, G. (1992). Pooling of unshared information during group discussion. In S. Worchel, W. Wood, & J. A. Simpson (Eds.), *Group process and productivity* (pp. 48–67). Newbury Park, CA: Sage.

Stasser, G., & Stewart, D. (1992). Discovery of hidden profiles by decision-making groups: Solving a problem vs. making a judgment. *Journal of Personality and Social Psychology, 63,* 426–434.

Stasser, G., Stewart, D., & Wittenbaum, G. M. (1995). Expert roles and information exchange during discussion: The importance of knowing who knows what. *Journal of Experimental Social Psychology, 31,* 244–265.

Stasser, G., Taylor, L. A., & Hannah, C. (1989). Information sampling in structured and unstructured discussions of three- and six-person groups. *Journal of Personality and Social Psychology, 57,* 67–78.

Stasser, G., & Titus, W. (1985). Pooling of unshared information in group decision-making: Biased information sampling during discussion. *Journal of Personality and Social Psychology, 48,* 1467–1478.

Stasser, G., & Titus, W. (1987). Effects of information load and percentage of shared information on the dissemination of unshared information during group discussion. *Journal of Personality and Social Psychology, 53*(1), 81–93.

Steiner, I. D. (1972). *Group processes and productivity.* New York: Academic Press.

Stewart, D., & Stasser, G. (1998). The sampling of critical, unshared information in decision-making groups: The role of an informed minority. *European Journal of Social Psychology, 28,* 95–113.

Stodgill, R. M. (1974). *Handbook of leadership: A survey of theory and research.* New York: Free Press.

Stoner, J. A. F. (1961). *A comparison of individual and group decisions involving risk.* Unpublished master's thesis, Massachusetts Institute of Technology.

Tajfel, H., & Turner, J. C. (1986). An integrative theory of intergroup conflict. In W. G. Austin & S. Worchel (Eds.), *Psychology of intergroup relations* (2nd ed., pp. 7–24). Chicago: Nelson-Hall.

Thibaut, J. W., & Strickland, L. (1956). Psychological set and conformity. *Journal of Personality, 25,* 115–129.

Turner, J. C. (1991). *Social influence.* Pacific Grove, CA: Brooks/Cole.

Turner, J. C., Hogg, M. A., Oakes, P. J., Reicher, S. D., & Wetherall, M. S. (1987). *Rediscovering the social group: A self-categorization theory.* Oxford: Basil Blackwell.

Turner, J. C., & Oakes, P. J. (1989). Self-categorization theory and social influence. In P. B. Paulus (Ed.), *Psychology of group influence* (2nd. ed., pp. 233–275). Hillsdale NJ: Erlbaum.

Wilke, H. A. M., & Kaplan, M. F. (in press). Task creativity and social creativity in decision-making groups. In C. M. Allwood & M. Selart (Eds.), *Creative decision-making in the social world.* Goteborg, Sweden: Kluwer Academic.

Williams, K. D., & Karau, S. J. (1991). Social loafing and social compensation: The effects of expectations of coworker performance. *Journal of Personality and Social Psychology, 61,* 570–581.

Wood, W. (1987). Meta-analytic review of sex differences in group performance. *Psychological Bulletin, 102,* 53–71.

Wood, W., & Karten, S. J. (1986). Sex differences in interactional style as a product of perceived sex differences in competence. *Journal of Personality and Social Psychology, 50,* 341–357.

Author Index

Note: Italicized page numbers refer to citations in references.

Subject Index

CABRINI COLLEGE LIBRARY
610 KING OF PRUSSIA RD.
RADNOR, PA 19087-3699

DEMCO